U.S. and Latin American Relations

GREGORY WEEKS

University of North Carolina, Charlotte

PEARSON
Longman

New York   San Francisco   Boston
London   Toronto   Sydney   Tokyo   Singapore   Madrid
Mexico City   Munich   Paris   Cape Town   Hong Kong   Montreal

Acquisitions Editor: *Vikram Mukhija*
Executive Marketing Manager: *Ann Stypuloski*
Production Manager: *Denise Phillip*
Project Coordination, Text Design, and Electronic Page Makeup: *TexTech, Inc.*
Cover Design Manager: *John Callahan*
Cover Designer: *Maria Ilardi*
Cover Image: *Courtesy of Planet Art*
Photo Researcher: *Rona Tuccillo*
Senior Manufacturing Buyer: *Alfred C. Dorsey*
Printer and Binder: *R. R. Donnelley & Sons / Crawfordsville*
Cover Printer: *R. R. Donnelley & Sons / Crawfordsville*

For permission to use copyrighted material, grateful acknowledgment is made to the copyright holders on the appropriate pages within the text, which are hereby made part of this copyright page.

Library of Congress Cataloging-in-Publication Data

Weeks, Gregory Bart.
   U. S. and Latin American relations / Gregory Weeks.
     p.   cm.
   Includes bibliographical references and index.
     ISBN-13: 978-0-321-27624-7
     ISBN-10:   0-321-27624-8
   1. Latin America—Relations—United States.   2. United States—Relations—Latin
    America.   I. Title.
   F1418.W28 2008
   327.7308—dc22   2007041365

Please visit us at www.ablongman.com

ISBN 13: 978-0-321-27624-7
ISBN 10:   0-321-27624-8

1 2 3 4 5 6 7 8 9 10—DOC—10 09 08 07

Brief Contents

Detailed Contents

PART II. CURRENT ISSUES

Preface

In his 2007 visit to Latin America, President George W. Bush wondered aloud why U.S. efforts to assist people in the region weren't more appreciated. In one speech he remarked, "I don't think America gets enough credit for trying to help improve people's lives."[1] The president's sentiments are not new. In 1901, Secretary of War Elihu Root complained that Cubans would never be granted independence "if they continue to exhibit ingratitude and entire lack of appreciation of the expenditure of blood and treasure of the United States to secure their freedom from Spain."[2] In 1926, a State Department official rationalized that after years of occupation in Central America, "If the United States has received but little gratitude, this is only to be expected in a world where gratitude is rarely accorded to the teacher, the doctor, or the policeman, and we have been all three."[3]

This persistent disconnect tells us something important. There are often gaps between the expectations of U.S. policy makers, the responses and actions of their Latin American counterparts, and the reaction from the Latin American (and in some cases the U.S.) public to policy initiatives. Why do such gaps exist? What kinds of similar historical continuities still exist? Where and when do we see different kinds of policies emerging from Latin America? *U.S. and Latin American Relations* argues that greater understanding requires a focus on power and, more precisely, the imbalance of power. For this reason, I employ realist theory from the scholarly literature on international relations, though I also explain how two other major theories—dependency theory and liberal institutional theory—can shed light on the relations between the United States and Latin American countries. Particular attention is paid to the strengths and weaknesses of each theoretical approach. Students can therefore link political history and current events to theories that serve as guides to explain the motivations of policy makers in different states, how political and economic power are used in the international system, and probable outcomes when interstate disputes arise.

The preceding quotes also show that we cannot hope to understand the relationships between the United States and Latin America unless we keep a keen eye on history. What does a secretary of war in 1901 have in common with a president in 2007? Why would they come to such similar conclusions after the passage of more than a century? We need to address these questions, and in this book I take care to emphasize the historical roots of U.S.–Latin American relations, which provide the foundation for understanding contemporary events.

Many books have been written on this topic, to the degree that reading all of them would be impossible unless one chose to do nothing else for a lifetime. What sets this book apart is its integration of theory, scholarship, history, and pedagogy. It serves not only as a theoretically and historically oriented analysis but also as a springboard for further learning and research.

Features

This book opens with an introductory chapter that establishes a theoretical context for studying relations between the United States and Latin America; the remainder of the book is split into two parts, one on historical background and one on current issues. Chapters 2 through 7 in Part I cover the period from Latin American independence in the early nineteenth century to the Cold War, highlighting the development of U.S. hegemony and shifts in relations that took place, in terms of both U.S. policy and the actions and perceptions of Latin American political leaders. It includes a case study of the Cuban revolution, which had a dramatic impact on policies in Latin American countries and in the United States. Chapters 8 through 11 in Part II detail critical contemporary issues: the politics of debt and trade, immigration, human rights and democracy, and drugs and terrorism. They go beyond the headlines to analyze how these issues have been addressed, the conflict and cooperation, and how U.S. power has been wielded and resisted.

This book goes beyond mere discussion and analysis. Each chapter includes a number of additional features that will help students dig deeper into the points being covered:

- A timeline of key events
- Excerpts from primary source documents
- An annotated selection of additional readings
- An annotated selection of Web sites
- Suggested topics for student research papers

The book also includes:

- A glossary for key concepts
- An extensive bibliography

Acknowledgments

Writing a textbook is a unique task. Not only does it require the synthesis of a large amount of information but also it must be done with the student reader in mind.

Special thanks go to my colleagues who read various drafts, provided me with feedback, and/or gave advice. They include Chris Blake, Christina Ewig, Brian Loveman, Christopher Mitchell, and Lars Schoultz. At the University of North

Carolina at Charlotte, students in both my Latin American Politics and U.S.–Latin American Relations courses read drafts and gave me invaluable suggestions. The book also went through multiple stages of anonymous external review, and for improving the book in numerous ways, I would like to thank Susan Berger, Fordham University; Darren Hawkins, Brigham Young University–Provo; Shannan Mattiace, Allegheny College; Jane Marcus-Delgado, City University of New York; Kirk Hawkins, Brigham Young University–Provo; Waltraud Morales, University of Central Florida; David Shirk, University of San Diego; David Scott Palmer, Boston University; Raul Madrid, University of Texas–Austin; and Russell Crandall, Davidson College.

At Longman, acquisition editor Ed Costello guided me through the initial process with tremendous energy. Afterward, Eric Stano juggled various roles to assist me in completing the manuscript. Finally, Vikram Mukhija brought the project to a successful conclusion.

My greatest gratitude goes to my family. My wife, Amy, was always there for me, as usual. Although my son, Benjamin, is probably too young to remember, he listened to every chapter as I read them aloud. My daughter, Julia, arrived when I was almost done writing a first draft and so was spared. Finally, I am deeply grateful to my parents, John and Deanna Weeks, whose own experiences in writing and editing a textbook were essential to me. They read every word of my book, made many editing suggestions, answered innumerable emails and instant messages, and were a constant source of support. For that and so much more, I dedicate this book to them.

Notes

1. Quoted in Baker and Brubaker 2007.
2. Quoted in Schoultz 1998, 150.
3. Quoted in LaFeber 1984, 301.

CHAPTER 1

The Theoretical Context of U.S. and Latin American Relations

Even the most casual observer of U.S.–Latin American relations knows that the relationship has been complex and often conflictive. A combination of wars, invasions, occupations, mutual suspicion (and occasionally open dislike), dictatorships, and/or differences in ideology represents a consistent obstacle to strong national friendships. However, relations have not always been negative. Periodically, Latin American political leaders have worked closely with the U.S. government in a spirit of partnership, and the United States has also offered new initiatives intended to show a willingness to establish a positive and friendly relationship. Yet, all too often, U.S. policy makers and the general public do not understand why Latin Americans routinely demonstrate indifferent or even hostile reactions to U.S. actions, and Latin Americans themselves often see ulterior motives in U.S. actions.

The relationship between U.S. and Latin American governments has had it all. Militarily, just in the past several decades the United States has been deeply involved in Central American civil wars, as well as invasion (most notably Panama). Economically, successive U.S. governments have sought to use economic pressure to oust Fidel Castro in Cuba, while engaging in negotiations over economic agreements with a host of other countries. This U.S. military and economic behavior has been accompanied by a tremendous movement of people, looking for opportunity and self-improvement. At the same time, President Hugo Chávez of Venezuela has endeavored to forge new political and economic links in Latin America to provide an alternative to the United States. Politically, starting especially in the 1990s, governments across the region have worked to protect democratic institutions in a number of countries, such as Guatemala, Paraguay, and Peru. The pervasive political violence that characterized the Cold War period is now gone, but new types of violence—a result of the drug trade— have emerged. How, then, can we make sense of it all? This book has three inter-twined purposes, focusing on theory, political history, and research.

The first is to articulate a theoretical framework, providing a guide to understand why governments behave in certain ways. The theoretical perspec-tive of the book comes from the "realist" school of international relations, which focuses on the state as a central actor in international relations and on the use of power, especially military and economic power, to achieve security in an anarchic system (i.e., there is no world government). In an anarchic world, states must either sink or swim because no other state or organization will step in with assistance. Every state must depend entirely on itself to advance its interests, and all states are doing so all the time.

In his classic study of realism, Kenneth Waltz argues that an actor is power-ful to the extent that he or she affects others more than they affect him or her.[1] Power, therefore, can easily be observed and is constantly present in the minds of policy makers. The history of U.S.–Latin American relations has always been characterized and shaped by significant differences in military and economic capabilities and the absence of effective international institutions to constrain the actions of the United States.

Although this book will address the nature of Latin America's economic dependency, it will not formally utilize dependency theory, which is another prominent approach in the literature on U.S.–Latin American relations. Depen-dency theory posits that Latin American underdevelopment is a result of domi-nation by more advanced economies, primarily the United States. The result is that Latin America suffers from constraints and barriers that prevent it from achieving its economic potential.

In this view, the global economy has fostered structural patterns that cannot be ignored. For example, U.S. companies have extracted natural resources— such as fruit, oil, or copper—in Latin America, then sold those products abroad, reaping tremendous profit but leaving little gain locally. Meanwhile, a small group of elites (both foreign and domestic) garnered the lion's share of national wealth and created a massive divide between rich and poor.

In its deterministic nature, however, this theory does not leave enough room for discussion of Latin American resistance to U.S. hegemony. In one of the most important works on dependency, Andre Gunder Frank concludes by arguing that only by destroying capitalism, breaking away from world imperialism, and embracing socialism can countries successfully counteract dependency.[2] Cardoso and Faletto offered a modified version (interestingly, Fernando Henrique Cardoso would later become a pro-market president of Brazil) that acknowledged the possibility of developing (at least to some degree) despite dependency, but autonomy would not be a realistic goal.[3] The bottom line of the theory is that true progress can never take place while contacts with the more powerful northern neighbor continued. In another seminal book on dependency, Evans posits that "dependent development" does take place, as foreign capital penetrates and creates diversified industrial sectors.[4] The end result, while admittedly industrial, remains seriously detrimental to the country as a whole because it continues to depend on foreign interests.

The dependency school has provided rich analyses of the challenges faced by less developed countries in Latin America but is less well equipped to explain autonomous actions initiated within the region vis-à-vis the United States. In other words, Latin American political leaders have often worked successfully and independently within the context of great power imbalance.

This is not to say that realism offers a perfect view of the relationship. The focus on realpolitik and the use of realist theory to understand U.S.–Latin American relations has many critics. As one has posited, "Even when done well, the realist argument has difficulty being precise in predictions about U.S. actions."[5] Similarly, another motes that the realist view fails to pinpoint precisely *why* the United States considers specific "Third World" regions such as Latin America to be important.[6] Nonetheless, in this book I argue that the factors of power and security should remain front and center, even while certain aspects of realist theory should be reexamined.

The third major theoretical approach in international relations—liberal institutionalism—denies realism's assumptions about how power leads to conflict. Instead, its adherents focus on harmony of interests and how countries can successfully get along. Thus, according to Rosecrance, as nations interact with each other, they develop a stake in each other's success. International institutions can serve as a means of reducing the problems associated with an anarchic world, thereby mitigating some of the worse elements of power politics.[7]

The theory envisions those institutions as taking on a life of their own. Even if they are created by powerful countries like the United States, they can become independently influential. Acceptance of their rules and norms spreads, and disregarding them raises more protest. As a result, political leaders will be more likely to accept them, thus limiting their range of policy options.

There is also a large body of literature arguing that democracies are more likely to promote peace and avoid war.[8] Although the chapters that follow will indeed discuss how some institutions have reduced conflict, the liberal institutional tradition does not adequately address the ways in which power politics has so often held sway in U.S.–Latin American relations.

For U.S. policy makers, Latin America has often represented both economic opportunity and a potential threat to U.S. national security. Viewed through the realist lens, U.S. policy at any given time often reflects a coherent internal logic. Latin Americans, whether politicians, rebels, or business elites, have had a keen appreciation for the power imbalance, and at times they have either accepted it, attempting to use it to their advantage (many dictators retained power in this manner), or they have worked to counteract it. The dynamics of power politics and the reactions to those dynamics constitute this book's framework.

A consistent theme in the book is the nature of "security." A subjective term, it revolves around policy makers' belief that the state is free from harm. Realism posits that states seek to protect their interests, but the manner in which they do so depends on how policy makers define threats to national security. Governments in the United States and Latin America often have differing perspectives on security, which in turn affects the dynamics of the U.S.–Latin America relationship, especially when those definitions are at odds.

Many variants of realist theory treat the state as a unitary actor, that is, regardless of the leadership, a state will do what's necessary to protect its vital interests. This takes the role of individuals out of the equation and assumes there wouldn't be much difference regardless of who was in charge of policy making. Realism "provides no framework for understanding the specific content of state policies and the ways in which these change over time."[9] There has been considerable debate over this point; as Keohane and Martin argue, international relations theory must "explain variations in state preferences" by developing "theories that begin with individuals and groups."[10]

This book joins the critics in asserting that the state should not be considered a unitary entity, but rather simply a sovereign one, where changing leadership affects how the key goals of political security and economic development are understood and articulated. People *do* matter, and have an independent impact on what policies ultimately are implemented. The analysis of state preferences and power, which are based on the perceptions of relevant policy makers, should be entirely consistent with realist theory.

Hegemony—meaning dominance of one country over others—and the application of U.S. interests should not be construed as so overwhelming that Latin America becomes only a passive actor following U.S. demands. There have been many instances when the sources of policies followed by Latin American governments originated from domestic concerns and therefore were not strictly reactions to U.S. policy. Efforts at state building, internal security, economic growth, and political stability, just to name a few, have often originated within Latin American countries themselves. At the same time, the United States has clearly been impossible to ignore. In this book, it will become clear that leaders of Latin American countries, and groups within countries, developed a wide range of reactions to U.S. policy. Being a hegemonic power does not mean total control. Latin Americans have often struggled against U.S. dominance and at times have been successful in that effort. These efforts have taken many forms, including interpretations of international law, the creation of regional organizations, the formation of rebellions and revolutions, the creation of nationalist policies, and even the production of a rich collection of literary works.

International factors also affect U.S. politics. This interplay has been labeled as "intermestic" in the international relations literature. Intermestic policy arises when domestic concerns strongly influence (or even determine) foreign policy decisions. The domestic audience, which itself is a complex web of voters, political parties, economic interests, lobbyists, and other actors, has been powerful in the formulation of U.S. policy toward Latin America. It is critical to understand not only *why* certain policies were followed but also *who* makes the decisions. Not only have there been heated battles between the U.S. executive and legislative branches for control over foreign policy but also at times other political actors have wielded tremendous influence.

This is also true in Latin America, where different political, economic, and social actors have viewed relations with the United States in very different ways. For example, democratically elected presidents and legislatures, military governments, guerrillas, human rights activists, reformers, business elites, workers, peasants and the urban poor view the U.S.–Latin American relationship in diverse ways and try to shape it accordingly. The region has traditionally been strongly presidential and highly centralized. As democracy spreads and new groups find voice, however, the policy context is becoming more multifaceted.

Realism tends to view international institutions as the product of states seeking to advance their core interests. There is an extended debate about their importance, framed by institutionalist theory.[11] This book considers institutions as the outcome when individual states come together to solve common problems, often related to security and/or economic development. However, institutions can take on lives of their own not anticipated by their creators and address areas that were not part of their original charter. The degree to which they do so is an important theme for the latter part of the book, especially with regard to human rights.

In short, there is no perfect theory, and several chapters (especially on human rights) will analyze some of realism's shortcomings. I strongly encourage students to engage different theories of international relations in the light of empirical evidence.

The second purpose of the book is to explain the historical and contemporary shifts in attitude and policy approaches that have affected the formation and implementation of policies, both in the United States and Latin America. There is much continuity to U.S. policy, to the point where at times the cliché "the more things change, the more they stay the same" seems to ring true, but at the same time important shifts have taken place over time. Latin American leaders, meanwhile, have not viewed the relationship in static terms, because their own interests changed. Although it is a truism to say that international relations contain elements of both continuity and change, to understand U.S.–Latin American relations, teasing out the interplay between the two is essential.

Theoretical Perspectives

	Realism	Liberal Institutionalism	Dependency
Core Beliefs	States act in a self-interested manner to achieve security	International institutions can constrain state behavior and promote cooperation	Less developed countries are exploited by the developed world
Key Actors	Individual states, regardless of what type of government	International institutions	Developed countries and corporations
Main Instruments	Military and economic power	The rules and norms of international institutions	Economic power
Theoretical Benefits	Explains the effects of power imbalance	Explains how states change behavior because of institutions	Explains the economic obstacles to autonomy in Latin America
Theoretical Shortcomings	Does not always adequately explain Latin American responses to hegemony and the complexities of policy making	Tends to overemphasize the power of international institutions	Does not adequately explain examples of Latin American autonomy

Source: Adapted from Snyder 2004.

Often, shifts in policy correspond to the U.S. perception of the international system and the threats perceived to be emanating from it. Just as the U.S. response to Latin American independence was crafted with an eye to the reactions of Spain, France, and Great Britain, Cold War and post–September 11 policies were aimed at dealing with enemies with origins outside the region, whether from Western Europe, the Soviet Union, or the Middle East. On many occasions, Latin Americans do not agree with U.S. assertions of imminent threat, and the debate over threats has continued unabated since the early nineteenth century.

Analysis of the Cold War period will highlight the persistent continuities, most notably the keen awareness of U.S. hegemony on the part of both U.S. policy makers and Latin Americans (whether presidents, diplomats, guerrillas, workers, or peasants). The rapid collapse of the Soviet Union drastically changed U.S. perceptions in the region, but political and economic dominance remained. Barely more than a decade later, the U.S. response to the terrorist attacks of September 11, 2001, would therefore represent far more continuity than change. Although the specific policy priorities would not be identical, U.S.

strategies would remain largely constant. The post–September 11 period echoes not only the Cold War but also U.S. responses to the wars of Latin American independence and the security issues arising during World War II.

Theory and political history provide a structure for understanding, but the third purpose of this book is to provide a guide to investigate topics in more detail and even to write research papers. Given the mass of data and dates, names and nations, it can be difficult to narrow down ideas and focus on specific issues and countries, much less to gather sources from the truly vast quantity of available books, government documents, articles, and Web sites. In addition to the general bibliography at the end of the book, the end of each chapter has a research section to serve as that guide.

Each research section has an annotated selection of books, with an emphasis on those containing useful overviews of the chapter's period or topic. Although these books are most often recent so that they incorporate as much updated scholarship as possible, the section also includes older reference works that have stood the test of academic time and therefore remain relevant. There are also specific government document collections that are well indexed and readily available (in some cases online) for students. The suggested readings are accompanied by possible research questions for students to explore as a way to develop term papers and research ideas. The subject matter of these questions comes from the chapter itself, but addressing the questions will require further study, with the bibliography as an initial guide. Each chapter also includes excerpts from prominent government documents, speeches, treaties, and agreements. Combined with the narrative, these documents offer a view into the world of diplomacy, negotiation, and international law.

Finally, the number of useful Web sites has skyrocketed but pales in comparison to the total number of Web sites on the topic. Therefore, the selected Web sites include those that have proved durable, credible, and/or useful for researchers. Most are in English, but a number of Spanish-only sites are also listed.

But what is Latin America? The answer is both simple and unsatisfactory. In general, for U.S. policy makers and scholars alike, Latin America refers to the places in the Western Hemisphere that were colonized by the Spanish and Portuguese. More specifically, that means Mexico, most of Central and South America, and parts of the Caribbean. Although the Dominican Republic and Haiti share the island now called Hispaniola (a variation of Española, or "Little Spain," so called by Columbus because of its physical resemblance to Spain), the latter was a French colony but is also often included. Aside from sharing the same colonial roots, a number of economic, political, and cultural similarities bind Latin American countries together. Yet we have to be aware at all times that the people who live within this vast region do not consider themselves part of a single bloc. Even the similarities—such as language—find very different expression, depending not only on the country in question but also regions and peoples within the same country. In fact, the idea that North Americans view such a wide variety of people as homogeneous leaves many Latin Americans shaking their heads. It is a trap that is easy to fall into, and although this book utilizes "Latin America" to describe regional trends, it also differentiates the relationships between the United States and different groups and governments within the region.

We must also keep in mind that U.S. interest has also shifted over time according to subregion. Given its proximity and shared border, the United States has for a long time paid very close attention to political developments in Mexico. Central America and the Caribbean (especially Cuba) were also of much greater concern than South America in the nineteenth century. South America became comparatively prominent only around World War II, as the global struggle brought the region directly onto the U.S. foreign policy radar and left it there for decades. Each chapter therefore addresses the shifting regional interests of the

Map 1.1 Latin America

Source: Latin America and the Caribbean. Volunteers for Prosperity. http://www.volunteersfor prosperity.gov/global-map/latin-america/index.html

United States and attempts to answer the question of why U.S. political leaders are particularly interested in certain parts of Latin America at any given time.

Structure

The book is divided into two sections. The first provides historical background and context, and the second covers contemporary issues, by examining critical current issues in U.S.–Latin American relations in the context of whether they appear to be generating more cooperation or conflict. Chapter 1 addresses the first half of the nineteenth century, particularly the wars for independence, nation building, and the U.S. concern for keeping European influence out of the hemisphere, exemplified by the Monroe Doctrine. This period also demonstrates how U.S. policy makers viewed the hemisphere and its potential for political and economic development.

Chapter 2 covers the latter half of the nineteenth century and the shifts in policy that result from the industrial revolution and the growth of U.S. economic influence. The assertion of power for economic reasons became known as "dollar diplomacy" and increased U.S. attempts to direct Latin American politics in a manner favorable to U.S. economic and strategic interests. It culminates in U.S. policy toward Cuba after the Spanish-American War expelled Spain from the region. During this period, Latin American reactions against U.S. hegemony become sharper.

Chapter 3 focuses on the first third of the twentieth century, as outright claims to hegemony and repeated intervention gave way to President Franklin Roosevelt's Good Neighbor Policy, which emphasized the beginning of an era of cooperation. At the same time, Latin American rebellions and reforms mark concerted efforts to avoid U.S. domination.

Chapter 4 describes the beginning of the Cold War, as U.S. policy shifted to combat the spread of Communism. The tenets of the Good Neighbor Policy soon disappeared, replaced by a renewed commitment to intervene precisely in those countries where Latin American reforms sought to establish greater national control over the economy.

Chapter 5 continues the same theme, covering the Cuban revolution and its immense impact on U.S. policy. During this period, U.S. concerns over Communism increased considerably. For U.S. policy makers, Fidel Castro himself became a symbol of Communist revolutions the United States was committed to derailing, while for many Latin Americans he was the leader of a movement intended to break away from U.S. hegemony.

Chapter 6 traces the remainder of the Cold War, as the United States continued to fight what it viewed as Communist infiltration in the hemisphere; its fight included supporting a variety of military governments. Central America, through revolution and armed rebellion against U.S.-supported regimes, became a focal point for U.S. policy, but attention to South America also became more intense, as the dictatorships in Argentina, Brazil, and Chile demonstrate.

Chapter 7 focuses on political economy, specifically the policies of debt and free trade. The politics of debt in the 1980s had lasting effects, and free trade, with agreements such as the North American Free Trade Agreement (NAFTA), remains hotly debated both in the United States and within Latin American countries, including sometimes violent responses.

Chapter 8 centers on immigration and the ways U.S. policy makers have addressed it, with specific attention to the dynamics of both legal and illegal immigrants in addition to refugees. It analyzes the factors affecting supply (why immigrants seek to come to the United States) and demand (why U.S. employers attract immigrants), the reactions to immigration in the United States, and the economic ramifications of immigration for Latin American countries.

Chapter 9 focuses on human rights, democracy, and the changing perceptions of the need to protect human rights. The U.S. government, along with some Latin American governments, has been concerned about Communism, drugs, and terrorism, which have given rise to conflict not only with Latin American political leaders and activists but also within the United States itself. The twin priorities of protecting individual liberties and combating "threats to public order" are sometimes difficult to reconcile.

Chapter 10 focuses on terrorism and violence in Latin America and U.S. attempts to eliminate it, particularly how the U.S.–Latin American relationship has changed since September 11, 2001. It discusses the intermestic nature of the formulation of antidrug and antiterrorist policies, the different strategies employed, and the very different way that many Latin Americans view the problem of drugs and related violence. The identification of terrorist threats in the region, the increased reliance on military solutions, and pressure to contribute to the global fight against terrorism have all had a significant impact on both the United States and Latin America.

Useful General Sources

Although the book provides sources on specific topics, there are several excellent places to start learning more about both past and current U.S. policy.

- **Papers Relating to the Foreign Relations of the United States**   Most commonly referred to as FRUS, these documents contain correspondence between the U.S. government (primarily the State Department) and U.S. diplomats in other countries, as well as a large number of documents. The series began in 1861 and new volumes are frequently published. The only limitation is that the volumes produced at any given time must contain documents that are approximately thirty years old. Increasingly, these volumes are being released online at the State Department's Web site: http://www. state.gov/www/about_state/history/frusonline.html.

- **Public Papers of the Presidents of the United States**   As the title suggests, this series collects each president's public papers, which means speeches, statements, and other papers that were originally released through the Office of the Press Secretary. It is fully indexed, and so it is easy to pinpoint policy statements about Latin America. The series dates back to the administration of Herbert Hoover, and some volumes are available online: http://www. gpoaccess.gov/pubpapers/search.html.

- **Weekly Compilation of Presidential Documents**   Every Monday, the U.S. government releases the presidential documents of the previous week. The online versions of these documents date back to 1993. Search options include keywords, so specific countries, presidents, agreements, and other topics are instantly available at http://www.access.gpo.gov/nara/nara003.html.

- **Department of State, Bureau of Western Hemisphere Affairs**   This part of the State Department deals with Latin America. Its Web site is useful because it contains press releases, government reports, congressional testimony, and legislation about U.S. policy toward Latin America. It is not necessarily comprehensive and may not contain *all* legislation that affects the region, but it is always updated and provides a good glimpse into current policies: http://www.state.gov/p/wha/

Different Theoretical Perspectives: U.S.–Venezuelan Relations

In 2006, President Hugo Chávez announced that Venezuela would seek to win the rotating seat reserved for Latin America and the Caribbean on the UN Security Council. Earlier in the year, Guatemala had already made known its desire for the seat. Under UN General Assembly procedures, if a region of the world cannot agree on a single candidate, then the General Assembly as a whole votes, and winning requires two thirds of all ballots cast.

An intense campaign ensued. President Chávez traveled all over the world, announced along the way all the votes he had garnered, and sought more during the meetings of the Non-Aligned Movement in Havana. Meanwhile, the administration of President George W. Bush made very clear that it did not want Venezuela on the Security Council. Its efforts to compel governments to vote for Guatemala even prompted the foreign minister of that country to remark, "In some countries I have to admit the U.S. has come on too strong in its opposition to Venezuela."[12]

A *realist* perspective would view the episode in terms of national interests and power. Although the United Nations can at times exert influence over international affairs, ultimately each state must do whatever possible to protect its own interests. Thus, the United States framed the choice in terms of security. Because the Security Council would be facing issues such as the nuclear ambitions of North Korea and Iran, it was not acceptable to have a country like Venezuela that would be interested only in "disrupting international events."[13]

(Continued)

To bring Guatemala to victory, the U.S. government sent signals to other Latin American countries that a vote for Venezuela would be punished. For example, the Bush administration privately informed the Chilean government that the cost of supporting Chávez would be "very high."[14] According to John Bolton, then the U.S. ambassador to the UN, "We had zero involvement—zero—until Venezuela declared its candidacy. And our concern from the outset has been the obstructionist and unhelpful behavior of Venezuela and the threat that it posed to orderly decision-making in the Security Council."[15]

The Venezuelan government also believed security was central, but in terms of checking U.S. power. A seat on the Security Council would provide the country with a platform from which to criticize U.S. policy, and Guatemala was considered too close to the United States to use that opportunity. In a situation of anarchy, the UN cannot put an effective brake on powerful countries, but at the very least it might serve as a vehicle for weaker countries to express their own views.

Thus, both U.S. and Venezuela policy makers used all means available to lobby for their respective interests, in the belief that the outcome would have an impact on their divergent perceptions of security.

A *liberal institutionalist* view would consider the evidence in a different light. That the U.S. government was so intent on keeping Venezuela off the Security Council points to the importance of that institution. Even though the rotating members of the Security Council do not have veto power, they can block resolutions, as occurred when Chile and Mexico voted against the use of force against Iraq in 2003. Given that reality, Presidents Bush and Chávez both attached considerable importance to which country would win the seat.

Despite the fact that the United States was a major driving force behind the creation of the UN, it has become an example of an international institution with a life of its own. If the United States chooses to ignore the UN, then it runs the risk of pursuing policies without assistance. As a consequence, the institution itself creates an incentive to build consensus and forge coalitions. As such, it constitutes a brake on the exertion of U.S. power abroad and instead promotes collective security and dialogue.

A *dependency theorist* would take a different tack. The problem is not power per se, but rather the reality that less developed countries are structurally constrained from independent action. Power is just a function of an inherently unequal international system, which is constantly exploited by more developed countries, especially the United States. Because they are created and financed by wealthy governments, even international institutions perpetuate dependent economic and political relationships.

Given its status as a state in the economic core of the international economic system, the U.S. government uses the United Nations to maintain its advantageous position, wielding its influence to counteract any effort by weaker states to assert themselves.

Especially because of the nature of veto power, the United Nations itself is dominated by a handful of countries, and little of consequence occurs unless the United States or other major powers acquiesce. A country like Venezuela may be able to make a public argument against or delay action through the UN, but ultimately cannot stop the United States (which, for example, invaded Iraq without UN support). The Bush administration bullies smaller countries into voting for its own choice because it costs nothing to do so and enhances U.S. economic and political power, and all parties understand that. But even if Venezuela were to win the seat, the effect would be minimal, because it would simply be operating within a structure that already favors the most powerful countries.

Notes

1. Waltz 1979, 192.
2. Gunder Frank 1967.
3. Cardoso and Faletto 1979.
4. Evans 1979.
5. Cottam 1994, 6.
6. Desch 1993, 6–9.
7. Rosecrance 1986.
8. See Kinsella 2005.
9. Hurrell 1996, 164–65.
10. Keohane and Martin 2003, 96.
11. For the essence of the debate, see Baldwin 1993.
12. Katz 2006.
13. Wadhams 2006.
14. Cavallo 2006.
15. United States Department of State Web site 2006.

HISTORICAL
BACKGROUND

CHAPTER 2

The Roots of U.S. and Latin American Relations

TIMELINE	
1807–1808	Napoleon Bonaparte invades Portugal and Spain
1811–1826	Most Spanish colonies and Brazil become independent
1811	No-Transfer Resolution passed by U.S. Congress
1822	United States first grants diplomatic recognition to independent Latin American states
1823	Monroe Doctrine proclaimed
1826	Simón Bolívar organizes first inter-American conference
1846–1848	War with Mexico, culminating in the Treaty of Guadalupe Hidalgo
1850	United States and Great Britain sign Clayton-Bulwer Treaty to share control over a canal
1854	Ostend Manifesto announced regarding U.S. interests in Cuba
1855–1857	William Walker fights in Nicaragua
1861–1865	U.S. Civil War
1862–1867	France invades and occupies Mexico
1878	French company begins work on a canal through Panama

At the dawn of the nineteenth century, the United States was a fledgling power, weaker than many European countries in both economic and military terms. The central government had effective control over only a small area of the continent, and disputes between it and the states were already well entrenched. It had continental aspirations, but only gradually would it begin moving its border westward. The power imbalance between the United States and Latin America was therefore not yet great, but it would rapidly swing in the U.S. direction in the first decades of the century. This chapter analyzes the challenges in establishing and maintaining relations between governments in the United States and Latin America and concludes with the post–Civil War period, at which time U.S. economic and military power began to increase markedly.

Latin America remained under the colonial control of Spain and Portugal (even though that was about to change), and its political and economic autonomy was very limited. Its European-origin inhabitants had not yet defined clear boundaries or even established firm control over territory; outlying areas were still dominated by indigenous groups. Although trade did exist with the United States, it did not yet contribute significantly to most of their economies, and interaction between the United States and Latin America had not yet developed significantly.

In the first half of the nineteenth century, U.S.–Latin American relations can be viewed in terms of newly independent countries (including the United States) trying to create new nations and to define their boundaries, their relationships with Europe, and their relationships with each other. Mutual wariness would quickly become evident. Wars over territory periodically erupted, nascent nationalism grew, and trade gradually increased as well. Following the end of the Civil War in 1865, the United States was continuing its economic growth and consolidating its position as an important (though not yet dominant) political, economic, and military power in the region. Security was paramount, because the continued existence of these states was no foregone conclusion. Following realist assumptions, political leaders in the United States viewed Latin America mainly in the context of European rivalries that threatened U.S. interests.

Most of Latin America became independent between 1811 and 1826, largely a result of the implosion of the once dominant Spanish empire. The legendary reign of Ferdinand and Isabella, who presided over the conquering of the "new" world beginning in 1492, was centuries past, replaced over time by a problematic combination of mismanagement, lethargy, and greed. The final straw, however, was that by 1808 the monarchy found it very difficult to maintain an empire while simultaneously being invaded by France. Something had to give. Even though he did not intend it, Napoleon played a key role in advancing the cause of Latin American independence.

When Spain was invaded, revolution did not immediately erupt across the region. Colonial elites had many reasons to be skeptical about independence.

As long as profit and social order were maintained, then little was to be gained. But sentiment varied greatly, as even elites were split, depending on the degree of their allegiance to Spain and their desire to maintain the colonial political and social hierarchy. Initially, local leaders created "caretaker" governments that would serve until colonial rule was restored. However, resentment between the Spanish-born ("Peninsulars," referring to the Iberian peninsula of Spain and Portugal) and native-born whites ("Creoles," from the Spanish word *criollo,* which in turn derived from the Latin *creare,* meaning "to create," referring to the fact that a new mixed race of people was being created), which had been bubbling along, soon boiled over. Creoles felt subjugated because Peninsulars were granted all privileges by Spain and wielded most of the political and economic power. In addition, when the Spanish monarchy was restored in 1814, local elites felt that they deserved autonomy in return for loyalty, but Ferdinand VII refused and instead sought to restore absolute control over his domain. This had the effect of severing ties with many colonial elites, who felt betrayed.

Latin America in the Era of Independence

Several geographical and political characteristics of Latin America at the time of independence greatly affected hemispheric relations. For example, when the United States recognized Mexico as an independent country in 1822, it included all of what is now the southwestern United States, a total of more than a million square miles. Meanwhile, Colombia included present-day Panama, the thin isthmus that pokes up from the northern tip of South America. In both cases, the United States would eventually go to war either to take or to control parts of those territories.

In addition, Latin American "independence" did not yet refer to the entire continent. The Dominican Republic, which shared the island of Hispaniola with Haiti, did not become fully independent until 1844 because Haiti had successfully invaded and occupied its territory. In Brazil, the Portuguese monarchs had sought refuge from Napoleon's onslaught, and in 1822 the king's son, Pedro I, proclaimed himself emperor. After negotiations, his father assented to independence, and the process was far less violent than in Spanish America. Brazil therefore became independent but remained closely tied to Portugal.

Neither did Cuba become independent at this point. Worried in particular about the possibility of a slave uprising if revolution was attempted, Cuban elites chose the safer route of remaining a colony. Cuba and the United States gradually developed very close ties, despite high taxes imposed by the Spanish crown and the general discouragement of non-Spanish trade. As it would be in the twentieth century, Cuba became a playground for wealthy Americans. The slave trade flourished, and after the U.S. Civil War, there arrived a wave of Southerners and their slaves. The influx from the United States also fostered boardinghouses and brothels. There were, as Pérez argues, "ties of singular intimacy" long before Cuba shed Spanish rule.[1]

More than once, serious plans were laid in the United States to buy or to seize Cuba from Spain. Southerners supported the idea either as a way to bring in another slave state or as a place where slaves could be sent if they became too much trouble for their owners. In 1852, Great Britain and France invited the United States to sign a joint treaty guaranteeing continued Spanish control of Cuba, ostensibly to promote stability on the island. Rejecting the idea, the United States government stated that there was a long-standing policy to acquire Cuba at some point. In 1854, the Ostend Manifesto (so named because the U.S. ministers to Spain, France, and England were meeting in Ostend, Belgium) spelled out why the United States should purchase Cuba and, if Spain were not willing to sell, stated that troops should take it by force to maintain order. In particular, the large slave population in Cuba, combined with weak Spanish rule, raised the possibility of a debilitating slave revolt that could spread to the United States. It is not likely that Northerners would have accepted the entrance of Cuba as another state, but it became a moot point, as the details of the manifesto were leaked, and the plan was quickly scuttled.

Security and U.S. Policy

As soon as the United States won its own battle against its former colonizer, the leadership quickly became concerned about developments south of its border. The direction of events was uncertain, and in the late eighteenth and early nineteenth centuries, U.S. policy makers had long debates about the course of action that would best suit U.S. interests. Even the definition of such interests was open to debate. They included keeping European influence out of the hemisphere as much as possible, acquiring territory then owned by Spain and France, and cementing the still fragile "united" states of America. The central question was, If the United States were to openly support the revolutionary movements in Latin America, what effect would that decision have on U.S. national interests?

National security was central, and a number of potential threats were immediately apparent. For example, what is now eastern Florida was Spanish territory, and if the Spanish empire fell apart, it was easy to imagine a foreign power moving in to take advantage of the situation. As British encroachments on U.S. sovereignty increased, such as seizing ships and forcing U.S. citizens to join the British navy, hawks in Congress clamored for a clear statement to deny any European incursions. In 1811, Congress passed the No Transfer Resolution, which proclaimed the right of the United States to occupy the Florida territory if another country sought to take it. It stated that if the United States were to "see any part of the said territory pass into the hands of any foreign power," then a "due regard to their own safety compels them to provide, under certain contingencies, for the temporary occupations of the said territory." It would then be "subject to a future negotiation."[2] The issue of eastern Florida remained unresolved until 1819, when a treaty with Spain ceded it to the United States in exchange only for not taxing Spanish ships any more than U.S. ships in the ports of Pensacola and St. Augustine for twelve years.

Other security threats to the United States at the time were both real and complex, to the point that historians continue to debate their relative importance. All tend to agree that the United States felt vulnerable on all flanks. European powers viewed the region as a potential source of aggrandizement, whether through trade or imperial expansion.

Spain itself, of course, represented a serious problem, but mostly in terms of its disintegration as opposed to its expansion. The fact that Spain managed to hold on to Cuba (as well as Puerto Rico) did serve to maintain its presence in the Western Hemisphere for almost a hundred more years, but the handwriting was on the wall for Spain as a global power. Spain did send troops to the Dominican Republic in 1861 in a short-lived effort to retake the former colony, and it attacked Peru in 1864 for not paying debts allegedly owed as a result of the independence wars. (A peace treaty was not signed until 1879.) But these events were isolated, the last gasps of a dying empire.

Great Britain was far more dangerous. The White House had barely been built when British soldiers torched it in the War of 1812. Britain also developed extensive trade relations in Central America and even went to South America, where, for example, over time it built the Chilean navy. From 1803 to 1811, the British navy disrupted trade between the United States and the rebellious Latin American colonies. In addition, a number of Caribbean islands were part of the British Empire. Until 1981, Belize would also remain a British protectorate in Central America and a constant source of border conflict with Guatemala. Great Britain invested heavily in Argentina as well, and in 1833 even took possession of a small group of islands off its coast (the Falkland Islands, or Islas Malvinas, as Argentina called them). In general, Britain competed—often successfully—with the United States for diplomatic and economic influence throughout the hemisphere.

Nonetheless, as the wars between the United States and Britain faded into the past, bilateral relations improved greatly. Treaties and agreements in the years immediately after the War of 1812 removed British opposition to U.S. westward expansion and served to delineate borders. Meanwhile, political leaders in the two countries very often shared the same suspicions about continental Europe, especially in terms of what would happen to the colonies of the crumbling and tattered Spanish empire.

The French represented a threat as a result of the French Revolution and the rise to power of Napoleon Bonaparte in the late eighteenth century. In 1800, France forced Spain to hand over the Louisiana territories. Given the importance of the Mississippi River for trade, Thomas Jefferson soon began negotiations to purchase the territories, with a deal finally completed in 1803. Back in Europe, with the intent of conquering Portugal, in 1807 Napoleon signed an agreement with Spain to allow an army of 28,000 French soldiers to march from

France to Lisbon. In early 1808, Napoleon decided to send soldiers to invade Spain as well. Thus began the occupation of the Iberian peninsula.

As Napoleon's quest to conquer Europe drained his resources, he largely turned away from the Western Hemisphere. A year after invading Spain, he issued a proclamation that France would not oppose revolution and independence in the Spanish colonies, "provided that these peoples do not form any relations with England."[3] This policy corresponded with U.S. interests but would shift after Napoleon's downfall; the new French government subsequently supported Spanish efforts to maintain its colonies. Spanish ministers also reminded France that the recognition of revolution in one area of the world could spell the end of colonial rule everywhere. France was therefore a periodic diplomatic thorn in the side of the United States, but after the Louisiana Purchase, it no longer represented a pressing threat.

Russia was also present. Initially, the tsar tried to help Spain regain her colonies, even with military assistance. It made sense to quash revolution; in the eyes of monarchs, the phenomenon has an annoying tendency to spread. Nonetheless, given its own conflict with France and the acknowledgment that Spain was beyond help, the tsar moved instead to expand Russia's presence in the Western Hemisphere and to establish both diplomatic and economic relationships with the new states. Most prominently, this meant aggressive actions to establish Russian economic influence in Brazil and in what would become California, in addition to a presence in Alaska.

There were, therefore, powerful European countries with a variety of interests—both political and economic—in the region at the time of the Latin American wars for independence, and most had sought to make arrangements that would disadvantage the others. Ultimately, U.S. leaders perceived more threat in the constant conniving than in the military or economic might of any one particular country, and eventually they would declare that Europe should simply stay out.

But threats to the national security of the United States were not only external. The country had existed for only a few decades and still wasn't very unified. During this early period, the dissolution of the Spanish empire posed a potentially disastrous challenge to the continued development of that unity. In particular, would the revolutionary fever spread through Florida, or through Louisiana, which had been purchased in only 1803? There was simply no assurance that these territories would remain part of the United States because they might decide they were better off alone. Policy deliberations therefore also kept that possibility closely in mind.

As presidents and members of Congress tried to figure out how to deal with Spanish American rebellion, they made no bones about the fact that U.S. interests were paramount and that the needs, desires, or goals of the rebels themselves were close to irrelevant. The U.S. government sent agents to different parts of Latin America and in some cases instructed them to provide moral support. But the rebels needed muskets, not vague pronouncements, and weapons were not forthcoming from the United States. Meanwhile, some of the U.S. diplomatic agents even fostered within Latin Americans a dislike for the United States, as they demonstrated their distaste for what they saw as uncouth rebels or took sides in factional disputes.

The official policy of the United States was "friendly" neutrality, intended to avoid antagonizing Spain while turning a blind eye as private ships left U.S. harbors with supplies. Revolutionaries often arrived to purchase weapons and even to build or purchase new ships. In 1816, the U.S. government "lent" some powder to a Venezuelan agent, claiming it was surplus. Despite constant protests by the Spanish government, there was very little enforcement of neutrality agreements. Yet official U.S. support never materialized.

It is clear that no policy maker had any faith in the ability of newly independent countries in the region to become stable, much less democratic. There is overwhelming evidence that the conventional wisdom in the United States was that Latin Americans were by nature incapable of much of anything. John Adams, for example, wrote that the idea of establishing democracy in the region was "as absurd as similar plans would be to establish democracies among the birds, beasts, and fishes."[4] There were indeed clear limits to the sympathy within the United States for the rebels. Congressional debate showed more interest in the Greeks (who at the time were seeking independence from the Ottoman Empire) than the Latin Americans, and Great Britain proved more generous with providing credit to Latin America.[5]

Though Latin America had followed the U.S. example of a revolutionary break with its former colonizer—another ragtag army fighting a European power—it was given little credit. In 1816, one observer told the U.S. Congress, "the struggle of liberty in South America will turn out in the end something like the French liberty, a detestable despotism."[6] Even in the late 1990s, as a senior U.S. Army officer surveyed U.S. military programs around the world, he spoke of Indonesia: "It's one of only a few formerly colonized countries in the world that has gained independence through revolution. There's us, Vietnam, and Indonesia."[7] Latin America didn't merit mention. Although tied to the United States in so many ways, whether geographical, political, cultural, or economic, it was still considered a backwater.

Nonetheless, at least on the surface Latin American countries emulated the political institutions of the United States. The new constitutions set up presidential systems with separation of powers and civil liberties, but these would become mixed with elements of French constitutional provisions and the Spanish constitution of 1812, a time when Spain was dabbling in republican government.[8] This mix meant the articulation of personal and political liberties with strong presidential governments, but in states of emergency (decided by some combination of the president and congress), all such liberties could be suspended.

For example, Venezuela adopted the first Latin American constitution in 1811. Section Two clearly lays out that all Venezuelans are guaranteed the rights of liberty, equality before the law, and security, thus echoing the U.S. Constitution and the amendments encapsulated in the Bill of Rights.[9] In Venezuela, there was also liberty (preamble and amendment five), security (amendment four), and law (five and six). Yet unlike the United States, Venezuela established Catholicism as its official religion (placed prominently as the first article), and article 134 gave the president and legislature (or, if the legislature could not be convened, only the president) all power necessary to put down "domestic violence." Those powers owed much to the French constitution, which evolved as revolution affected public order, and by 1797 it allowed the government to establish a state of siege to combat "internal security." Future constitutions, in Venezuela (where that first constitution lasted only eight years) and elsewhere, would reinforce this hybrid foreign influence. And, as in the United States, Latin American political elites were not eager to extend rights and liberties to all their fellow citizens. Many shared the same doubts as U.S. policy makers regarding whether their countries could (or should) become democracies.

The "founding fathers" of Latin America—the generals fighting for independence—such as Simón Bolívar (Venezuela), Augustín de Iturbide (who eventually proclaimed himself emperor of Mexico), José de San Martín (Argentina), and Bernardo O'Higgins (Chile), generally rejected the model of federalism and limited government developed in the United States and instead emphasized centralism and a strong executive. Although they disagreed about the precise nature of the new political systems (and many different political experiments would be made, with more than a hundred constitutions promulgated in the nineteenth century), they were united in a vision of a strong government capable of restoring and then maintaining order; Bolívar even advocated a president-for-life position. Their charters therefore resembled that of the United States but developed their own distinct flavors according to the security concerns of the era.

The nature of these political foundations also meant that for decades the policy process in Latin America would be dominated by the executive branch. Presidents, not legislators, would determine how to interact with the United States. Thus, the political leanings of the president would resolve the question of whether the country would work closely with the United States.

Recognition of the New Nations

Two series of events in the 1820s further defined the U.S. attitude toward the new nations and its relationship with them. First, in 1822 the United States granted diplomatic recognition to five Latin American countries (Argentina, Chile, Colombia, Mexico, and Peru). Essentially, that meant the United States had formally declared that these new nations had the right to exist independently and would therefore enter into full diplomatic relations with them. The decision was based almost entirely on the idea, expressed most clearly by Thomas Jefferson, that if a government had de facto control then it deserved recognition.[10] In other words, ideology or attitude toward the United States did not matter. The main criterion was simply having control of territory and people. This diplomatic recognition had more of a symbolic impact than anything else. The United States was in no hurry to establish trade relations or have much interaction at all with these new, weak, bloodstained countries that U.S. investors and politicians alike viewed as backward and uncivilized. Nonetheless, it did provide an example for other countries to follow, because the United States was the first country outside Latin America to grant recognition.

The decision to recognize had been a matter of debate for years, but no consensus had been reached. One reason was that the most vocal proponent of granting recognition, Henry Clay, was speaker of the House of Representatives, and his efforts were viewed as an attempt to give diplomatic power to Congress, which presidents saw as their sole domain. Secretary of State John Quincy Adams wrote that Clay's insistence was an attempt "to control or overthrow the Executive."[11] It was also part of an effort to launch Clay's own presidential bid and contained some personal elements as well, in that Clay had wanted President Monroe to choose him as secretary of state.

In this era, the boundaries of executive, legislative, and judicial powers in the country were still fluid, which raised the stakes, and that struggle over control has never disappeared. In particular, it continues to emerge whenever the president and the congressional majority disagree on policy. Ultimately, President James Monroe used his authority to grant recognition, and subsequent federal court decisions upheld that authority.

Latin American responses to these developments were laced with caution and even suspicion. Simón Bolívar, whose leadership made him known as the liberator of the Spanish American colonies, convened a conference of American states (the Congress of Panama) in 1826 with the hope of creating a loose confederation that would foster trade and provide protection against external enemies. His argument that this new arrangement "seems destined to form a league more extensive, more remarkable, and more powerful than any that has ever existed on the face of the earth" was certainly exaggerated, but it did mark the beginning of many attempts to bring the countries of the region together. Bolívar invited Great Britain (given its wartime assistance) and only belatedly the United States (whose delegates were sent but never arrived because of transportation problems, illness, and even death—congressional debate over even sending them was intense). Bolívar's attitude was, as he wrote in 1829, that the United States "seem destined by Providence to plague America with torments in the name of freedom."[12]

After all, it is fair to ask why Latin American leaders would have confidence in the intentions and actions of the United States. During the wars for independence, the United States had been neutral and so had not demonstrated open support for fellow revolutionaries; negotiations with Spain took precedence. From the beginning, U.S. diplomats often failed to demonstrate that the United States had any profound interest in the region.

Simón Bolívar, Views on the Congress of Panama (1826)

The Congress of Panamá will bring together all the representatives of America and a diplomat-agent of His Britannic Majesty's government. This Congress seems destined to form a league more extensive, more remarkable, and more powerful than any that has ever existed on the face of the earth. Should Great Britain agree to join it as a constituent member, the Holy Alliance will be less powerful than this confederation. Mankind will a thousand times bless this league for promoting its general welfare, and America, as well as Britain, will reap from it untold benefits. A code of public law to regulate the international conduct of political bodies will be one of its products.

1. The New World would consist of independent nations, bound together by a common set of laws which would govern their foreign relations and afford them a right to survival through a general and permanent congress.
2. The existence of these new states would receive fresh guarantees.
3. In deference to England, Spain would make peace, and the Holy Alliance would grant recognition to these infant nations.
4. Domestic control would be preserved untouched among the states and within each of them.
5. No one of them would be weaker than another, nor would any be stronger.
6. A perfect balance would be established by this truly new order of things.
7. The power of all would come to the aid of any one state which might suffer at the hands of a foreign enemy or from internal anarchic factions.
8. Differences of origin and color would lose their influence and power.
9. America would have nothing more to fear from that tremendous monster [the black population] who has devoured the island of Santo Domingo, nor would she have cause to fear the numerical preponderance of the aborigines.
10. In short, a social reform would be achieved under the blessed auspices of freedom and peace, but the fulcrum controlling the beam of the scales must necessarily rest in the hands of England.

Source: Simón Bolívar, "Views on the Congress of Panamá." In Vicente Lecuna (comp.) and Harold A. Bierck Jr. (ed.). *Selected Writings of Bolívar, Vol. 2, 1823–1830* (New York: Colonial Press): 561–62.

Nation Building and International Relations in Latin America

There was, however, no monolithic Latin American relationship with the northern neighbor. In many countries, political competition after independence revolved around liberals and conservatives, who had very different views. Bearing no resemblance to U.S. definitions, in Latin America "liberal" referred (with some regional variation) to those who looked to the United States and Europe as political models, advocating republican and democratic values (though with clear restrictions on who could participate), separation of church and state, the dismantling of the traditional aristocracy, and the rapid growth of trade and production. "Conservative" had opposite connotations, being more traditional, nationalist, and close to the Catholic Church. In general, liberals were more interested in alliances with U.S. politicians and business leaders.

The emergence of these political differences also came in the context of the development of new states and uncertain ideas about nationality. These new states were to varying degrees born dependent on the economies of Europe. The capitalist classes, already enjoying strong ties to their counterparts in the more developed world, worked to create states that served their economic interests and were centralized in the capital.

In the case of South America, for example, Centeno argues that the state's fiscal capacity (that is, the ability of these new states to establish effective economic administration, impose and collect taxes, and otherwise impose the rule of law) remained almost nonexistent, and instead there were "only perpetually bankrupt beggar states."[13] But Centeno also notes that the key reason for the weakness of these states was that wars rarely occurred. "Total wars," with full mobilization (and militarization) of the population, many deaths, and a crusade mentality, have always been lacking in Latin America. Instead, there have been "limited wars" that are smaller geographically, originate in economic or frontier conflicts, and may not even affect a large proportion of the citizenry.[14]

To this day there has never been a South American continental war. Unlike Europe, where such wars solidified national identity and forced states to develop their own means of financing their security, in Latin America limited wars meant that the sense of being in a collective enterprise did not extend much beyond the capitals and major cities, and the state simply incurred debt to fund the fighting.

For U.S.–Latin American relations, these issues would have important consequences. First, the failure of Latin American countries to become financially independent would soon trouble U.S. policy makers because European governments would begin intervening in order to collect. Second, Latin American perceptions of "security" were much more internally oriented. It was considered more important to consolidate control over the country's territory than to concentrate on external enemies, which left them more open to influence. As Loveman argues, Latin American leaders had to construct "la Patria" (the nation or "fatherland") in the face of a highly divided population (often including indigenous groups, which persistently resisted encroachment on their territory), and they did so through the use of some type of military force.[15]

One core idea of realism is that the state's primary goal is security. The United States defined security in terms of freedom from European aggression, but the weaker Latin American states viewed security largely as control over internal opposition. Although immediately after independence they faced threats from Spain (and, in Central America, from Great Britain), their main concern would be European efforts to collect debt. Over time, this meant that the United States would be successful in taking advantage of internal conflict and thereby imposing its own version of security over the region.

Argentina provides a glimpse into these dynamics. Its capital, Buenos Aires, was an integral and flourishing part of the Spanish economic empire, but revolution forced its elites to adopt new institutions as a way to maintain their prominence and to create order out of revolutionary chaos. The caudillo of Buenos Aires province, Juan Manuel de Rosas, fought successfully to take over the government, established a harsh dictatorship, and ruled in 1829 through 1832 and then again from 1835 to 1853. Like other Argentine leaders, Rosas encouraged foreign investment and trade with Europe, especially with Great Britain, where there was great interest in Argentine cattle. From this combination of political repression and foreign economic presence emerged a state marked by corruption, weak control over distant provinces, and dependence on foreign capital. By the end of the nineteenth century, Argentina was widely considered an up-and-coming economic power, and Buenos Aires was imbued with European flavor. It did not, however, effectively counter the expansion of U.S. political influence in the region.

The Origins of the Monroe Doctrine

The next critical definition of U.S. policy came at the end of an annual presidential message to Congress in 1823 by James Monroe. Several paragraphs outlined the U.S. view on European activity in the Western Hemisphere, and a new doctrine was born. Without it, Monroe's name may have passed into the relative obscurity of the Fillmores, Arthurs, and Harrisons. Instead, the Monroe Doctrine is the most enduring symbol of U.S. interest in Latin America. It stated simply that the United States would stay out of Europe's business and expected the reverse to hold as well. If Europe tried to "extend its political system" in Latin America, it would be viewed as "endangering our peace and happiness."

The idea that European meddling was unacceptable already had deep roots and was a logical extension of the anti-Europe sentiment that had found voice since the U.S. revolution. Up to that point, all U.S. presidents had at some time openly advocated isolationism. Monroe's speech was distinctive, however, because it shifted from isolationism to a more active expression of hemispheric hegemony. The speech itself was directed at Russia and at the Holy Alliance (which in addition to Russia included Austria, France, and Prussia). The former was encroaching on U.S. territory in the Pacific Northwest. Meanwhile, rumors were flying that the latter, in its quest to stem the growth of republican political systems, sought to aid Spain in restoring its control over the former colonies. (It is far from clear whether those rumors were true.) Hearing these rumors, the British had approached the Monroe administration in hopes of jointly declaring their opposition to further colonization in the region. After discussions within

The Monroe Doctrine (1823)

[T]he occasion has been judged proper for asserting, as a principle in which the rights and interests of the United States are involved, that the American continents, by the free and independent condition which they have assumed and maintain, are henceforth not to be considered as subjects for future colonization by any European powers. . . . Of events in that [European] quarter of the globe, with which we have so much intercourse and from which we derive our origin, we have always been anxious and interested spectators. The citizens of the United States cherish sentiments the most friendly in favor of the liberty and happiness of their fellowmen on that side of the Atlantic. In the wars of the European powers in matters relating to themselves we have never taken any part, nor does it comport with our policy so to do. It is only when our rights are invaded or seriously menaced that we resent injuries or make preparation for our defense. With the movements in this hemisphere we are of necessity more immediately connected, and by causes which must be obvious to all enlightened and impartial observers. The political system of the allied powers is essentially different in this respect from that of America. This difference proceeds from that which exists in their respective Governments; and to the defense of our own, which has been achieved by the loss of so much blood and treasure, and matured by the wisdom of their most enlightened citizens, and under which we have enjoyed unexampled felicity, this whole nation is devoted. We owe it, therefore, to candor and to the amicable relations existing between the United States and those powers to declare that we should consider any attempt on their part to extend their system to any portion of this hemisphere as dangerous to our peace and safety. With the existing colonies or dependencies of any European power we have not interfered and shall not interfere. But with the Governments who have declared their independence and maintained it, and whose independence we have, on great consideration and on just principles, acknowledged, we could not view any interposition for the purpose of oppressing them, or controlling in any other manner their destiny, by any European power in any other light than as the manifestation of an unfriendly disposition toward the United States.

Our policy in regard to Europe, which was adopted at an early stage of the wars which have so long agitated that quarter of the globe, nevertheless remains the same, which is, not to interfere in the internal concerns of any of its powers; to consider the government de facto as the legitimate government for us; to cultivate friendly relations with it, and to preserve those relations by a frank, firm, and manly policy, meeting in all instances the just claims of every power, submitting to injuries from none. But in regard to those continents circumstances are eminently and conspicuously different. It is impossible that the allied powers should extend their political system to any portion of either continent without endangering our peace and happiness; nor can anyone believe that our southern brethren, if left to themselves, would adopt it of their own accord. It is equally impossible, therefore,

(Continued)

that we should behold such interposition in any form with indifference. If we look to the comparative strength and resources of Spain and those new Governments, and their distance from each other, it must be obvious that she can never subdue them. It is still the true policy of the United States to leave the parties to themselves, in the hope that other powers will pursue the same course. . . .

Source: http://usinfo.state.gov/usa/infousa/facts/democrac/50.htm

the administration, Monroe decided it did not make sense to issue an anti-Europe declaration along with a European power.

Initially, it was hard for anyone to take Monroe's doctrine too seriously. The United States was still in no position to be taking on European powers militarily. Great Britain had the most powerful navy in the world, and France's was also formidable. Europe's response was to scoff at the idea (and the British were annoyed that Monroe had rejected their offer of a joint declaration). Battling the British at home was a far cry from sending an army to, for example, the far reaches of the south Atlantic coast. Only ten years later, Britain seized the Falkland Islands (Islas Malvinas) off the coast of Argentina. These islands once again became prominent in 1982, when an Argentine dictatorship invaded in an attempt to incite a surge of nationalism. Both in 1833 and in 1982, the United States made no protest as British forces defeated Argentina, and in 1982 it actively aided Britain with intelligence.

The Monroe Doctrine was never applied uniformly, as other European incursions periodically occurred. The United States also made clear that the doctrine should not be interpreted as a desire to create security agreements or treaties with Latin American countries. It was a unilateral policy. The U.S. minister to Mexico stated erroneously that the doctrine was a "pledge," but the U.S. government was quick to explain that he was mistaken.[16] In the 1820s and 1830s, several Latin American leaders invoked the doctrine when confronted by European militaries, but their requests were ignored. In the case of the Falkland Islands/Islas Malvinas, the United States noted that the British had laid claim to the islands before independence, and so the doctrine did not apply.[17] In 1838, the French blockaded the port of the Argentine capital, Buenos Aires, but the United States chose not to respond. There were few in the United States interested in transforming Monroe's words into a fixed policy, which would represent entangling alliances that could push the country toward war against its best interests. The "doctrine" was selective, and indeed the United States was usually in no position to enforce it anyway.

This response disappointed a number of Latin American leaders, who for a brief time entertained the hope that Monroe was reaching out to his neighbors. The United States was the only country to offer any sort of rhetorical defense against European efforts at economic domination. European countries were far more apt to intervene than the United States, and so Argentina, for example, believed the United States might at least be able to prevent European meddling. Perhaps some measure of unity could offer protection against this common enemy.

For many in the United States, policy makers and academics alike, the Monroe Doctrine was wholly beneficial for all involved, most especially Latin Americans. As one U.S.–Latin America textbook put it in 1920, the doctrine had "saved South America from the kind of exploitation to which the continents of Africa and Asia have, during the past generation, fallen a prey."[18] Because it did not engage in traditional colonization, the idea that the United States had any hand in exploitation would not be widely debated until several decades later.

At the time, authority over Latin American states remained in question, as regional caudillos fought each other for access to the resources available only to those who controlled the government. In Argentina, the destructive nature of these battles was captured in a book entitled *Civilization or Barbarism*, published in 1845. After describing the viciousness of Rosas and a regional caudillo (Facundo Quiroga), Sarmiento asks simply, "Have Facundo or Rosas ever done the least thing for the public good, or been interested in any useful object? No. From them come nothing but blood and crimes."[19] In much of Latin America, security concerns were largely turned inward, which left these new states more open to foreign encroachment. The inability of Latin American countries to shake free of European domination underlined the growing power imbalance with the United States.

The fledgling Central American Confederation (what are now Guatemala, El Salvador, Honduras, Nicaragua, and Costa Rica) requested U.S. assistance to counter British border encroachment, military threat, and commercial domination in the 1820s and 1830s. At first the U.S. government ignored the requests, and then it proceeded to negotiate a solution directly with Great Britain, without Central American input. In the 1820s, the United States received and then denied requests for formal alliances with Brazil, Chile, and Colombia and refused to give assurances to Mexico and the Provinces of the Rio de la Plata (which would later become Argentina and Uruguay) that the United States would guarantee protection under the Monroe Doctrine.

In general, the United States had little strategic or economic interest in South America in the first half of the nineteenth century, and there was little reason to enforce the Monroe Doctrine. For example, the British, French, and Portuguese were more active in trade with Argentina and Brazil. For the most part, the United States focused on Mexico and the Caribbean, which were closer geographically and therefore more important economically and strategically. Not until the turn of the twentieth century, when the United States had become an industrial power, did its attention begin to include the entire region, and even then the northern parts of Latin America remained the most vital.

The most egregious flouting of the Monroe Doctrine occurred between 1862 and 1867, when France invaded Mexico and even installed an emperor—Maximilian—to rule. In fact, some Mexican elites had been searching Europe for an available monarch and finally through France found their candidate. For Napoleon III (the nephew of Napoleon Bonaparte), it was an opportunity to seize Mexican customs houses and thereby force repayment of loans to French creditors (Clamoring for their money, along with Spanish and British creditors). With the backing of the French army, which had been sent two years earlier to pave his way, Maximilian arrived in Mexico City in 1864. Celebrations of Cinco de Mayo (which tend to be more popular, though much less understood, in the United States than in Mexico) in fact go back to a battle on May 5, 1862, in which a Mexican force (which included future presidents Benito Juárez and Porfirio Díaz) in Fort Guadalupe repelled a French attack.

Despite the invasion, the United States made minimal protests. President Abraham Lincoln told the Mexican minister that in the case of European aggression, the U.S. would not be in a position to come to Mexico's aid. Domestic issues were more important. Given the outbreak of civil war, the U.S. could ill afford to have France recognize and supply the Confederacy, so Lincoln preferred to remain neutral. Only after the civil war ended did the United States turn its attention to Mexico, and rumors of intervention flew. Action by the U.S. government was concentrated on pressuring France to withdraw, even with hints of war. Ultimately, Mexican soldiers themselves did much of the job. In 1867, shortly after the last French troops left, Maximilian was executed, and the experiment was over.

Manifest Destiny

As the newly formed Latin American nations struggled to define their politics and even their borders, the United States remained restless, constantly looking to the west. The term "Manifest Destiny" was attributed to a newspaper reporter in 1845, but it reflected a belief that had been present for decades, namely, that the true destiny of the United States was to continue westward expansion. Beyond the mystical imagery, however, the expansion of economic and military power was also important. Control over the west would fortify the country and make it far stronger economically. Utilizing the U.S. military to achieve such goals seemed wholly appropriate to U.S. policy makers.

It was well known that all manner of indigenous peoples and Mexicans lived in those territories, but this was no obstacle. Those "heathens" would be "civilized" or simply moved out of the way. Politicians and the general public alike embraced the concept of Manifest Destiny. The former viewed it as a way to increase their political power (creating new states, of course, also immediately became wrapped up in the debate over slavery), and the latter saw an opportunity to make their fortunes. The west was sparsely populated and virtually lawless, given the weak Mexican government. Why not just take it?

For years, U.S. presidents had sent representatives to Mexico with the goal of purchasing part of it. In the years following independence, the United States floated offers of $1 million to move the border to the Río Grande. These offers were always rejected, and Mexican leaders became concerned about the many settlers moving in from the southern and eastern United States, the majority of whom stayed in Texas. The infamous battle of the Alamo in 1836, in which General Antonio López de Santa Anna wiped out a force of Texans who had declared Texas's independence, symbolized the deteriorating Anglo-Mexican relationship. (Several months later, the Texans won several decisive battles, even capturing Santa Anna.) The following year, the United States recognized the independence of Texas, and subsequently debate arose about incorporating Texas as a new state.

Although liberals in Mexico tended to be more sympathetic to the United States and viewed it as a political and economic model, by the 1840s, Mexicans of all political stripes became more united as U.S. annexation of Texas seemed increasingly likely. The religious and racial superiority expressed in Manifest Destiny troubled even liberals, who had come to view it as an attempt to exterminate Hispanic culture. They emphasized how Mexican culture was more civilized than that in the United States, especially given the abolition of slavery in Mexico.

In 1844, James Polk was elected president, and he came to office with the publicly stated goal of reacquiring Texas, which, as part of the 1819 Adams–de Onís Treaty, remained in Spanish (and then Mexican) hands, though its Anglo residents had declared an independent republic. The following year, the U.S. Congress formally asked Texas if it wished to join the Union, an offer that was accepted. The idea of annexing Texas had been raised in the past (John Quincy Adams had tried to acquire it from Spain in 1819 and then wanted to buy it from Mexico), but because it would become a slave state, Northerners had resisted the decision for decades. Gradually, Texas became entwined with the rest of the west and the realization of Manifest Destiny. Shifting political alliances within the United States continued to provide majorities in Congress that supported and funded the entire project.

The United States thus annexed Texas in 1845, which only increased its thirst for pushing west all the way to the Pacific Ocean. At the same time, Mexican leaders were angered by the loss of the Texas territory, as well as the Polk administration's request for even more territory. The combination of these factors led to war. What is now generally known in the United States as the Mexican-American War was then popularly known as "Mr. Polk's War." In Mexico, it is the "the War of the Northern Aggression" or "the War of the United States against Mexico."

The war with Mexico lasted two years and ended in 1848 with the Treaty of Guadalupe Hidalgo. For $15 million, the United States took possession of the west. The Rio Grande became the southern border with Mexico, and everything north of the river and west of Texas was then part of the United States. In a short span of time, Mexico had lost approximately half its land (though only a small percentage of the total Mexican population resided there) and rich natural resources. Discussions had emerged in the United States about pushing even

Map 2.1 Mexican Cession

Source: Mexican Cession. U.S. Army Chaplain Center and School. http://www.
usachcs.army.mil/history/brief/chapter_2.htm

further south into Mexico, but they stalled because there was no appetite within
the U.S. Congress for bringing a large population of Mexicans into the Union.
The Gadsden Purchase of 1853, through which the United States purchased what
would become southern Arizona and New Mexico, finalized the transfer of land.

The United States was triumphant and even self-congratulatory. In his
widely used 1943 text on U.S.–Latin American relations, Samuel Bemis wrote,
"The United States acquired the whole western territory from the Mississippi
River to the Pacific Ocean without unjustly despoiling any civilized nation, and
this statement holds good for the war with Mexico."[20] However, Mexicans, who
felt both civilized and despoiled, carried resentment that only slowly faded and
has never disappeared. In 2001, the General Accounting Office of the United
States began an investigation into Mexican land claims that were legally protected by the 1848 treaty but were subsequently ignored. Violence has periodically erupted over land ownership disputes, as descendants of Mexicans who
lived in the territories produce pre-1848 land grants demonstrating their claims.
Mexican concepts of security, therefore, have always been highly attuned to the
United States.

The war took a considerable toll on Mexico, which would plunge into civil
war as political divisions and mutual blaming—already a serious problem—
became ever more bitter. Chronic instability would eventually contribute to the
French invasion, as exasperated conservative elites invited an updated colonialism. For their part, liberals began a series of reforms in 1857 that blamed the
clergy, the military, and indigenous populations for Mexico's inability to defend

Treaty of Guadalupe Hidalgo (1848)

The United States of America and the United Mexican States animated by a sincere desire to put an end to the calamities of the war which unhappily exists between the two Republics and to establish Upon a solid basis relations of peace and friendship, which shall confer reciprocal benefits upon the citizens of both, and assure the concord, harmony, and mutual confidence wherein the two people should live, as good neighbors have for that purpose appointed their respective plenipotentiaries . . . Who, after a reciprocal communication of their respective full powers, have, under the protection of Almighty God, the author of peace, arranged, agreed upon, and signed the following: Treaty of Peace, Friendship, Limits, and Settlement between the United States of America and the Mexican Republic.

Article V

The boundary line between the two Republics shall commence in the Gulf of Mexico, three leagues from land, opposite the mouth of the Rio Grande, otherwise called Rio Bravo del Norte, or Opposite the mouth of its deepest branch, if it should have more than one branch emptying directly into the sea; from thence up the middle of that river, following the deepest channel, where it has more than one, to the point where it strikes the southern boundary of New Mexico; thence, westwardly, along the whole southern boundary of New Mexico (which runs north of the town called Paso) to its western termination; thence, northward, along the western line of New Mexico, until it intersects the first branch of the river Gila; (or if it should not intersect any branch of that river, then to the point on the said line nearest to such branch, and thence in a direct line to the same); thence down the middle of the said branch and of the said river, until it empties into the Rio Colorado; thence across the Rio Colorado, following the division line between Upper and Lower California, to the Pacific Ocean.

Article XI

Considering that a great part of the territories, which, by the present treaty, are to be comprehended for the future within the limits of the United States, is now occupied by savage tribes, who will hereafter be under the exclusive control of the Government of the United States, and whose incursions within the territory of Mexico would be prejudicial in the extreme, it is solemnly agreed that all such incursions shall be forcibly restrained by the Government of the United States whensoever this may be necessary; and that when they cannot be prevented, they shall be punished by the said Government, and satisfaction for the same shall be exacted all in the same way, and with equal diligence and energy, as if the same incursions were meditated or committed within its own territory, against its own citizens.

(Continued)

Article XII

In consideration of the extension acquired by the boundaries of the United States, as defined in the fifth article of the present treaty, the Government of the United States engages to pay to that of the Mexican Republic the sum of fifteen millions of dollars.

Source: http://www.yale.edu/lawweb/avalon/diplomacy/mexico/guadhida.htm

itself. Civil conflict would eventually result in the dictatorship of Porfirio Díaz. Mexico, like Argentina, would also consistently assert its foreign policy independence from the United States and refuse to hew to the U.S. line.

Although the war with Mexico is the most famous example of Manifest Destiny in action, it appeared in other ways as well. For example, in the 1850s, the United States began a comprehensive land survey of all Latin America that was part of an overall plan to expand railroads for commerce. In addition, immediately after the war, in the eyes of U.S. policy makers the new extension of the United States required a transport route to connect the Pacific and Atlantic oceans. Railways were not yet widespread and, in any case, were extremely slow, so a canal cut through a Central American country would serve perfectly as a route. Several locations in the isthmus of Central America were promising, but Great Britain still had more naval power and economic presence there than the United States.

For the United States, the strategic and economic importance of such a canal spurred an effort to come to an agreement with Britain about its potential construction. At that time, neither country yet had the capital or the political will to begin the project, which would be a massive undertaking, but the threat that Britain might build a canal and control the crossing alarmed U.S. administrations. In 1850, the two sides signed the Clayton-Bulwer Treaty (named for the U.S. secretary of state and the British minister to the United States). The two countries agreed that if a canal were built, neither side would have exclusive control over it; that they would agree not to "occupy, or fortify, or colonize, or assume, or exercise any dominion over Nicaragua, Costa Rica, the Mosquito coast, or any part of Central America"; and that together they would guarantee its neutrality.[21] In one sense, it represented a diplomatic victory for the United States because it symbolized a real block on British power, which at the time was still considerable.

The treaty obviously violated the spirit of the Monroe Doctrine by acceding to British influence in Central America, and the administration of Zachary Taylor received heavy domestic criticism. But with civil war clearly on the horizon, many in the administration and Congress believed that other issues were far more pressing and so were content with the agreement. The treaty would remain in force for another fifty years, until President Theodore Roosevelt decided to seize land and build a canal.

The treaty was remarkable for its intentional neglect of those countries that might house the canal. Whether the final location would be Nicaragua or Panama (which was still northern Colombia), the attitude of those governments was not considered in the writing of the treaty. That the land could be had was taken for granted. Several times already, when faced with a perceived European threat in Latin America, the United States had met only with representatives of the European country. This strategy was subsequently repeated many times.

Even before the existence of a canal, transit through the isthmus had become a matter of national security. The United States landed troops in Panama in 1856 to protect U.S citizens; this became known as the "watermelon war" because a Panamanian vendor attacked a drunken traveler who refused to pay for a slice of watermelon, and the fight became a riot. According to a British prime minister, referring to U.S. interest in the area, "These Yankees are most disagreeable fellows to have to do with about any American Question; They are on the spot, strong, deeply interested in the matter, totally unscrupulous and dishonest and determined somehow or other to carry their Point."[22]

Panamanians often agreed. In 1850, Colombia offered concessions to a U.S. company to build a railroad in what would become Panama to accommodate the large number of people who were traveling from the east coast of the United States to California's gold fields. The result was not only profit but also de facto political control. Private soldiers of fortune replaced national police, and U.S. troops routinely landed in response to disorder, all of which clearly violated the Clayton-Bulwer Treaty. From a realist perspective, for the U.S. government, even private citizens could contribute to the expansion of U.S. power and economic welfare, and so they were encouraged. From the Panamanian perspective, the railroad had brought some measure of prosperity, but it accrued mostly to foreigners, and along with it came unemployment (many foreign workers, such as Africans, Chinese, and Irish, were imported to build the railroad), racial violence (including lynchings), inflation, and ever more exotic diseases. The state of U.S.–Panamanian relations remained uneasy. The relationship with Colombia was less troublesome for the time being, as successive Colombian governments received payments through the agreements the U.S. companies had signed. Relations between Panama and Bogotá worsened, however.

The foundations of Manifest Destiny also seemed to encourage adventurers and filibusters (defined as those who raise private armies to take action in a foreign country) lured westward with dreams of riches, who soon discovered that mining was backbreaking and often yielded nothing. Filibusters saw in Latin America a combination of investment opportunity and weak states. The most prominent of these wanderers was William Walker, who actually became president of Nicaragua in 1855. In the 1850s he went west, but instead of seeking gold, he started a colony in Baja California and proclaimed it independent of

Mexico in 1853 (with Ensenada as the capital). Given its shaky relationship with Mexico, the U.S. government shut down his recruitment office in San Francisco and arrested him when he came back to the United States the following year. Undaunted and out of jail, he heard about civil war in Nicaragua, went there with a force of soldiers for hire, and joining forces with Nicaraguans, took the capital in 1855.

The two factions soon began to see that their dispute was less important than the fact that a Yanqui was gaining control of the country. Even other countries, such as Costa Rica, sent troops to force him out. Trying for the appearance of legitimacy, Walker held a fraudulent election and made himself president, even though the Nicaraguan constitution clearly stated that the president must be native-born. A native Southerner, he announced the reestablishment of slavery, which brought in money from Southern investors, but widespread opposition ultimately led to his defeat in 1857. Concerned over antagonizing the United States, Nicaraguan leaders allowed him to return to United States, where he was treated like a popular hero. In fact, a Broadway musical, *Nicaragua, or General Walker's Victories* celebrated his exploits. He met his demise in 1860, when, yet again, he returned to Central America and fought for control of a Honduran port. Chased into the jungle, he was cornered and shot.

The entire sordid episode demonstrates not only the disdain of some U.S. citizens for Latin American sovereignty but also another contribution to the persistent suspicion and distrust that permeated U.S.–Latin American relations. From the Nicaraguan perspective, it did not matter if the U.S. government was directly involved or not. Walker received money from the United States, he was never effectively deterred, and so he seemed just another part of a U.S. plan to dominate the region. A New York congressman succinctly summed up the reaction of U.S. politicians: "We northern Democrats believe that the Government should, by conquest, do certain things; but that this business of Walker was committing petty larceny. We northern Democrats are rather in favor of national grand larceny."[23]

In Nicaragua, the Walker episode had several effects. Liberal support for him discredited their party, thus ushering in a relatively stable (though not democratic) period of conservative rule in Nicaraguan politics. The backlash against the United States took the concrete form of leading Nicaraguan governments to attract French investment for a canal. Only when that effort failed did a French company go to Panama instead, where in 1878 it signed a contract and began work. Chapter 3 discusses how the United States bought out the company and continued the work.

One effect of Manifest Destiny was to reveal the difficulties Latin American countries had in confronting U.S. exercises of power. Even though the United States was not yet a global military power, the fractious nature of Latin American politics precluded any concerted effort to develop a strong response. Internal order was such a high priority that the United States was able to play off different sides for its own gain.

Summary and Conclusion

During this initial period, after most of Latin America gained its independence from Spain and Portugal, certain patterns emerged that would prove to be durable. In realist terms, the imbalance of power, though not as large as it would be by the end of the century, was becoming evident. The United States quickly viewed the area as its domain, pushing Europe out as much as possible while taking some extra land for itself. The U.S. policy makers believed that Latin Americans were not capable of effective self-rule, economic progress, or other signs of "civilization," which made it easy to rationalize any action, whether conquest, subjugation, or intimidation. One result was that Latin American leaders developed a suspicion of U.S. policies and the diplomats who tried to explain them, not to mention the U.S. adventurers who roamed the region of their own accord.

Further, the formulation of U.S. policy was based primarily on a combination of domestic politics and response to European machinations and investment. Especially because politicians did not believe Latin Americans capable of stability, they pursued policy objectives with little or no regard for Latin American opinions. Even clearly stated policies, such as the Monroe Doctrine, were routinely sidestepped if they did not correspond to the current notions of national security.

Instability was a product of political growing pains, as Latin American countries struggled to create new states and to establish authority over them. Suspicions regarding U.S. actions increased, but many leaders periodically still looked to the United States as a potential ally. Both security and economic development depended on domestic order, and it was to that end, and not toward external enemies, that many national resources were dedicated.

The struggle for stability and nationhood drained already weakened economies, thus making it more difficult to establish effective foreign policies. Torn asunder by civil conflict, Latin American countries lacked the resources and stable leadership to counterbalance the growing assertion of U.S. military and economic power. Power would beget power, which U.S. governments were not hesitant to use if (and only if) they believed U.S. security was at stake.

But it would not be accurate to assert that the United States dominated the region in the first half of the nineteenth century. Its policies focused primarily on Mexico and the Caribbean. Given its geographical proximity, trade and investment in Central America was growing, but the British remained the region's most important foreign trading partner. In South America, European influence was unquestionably greater than that of the United States. But beginning mid-century, a slow shift began that would accelerate as the United States industrialized and investors sought out new markets. Even distant South America had tremendous potential, a land of opportunity with a lighter skinned and therefore more "advanced" population. The Southern Cone (Argentina, southern Brazil, Chile, Paraguay, and Uruguay) could be a "new west" that was ripe for U.S. investment.

Industrialization would thus deepen U.S. interest in Latin America. For decades an agrarian nation, the U.S. economy exploded as the population grew, railroads were laid, and factories were built. Entrepreneurs viewed Latin America as a source of unlimited profit, a bountiful combination of rich natural resources, cheap labor, and governments eager for wealth to come their way. From the perspective of the U.S. government, this investment was essential for the economic prosperity of the United States, and presidents were responsive to any flash of Latin American nationalism that might endanger them. The era of dollar diplomacy was underway, which is explained in Chapter 3.

Research Questions

1. To what degree did the U.S. Constitution and its framers influence the development of Latin American constitutions? In what key ways were the two political models different, and why?
2. Assess the relative importance of domestic and international factors in the U.S. decision to grant diplomatic recognition to the newly independent Latin American states.
3. Why did President Monroe create his doctrine? To what degree did European countries take it seriously?
4. How did the newly independent countries of Latin America respond to the Monroe Doctrine? To what degree did regional differences in response exist?
5. Compare and contrast the political and economic influence of the United States in Central America and the Caribbean versus South America.

Further Sources

Books

DAVIS, HAROLD EUGENE, JOHN J. FINAN, and F. TAYLOR PECK. *Latin American Diplomatic History: An Introduction* (Baton Rouge: Lousiana State University Press, 1977). Especially for the nineteenth century (six of the book's eleven chapters), the book provides a fresh approach, namely, the Latin American views on diplomacy and reactions to U.S. policies.

LEWIS, JAMES E. *The American Union and the Problem of Neighborhood: The United States and the Collapse of the Spanish Empire, 1783–1829* (Chapel Hill: University of North Carolina Press, 1998). An interesting historical interpretation of U.S. policy toward Latin American revolutions, with the thesis that maintaining the fragile union in the United States was the primary policy determinant. It also has a useful bibliography for early U.S.–Latin American relations.

MANNING, WILLIAM R. *Diplomatic Correspondence of the United States Concerning the Independence of the Latin American Nations* (1925–1926, 3 vol.) and *Diplomatic Correspondence of the United States: Inter-American Affairs 1831–1860* (1932–1939, 12 vol.). These are collections of primary documents from independence until 1860. There are both lists of the documents and an index, which makes it particularly valuable for research.

SCHOULTZ, LARS. *Beneath the United States: A History of U.S. Policy toward Latin America* (Cambridge: Harvard University Press, 1998). This book details the attitudes of U.S.

policy makers since Latin American independence, which provides rich and often amusing narrative on the dismissive and superior attitude that those policy makers have held. It is well-written and an excellent historical guide. In addition, there is a very large companion bibliography at http://www.unc.edu/~schoultz/bibliography. html

Web Sites

American Diplomacy 1778 to the Present: Treaties, Agreements and Correspondence. This is the Avalon Project of Yale Law School, which contains the full text of many written agreements between Latin American countries and the United States. A large number of them are from the eighteenth and nineteenth centuries. http://www.yale.edu/lawweb/ avalon/amerdipl.htm

 Constitutions of the Americas. Offered online through Georgetown University, the Web site contains the text of every Latin American constitution. The only drawback arises if you do not read Spanish because they are all in their original form, but it is possible to utilize an online translator (such as Babel Fish translation at http://babelfish.altavista. com/translate.dyn) that can transform each document into English. http://www.pdba. georgetown.edu/Constitutions/constudies.html.

 The Mexican-American War and the Media. From the Department of History at Virginia Tech, this site is a collection of newspaper articles from the United States and Britain of the time, timelines, images, and links to the documents associated with the war. It does not devote much attention to the Mexican side. For further research, it also provides links to extensive bibliographies: http://www.history.vt.edu/MxAmWar/index. htm.

 For a more pro-Mexico perspective, *Invasión Yanqui: The Mexican War* at http:// www.humanities-interactive.org/invasionyanqui/ is presented by the Texas Council for the Humanities Resource Center and contains images, commentary, essays, and bibliographical links.

Notes

1. Pérez 1990.
2. Quoted in Holden and Zolov 2000, 6.
3. Robertson 1967, 73.
4. Quoted in Schoultz 1998, 5.
5. Gleijeses 1992.
6. Quoted in Newton 1991, 11.
7. Quoted in Priest 2003, 223.
8. Loveman 1993, 40–41.
9. For text of this and other constitutions, see the Georgetown University *Political Database of the Americas*, http://pdba.georgetown.edu/Constitutions/constudies.html.
10. Weeks 2001.
11. Quoted in Lewis 1998, 102.
12. Quoted in Holden and Zolov 2000, 18.
13. Centeno 2002, 28.
14. Centeno 2002, 21.
15. Loveman 1999.
16. Davis 1977, 73.
17. Goodwin 1991.

18. Latané 1920, 331.
19. Sarmiento 1961, 144.
20. Bemis 1943, 74.
21. Quoted in Holden and Zolov 2000, 35.
22. Quoted in Callcott 1968, 27.
23. Quoted in Bermann 1986, 83.

CHAPTER 3

The Rise of U.S. Hegemony

TIMELINE

1889	First Pan American Conference
1891	USS *Baltimore* incident in Chile
1895	Olney Doctrine announced
1896	Calvo Clause
1898	Spanish-American War
1899	United Fruit Company is formed
1901	Hay-Pauncefote Treaty
1901	U.S. Congress passes the Platt Amendment
1903	Panama becomes independent from Colombia

Following the Civil War, the United States began to industrialize in earnest, and the government followed a largely laissez-faire economic strategy to encourage economic growth. It was a time when investors such as Carnegie, Rockefeller, and Vanderbilt became immensely wealthy through a combination of shrewd investment, ruthless treatment of competitors and labor, and a constant eye toward new opportunities. Industrialization, which entailed factories as well as railroads to transport the products coming almost constantly out their factory doors, created a seemingly never-ending need for raw materials. The ability to maintain wealth itself, meanwhile, required new opportunities beyond the borders of the United States to grow. Latin America, with its relatively untapped resources and proximity, seemed to represent a perfect avenue. Soon the U.S. government would begin using force to pursue economic and political interests. The chapter concludes at the turn of the twentieth century, when the era of intervention began in earnest.

Moreover, the U.S. domestic market was soon saturated. Despite industrialization, the U.S. economy suffered periodic depressions—one in each of the last three decades of the nineteenth century. The panic associated with the first economic slowdown after the Civil War led to a new interest in pursuing foreign markets, and that interest would continue growing. By 1881, newspapers had begun arguing that South America was "the great market for our surplus manufactures . . . [which] lies at our door neglected," and a steel industry publication informed the U.S. State Department that the government should "see to it" that steel had adequate foreign markets.[1] What was good for business was good for the country, and so the U.S. government would begin exerting its diplomatic, economic, and military leverage in new ways.

The term "dollar diplomacy" would become widely used in the early twentieth century, but its seeds had been sown much earlier. In practice, it meant a symbiotic relationship between government and business, to the point that the U.S. government would use private economic interests as rationale for policy toward Latin America, particularly with regard to debt repayment. Investors would help spread U.S. political influence, while U.S. policy would reflect their needs. The emphasis on national security had not disappeared, but the threats to U.S. borders were less dire than in the past.

For these reasons, dependency theory has much to say about the era. In a study of Central America, Lester Langley and Thomas Schoonover argue the following:

> The comprador elite, consisting of representatives of the small professional and artisan class as well as the socially prominent, permitted foreign interests to maximize their production of wealth. After the 1870s, metropole influence spread into all areas of Central American life: education, the professions, the military, local administration, and even public service.[2]

Nonetheless, realist propositions are also compelling. Economic expansion can be seen as one element in an overall project to expand U.S. influence. Policy in

Latin American countries also reflected a conscious effort to resist U.S. hegemony, both politically and militarily.

Political leaders in Latin America were struggling to recover from civil wars, liberal-conservative conflict, economic crises, bickering between capitals and outlying areas, border disputes, and other common problems facing the first few generations of newly independent states. They had neither the unified political support nor the military strength required to counter U.S. influence. At times, in fact, they welcomed it. Much of the political unrest revolved around the persistent battles between liberals and conservatives, and those groups out of power would often appeal to the United States for assistance. Some political and economic elites had much to gain by a U.S. presence, which could bring stability and profit. The United States stepped neatly and easily into this political maelstrom.

Meanwhile, in part precisely because Latin American politics were so unpredictable, U.S. views of Latin Americans had not changed significantly, if at all. President Ulysses S. Grant's minister to Central America referred to Nicaragua's foreign minister as a "mendacious negro statesman."[3] According to Secretary of State James Blaine, Latin Americans "require external pressure to keep them from war; when at war they require external pressure to bring them to peace."[4] The U.S. policy was often framed in paternalistic terms, with Latin Americans portrayed as unruly children who at times needed a whipping.

With the exceptions of Great Britain, Spain, and to some degree Germany, Europe was generally easing itself out of the region. Table 3.1 compares the growth of U.S., British, and German trade. In relative terms, U.S. trade with Latin America in 1890 was not dominant and in some cases lagged behind, whereas in two more decades it had expanded considerably.

After the Mexico debacle, French interest was limited to economic enterprise, including an unsuccessful private-sector stab at building a canal through Panama. Spain was pouring resources into Cuba as colonial unrest became more violent. The Ten Years' War (1868–1878) had wreaked havoc on the island and seriously damaged to Spanish and U.S. economic interests. As in the past, however, the U.S. government was less concerned about the Spanish presence than it was about other foreigners who might take advantage of the situation.

Central America and the Pursuit of a Canal

The focus of U.S. policy continued to be the Caribbean, but interest in Central America and even South America expanded as well, and the developments that led up to the construction of a canal in Panama highlight the imbalance of power and the readiness of the U.S. government to wield military power for its interests. United States policy toward Central America reflected a combination of economic opportunism and national security because it was the route between the oceans and had long been dominated by Great Britain. There was also a significant German economic presence in Guatemala. Presidents and their secretaries

Table 3.1 External Trade with Germany, the United Kingdom, and the United States (in current values), 1890 and 1913

Country	1890 (Import/Export)	Trading Partners	1913 (Import/Export)
Argentina	12/12	Germany	84/62
	58/19	UK	154/129
	9.3/6.1	US	73/25
Chile	16/6.4	Germany	81/84
	29/46	UK	99/153
	5.2/8.5	US	55/83
Colombia	1,636/2,475	Germany	4/3.2
	4,990/4,835	UK	5.8/5.6
	1,218/4,636	US	7.6/19
Costa Rica	1,262/—	Germany	2.9/1.1
	1,449/—	UK	2.8/9.3
	2,225/—	US	9.6/11
Mexico	3.7/1.7	Germany	25/16
	8.5/14	UK	26/31
	29/43	US	97/232
Uruguay	2.8/1.0	Germany	7.8/13.0
	8.8/3.9	UK	12/7.7
	2.4/2.0	US	6.4/2.8

Source: International Historical Statistics: The Americas, 1750–1993, 4th ed. (New York: Stockton Press, 1998).

of state openly insisted that no European power be allowed to control a canal. After the French began construction in 1879, President Rutherford B. Hayes stated, "The policy of this country is a canal under American control."[5] Nicaragua received the lion's share of attention regarding a canal, and over the years a variety of agreements surfaced but for various reasons (such as U.S. unwillingness to commit itself to maintaining order) did not come to fruition.

As the idea of a canal became more popular, U.S. policy makers promoted political stability in Central America to foster investment and security. The battles between liberals and conservatives were still hard fought and bitter, with conservatives more skeptical of a U.S. presence. Stepping into this political whirlwind, U.S. diplomats announced that only a union of Central American countries could effectively solve the problem. Simón Bolívar had dreamed of such a union, and now his old nemesis was actively encouraging it.

Unfortunately, the United States ran into the same obstacles that Bolívar had experienced. In particular, Central American countries were strongly nationalistic, and many were simply unwilling to give up sovereignty to some central political body. Interstate conflicts were common, which in the minds of many Central American leaders underlined the continued need for national armies and secure borders. The combination of liberal-conservative disputes with the widely different national goals of five countries (Costa Rica, El Salvador, Guatemala, Honduras, and Nicaragua) precluded any lasting union.

Despite these persistent failures, U.S. policy makers continued to view Central America as an important area for U.S. economic expansion. When depression hit the United States in 1873, President Grant and his minister to Central America (a title reflecting the hope of a united region) worked with Central American liberals to build railroads for the transit of goods, to provide concessions for U.S. business, and to exclude Europe as much as possible. Once the economy of the United States recovered, investment in Central America grew. Coffee was the largest industry, but a host of other agricultural sectors, such as sugar, cotton, chicle, cocoa, rubber, and timber (including expensive woods like mahogany, cedar, and rosewood), came under the control of U.S. businesses. United Fruit, which would later be a foundation for dollar diplomacy, was not yet a cash crop. Difficulties in transportation, unpredictable weather, and political instability limited profits until later in the nineteenth century. The banana, introduced to U.S. markets in 1866, for years remained a curiosity rather than the diet staple it is today.

Despite the expansion of U.S. investment in Central America, the prospect of a canal was always the main priority of U.S. policy. Presidents mentioned it regularly in speeches, and Central America would not receive such concentrated attention again until Marxist-inspired revolutions swept the region in the 1970s and 1980s. President Grant stated in 1869 that a canal was essential to U.S. security and established a commission to investigate a possible Panama route. In 1880, President Hayes announced that if any existing treaty (i.e., Clayton-Bulwer) stood in the way of U.S. control, then the treaty needed to be renegotiated. In his inaugural address of 1881, James Garfield said that he agreed with his predecessor and would act to promote U.S. interests in a canal.

The possible locations for a canal had been narrowed to Nicaragua and Panama, with Costa Rica a distant third. All involved felt that the presidents and congresses of the two countries could be convinced to accept U.S. dominance over a canal zone. At times, agreements with Nicaragua reached advanced stages, foundering only on the unwillingness of the U.S. Congress to commit to the protection of Nicaraguan sovereignty. The stickier problem was the British reaction because the Clayton-Bulwer Treaty clearly stated that the United States could not build a canal without British participation. Consequently, years of negotiation by different U.S. presidents and secretaries of state centered on eliminating Clayton-Bulwer. The treaty could not be unilaterally abrogated without risking a backlash, but every effort was made to find legal loopholes that would convince the British government that the treaty was null and void. This effort required considerable legal gymnastics. For example, Secretary of State Blaine argued that when the treaty was written, the United States had assumed that any canal would be built with British financial assistance, and since the United States no longer needed British help, the treaty was invalid. No one had ever made such an assumption formally, but according to Blaine, it was "inferable from every line of it."[6] Needless to say, such arguments did not convince anyone, and the British made it clear that they expected full compliance with the treaty.

Promotion of a U.S.-controlled canal dovetailed with commerce. When liberal governments began retaking power in Central America in the 1880s (or even earlier in some cases), they were eager to attract foreign capital. Using strategies that would be copied even into the twenty-first century, they offered tax breaks, legal exemptions, promises of docile labor, and similar incentives to entice investment. From the perspective of U.S. investors, such concessions were the only way to offset other costs, including lack of infrastructure, unpredictable and sometimes violent weather, political instability, disease, and a workforce that did not always remain content with low wages and miserable working conditions. Soon foreign companies (primarily from the United States and Great Britain) dominated not only commerce but also banking and owned increasing acreage of arable land.

At the end of the century, a multitude of pressures began pushing U.S. policy makers to a more active pursuit of a canal. Along with increased investment, vocal proponents—including future president Theodore Roosevelt—of increased naval power gained influence, and a canal would be essential for naval strength in both the Atlantic and Pacific oceans. Meanwhile, competition from outside the hemisphere was fading fast. Once the efforts of a French entrepreneur, Ferdinand de Lesseps, to build a canal failed, the French government's interest also evaporated. De Lesseps had formed a corporation, begun work, and then gone bankrupt. Great Britain was in the process of disengaging from Central America, even on the Mosquito Coast of Nicaragua, where it had been active for years. The costs of maintaining the British Empire elsewhere in the world made Central America a much lower priority.

These events left the United States with three objectives to accomplish: First, choose a canal site. Second, by some means, gain control of that site. Third, negotiate a new agreement with Britain to be rid of the Clayton-Bulwer Treaty.

In the late 1880s, the U.S. government commissioned studies to determine the most propitious location for a canal. Soon the British government realized the United States was determined in its efforts, and therefore the treaty could become a source of discord. At the time, Britain was facing all the challenges inherent in maintaining an empire, especially in Asia and Africa, as well as potential adversaries in France, Russia, and Germany, and its government was more than willing to remain in the good graces of the United States and avoid an unwanted crisis.

Beginning in 1898, the two countries agreed to replace Clayton-Bulwer, and the details were slowly hammered out over the next three years. The British wanted the canal to be demilitarized (similar to the Suez Canal), but many in the United States (most vocally Theodore Roosevelt, then governor of New York) insisted that the United States be allowed to protect a canal by force if necessary. In 1901, the Hay-Pauncefote Treaty found a middle ground, with the language of neutrality but a guarantee of U.S. protection: "The United States . . . shall be at liberty to maintain such military police along the canal as may be necessary to protect it against lawlessness and disorder."[7] The canal was now officially a U.S.-only project.

In 1901, a U.S. government commission (the Walker Commission, named for its chair, Admiral John G. Walker) recommended Nicaragua as the best site, and the United States purchased exclusive rights to build for $5 million. The Panama route had been deemed too expensive because the company in France that owned the rights (de Lesseps's own corporation had gone into receivership, and new investors took control) wanted a large sum to transfer its interests in the venture. Although Costa Rica never received much serious attention, to cover all its bases, the United States also bought exclusive rights to any future canal on its territory.

Alarmed by the interest in Nicaragua, the French company that owned rights in Panama cut its asking price, and a second Walker Commission report switched its recommendation to Panama. At the same time, President José Santos Zelaya of Nicaragua was refusing to accept certain conditions the United States demanded, especially full judicial control in the canal zone. Colombia, on the other hand, which still controlled Panama (as mentioned in Chapter 2), was ready to negotiate that route.

In 1902, the U.S. Congress debated and then passed the Spooner Amendment, which authorized the president to purchase the property and concessions of the French for $40 million and, only if unsuccessful, to turn to Nicaragua. As usual, the debate barely touched on the effects U.S. action would have on the countries in question. By this time, Theodore Roosevelt was president, and he was intent on Panama, and so negotiations with Colombia were underway even before congressional debate was finished.

The United States and Colombia came within a hair's breadth of ratifying the Hay-Herrán Treaty, which would have given the United States the rights to a six-mile-wide strip of land in return for an initial lump sum of $10 million and annual payments of $250,000. It was ratified by the U.S. Congress in early 1903, but then was rejected by the Colombian congress. That decision was based in part on the belief that greater financial benefits could be wrangled from the U.S. and in part as a negative reaction to the landing of U.S. troops in Panama in 1902 without notifying local authorities. Although the Colombian government hoped to renew negotiations, the treaty's rejection cemented in Roosevelt's mind the need for intervention.

Very quickly, Roosevelt and his advisers came up with justifications for violating Colombian sovereignty. Most important, they claimed, was that the canal was not being built for profit but for the benefit of all humankind. They argued it would also serve to bring civilization to Panama and respect for human rights (both of which would be learned through the presence of U.S. citizens), which was important because, according to Roosevelt, Colombians were "of fatuous weakness, of dismal ignorance, cruelty, treachery, greed, and utter vanity."[8] Finally, the United States said it had been protecting Colombian sovereignty,

Colombia had benefited from that protection, and therefore it was no position to block the canal. This tortured logic prompted the Roosevelt administration to precipitate a Panamanian uprising against Colombia.

Roosevelt wasted little time. Panamanians had long resented Colombian rule and did not need much encouragement to start an all-out fight for independence. In November 1903, the uprising began, and the U.S. Navy was instructed to prevent Colombian forces from arriving. Once again, the argument went that a canal would benefit the entire world and civilization in general, so it was unacceptable to allow the Colombian government to interfere, even when it was simply attempting to maintain its sovereignty.

Panamanian "independence" came only two days later. The United States immediately recognized the new government and began writing a treaty. The Hay–Bunau Varilla Treaty was written in New York City without any representatives from Panama. The terms were the same as Hay–Herrán, except the canal zone would be ten miles wide instead of only six. As plans for construction began, the United States also successfully pressured the new Panamanian president to disband the army; the United States would be protecting the country's sovereignty, the argument went, so an army would only be a hindrance. Moreover, as President Taft stated in 1906, the United States desired to "advise all political parties in the Republic of Panama that in order to avoid obstruction to the building of the canal, the United States will not permit revolutions in that republic."[9]

The first ship passed through the canal in 1914, and from that moment onward, the entire area was central to U.S. security. An attack on the canal would mean a serious disruption of trade. For the entire twentieth century, the administration of the canal would be a source of tension between the United

Map 3.1 Panama and the canal

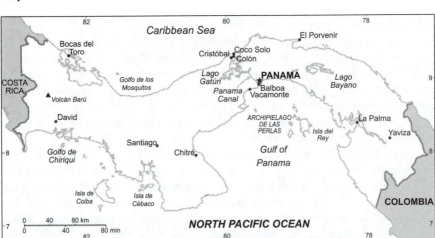

Source: Panama. Central Intelligence Agency World Factbook. https://www.cia.gov/library/publications/the-world-factbook/geos/pm.html

Photo 3.1 Panama Canal.

States and Panama, marked by strenuous Panamanian efforts to take greater control of its operation.

U.S. Investment and "Banana Republics"

Given the governments' efforts to develop rapidly with the help of foreign capital, debt was piling up in all of Central America. Investors wielded tremendous political and economic influence because the debt would begin to prompt foreign governments to send troops as a means of forcing repayment. Domestic industry was barely forming, and this economic penetration left Central American governments heavily dependent on a continued flow of foreign capital. The most famous example of dependence and control is the fruit industry. By the 1880s, bananas and other exotic fruits had become profitable in U.S. markets, and several companies had gradually bought extensive tracts of land in Central America and the Caribbean. In 1899, the two largest companies merged and became United Fruit Company.

United Fruit built its own railroads, steamships, housing, schools, radio, and telegraph and was always adept at either currying favor with the government in power or, if the government did not prove pliable enough, working with the opposition. Given its rapid growth, it also attracted attention from the U.S. political elite, and over time some highly influential policy makers would be United Fruit stockholders or even directors. Within Central America, the company would become a negative symbol of U.S. imperialism.

Nevertheless, Central American governments often supported United Fruit. It was building infrastructure, it was combating disease (which had always plagued previous efforts to increase worker productivity), and despite generous exemptions, it provided badly needed tax revenue. Over time, the costs would prove to be very high, but at least initially the company was bringing in capital and expertise that did not exist locally.

O. Henry's 1904 novel *Cabbages and Kings,* set in a fictional Central American country, introduced the term "**banana republic.**" It refers to "this small, maritime banana republic" and how these small "nations play at government and intrigue until some day a big, silent gunboat glides into the offing and warns them not to break their toys."[10] Such was banana diplomacy.

Debt and Intervention

Countless other U.S. companies established themselves in Central America, and the issue of debt became more and more prominent. Failure (or refusal) to pay debt had become tantamount to a direct insult to the United States. In Nicaragua, President José Santos Zelaya discovered this the hard way. On the sparsely populated Atlantic coast of Nicaragua, the Miskito Indians were granted autonomy from the central government (an arrangement similar to reservations in the United States, though with more authority for self-rule), and by the 1890s the area had also become popular for U.S. investors and traders, who soon outnumbered the British who had been active there for decades. The Miskito coast was particularly attractive because the local government (such as it was) had lax regulations and tax codes and did not answer to authorities in the faraway Nicaraguan capital of Managua.

President Zelaya rued the amount of revenue his government was unable to collect. His nationalist attitude would periodically spark conflict with the United States, as would altercations (including shootings) between Nicaraguans and U.S. citizens in Bluefields, the main town on the Miskito coast. The situation deteriorated further in 1894, when, in response to a Honduran invasion, Zelaya imposed martial law in Bluefields and began imposing (or simply enforcing) taxes. The Miskito Indians were soon compelled to accept Nicaraguan rule, but the stage had been set for a showdown with the United States.

Zelaya's intransigence irritated U.S. businessmen, who in the 1890s were coming to Bluefields for the banana and mahogany industries. They did what they could to aid a rebellion in 1899, but to their dismay Zelaya was successful in putting down the revolt. The U.S. minister reported that U.S. businessmen "have many complaints of long standing against the Zelaya government" and "desire aggressive action, aided by [U.S.] military power, which is not permissible under present conditions."[11] However, their complaints would not reach a consistently sympathetic presidential ear until Theodore Roosevelt took office.

Nicaragua is the perfect example of the evolution of the U.S. response to crises involving U.S citizens. In the 1890s, warships off the coast of Bluefields were a not uncommon sight, as the U.S. government sent a visible reminder that the Nicaraguan authorities had better treat U.S. citizens well or suffer the consequences. The principle of using military force to back up investment had become so vexing to Latin Americans that Carlos Calvo, a noted Argentine legal scholar, developed what became known as the Calvo Clause, a legal doctrine insisting that no government should intervene in another country's affairs for the purposes of protecting its own citizens. Because Argentina had suffered foreign intervention and also had aspirations to become a hemispheric leader, its intellectuals developed concepts in international law intended to limit foreign (especially U.S.) intervention. In some countries, the Calvo Clause would be translated into the practice of using contractual clauses by which foreigners would agree not to call on their own government for aid. Even in countries such as Nicaragua that did not commonly utilize such a clause, the general idea was the same. The United States had become more active in its foreign policy, and Latin American governments were beginning to resist it.

Calvo Clause (1896)

America as well as Europe is inhabited today by free and independent nations, whose sovereign existence has the right to the same respect, and whose internal public law does not admit of intervention of any sort on the part of foreign peoples, whoever they may be. . . . Aside from political motives these interventions have nearly always had as apparent pretexts, injuries to private interests, claims and demands for pecuniary indemnities in behalf of subjects. . . . According to strict international law, the recovery of debts and the pursuit of a private claim does not justify *de plano* the armed intervention of governments, and, since European states invariably follow this rule in their reciprocal relations, there is no reason why they should not also impose it upon themselves in their relations with nations of the new world. . . .

It is certain that aliens who establish themselves in a country have the same right to protection as nationals, but they ought not to lay claim to a protection more extended. If they suffer any wrong, they ought to count on the government of the country prosecuting the delinquents, and not claim from the state to which the authors of the violence belong any pecuniary indemnity. . . .

The rule that in more than one case it has been attempted to impose on American states is that foreigners merit more regard and privileges more marked and extended than those accorded even to the nationals of the country where they reside. This principle is intrinsically contrary to the law of equality of nations. . . .

To admit in the present case governmental responsibility, that is the principle of an indemnity, is to create an exorbitant and fatal privilege, essentially favorable to the powerful states and injurious to the weaker nations, establishing an

(Continued)

unjustifiable inequality between nationals and foreigners. From another standpoint, in sanctioning the doctrine that we are combating, one would deal, although directly, a strong blow to one of the constituent elements of the independence of nations, that of territorial jurisdiction; here is, in effect, the real extent, the true significance of such frequent recourse to diplomatic channels to resolve the questions which from their nature and the circumstances in the middle of which they arise come under the exclusive domain of the ordinary tribunals. The responsibility of governments toward foreigners cannot be greater than that which these governments have toward their own citizens.

Source: Donald R. Shea, *The Calvo Clause: A Problem in Inter-American and International Law and Diplomacy* (Minneapolis: University of Minnesota Press, 1955): 17–19.

The Evolution of Cuban "Independence"

The Caribbean was also a central concern to U.S. policy makers, as developments in Cuba appeared to pose a potentially serious security threat. For Creoles, if not the rest of the population, the 1868 Cuban declaration of war against Spain included the goal of annexation to the United States. Creoles hoped to copy the example of Texas, a sovereign government that willingly became a U.S. state. Such efforts were doomed, however, by U.S. unwillingness not only to annex a slave state (now impossible after the Thirteenth Amendment to the Constitution) but also to assimilate a nonwhite population. As this unwillingness became clear, Cuban interest in joining the United States decreased because the only viable means would be as a protectorate, and Cuba would neither be sovereign nor a state. During the Ten Years' War, the U.S. government maintained its position of support for Spain and became disgruntled by damage to U.S. citizens' property.

Having demonstrated its ability to quash the revolution, after the war ended in 1878 Spain appeared more willing to negotiate compromises with Cuba, including expansion of trade with the United States and reduction of taxes and tariffs. The subsequent increase of financial ties with the United States would have lasting consequences. In particular, as prices for sugar (Cuba's main export) plummeted in the 1880s, Cubans turned to creditors in the United States for emergency assistance, pledging their land as collateral. When, as often happened, they were unable to repay, creditors took the land. The United States was already Cuba's primary trading partner, so Cuba's depression set the stage for full-fledged domination of all sectors of the economy. In addition to sugar, U.S. investors were active in railroads, cattle, coffee, manganese and nickel mining, boarding houses, general stores, banks, and steamships. Citizens of the United States, who had already been coming to the island, arrived in greater numbers to live and work. It had become clear that Spain could not keep up economically with the United States. Cubans wanted credit and export markets, and in both areas the dying Spanish empire lacked resources after the Ten Years' War.

For a decade or more, the U.S.–Cuban–Spanish relationship was largely amicable, but tensions arose from two sources. The first was the continued Cuban fervor for independence, and "Cuba libre" ("free Cuba") did not refer solely to Spain. The Creole idea of annexation has faded, and a conflict over the precise nature of Cuban independence seemed inevitable. But as has always been the case, U.S. domestic politics strongly influenced U.S. foreign policy, and in 1894 domestic problems precipitated a crisis. Facing yet another economic depression, as well as a bitterly fought presidential election, the U.S. Congress passed a **tariff** that imposed a hefty tax on Cuban sugar, which had previously enjoyed almost completely free access to U.S. markets. Spain responded with tariffs of its own, but the damage was soon evident. Because Cuba relied almost entirely on the U.S. market, many Cubans faced bankruptcy, whether they were sugar growers, suppliers, or even just part of the chain of merchants who made their living from U.S.-Cuban commerce.

Given Spain's inability to assist its colony in any meaningful way, many Cubans joined rebel forces, a development that, by the 1890s, alarmed Cuban landowners and urban economic elites, who felt pressure from all directions. Staying with Spain was untenable and almost pointless, given its economic and military impotence, but becoming independent was an equally unpleasant idea. Independence would very likely mean a revolt from below, which would become a direct (and violent) challenge to the entire racial and social class structure. So these elites, who maintained their own representatives in large U.S. cities such as New York, appealed directly to the United States to step in and take Spain's place. However, they were still unable to generate U.S. support for such a decision because policy makers had little respect for them. President Grover Cleveland told his secretary of state that the Cuban insurgents were "the most inhuman and barbarous cutthroats in the world."[12]

The United States continued to insist that Spain must make more concessions and grant more autonomy, while it maintained order by using a military presence. The hope was that such compromises would take the steam out of the revolutionary movement and restore the elite's faith in the Spanish ability to rule. In 1897 and early 1898, Spain made sweeping changes, even a new constitution for the island. The effect became the opposite of what both Spain and the United States wanted. Most Spaniards in Cuba felt betrayed, because they believed that autonomy would quickly lead to complete control by Cubans. Economic elites in general believed that Spain was essentially giving up, and that notion was reinforced by the Spanish military's inability to curb the growing insurrectionary forces sweeping from the mountains of eastern Cuba toward the west. For the rebels, Spain's concessions made the mother country look even weaker and bolstered their calls for independence.

Into 1898, President William McKinley began to realize that unless the United States took action, Spain would lose Cuba. Because policy makers believed Cubans to be incapable of effective self-rule, that outcome was unacceptable. In that view, the many interests of U.S. citizens in Cuba would be in peril if a band of ragtag rebels managed to take power. McKinley tried to push both sides toward a cease-fire and negotiations. Ultimately, Spain agreed to a cease-fire, but the insurgents refused. Spain was losing the war, and McKinley felt that the time had come for intervention.

By the time McKinley sent troops, U.S. public attention was focused squarely—even obsessively—on the island. The president and Congress alike were swept up in the fever. Intermestic issues were also present. Republicans did not want to appear soft and, knowing that they would face William Jennings Bryan, a formidable opponent, in the 1898 elections, decided that being more aggressive would play better in public opinion. From their morning newspapers, people in the United States had been reading for some time about Spanish atrocities (especially the forced movement of Cubans—called "reconcentration"—to deprive guerrillas of support) and so were primed to use military might. So-called yellow journalists, led by William Randolph Hearst's *New York Journal*, wrote lurid stories that were accompanied by even more suggestive drawings and cartoons.

In this context, in February 1898 a U.S. battleship, the *Maine*, blew up in Havana harbor, killing 266. Did Spain deliberately attack the ship? An immediate naval investigation concluded that an underwater mine had caused the explosion, despite the fact that the water around the ship was so muddy that divers could see virtually nothing, and even though the theory of an internal explosion was credible, given similar catastrophes in the past several years. Most analyses since then have concluded the latter, but at the time the president told Congress and the public that it was an act of sabotage, thus inflaming public opinion.

In April 1898, McKinley formally requested that Congress authorize him to take whatever measures were necessary to oust the Spanish from Cuba. Congress did grant him that authority, though it included a restriction. The Teller Amendment, authored by a Colorado senator who wanted to make sure that Cuba's sugar would not compete with his state's crop of beet sugar, prohibited the president from annexing Cuba:

> [T]he United States hereby disclaims any disposition or intention to exercise sovereignty, jurisdiction, or control over said island, except for the pacification thereof, and asserts its determination, when that is accomplished, to leave the government and control of the island to its people.[13]

Cuba would therefore not become part of the United States, but the president could still occupy the island for pacification. Because no one defined "pacification," the amendment gave McKinley and his successors the legal justification to occupy Cuba indefinitely.

Soon thereafter, the United States invaded. The war itself would last only from April 21 to August 12. The War of Cuban Liberation suddenly became the Spanish-American War, financed and controlled by the United States. The irony is obvious: the name of a war for independence begun by Cubans in Cuba would not even mention Cuba. Although the war was ostensibly a joint U.S.-Cuban effort to expel Spain, Cubans were clearly held in very low regard. Theodore Roosevelt, who was secretary of the Navy and volunteered to fight (he recruited the so-called Rough Riders), later wrote, "We should have been better off if there had not been a single Cuban with the army. They accomplished literally nothing, while they were a source of trouble and embarrassment."[14] Roosevelt famously referred to the conflict as a "splendid little war," and for him and many others, the less Cubans were involved, the more splendid it was.

As Spanish troops surrendered to the oncoming forces, the negotiations excluded Cubans, and control over territory was left entirely to U.S. soldiers. In some cases (such as the city of Santiago), Cuban troops were not even allowed to enter. By the summer, many Cuban soldiers, tired of being openly scorned and insulted, officially broke ties with the United States. As far as the war was concerned, this had little effect. The tide had turned, and by August Spain was ready to discuss the terms of its departure.

The end of Spanish rule in the Western Hemisphere was outlined in the Treaty of Paris. It transferred control over Cuba from Spain to the United States and did not even allude to or hint at Cuban independence. In practice, Cuba became a de facto U.S. colony until "pacification" was complete. As in all other matters important to Cuba, the treaty was written not only without any Cubans present but also without consulting any Cuban leaders. The U.S. military began its occupation on New Year's Day of 1899.

The treaty also brought Puerto Rico, Guam, and the Philippines into the U.S fold (and Hawaii was annexed during the war), which greatly enlarged the U.S. presence in the Pacific Ocean and the Caribbean. McKinley sent governors and troops to begin "civilizing" the new territories. The "Spanish-American" war thus encompassed much more than just Cuba.

From the perspective of the U.S. government, Cubans needed to be taught self-rule, which would require a long period of occupation. As historian Hugh Thomas writes, "In the light of this expectation, and of their own prejudices, these officers sought with dedication and without sparing themselves, to recast Cuban society, such as it was, in the mould of North America; all the corruption, the incompetence and makeshift devices lying between law and custom were to be swept immediately away; and from this well-meant effort much ill was later to flow."[15] Most Cubans, who had been fighting Spain for decades, bristled at the idea of an extended U.S. presence intended to "improve" them. Although some, especially those who owned property, welcomed the U.S. presence to protect them from the dangers of disorder, elections would demonstrate that a majority of elites wanted to be fully independent. Hoping to exclude the "rabble" from elections, the United States restricted suffrage to approximately five percent of the population, but independence-minded candidates nonetheless won municipal elections in 1900 and also seats on the constitutional assembly.

But the McKinley administration was in a bind. The Teller Amendment prohibited outright annexation, the occupation had no legal justification, and there were calls from Congress to pull out. Meanwhile, the Cuban constitutional assembly was refusing to accept any limits on Cuban sovereignty in its new constitution. The administration did have political allies, such as Senator

Orville H. Platt of Connecticut, chair of the Senate Committee on Relations with Cuba, however. In 1901, Congress would enact the Platt Amendment.

According to its dictates, Cuba would become a protectorate of the United States. Military occupation would end, but Cuban leaders would be forced to ask for U.S. permission before entering into treaties with other countries, could not take on public debt beyond limits set by the United States, and had to lease certain areas of the island (such as Guantánamo Bay, which has remained under U.S. control ever since) to the U.S. government. Most important, the United States reserved the right to send its own military to the island at any time "for the preservation of Cuban independence, the maintenance of a government adequate for the protection of life, property, and individual liberty, and for discharging the obligations with respect to Cuba imposed by the Treaty of Paris on the United States, now to be assumed and undertaken by the government of Cuba."

Platt Amendment (1901)

[I]n fulfillment of the declaration contained in the joint resolution approved April twentieth, eighteen hundred and ninety-eight, entitled "For the recognition of the independence of the people of Cuba, demanding that the Government of Spain relinquish its authority and government in the island of Cuba, and withdraw its land and naval forces from Cuba and Cuban waters, and directing the President of the United States to use the land and naval forces of the United States to carry these resolutions into effect," the President is hereby authorized to "leave the government and control of the island of Cuba to its people" so soon as a government shall have been established in said island under a constitution which, either as a part thereof or in an ordinance appended thereto, shall define the future relations of the United States with Cuba, substantially as follows:

"I. That the government of Cuba shall never enter into any treaty or other compact with any foreign power or powers which will impair or tend to impair the independence of Cuba, nor in any manner authorize or permit any foreign power or powers to obtain by colonization or for military or naval purposes or otherwise, lodgement in or control over any portion of said island."

"II. That said government shall not assume or contract any public debt, to pay the interest upon which, and to make reasonable sinking fund provision for the ultimate discharge of which, the ordinary revenues of the island, after defraying the current expenses of government shall be inadequate."

"III. That the government of Cuba consents that the United States may exercise the right to intervene for the preservation of Cuban independence, the maintenance of a government adequate for the protection of life, property, and individual liberty, and for discharging the obligations with respect to Cuba imposed by the treaty of Paris on the United States, now to be assumed and undertaken by the government of Cuba."

"IV. That all Acts of the United States in Cuba during its military occupancy thereof are ratified and validated, and all lawful rights acquired thereunder shall be maintained and protected."

"V. That the government of Cuba will execute, and as far as necessary extend, the plans already devised or other plans to be mutually agreed upon, for the sanitation of the cities of the island, to the end that a recurrence of epidemic and infectious diseases may be prevented, thereby assuring protection to the people and commerce of Cuba, as well as to the commerce of the southern ports of the United States and the people residing therein."

"VI. That the Isle of Pines shall be omitted from the proposed constitutional boundaries of Cuba, the title thereto being left to future adjustment by treaty."

"VII. That to enable the United States to maintain the independence of Cuba, and to protect the people thereof, as well as for its own defense, the government of Cuba will sell or lease to the United States lands necessary for coaling or naval stations at certain specified points to be agreed upon with the President of the United States."

"VIII. That by way of further assurance the government of Cuba will embody the foregoing provisions in a permanent treaty with the United States."

Source: http://www.ourdocuments.gov/doc.php?doc=55&page=transcript

Platt's document was presented to the Cuban assembly writing the new constitution to inform its members that they could either include it as part of their constitution or suffer indefinite occupation. After acrimonious debate, the assembly finally agreed by a single-vote majority. As Secretary of State Elihu Root said without a trace of irony, "If they continue to exhibit ingratitude and entire lack of appreciation of the expenditure of blood and treasure of the United States to secure their freedom, the public sentiment of this country will be more unfavorable to them."[16] For the next thirty years, Cuban political affairs would be directed in large part from Washington, D.C.

The Importance of South America

Only occasionally did U.S. presidents regard anything south of Panama as an important strategic or economic interest. Two examples demonstrate the low but slowly growing salience of South America. With regard to Chile, the United States wielded its newfound political might, and in Venezuela it was asserting— and even extending—the dictates of the Monroe Doctrine. In both cases, it was reacting primarily to European influence.

The War of the Pacific

In 1879, Chile went to war with Bolivia and Peru in the War of the Pacific. At stake was a small piece of coast in western Bolivia that Chile invaded. Peru was involved because it had previously signed an alliance with Bolivia that became operational if either country were attacked. Although this desolate patch of land contained silver and copper mines, its main economic attraction was guano, or bird droppings. Built up over the centuries, these mounds of bird droppings were a rich source of fertilizer for Europe, where demand was growing at a tremendous rate. The so-called guano war was a fight to determine who would control the industry, and for Bolivia, it also meant protecting its only access to the ocean.

The conflict itself was not automatically a high priority for the United States. More troubling was the high-profile presence of the British, who were actively working with the Chilean navy, as well as Germans and French. Chile was distant, but for U.S. policy makers the war could turn into an excuse for an expanded European presence. Suspicions ran high. By 1881, the United States actively tried to make its presence felt and serve as arbiter between the two sides. Ultimately, this effort was rebuffed (with U.S. envoys alienating both sides), and the matter was settled through a Chilean military victory in 1883, which meant the temporary occupation of Lima, as well as Bolivia's loss of access to the Pacific Ocean.

The U.S. response to Chile's 1891 civil war also heightened tensions. Ostensibly to protect its citizens, U.S. ships were sent to wait off the coast. One of these was the USS *Baltimore*. Meanwhile, by its words and actions the United States had shown a clear preference for the government in the civil war—for example, it had blocked the arrival of a ship containing arms for the insurgents—which became a serious problem when that government was defeated. The new Chilean leaders were convinced, with good reason, that they had no reason to trust U.S. diplomats or sailors. As one U.S. diplomat wrote, the "feeling of animosity against Americans is very decided . . . in social gatherings and in groups of Chileans on street corners, when I have passed, I have heard chants of 'abajo los Yankees (down with the Yankees).'"[17]

Within that atmosphere, in late 1891, sailors from the *Baltimore* went ashore to Valparaíso, Chile's main port. Like other port cities in the world, it provided ample opportunity for sailors to lose their money in bars and bordellos, and the United States and Chile would come to the brink of war because of a drunken brawl. Insults led to fighting, which then erupted into mob violence, with U.S. sailors being chased and beaten (in two cases fatally). The administration of Benjamin Harrison demanded an apology and reparations, while the Chilean justice system slowly reviewed the incident and then laid the blame on U.S. sailors for inciting the violence. In 1892, the courts even sought to indict them.

Diplomatic efforts stalled, and Harrison went to Congress and requested that it be ready to take action: "We must protect those who, in foreign ports, display the flag or wear the colors of this Government against insult, brutality, and death, inflicted in resentment of the acts of their Government, and not for any fault of their own."[18] The Chilean minister suggested that President Harrison was either wrong or lying when he claimed (based on a U.S. Navy report) that Chileans were to blame.

As quickly as it had escalated, the furor died down. The Chilean government, which had just emerged from civil war, realized that it was almost at war with a much stronger country. The Chilean navy was well equipped in Latin American terms, but the government's resources were hardly adequate to sustain a war either financially or politically. Chile had also received news from England, where an official of the Foreign Office claimed that if the United States did not receive what it demanded, then President Harrison planned to declare war and seize nitrate territories.[19] The Chilean government offered to pay reparations and distanced itself from the statements of its minister. Nonetheless, as a British diplomat noted, the affair had created a "passionate sense of hatred toward the United States, which will take a long time to remove."[20]

Venezuela and the Olney Doctrine

Another important conflict in South America was geographically much closer to the United States. For years there had been a border dispute between Venezuela and British Guiana. Neither the Dutch (who had originally claimed Guiana and then ceded it to Britain) nor Spain had ever explicitly mapped out the borderline. Only in the mid-nineteenth century did Britain finally do so, to Venezuela's determined dissatisfaction. In the 1870s, Venezuela pushed the issue and demanded negotiations to settle the matter. In that effort, Venezuelans turned to the United States for support. Although the Monroe Doctrine was only sporadically affirmed, to Venezuelan leaders this seemed a perfect time to invoke it. Predictably, for a number of years U.S. administrations either did not respond or did so vaguely. This northern tip of South America was not strategically important (though the head of the Orinoco River was becoming significant for trade), and so it was deemed not worth the political effort to become involved in the conflict.

The discovery of gold increased Venezuelan interest in the territory, and matters finally came to a head in 1887, when Venezuela demanded that Great Britain vacate part of the disputed territory. Yet again Venezuela appealed to the United States, citing Britain's "insatiable thirst for conquest" as a rationale for invoking the Monroe Doctrine.[21] Once settled into his second term of office in 1893, President Grover Cleveland finally made the issue a foreign policy priority. Perhaps the British were indeed becoming too aggressive in the region, as their influence in Central America remained significant.

In 1894, Cleveland mentioned British encroachment in his State of the Union address, and the U.S. Congress passed a joint resolution encouraging U.S. participation in arbitration. In 1895, Cleveland instructed Secretary of State Richard Olney to craft a message that would be delivered to the British. It had two parts: the first asserted U.S. interests in the hemisphere, and the second proposed U.S involvement in arbitration. It would become known as the Olney Doctrine.

The foundation of Olney's message was, of course, a reiteration of Monroe's words. What made it different was the bolder proclamation that the United States was "practically sovereign on this continent, and its fiat is law upon the subjects to which it confines its interposition." Deconstructing Olney's nineteenth-century language shows a simple and forceful message: the United States was the hegemonic power in the region and felt perfectly justified in using its might to protect its interests, which went well beyond Monroe's original intent.

Olney Doctrine (1895)

Since the close of the negotiations initiated in 1893, Venezuela has repeatedly brought the controversy to the notice of the United States, has insisted upon its importance to the United States as well as to Venezuela, has represented it to have reached an acute stage—making definite action by the United States imperative—and has not ceased to solicit the services and support of the United States in aid of its final adjustment. . . . [T]he Government of the United States has made it clear to Great Britain and to the world that the controversy is one in which both its honor and its interests are involved and the continuance of which it can not regard with indifference.

That there are circumstances under which a nation may justly interpose in a controversy to which two or more nations are the direct and immediate parties is an admitted canon of international law. The doctrine is ordinarily expressed in terms of the most general character and is perhaps incapable of more specific statement. . . . President Monroe, in the celebrated Message of December 2, 1823 . . . declared that the American continents were fully occupied and were not the subjects of future colonization by European powers. . . . It was realized that it was futile to lay down such a rule unless its observance could be enforced. It was manifest that the United States was the only power in this hemisphere capable of enforcing it. It was therefore courageously declared not merely that Europe ought not to interfere in American affairs, but that any European power doing so would be regarding as antagonizing the interests and inviting the Opposition of the United States.

That America is in no part open to colonization, though the proposition was not universally admitted at the time of its first enunciation, has long been universally conceded. We are now concerned, therefore, only with that other practical application of the Monroe doctrine the disregard of which by an European power is to be deemed an act of unfriendliness towards the United States. The precise scope and limitations of this rule cannot be too clearly apprehended. It does not establish any general protectorate by the United States over other American states. . . . It does not contemplate any interference in the internal affairs of any American state or in the relations between it and other American states. It does not justify any attempt on our part to change the established form of government of any American state or to prevent the people of such state from altering that form according to their own will and pleasure. The rule in question has but a single purpose and object. It is that no European power or combination of European powers shall forcibly deprive an American state of the right and power of self-government and of shaping for itself its own political fortunes and destiny.

If . . . for the reasons stated the forcible intrusion of European powers into American politics is to be deprecated—if, as it is to be deprecated, it should be resisted and prevented—such resistance and prevention must come from the United States. They would come from it, of course, were it made at the point of attack. But, if they come at all, they must also come from it when any other American state is attacked, since only the United States has the strength adequate to the exigency.

Is it true, then, that the safety and welfare of the United States are so concerned with the maintenance of the independence of every American state as against any European power as to justify and require the interposition of the United States whenever that independence is endangered? The question can be candidly answered in but one way. The states of America, South as well as North, by geographical proximity, by natural sympathy, by similarity of governmental constitutions, are friends and allies, commercially and politically, of the United States. To allow the subjugation of any of them by a European power is, of course, to completely reverse that situation and signifies the loss of all the advantages incident to their natural relations with us. But that is not all. The people of the United States have a vital interest in the cause of popular self-government. They have secured the right for themselves and their posterity at the cost of infinite blood and treasure. They have realized and exemplified its beneficent operation by a career unexampled in point of national greatness or individual felicity. They believe it to be for the healing of all nations, and that civilization must either advance or retrograde accordingly as its supremacy is extended or curtailed. Imbued with these sentiments, the people of the United States might not impossibly be wrought up to an active propaganda in favor of a cause so highly valued both for themselves and for mankind. But the age of the Crusades has passed, and they are content with such assertion and defense of the right of popular government as their own security and welfare demand. It is in that view more than in any other that they believe it not to be tolerated that the political control of an American state shall be forcibly assumed by a European power.

. . . To-day the United States is practically sovereign on this continent, and its fiat is law upon the subjects to which it confines its interposition. Why? It is not because of the pure friendship or good will felt for it. It is not simply by reason of its high character as a civilized state, nor because wisdom and justice and equity are the invariable characteristics of the dealings of the United States. It is because, in addition to all other grounds, its infinite resources combined with its isolated position render it master of the situation and practically invulnerable as against any or all other powers.

All the advantages of this superiority are at once imperiled if the principle be admitted that European powers may convert American states into colonies or provinces of their own. . . .

There is, then, a doctrine of American public law, well founded in principle and abundantly sanctioned by precedent, which entitles and requires the United States to treat as an injury to itself the forcible assumption by a European power of political control an American state. The application of the doctrine to the boundary dispute between Great Britain and Venezuela remains to be made and presents

(Continued)

no real difficulty. Though the dispute relates to a boundary line, yet, as it is between states, it necessarily imports political control to be lost by one party and gained by the other. The political control at stake, too, is of no mean importance, but concerns a domain of great extent . . . and, if it also directly involves the command of the mouth of the Orinoco, is of immense consequence in connection with the whole river navigation of the interior of South America. . . .

. . . It being clear, therefore, that the United States may legitimately insist upon the merits of the boundary question being determined, it is equally clear that there is but one feasible mode of determining them, viz., peaceful arbitration. . . .

In these circumstances, the duty of the President appears to him unmistakable and imperative. Great Britain's assertion of title to the disputed territory combined with her refusal to have that title investigated being a substantial appropriation of the territory to her own use, not to protest and give warning that the transaction will be regarded as injurious to the interests of the people of the United States as well as oppressive in itself would be to ignore an established policy with which the honor and welfare of this country are closely identified. . . .

Source: U.S. Department of State, *Papers Relating to the Foreign Relations of the United States* (FRUS), 1895: 545–62.

The British rejected the idea that the United States had any right to be involved at all. In other words, even the Monroe Doctrine was invalid. That is how the matter stood for most of 1895, while both sides tried to resolve the problem. Cleveland asked Congress to set up a commission to investigate the boundaries in question, and in early 1896, Great Britain backed down and accepted negotiation. The commission itself included no Venezuelans (who were, in fact, never consulted at all), and the agreement concluded in 1899 gave the British government most of what it wanted, namely, a continuation of the status quo. Given that the entire unpleasant business was nearing its end, Cleveland had no desire to antagonize Britain with an unfavorable settlement.

Although Britain did not explicitly acknowledge U.S. hegemony, its acquiescence to demands meant the same in practice. Not long after the Venezuela conflict, Britain would accept the demise of the Clayton-Bulwer Treaty as well. Recognition was dawning that the United States was a formidable power—a feeling that would solidify after the Spanish-American War—and that rapprochement was preferable to enmity. If the United States wanted to establish dominion over its "neighborhood," so be it.

Conflicting Visions of Pan-Americanism

Ever since independence was won from Spain, many Latin American leaders—most notably Simón Bolívar—had advocated regional unity. Unity did not necessarily mean union, which only a few desired, but hemispheric agreements that would bolster economic growth and security for all. The concept of

Pan-Americanism in general refers to the notion that there is a commonality among the republics of the Americas that should bind them together. The problem, of course, lay in articulating how that should happen, who should lead the effort, and who would benefit the most from the interaction. The "modernist" literary movement in Latin America around the turn of the century marked a new self-reflection of Spanish American culture. The Nicaraguan poet Rubén Darío called for "Pan Hispanism," which deliberately excluded the United States. In his poem "Salute of the Optimist" ("Salutación del optimista"), Darío calls for the "fertile Hispanic blood" to awaken and to "sing new hymns" of glory.[22]

Meetings convened periodically in Latin American cities, with widely varying participation and results. For example, the United States refused to attend a conference on creating hemispheric law, on the grounds that U.S. and Latin American legal systems were too different. In general, the United States showed no interest and preferred to deal directly with individual governments, and even within Latin America, the delegates found it difficult to reach consensus on most issues.

Under Secretary of State James Blaine's direction, in 1889 the United States hosted an inter-American conference in Washington, D.C., the First American International Conference, more commonly known as the first Pan-American Conference. The impetus was the U.S. economic crisis and need to cultivate foreign markets, and the conference came on the heels of a special government commission that had issued a report detailing the tremendous economic possibilities in Latin America. All countries could send as many delegates as they wished. The Latin American countries sent between one and three each, the majority of whom were diplomats, and the United States sent ten, all of them businessmen and most of whom spoke no Spanish.

The two essential goals for Blaine (who, though he had resigned in the meantime, attended as a nondelegate) were a customs union and an arbitration system for international disputes. The delegates were hopelessly split, and Argentina led the opposition to both ideas. A customs union would limit a country's control over its tax income, and many feared that a fixed system of arbitration would end up favoring the stronger countries, especially the United States. Along with Brazil, Argentina offered a proposal that would formally oppose territorial conquest, and the U.S. delegates refused to accept it. Nationalism, combined with skepticism of U.S. motives, stalled all major proposals. Yet the fact that all countries of the "Americas" (with the sole exception of the Dominican Republic, which did not attend) came together was, in itself, an accomplishment that eventually led to a series of organizations (the Commercial Bureau of the American Republics in 1889 became the International Bureau of the American Republics in 1902, and in turn the 1910 Pan-American Union) that would become today's Organization of American States in 1948.

Suspicions of a U.S. drive to hegemony permeated this and many future conferences. As the famous Cuban nationalist leader José Martí reported from the meetings, the United States was "glutted with unsaleable merchandise and determined to extend its dominions in America."[23] Latin American representatives reiterated the same sentiment, even openly, but for the most part continued to attend. They did not necessarily trust their giant northern neighbor, but its presence was impossible to ignore.

Summary and Conclusion

At the dawn of the twentieth century, the United States was a country with tremendous military and economic power, which was reflected in its relationship with Latin America. That region still suffered both economic dependence and political instability. As a result, it was widely agreed in the United States that, as one scholar of the time put it, "Economic imperialism is very wholesome when carried out with discretion . . . [and] will also often be of great assistance to the backward countries that cannot follow the progress of the nations."[24] This was, as Samuel Bemis put it, "protective imperialism."[25] The consensus was that the United States was helping countries that otherwise would remain mired in near barbarism, and so the mantle of "protection" not only was wholly justified but also should be applauded. It is undeniable that U.S. efforts did bring some measure of advancement in Latin America—especially in combating disease—but reaction in the region to U.S. policy also demonstrates that its presence and actions were not universally admired.

The effects of the increasing military and economic dominance of the United States would soon be manifest. European countries were largely ceding control in the region, and there were no remaining obstacles to U.S. actions. The era of dollar diplomacy would merge seamlessly with military intervention and occupation. Chapter 4 addresses the expansion of U.S. military action and the resentment it fostered.

Research Questions

1. How did the United Fruit Company manage to become so powerful in parts of Latin America? In what countries was it most influential, and why?
2. What was the relative weight of domestic and international factors in the decision by the United States to declare war on Spain and initiate the Spanish-American War?
3. When responding to conflicts in the latter half of the nineteenth century, were U.S. actions based primarily on economic or political factors? Was there a regional difference, for example, between Central America and South America?
4. Analyze the attempts made in the nineteenth century to establish Pan-American union or inter-American agreements. Who favored such proposals? What were the primary obstacles?
5. Discuss how well realist theory serves to explain U.S. policy toward Latin America after the Civil War. Does dependency theory offer a compelling alternative?

Further Sources

Books

HARRISON, LAWRENCE E. *The Pan-American Dream: Do Latin America's Cultural Values Discourage True Partnership with the United States and Canada?* (New York: Basic Books, 1997). A provocative and controversial account of the failures of Pan-Americanism, blaming it on Latin American culture, especially its "Ibero-Catholic" background.

JOHNSON, JOHN J. *Latin America in Caricature* (Austin: University of Texas Press, 1980). An excellent collection of political cartoons from U.S. newspapers, along with commentary. Most of the cartoons date back to the nineteenth and early twentieth centuries and demonstrate the paternalistic and even racist ways in which the U.S. press portrayed Latin Americans.

LAFEBER, WALTER. *The New Empire: An Interpretation of American Expansion, 1860–1898* (Ithaca, N.Y.: Cornell University Press, 1963). A prominent (and also controversial) account of the rise of the United States in the latter half of the nineteenth century, utilizing a deterministic economic argument that emphasizes the drive for more markets. Although the book is general, it includes sections on Pan-Americanism, Chile, Cuba, Brazil, Nicaragua, and Venezuela.

LANGLEY, LESTER D., and THOMAS SCHOONOVER. *The Banana Men: American Mercenaries and Entrepreneurs in Central America, 1880–1930* (Lexington: University Press of Kentucky, 1995). A historical account of the banana industry in Central America from a "world systems" perspective, focusing on the investors who had an enormous impact on the region.

LEONARD, THOMAS M. *United States–Latin American Relations, 1850–1903: Establishing a Relationship* (Tuscaloosa: University of Alabama Press, 1999). A good collection of essays by historians detailing the relationships between the United States and specific Latin American countries.

Web Sites

The United Fruit Historical Society, Inc. A Web site created by two Ph.D. history students at Stanford University. It provides a good overview of the company, biographies of important figures, a company chronology, and also a large bibliography for further study. http://www. unitedfruit.org/.

The World of 1898: The Spanish-American War. This Web site, based at the Hispanic Division of the U.S. Library of Congress, provides a chronology and index of people, places, and events. It has presentations on Cuba, the Philippines, Puerto Rico, and Spain. http://www.loc.gov/rr/hispanic/1898/.

Another useful Web site on the Spanish-American War is *Crucible of Empire: The Spanish-American War*, produced by the Public Broadcasting System. In particular, it includes a bibliography, links to other sites, and a short discussion (with examples of political cartoons and headlines) of "yellow journalism." http://www.pbs.org/crucible/

The Panama Canal is the official site of the canal. It contains a large amount of information, both historical and current, including the canal's legal and historical foundations, its administration, photos (including a live camera), news, and press releases. http://www. pancanal.com/eng/index.html/

Notes

1. Quoted in LaFeber 1963, 20–21.
2. Langley and Schoonover 1995, 22.
3. Quoted in Schoonover 1991, 56.
4. Quoted in Schoultz 1998, 94.
5. Quoted in Leonard 1991, 39.
6. Healy 2001, 49.
7. Quoted in Holden and Zolov 2000, 84.
8. Quoted in Schoultz 1998, 164.
9. Quoted in Conniff 2001, 74.
10. Henry 1904, 132.
11. Quoted in Bermann 1986, 137.
12. Quoted in Schoultz 1998, 128.
13. Quoted in Holden and Zolov 2000, 73.
14. Quoted in Pérez 1983, 201.
15. Thomas 1998, 436.
16. Quoted in Pérez 1983, 325.
17. Quoted in Sater 1990, 60.
18. Quoted in Sater 1990, 64.
19. Pike 1963, 78.
20. Quoted in Sater 1990, 67.
21. Quoted in Schoultz 1998, 110.
22. Quoted in Aching 1997, 160.
23. Quoted in Smith 2000, 19.
24. Gil 1911, 170.
25. Bemis 1943, 140.

CHAPTER 4

The Era of Intervention and the Good Neighbor

TIMELINE	
1902	Debt crisis in Venezuela; Drago Doctrine
1904	"Roosevelt corollary" to the Monroe Doctrine
1905	Dominican Republic goes into receivership
1910–1917	Mexican revolution
1912	U.S. Marines arrive in Nicaragua
1916–1917	"Punitive Expedition" in Mexico
1925–1933	Machado dictatorship in Cuba
1929	Stock market crash and beginning of global depression
1933	Franklin Roosevelt announces Good Neighbor Policy
1934	Platt Amendment abrogated

After the turn of the twentieth century, the United States was an acknowledged global power in both economic and military terms. The country had industrialized and begun to pursue foreign markets with more vigor. Foreign policy had also been transformed; it was more aggressive and more often backed by military might. Most U.S. political leaders viewed the country's role as that of bringing the light of civilization to the rest of the world. That coincided perfectly with national security and economic growth, because U.S. actions in the less developed world would also bring the forced stability that U.S. investors desired. All of this was readily apparent in Latin America, where U.S. power would be wielded on behalf of U.S. interests. The first third of the twentieth century hews closely to the expectations of realist theory, as U.S. leaders were well aware of the power imbalance and used it openly to advance national interests, both political and economic. This chapter examines the extension of U.S. power in this period, which ends with a significant shift in U.S. policy, marked by the Good Neighbor Policy.

In Central America and the Caribbean, most countries were still reeling from the conflicts between liberals and conservatives that had brought on sometimes rapid and usually violent changes of government. Eager for foreign capital, presidents and dictators accepted and even invited U.S. investment for their own benefit. In South America, where U.S. attention was less avid, countries like Argentina and Chile were outpacing their neighbors economically but remained too weak to challenge U.S. hegemony. It would be an age of imperialism, as no country in the hemisphere was able to stop the northern juggernaut.

The intense and rapid chain of events that brought Cuba and other territories into the U.S. orbit and established even more firmly the imprint of U.S. economic influence was capped in December 1904 by the "Roosevelt corollary" to the Monroe Doctrine. Just as Monroe before him had done, President Theodore Roosevelt used the occasion of his annual address to Congress to publicly outline the U.S. response to Latin American political affairs and the European presence there. Although the Olney Doctrine had already expanded the original idea of keeping the region free of European encroachment, Roosevelt took it to an entirely new level when he announced that in certain situations the United States would act as an "international police power." The notion that a stronger country could and should assert its hegemonic position was taken for granted. Indeed, the self-interest of the United States was portrayed as positive for all concerned.

The rationale for such a statement was the pressing dilemma of Latin American governments finding themselves unable to pay debts to foreign creditors. In 1902, Great Britain, Germany, and Italy combined to attack Venezuela when its president showed himself unwilling to pay. Under bombardment, he agreed to bring the case to arbitration, but the presence of European warships in the hemisphere was something Roosevelt committed himself to avoiding. The solution, he told Congress, was for the United States to control a country's finances if

The Roosevelt Corollary (1904)

It is not true that the United States feels any land hunger or entertains any projects as regards the other nations of the Western Hemisphere save such as are for their welfare. All that this country desires is to see the neighboring countries stable, orderly, and prosperous. Any country whose people conduct themselves well can count upon our hearty friendship. If a nation shows that it knows how to act with reasonable efficiency and decency in social and political matters, if it keeps order and pays its obligations, it need fear no interference from the United States. Chronic wrongdoing, or an impotence which results in a general loosening of the ties of civilized society, may in America, as elsewhere, ultimately require intervention by some civilized nation, and in the Western Hemisphere the adherence of the United States to the Monroe Doctrine may force the United States, however reluctantly, in flagrant cases of such wrongdoing or impotence, to the exercise of an international police power. If every country washed by the Caribbean Sea would show the progress in stable and just civilization which with the aid of the Platt Amendment Cuba has shown since our troops left the island, and which so many of the republics in both Americas are constantly and brilliantly showing, all question of interference by this Nation with their affairs would be at an end. Our interests and those of our southern neighbors are in reality identical. They have great natural riches, and if within their borders the reign of law and justice obtains, prosperity is sure to come to them. While they thus obey the primary laws of civilized society they may rest assured that they will be treated by us in a spirit of cordial and helpful sympathy. We would interfere with them only in the last resort, and then only if it became evident that their inability or unwillingness to do justice at home and abroad had violated the rights of the United States or had invited foreign aggression to the detriment of the entire body of American nations. It is a mere truism to say that every nation, whether in America or anywhere else, which desires to maintain its freedom, its independence, must ultimately realize that the right of such independence can not be separated from the responsibility of making good use of it.

In asserting the Monroe Doctrine, in taking such steps as we have taken in regard to Cuba, Venezuela, and Panama, and in endeavoring to circumscribe the theater of war in the Far East, and to secure the open door in China, we have acted in our own interest as well as in the interest of humanity at large. There are, however, cases in which, while our own interests are not greatly involved, strong appeal is made to our sympathies. Ordinarily it is very much wiser and more useful for us to concern ourselves with striving for our own moral and material betterment here at home than to concern ourselves with trying to better the condition of things in other nations. We have plenty of sins of our own to war against, and under ordinary circumstances we can do more for the general uplifting of humanity by striving with heart and soul to put a stop to civic corruption, to brutal lawlessness and violent race prejudices here at home than by passing resolutions and

(Continued)

wrongdoing elsewhere. Nevertheless there are occasional crimes committed on so vast a scale and of such peculiar horror as to make us doubt whether it is not our manifest duty to endeavor at least to show our disapproval of the deed and our sympathy with those who have suffered by it. The cases must be extreme in which such a course is justifiable. There must be no effort made to remove the mote from our brother's eye if we refuse to remove the beam from our own. But in extreme cases action may be justifiable and proper. What form the action shall take must depend upon the circumstances of the case; that is, upon the degree of the atrocity and upon our power to remedy it. The cases in which we could inter-fere by force of arms as we interfered to put a stop to intolerable conditions in Cuba are necessarily very few. Yet it is not to be expected that a people like ours, which in spite of certain very obvious shortcomings, nevertheless as a whole shows by its consistent practice its belief in the principles of civil and religious lib-erty and of orderly freedom, a people among whom even the worst crime, like the crime of lynching, is never more than sporadic, so that individuals and not classes are molested in their fundamental rights

Online source: http://ourdocuments.gov/content.php?page=transcript&doc=56

they "had invited foreign aggression" through fiscal mismanagement. In other words, U.S. security was at stake if Latin American countries could not fulfill their obligations, which, in his opinion, provided more than enough justifica-tion for intervention.

The Drago Doctrine

The Latin American response to the 1902 Venezuelan crisis was different, and decidedly counterhegemonic. Luis Drago, the Argentine minister to the United States, wrote a document (later referred to as the Drago Doctrine) asserting that no government had the right to collect public debt by force. Appealing to the Monroe Doctrine's emphasis on resistance to the expansion of external influ-ence, Drago envisioned a multilateral inter-American response to debt, very likely with Argentina at the forefront. Although applauded by many, it was largely ignored in the United States, which was not interested in sharing leader-ship with other nations or in committing itself to multilateral action. The Nicaraguan poet Rubén Darío, who in 1904 wrote the poem "To Roosevelt," sums up the Latin American reaction lyrically: "You're rich / You combine the worship of Hercules with the worship of Mammon; / and lighting the way for easy conquest."[1]

European governments ignored the Drago Doctrine, and The Hague's Court of Permanent Arbitration ruled that creditor countries had the right to use force to collect debts. As always, for the United States the essential reasons for interven-tion were rooted not in any sense of hemispheric solidarity or international law, but rather in a calculation of what foothold potentially hostile European countries

The Drago Doctrine (1902)

[T]his government has deemed it expedient to transmit to your excellency some considerations with reference to the forcible collection of the public debt suggested by the events that have taken place.

Among the fundamental principles of public international law which humanity has consecrated, one of the most precious is that which decrees that all states, whatever be the force at their disposal, are entities in law, perfectly equal one to another, and mutually entitled by virtue thereof to the same consideration and respect.

The acknowledgment of the debt, the payment of it in its entirety, can and must be made by the nation without diminution of its inherent rights as a sovereign entity, but the summary and immediate collection at a given moment, by means of force, would occasion nothing less than the ruin of the weakest nations, and the absorption of their governments, together with all the functions inherent in them, by the mighty of the earth. . . .

This is in no wise a defense for bad faith, disorder, and deliberate and voluntary insolvency. It is intended merely to preserve the dignity of the public international entity which may not thus be dragged into war. . . .

As these are the sentiments of justice, loyalty, and honor which animate the Argentine people and have always inspired its policy, your excellency will understand that it has felt alarmed at the knowledge that the failure of Venezuela to meet the payments of its public debt is given as one of the determining causes of the capture of its fleet, the bombardment of one of its ports, and the establishment of a rigorous blockade along its shores. If such proceedings were to be definitely adopted they would establish a precedent dangerous to the security and the peace of the nations of this part of America. . . .

Such a situation seems obviously at variance with the principles many times proclaimed by the nations of America, and particularly with the Monroe Doctrine, sustained and defended with so much zeal on all occasions by the United States, a doctrine to which the Argentine Republic has heretofore solemnly adhered. . . .

The only principle which the Argentine Republic maintains and which it would, with great satisfaction, see adopted, in view of the events in Venezuela, by a nation that enjoys such great authority and prestige as does the United States, is the principle, already accepted, that there can be no territorial expansion in America on the part of Europe, nor any oppression of the peoples of this continent, because an unfortunate financial situation may compel some one of them to the fulfillment of its promises. In a word, the principles which she would like to see recognized is: that the public debt can not occasion armed intervention nor even the actual occupation of the territory of American nations by a European power.

The loss of prestige and credit experienced by the States which fail to satisfy the rightful claims of their lawful creditors bring with it difficulties of such magnitude as to render it unnecessary for foreign intervention to aggravate with its oppression the temporary misfortunes of insolvency. . . .

(Continued)

> At this time, then, no selfish feeling animates us, nor do we seek our own advantage in manifesting our desire that public debt of States should not serve as a reason for an armed attack on such States. . . .
>
> I address you . . . that you may communicate to the Government of the United States our point of view regarding the events in the further development of which that Government is to take so important a part. . . .
>
> Source: U.S. Department of State, *Papers Relating to the Foreign Relations of the United States, 1903* (Washington, D.C.: Government Printing Office, 1904): 1–5.

may have been gaining. In this sense, Roosevelt accomplished his foreign policy goal because no European power would ever again attempt to collect debts with military force.

Understanding U.S.–Latin American relations in the first third of the twentieth century requires full cognizance of U.S. policy makers' perception that national security was at stake. Security, however, blended seamlessly with economic growth. Dollar diplomacy did not always reflect outright U.S. government support for private interests, but it generally did respond to the notion that expansion of the U.S. economy was essential for the nation's well-being and, by extension, its place in the international system. Dependency theorists would disagree and posit that this period marked an intensification of the process of economic domination. As U.S. companies penetrated Latin America, they made it impossible for domestic capital to materialize. Instead, Latin American leaders were beholden to foreign investors, who ensured that their own interests would remain safe. The periodic intervention of the U.S. government solidified these relationships, and so autonomous economic development didn't occur.

Debt and the Dominican Republic

During this period, only rarely did the United States believe that it might become a direct target of a European country, and Germany was the only country viewed seriously in that manner. The concept of security was therefore focused on how countries from outside the hemisphere were displacing U.S. political influence or perhaps were acting to block U.S. investors from gaining access to lucrative Latin American markets. That alone was sufficient to prompt U.S. presidents to take decisive measures.

The Dominican Republic was the first clear example of how the Roosevelt corollary would be wielded in practice, but it also demonstrates the complexities of dollar diplomacy because intervention came in response to the recognition that U.S. interests had helped bring a country to the brink of financial ruin. For decades, foreigners had controlled Dominican finances, and in 1892 a U.S. company bought the country's debt from a Dutch firm. With the aid of the

Dominican dictator Ulises Heureaux, the company's president attempted to shift the economy toward the export of cash crops.

The strategy failed. In 1899, Heureaux was assassinated, and the U.S. company was completely discredited. The national debt had risen to $32 million, and there was no sign that it could be paid off. There was also, of course, the specter of European intervention to collect debts. Specifically, the creditors were Belgian, French, German, Italian, and Spanish. President Roosevelt was not anxious to take on the debt of another country, but with the Venezuela imbroglio fresh in his mind, he finally decided (after he had been reelected in 1904) that such a decision was in the best interest of the United States. Negotiations yielded an agreement in 1905 that would "restore the credit, preserve the order, increase the efficiency of the civil administration and advance [the] material progress and welfare of the Republic."[2] The decision was not popular in the U.S. Senate, and Roosevelt had to push it through by executive order until it was formally ratified in 1907.

Taking over the Dominican debt involved managing all of the customs houses, which at the time were the primary source of revenue for Latin American countries, especially in the absence of any effective domestic income tax. The United States collected the revenue and then made arrangements for repaying creditors. In other words, the situation was one of receivership, in which an agent appointed by the United States had the legal right to control Dominican revenue and pay out whatever was necessary. Roosevelt also sent ships to Dominican waters to ensure that no European country would feel tempted to take its funds by force. As it turned out, however, European leaders assured Roosevelt that they accepted U.S. hegemony as long as their citizens were repaid.

Case Study in Dollar Diplomacy: Nicaragua

The downfall of Nicaraguan president José Santos Zelaya and the aftermath illustrate not only how the United States took power politics for granted but also the blurring of public and private interests. After the Roosevelt administration decided to build the canal in Panama, U.S.–Nicaraguan relations deteriorated. Zelaya was actively involved in regional political intrigue, especially in countering the growing influence of Guatemala (though he also invaded Honduras in 1907), and over time the Roosevelt and Taft administrations believed his actions to be destabilizing. Zelaya, who felt spurned when Nicaragua was not chosen as the canal site, made no attempt to curry favor either with the U.S. government or with U.S. investors in his country.

Within this context, in 1909 there was yet another uprising in Bluefields, the part of the coast where foreign influence had always been high. By that time, U.S. citizens outnumbered the British, so the majority of foreigners supported U.S. intervention. Zelaya's troops arrested two U.S. citizens who had played a role in the rebellion (by laying mines) and executed them for crimes against the government. If there had been any hesitance in Washington to overthrow Zelaya, it evaporated immediately. Soon Secretary of State Philander Knox argued that Zelaya's government was "a blot upon the history of Nicaragua," and that "it is equally a matter of common knowledge that under the regime of President Zelaya republican institutions have ceased in Nicaragua except in name, that public opinion and the press have been throttled, and that prison has been the reward of any tendency to real patriotism."[3]

Pressured by insistent calls from all quarters of the U.S. government to force him out, within a month, Zelaya resigned and fled the country. Trouble began immediately, as there was no choice of president who satisfied both the United States and a majority of Nicaraguan elites. So in 1912, the first U.S. Marines landed in Nicaragua to keep order, but it would become a full-fledged occupation. The soldiers were in the country almost constantly (with the exception of some periods between 1925 and 1927) until 1933 in support of conservative presidents. The national security of the United States was also taken into account through the 1914 Bryan-Chamorro Treaty. In that agreement, the United States paid Nicaragua $3 million (which would go directly toward debt repayment) and in exchange received exclusive rights to build a canal if it decided to do so and the right to lease Nicaraguan territory on the Caribbean and Gulf of Fonseca for ninety-nine years (with the option to renew for another ninety-nine years). Intervention in Nicaragua thus also served the purpose of shoring up the U.S. military presence in the region.

Occupation included seizing control over the country's finances, so U.S. representatives oversaw Nicaragua's customs revenue, national bank operations, railroads, and budget-making process. The Roosevelt corollary had made control of money an inevitable part of U.S. actions. Although undertaken by President Taft and his successors (not until Franklin Roosevelt's first term would the marines finally leave), the situation was the epitome of Theodore Roosevelt's corollary. From that perspective, if Nicaraguans were incapable of taking care of themselves, and if that state of affairs adversely affected the U.S. economy (whether because of trade disruption or because of harassment of investors and their interests) and national security, then it was only natural for the U.S. government to take action. For Taft, there was simply no doubt:

> The United States has contributed much to the cause of peace by assisting countries weak in respect to their internal government so as to strengthen in them the cause of law and order. This relationship of guardian and ward as between nations and countries, in my judgment, helps along the cause of international peace and indicates progress in civilization.[4]

The combination of U.S. occupation and corrupt conservative governments sparked a rebellion in 1926. Augusto César Sandino was a widely traveled Nicaraguan who believed his country was suffering from national shame because of its evident lack of sovereignty. With the slogan "liberty or death," he rejected efforts at negotiated settlements and rallied his supporters to continue fighting. His attitude soon gained the attention of U.S. authorities, who proclaimed his activities illegal. Sandino became a national hero and a black eye for the U.S.

government, which had no interest in having the U.S. public read lurid headlines about casualties.

Within a year, Sandino was leading a **guerrilla** force that harassed and attacked U.S. occupation forces regularly. He was impossible to find because he seemed to melt into the countryside without a trace. As U.S. Marines trudged through rivers, mountains, and rainstorms, often beset by illness, the Nicaraguans they encountered viewed them primarily through a lens of nationalist suspicion and distrust.

In 1927, President Calvin Coolidge sent Henry Stimson (a former secretary of war) to Nicaragua on an official trip to assess the situation and meet with the Nicaraguan president. Stimson reported that free elections were essential because political differences tended to be decided through revolution. Next, Nicaragua required a trained constabulary force to ensure the country did not descend into chaos once U.S. forces were gone. The Agreement of Tipitapa (named for the lake near where the meetings were held) stipulated that supervised elections would be held in 1928 and that all rebels would lay down their arms (Sandino refused to accept the agreement). Soon, U.S. marines began training a national guard military force to maintain order once the marines had departed (which occurred in 1933).

To head the national guard, Nicaraguan President Juan Sacasa (elected in 1932) chose Anastasio Somoza. Somoza was ruthless, cunning, and very adept at maintaining the support of the U.S. government. Soon after assuming his position, he managed to have Sandino arrested and murdered, which made Sandino a symbol for anti-Somoza, anti-U.S. rebels (the Sandinistas) decades later. In 1936, Somoza overthrew Sacasa, and for more than forty years, he and then his sons ruled Nicaragua.

President Roosevelt felt a certain distaste for Somoza but accepted him. In 1934, as Somoza maneuvered his way into power, the U.S. minister in Nicaragua advocated taking action to block him. Secretary of State Cordell Hull's response was:

> It has for many years been said that the United States has sought to impose its own views upon the Central American states, and that to this end, it has not hesitated to interfere or intervene in their internal affairs. This criticism has been made particularly with regard to our relations with Nicaragua. We therefore desire not only to refrain in fact from any interference, but also from any measure which might seem to give the appearance of such interference.[5]

Somoza was therefore free to seize power and to construct a personalistic dictatorship, during which he amassed tremendous personal wealth and aggressively fought off any opposition. The U.S. policy of noninterference became a sort of tacit support, which bolstered Somoza's position. It was then that President Roosevelt is said to have made the famous, possibly apocryphal, remark about Somoza: "He is a son of a bitch, but he's *our* son of a bitch" (though some say the quote was aimed at Dominican dictator Rafael Trujillo). When the Cold War began, the U.S. government supported him more openly and rewarded his virulent anti-Communist rhetoric. These sorts of policies are consistent with realist theory, as they were based entirely on the perception of U.S. interests, with virtually no attention to the effect on the country in question.

Nicaraguan politics would remain intimately tied to the United States until the 1990s, with rebellions of varying sizes against U.S.-supported governments. As a U.S. reporter noted in the late 1920s, "In 1909, the U.S. took a bear by the tail, and it has never been able to let it go. . . .Once in, [the United States] found that it could not get out. It tried to get out, and disaster struck Nicaragua, and dragged it in again."[6]

The Dominican Republic

Events in Nicaragua were mirrored in the Dominican Republic, where U.S. intervention would also have long-term political ramifications. In the Dominican Republic, decades of U.S. occupation and economic control were giving way to pressures within the United States to hand power back to Dominicans. The U.S. policy makers once again believed that a combination of elections (a free election was held in 1924) and a constabulary would provide the necessary conditions for an orderly withdrawal (though control over customs houses would not end until 1941). The United States had earlier established a national guard, which had spent much of its time fighting guerrillas. Rafael Trujillo, who had joined the force in 1918, was chosen to head it when the marines left the country, and he was cut from the same cloth as Somoza. In 1930, he oversaw a fraudulent election, became president, and then ruled in a notoriously brutal and corrupt fashion with the full support of the United States until near the end, when was finally viewed as too extreme, which led to his U.S.-aided assassination in 1961. The struggle for power after his death brought about a U.S. invasion in 1965, which is discussed in Chapter 5.

Controlling Cuba

A very similar state of affairs could be found in Cuba. With the Platt Amendment, the United States had already committed itself to intervention and, at times, occupation, and U.S. soldiers found themselves in Cuba from 1906 to 1909. But in Cuba, unlike Nicaragua, there was a large U.S. population and numerous U.S. companies, such as United Fruit and Hershey. As Louis Pérez argues, "Political culture, social formations, economic structures, and, in the end, the very function of the state were shaped by and around the expanding North American presence in Cuba."[7]

Dollar Diplomacy and Debt

In the early 1920s, large U.S. banks initiated a plan of extending loans to Latin American countries, one of the signs that U.S. policy makers were expanding their conceptions of security to include protection of economic interests. Economic power—that is, the ability of U.S. investors to use their money to extract sweetheart deals from Latin American governments—was often augmented by the might of the U.S. military, or at least with the overhanging threat of intervention.

These governments were short of capital—the 1920–1921 period had seen a sharp drop in export earnings—while the U.S. economy was picking up steam. Between 1922 and 1928, the banks lent $2 billion. Given its size, Brazil took on the largest amount of debt, but in per capita terms the greatest debtors were Bolivia, Cuba, and Uruguay. All countries, however, took on more debt in the 1920s, as New York was overtaking London as the banking center for Latin American debt. At the same time, the United States at times controlled customs revenue in Cuba, Haiti, the Dominican Republic, Nicaragua, Peru, Ecuador, Honduras, and Bolivia.

Debt was overcoming countries in Central America. By 1909, Honduran debt, dating all the way back to 1867, reached $120 million, compared with annual revenues of approximately $1.65 million. Although the U.S. government did not make Honduras into a financial protectorate, it did step in to negotiate changes of government, and United Fruit also jockeyed to benefit from the government's financial woes. Guatemalan debt was approximately $10.5 million, and the British government made insistent calls for accelerated repayment. The U.S. State Department disliked Guatemalan president Manuel Estrada Cabrera so much that it did not issue the normal anti-Europe response when the British government threatened the use of force. Estrada finally began paying in 1913. Even Costa Rica, traditionally the most stable Central American country, experienced firsthand a taste of dollar diplomacy. The U.S. government approved a $13 million deal whereby private investors paid British creditors and reserved the right to appoint a customs collector if Costa Rica defaulted.

Thus, before the stock market crashed, dollar diplomacy had reached its zenith. Because debt could always be financed through new loans and because the U.S. government had shown itself so willing to guarantee stability, U.S. investors believed Latin American governments to be a source of unending profit. Moreover, U.S. officials believed they were simply helping Latin American governments accomplish what they were otherwise incapable of achieving.

In Latin America, the loans were often accompanied by corruption and enrichment of political and economic elites, especially in those countries with dictatorships. Many of the loans were ostensibly for public works projects, and although projects such as sanitation, roads, hospitals, and schools were built, the relatively low expenditures showed that funds were disappearing into the pockets of both national and local elites. The fact that loans did not spur rapid economic growth made the issuance of new loans inevitable. Rumblings from the poorer classes would accelerate in the 1930s; they had never benefited much from the apparent prosperity of the 1920s and were devastated by the subsequent depression.

The expansion of U.S. economic interests expanded beyond Central America and the Caribbean. By the time of the Good Neighbor Policy, the U.S. economic presence in Latin America had reached into every country. In South America, U.S. products accounted for 16.2 percent of imports in 1913 and by 1927 had grown to 26.8 percent. In the entire region, U.S. investments went from $1.6 billion in 1914 to $5.4 billion in 1929. Most U.S. companies were involved in the production and export of primary goods in both mining and agriculture. Facing less and less foreign competition, they settled into such industries as fruit, copper and other metal mining, coffee, rubber, sugar, tobacco, and oil.

Woodrow Wilson: More Continuity Than Change

When Woodrow Wilson was elected president in 1912, a new progressive era seemed to be dawning. He and his first secretary of state, William Jennings Bryan, openly criticized every aspect of dollar diplomacy. Wilson himself has gone down in history as the "idealist" former political science professor who tried in vain to establish a League of Nations that would finally bring peace to the world. In spite of this common image, the remarkable aspect of his policy toward Latin America was that it was virtually identical to that of Roosevelt and Taft. If anything, it involved *more* intervention.

Wilson showed public concern over the degree of European (especially British) control over Latin American economies, which he believed was an Old World imperialist obstacle to true independence. In 1913, he promised that the United States would act to promote "true constitutional liberty" in the region and said, "We must show ourselves friends by comprehending their interest whether it squares with our own interest or not."[8] Although his rhetoric was short on specifics, his actions spoke volumes and reflected an inherent contradiction: to protect Latin America from foreign political and economic interference, the United States would have to interfere.

Like other presidents before him, Wilson viewed Latin America in openly paternalistic terms and considered stability to be the essential element missing in Latin American politics and economics. Moreover, U.S. national interests were closely tied to regional stability. Even though Wilson may have disagreed with the degree to which business interests had influenced policy, he heartily agreed that economic opportunities would spur the U.S. economy and bring prosperity to the host country. During his two administrations, the U.S. government aggressively defended what it perceived to be its interests.

In the Dominican Republic, for example, Roosevelt and Taft had rearranged the country's finances, but Wilson proved even more active by occupying the entire country from 1916 until 1924, on the pretext that the Dominican government had exceeded the debt ceiling established in 1907. The occupation was the product of Wilson's brand of idealism, which emphasized the **white man's burden**. More civilized (and lighter skinned) countries like the United States had the obligation to teach their less civilized (and darker skinned) neighbors how to run a country. In addition to the now common control over customs houses, U.S. troops built roads, schools, and other infrastructure and improved sanitation and health conditions. In return, they (as well as the president himself) hoped for gratitude. What they often received was hostility, and they never understood why.

Woodrow Wilson and Mexico

The way Wilson responded to revolution in Mexico provides an excellent example of how intervention remained central to U.S. policy, despite changes of administration. Porfirio Díaz had taken power in 1876 and created a dictatorship imbued with liberal values, meaning that he invited foreign investment while promising (and usually delivering) the order demanded by investors for economic development and modernization to flourish. However, by the early twentieth century and especially after a 1907 depression, discontent arose in various quarters. Peasants and urban workers felt exploited by both domestic and foreign land and factory owners, and part of Díaz's promise of prosperity involved denying rights to these workers. Simultaneously, many domestic elites hit hard by the depression looked with dismay at foreign entrepreneurs, whose access to capital was undiminished, and they also resented the growing control of Díaz's government, which restricted regional decision making.

In 1910, armed struggle broke out, and the following year Díaz was toppled and Francisco Madero became president. President Taft accepted the new government, but his ambassador, Henry Lane Wilson, disliked Madero intensely and soon began conspiring with former *porfiristas* to overthrow him. Victoriano Huerta became his chosen favorite, and in 1913, with the ambassador's full support, Huerta's forces led a coup d'état and killed Madero in the process. But Woodrow Wilson had just taken office, and as soon as he learned of the plot, he recalled the ambassador. He then sent an official to talk to Huerta to determine what should be done.

The report was not comforting. The overall assessment was that "General Huerta is an ape-like old man, of almost pure Indian blood. He may also be said to subsist on alcohol."[9] This offended Wilson in several ways. He was a strong proponent of democracy, and clearly Huerta had never won an election. But his moral rectitude also demanded that, as a civilized country, the United States must work to help Latin American governments learn good governance. The only way to do so was to oust any leader who did not live up to his standards. For Huerta, first the United States refused to recognize his government. However, Wilson also opened the U.S. border to allow arms shipments for anti-Huerta rebels and then in 1914 sent U.S. Marines to occupy Veracruz, a port city important for its customs revenue. Faced with diplomatic and military intervention, Huerta resigned and fled.

Despite Wilson's vocal preferences for "upstanding" leaders, he was not deaf to national security concerns and the legacies of the Monroe Doctrine, which came into play when World War I broke out in 1914. Many in Washington had become convinced that British oil interests were conspiring in Mexico, desperate to maintain oil supplies for the British military. Although Wilson eventually decided that British interests did not conflict with U.S. interests, the European war would become more important in the formulation of U.S. policy. Meanwhile, Mexican politics disintegrated ever further, as several rival groups fought each other. In 1915, Wilson extended diplomatic recognition to Venustiano Carranza, who came the closest to the president's idea of an effective leader.

In 1916, the rebel leader Pancho Villa, who in the past had already killed some U.S. citizens residing in Mexico, crossed the border into Columbus, New Mexico, in a raid that left nineteen dead. For Wilson, an attack on U.S. soil by someone the U.S. government viewed as a terrorist demanded retribution. The matter had again shifted from morals to national security. It was deemed unthinkable to allow the impression that the United States could be assaulted without punishment. In response, Wilson sent a "punitive expedition" of 6,000 soldiers under the command of Gen. John J. Pershing, known for his successful battles against the Apaches. In 1916 and 1917, they probed all over northern Mexico, as far as a hundred miles south of the U.S. border, but never rooted out Pancho Villa, who moved around the vast territory with knowledge of the terrain and sympathy from the local population. Eventually the expedition clashed with the Mexican army, leaving fourteen U.S. soldiers dead. Wilson had to choose between declaring war on Mexico or pulling out, and he opted for the latter.

The decision to remove the troops was based largely on U.S. concern over World War I. Mexico was an unwelcome distraction at a time of great political turmoil in Europe. Moreover, the German Kaiser, knowing the United State would join forces with the British, was eager to keep it out of the war. To this end, he concocted a plan to create war between the United States and Mexico, which would keep the country too occupied to involve itself in Europe. Germany's foreign secretary sent a telegram to his representative in Mexico, telling him to offer Mexico the territories lost in 1848 in return for joining Germany and going to war with the United States. Mexico could be protected because, in the stilted language of telegrams, "ruthless employment our U-boats now prospect offers."[10] The British intercepted the "Zimmerman telegram" and eagerly relayed it to President Wilson as the spark that would bring the United States to Europe.

Once Wilson brought the United States into World War I (and after President Carranza officially rejected Zimmerman's offer), his attention toward Mexico waned. The main exception related to Mexico's new constitution, drafted in 1917. Article 27 gave the Mexican state the right to nationalize mineral resources (such as oil) and to expropriate private property. Seeing it as an assault on U.S. investments specifically and commerce more generally, Wilson threatened to withdraw recognition, but the issue was not settled before both Wilson and Carranza were out of power. Wilson finished his two terms and was replaced by Warren Harding, and Alvaro Obregón ousted Carranza. Harding denied Obregón recognition while the oil issue remained pending. The dispute lumbered on, and finally in 1923 the Bucarelli Agreement (named for Bucarelli Street in Mexico City, where the meeting took place) exchanged diplomatic recognition for a Mexican declaration that oilfield owners could maintain ownership as long as they proved that drilling or other "positive" signs of use were ongoing. Nonetheless, the agreement—which was not a treaty—did not prevent further seizures of oilfields and constant legal and diplomatic wrangling.

The question of oil remained unresolved into the 1930s, a time when the revolution was being channeled into a political party, the Mexican Revolutionary Party, which was was created in 1938. (It would become the Institutional Revolutionary Party, or PRI, which dominated Mexico until 2000.) The watershed event of the oil dispute occurred in 1938 under President Lázaro Cárdenas, who nationalized oil industries. In a direct challenge to the demands of U.S. businesses, he said, "It is a good time to see if England and the United States, which talk so much about democracy and respect for the sovereignty of other countries, will in fact stand up to their spoken convictions when Mexico exercises its rights."[11]

The timing turned out to be perfect. Not only was President Franklin Roosevelt pursuing more cordial ties with Latin America but also he had an eye on conflicts in Europe and therefore did not wish to become involved in a lengthy dispute with Mexico that might eventually jeopardize hemispheric solidarity. Instead, the two governments began a series of discussions that would lead in 1941 to an agreement on compensation for the lost property. President Cárdenas had successfully overcome powerful U.S. business interests.

The Mexican revolution and its legacy, with its strong nationalist flavor, fostered a curious relationship with the United States. Economic dependence entailed a persistent need to negotiate agreements on trade, immigration, and investment, but it would be tempered by a streak of firm Mexican independence in both domestic and foreign policy. Whether the topic was oil companies, Fidel Castro in Cuba, socialism in Central America, or a distant war to topple Saddam Hussein in Iraq, Mexican presidents would show themselves willing to withstand U.S. pressures by pursuing policies that openly defied the stated desires of the U.S. political leadership.

Wilson and Pan-Americanism

President Wilson had been aggressive in the case of Mexico, but not all of his initiatives involved intervention. He was active in promoting Pan-American agreements, building on the foundations laid by James Blaine twenty-five years earlier. The U.S. commitment to Pan-American ideals was shaky and had generally been associated with establishing reciprocal trade agreements. Wilson acted to bring Latin American countries together to resolve disputes. In 1915, six countries had worked with the disparate parties in the Mexican civil war, albeit with little success. In 1916, Wilson proposed a Pan-American Treaty based on "the solid, eternal foundations of justice and humanity."[12] There was some resistance to the idea, especially from Chile, whose governments were always leery of any agreement that might question the territory conquered in the War of the Pacific (1879–1883). The outbreak of World War I also had a dampening effect by distracting Wilson and the U.S. Congress from their southern neighbors.

The greatest obstacles to Pan-American unity, however, were Wilson's own foreign policy decisions in Latin America. It was hardly convincing to proclaim "the principles of absolute political equality among the states" while simultaneously chasing around northern Mexico and while invading and occupying multiple countries in Central America and the Caribbean.[13] In addition, Chile was opposed because it did not want to submit its border dispute with Peru to international arbitration. Two other powerful South American countries—Argentina and Brazil—also showed a distinct lack of interest, and he was forced to drop it. Wilson himself seemed never to waver from the belief that he was acting according to the highest principles of morality, even as he acted strictly in the interests of U.S. security.

Cuba under the Platt Amendment

Meanwhile, Cubans had begun to chafe under the Platt Amendment, which constrained the decision-making latitude of Cuban leaders and did not resolve any of the liberal-conservative disputes that had carried over from the colonial period and erupted as soon as the first Cuban president, Tomás Estrada Palma, a conservative installed by the U.S. government, took office. In fact, in some ways it tended to exacerbate disputes. Both liberals and conservatives commonly appealed to the United States to intervene when political conflict became acute, and both sides believed they would benefit from intervention. The U.S. government also kept a keen eye on the protection of the increasing numbers of U.S. citizens and their property within Cuba. The expansion of U.S. interests encompassed all areas of the Cuban economy and its society, though the cultivation and export of sugar was the most prominent economic activity.

In 1906, political disorder fostered precisely to seize U.S. attention prompted the Theodore Roosevelt administration to send marines (2,000 initially, with more than 5,000 soon to arrive) as a way to quell the violence, and Secretary of War William Howard Taft became governor of the island for a short time. Marines arrived again in 1912 and then stayed between 1917 and 1922. Very often, the presence of troops (or at times only the appearance of a ship at a port) was a direct response to strikes or some other form of labor agitation, which was of grave concern to U.S. business leaders in Cuba.

By the 1920s, a resurgent nationalism was beginning to surface in Cuba, fueled by an economic boom (dependent almost entirely on high sugar prices) after World War I and the realization that not only was Cuban sovereignty nonexistent but also the United States seemed unwilling to depart. Cuban merchants in particular struggled to obtain greater political voice. They viewed the U.S. presence not as protection but rather as meddling.

The beginning of the end of the Platt Amendment began in 1925, when Gerardo Machado was elected president. He cultivated the support of Cuban merchants as well as the U.S. government, and for several years he worked to spur economic development. He received loans from U.S. bankers, which, of course, had to be approved by the U.S. government, and also repressed labor to make Cuba more attractive for investment. Even in the face of growing domestic opposition, in 1927 he used a combination of corruption and intimidation to gain support for a reelection bid (he ran unopposed in 1928) and to convene a constitutional commission to increase the presidential term from four to six years. Cuban democracy was becoming even more of a fiction as Machado viciously attacked his opposition, especially labor.

A combination of events culminated in the abrogation of the Platt Amendment in 1934. The depression beginning in 1929 hit Cuba very hard, which exacerbated domestic opposition. A year later, the United States passed the Smoot-Hawley tariff, which immediately made Cuban sugar too expensive for U.S. consumers. The overall economic effect of these two factors was devastating. Lacking revenue to respond effectively to the crisis, Machado took the country even further into debt to pay for emergency social programs. As unrest escalated (including an unsuccessful coup in 1931), Cuban elites appealed once again to the United States to unseat Machado. He was seen as the obstacle to meaningful economic change, and despite distrust of the United States, many Cuban elites viewed their northern neighbor as the only force strong enough to effect political change.

In 1933, newly inaugurated President Franklin Roosevelt sent a mediator to negotiate a settlement that would not include overt U.S. intervention. The proposals, however, involved more U.S. influence over Cuban politics as a way to restore order, which did not please those in the opposition who wanted the United States to assist in the process of political mediation but not to take over the country again. Ultimately, Cubans themselves created the conditions for his ouster. A general strike gripped the country in mid-1933, and even the United States called openly for Machado to step aside. With that declaration, Machado's supporters—even the army—saw the handwriting on the wall and quickly deserted him. The dictator then fled the country.

The new president lacked widespread support, and immediately a group of disgruntled lower-ranking army officers began organizing with the goal of forcing the government to accept its demands. But what began as an attempt to redress problems escalated into a coup as other Cubans joined together in the so-called Sergeants' Revolt. Led by Sergeant Fulgencio Batista, the troops forced out higher-ranking officers and installed a new civilian president, Ramón Grau San Martín. In a fever of nationalism and reform (which included, among many other things, minimum wages, maximum hours, and workers' compensation), Grau announced the end of the Platt Amendment.

In the United States, Grau's talk and action greatly alarmed the government and investors, both of which felt they had much to lose if Grau remained in office. Roosevelt refused to extend diplomatic recognition, which put Grau in limbo and encouraged even more political conflict. Within months, however, the U.S. government turned directly to Batista, asking him to oust Grau. In late 1933, Batista complied and installed a new president. The United States immediately recognized him. Cuban political stability was thus restored and, combined with the Good Neighbor Policy emphasis on improved relations, prompted the Roosevelt administration to abrogate the Platt Amendment. The only exception was U.S.

control over naval bases. Cuba was compelled to agree that Guantánamo Bay would remain in U.S. hands for perpetuity.

From 1906 until 1934, Cuban politics was characterized by rapid, often violent changes of government, accompanied by U.S. intervention and, at times, control over the country's finances. The result was a political dependence on the United States on the part of many Cuban elites that never fully disappeared, despite periodic flashes of nationalism.

The Good Neighbor Policy

In 1933, President Roosevelt initiated a policy that would resonate within Latin America because, for the first time, a U.S. president seemed to be shedding the traditional mantle of power politics and hegemony. Roosevelt stated, "The essential qualities of a true Pan Americanism must be the same as those which constitute a good neighbor, namely, mutual understanding, and, through such understanding, a sympathetic appreciation of the other's point of view." Latin American leaders, though understandably wary, were willing to support Roosevelt and work with him on a vision of hemispheric understanding. As was clear from the continued intervention in Cuba, however, the policy did not represent a rejection of the use of power to advance U.S. interests.

FDR's Good Neighbor Speech (1933)

I rejoice in this opportunity to participate in the celebration of "Pan American Day" and to extend on behalf of the people of the United States a fraternal greeting to our sister American Republics. The celebration of "Pan American Day" in this building, dedicated to international good-will and cooperation, exemplifies a unity of thought and purpose among the peoples of this hemisphere. It is a manifestation of the common ideal of mutual helpfulness, sympathetic understanding and spiritual solidarity.

There is inspiration in the thought that on this day the attention of the citizens of the twenty-one Republics of America is focused on the common ties—historical, cultural, economic, and social—which bind them to one another. Common ideals and a community of interest, together with a spirit of cooperation, have led to the realization that the well-being of one Nation depends in large measure upon the well-being of its neighbors. It is upon these foundations that Pan Americanism has been built.

This celebration commemorates a movement based upon the policy of fraternal cooperation. In my Inaugural Address I stated that I would "dedicate this Nation to the policy of the good neighbor—the neighbor who resolutely respects himself and, because he does so, respects the rights of others—the neighbor who respects his obligations and respects the sanctity of his agreements in and with a world of neighbors." Never before has the significance of the words "good neighbor" been so manifest in international relations. Never have the need and benefit of neighborly cooperation in every form of human activity been so evident as they are today.

Friendship among Nations, as among individuals, calls for constructive efforts to muster the forces of humanity in order that an atmosphere of close understanding and cooperation may be cultivated. It involves mutual obligations and responsibilities, for it is only by sympathetic respect for the rights of others and a scrupulous fulfillment of the corresponding obligations by each member of the community that a true fraternity can be maintained.

The essential qualities of a true Pan Americanism must be the same as those which constitute a good neighbor, namely, mutual understanding, and, through such understanding, a sympathetic appreciation of the other's point of view. It is only in this manner that we can hope to build up a system of which confidence, friendship and good-will are the cornerstones.

In this spirit the people of every Republic on our continent are coming to a deep understanding of the fact that the Monroe Doctrine, of which so much has been written and spoken for more than a century was and is directed at the maintenance of independence by the peoples of the continent. It was aimed and is aimed against the acquisition in any manner of the control of additional territory in this hemisphere by any non-American power.

Hand in hand with this Pan American doctrine of continental self- defense, the peoples of the American Republics understand more clearly, with the passing years, that the independence of each Republic must recognize the independence of every other Republic. Each one of us must grow by an advancement of civilization and social well-being and not by the acquisition of territory at the expense of any neighbor.

In this spirit of mutual understanding and of cooperation on this continent you and I cannot fail to be disturbed by any armed strife between neighbors. I do not hesitate to say to you, the distinguished members of the Governing Board of the Pan American Union, that I regard existing conflicts between four of our sister Republics as a backward step.

Your Americanism and mine must be a structure built of confidence cemented by a sympathy which recognizes only equality and fraternity. It finds its source and being in the hearts of men and dwells in the temple of the intellect.

We all of us have peculiar problems, and, to speak frankly, the interest of our own citizens must, in each instance, come first. But it is equally true that it is of vital importance to every Nation of this Continent that the American Governments, individually, take, without further delay, such action as may be possible to abolish all unnecessary and artificial barriers and restrictions which now hamper the healthy flow of trade between the peoples of the American Republics.

I am glad to deliver this message to you, Gentlemen of the Governing Board of the Pan American Union, for I look upon the Union as the outward expression of the spiritual unity of the Americas. It is to this unity which must be courageous and vital in its element that humanity must look for one of the great stabilizing influences in world affairs.

Source: Franklin Roosevelt, *The Public Papers and Addresses of Franklin D. Roosevelt*, vol. 2 (New York: Random House, 1938): 129–33.

Although Roosevelt had given official voice to this Good Neighbor Policy, it was not entirely original and was intermestic, responding to political pressures within the United States that had gained ground in the 1920s. After Wilson left office, U.S. political parties and their constituents' interest in Latin America had dwindled. There were periodic diplomatic negotiations, such as the 1923 General Treaty of Peace and Amity with Central American countries that would deny diplomatic recognition to any government taking power through a coup and end political interference between the countries. In other cases, however, such as during the Sixth Pan-American Conference in 1928, the United States flatly rejected pleas to open its markets by reducing tariffs. In general, as the 1920s wore on, the primary concern of both politicians and the public in the United States was to reduce its presence and public expenditure in Latin America.

When the blood of U.S. soldiers was shed in Nicaragua, resistance grew to fighting in other countries, especially when the "national interest" seemed ill defined. The stock market crash of 1929 and ensuing depression broadened the scope of isolationism because it became difficult to justify spending any money outside the United States. President Hoover supported being a better neighbor and bringing troops home, but he did not develop a coherent policy.

For Roosevelt, the policy was framed as something that benefited everyone. Not only would it end costly occupations, but it would also promote good will at a time of tremendous global uncertainty, especially given the rise of fascism in Europe. There were crucial strategic areas in Latin America (most notably the Panama Canal), but various countries also had important natural resources, so hostile governments or foreign intervention could therefore threaten U.S. access to them. The administration therefore could argue that it was entirely positive for the United States.

The practical impact of the Good Neighbor Policy was felt almost instantly. In 1934, the United States cut many tariffs and established reciprocal trading agreements. For Latin American presidents, this welcome move brought badly needed foreign exchange, though it would also have the effect of further tying some economies (such as Cuba's) to the United States. It also meant ending the sometimes decades-long era of occupation. In 1933 at the Seventh International Conference of American States, the U.S. delegation agreed to the Convention on the Rights and Duties of States that included "No state has the right to intervene in the internal or external affairs of another," though the U.S. argued it would also adhere to "the law of nations as generally recognized and accepted," which was understood as allowing intervention to protect its own citizens.[14] This meant accepting the essence of the Calvo Doctrine with its rejection of intervention, which the U.S. had refused to accept decades earlier.

The United States negotiated a new treaty with Panama as well. In 1931, Acción Comunal, a nationalist organization, took power through a coup. It was dedicated to reducing the U.S. presence and had the slogan "Panama for the Panamanians."[15] The government began pressing for a reform of the 1903 treaty, and in Franklin Roosevelt finally found a willing ear. The result was a new treaty in 1936 (though a reluctant U.S. Congress would not vote favorably on it until 1939), which eliminated Panama's protectorate status, raised the annual payment for the canal, and offered a number of other changes; for example, Panamanians had previously been banned from operating radio stations. The treaty bolstered the position of Acción Comunal's leadership, which moved to utilize the national police (Panama was still prohibited from raising a military) for its own political ends.

There were still some snags along the way. For example, when the Roosevelt administration refused to recognize the Grau government in Cuba in 1933, they argued that it did not constitute "intervention," especially because it was intended to forestall the need for military action. Yet, despite such caveats, U.S. policy did represent something new.

The Good Neighbor Policy soon explicitly encompassed hemispheric security as well. The rise of the Nazi party and Adolf Hitler's ascension to power in Germany in 1933, the Japanese invasion of China in 1937, and the eruption of other conflicts raised the distinct possibility that war in Europe or even Asia was in the offing. By 1935, Roosevelt began to push for inter-American agreements to address potential extrahemispheric threats. Chapter 5 addresses the policy shift back toward security and the Latin American response to it.

Summary and Conclusion

In the first third of the twentieth century, U.S. political and economic influence in Latin America grew, and the imbalance of power became even more apparent. Regardless of the different stated public positions of U.S. presidents, the relationship with Latin America remained based firmly in the concept of security, and the advancement of U.S. economic development became intertwined with security. The U.S. government proudly proclaimed its hegemonic position, which perhaps was a simple extension of Manifest Destiny. Power thus was transformed into a historic mission.

The specter of European intervention was still relevant, and the Roosevelt corollary to the Monroe Doctrine was the response, a way for the United States to prevent European incursion and, as policy makers of the time believed, to help Latin American countries arrange their affairs properly, which they seemed unable to do on their own. Dollar diplomacy, with its tight (though not unwavering) connection between government and business, went hand in hand with the Roosevelt corollary. Under President Wilson, who espoused a deeply felt moral obligation to bring democracy to the rest of the world, U.S. troops were sent to more countries, and occupation was the norm in countries such as Cuba, the Dominican Republic, and Nicaragua. This combination meant that hegemony and "democratic promotion" were one and the same.

With only a few exceptions, such as Venezuela, the U.S. government showed little interest in South America, choosing to focus, at times very intensely, on Mexico, Central America, and the Caribbean. However, U.S. businesses were beginning to demonstrate great interest in the entire region. The era of dollar diplomacy had seen U.S. investors and troops move ceaselessly, as diplomacy and money worked closely together. Only with President Franklin Roosevelt's enunciation of the Good Neighbor Policy did the United States assert the integrity and sovereignty of Latin American countries.

The Good Neighbor Policy poses a challenge to a realist perspective of this era. It seemed to turn security on its head in favor of an intermestic policy that sought to placate domestic interests in the context of economic depression. Nonetheless, Roosevelt did not disregard security, as demonstrated by his vigilant eye on Europe and Asia and his use of military and political leverage against Latin America when deemed necessary. Moreover, as Chapter 5 discusses, the time of the good neighbor was a policy hiccup, to be rather rapidly jettisoned in the face of a new postwar threat.

In Latin America, some politicians and business leaders endeavored to take whatever gain they could from the U.S. presence, thus acknowledging (and even accepting) the power imbalance. Many elites made handsome profits and/or were catapulted to positions of political authority. Beyond this small group, however, brewed a nationalist and increasingly anti-U.S. sentiment, fueled by poverty, occupation, and mistreatment. These movements would require long incubation before they would explode, but their roots lay in the first third of the twentieth century. There is a direct causal link between U.S. policy and the creation of organizations and rebellions that would later during the Cold War be viewed as subversive and Communist.

Latin American invocation of international law also continued, as the Drago Doctrine was another step (building on Calvo's thesis of nonintervention) toward using reasoned legal arguments to counter U.S. hegemony. Although they had no immediate policy impact, together they constituted the first halting steps toward the creation of international regimes.

Ironically, the nonintervention angle of the Good Neighbor Policy had the direct result of snuffing out any chances of democracy in numerous countries. Not only did President Roosevelt not intervene when violent changes of government occurred but also he and his cabinet refused even to condemn them. Dictators who would later become international icons of brutality and corruption, such as Somoza and Trujillo, owed their positions in part to the Good Neighbor Policy. But the clouds of war were already dark, and by the end of World War II the Good Neighbor Policy would be largely discarded, replaced by the exigencies of a new, "colder" conflict.

Research Questions

1. During the first third of the twentieth century, to what degree was U.S. intervention (both political and economic) requested by Latin American political elites versus simply being imposed?

2. What were the most prominent responses by Latin American leaders to dollar diplomacy? How effective were they at challenging U.S. hegemony?
3. When President Woodrow Wilson took office, what were the most important changes in U.S. policy toward Latin America, and what aspects of that policy remained the same?
4. In what specific ways did the Good Neighbor Policy represent a significant shift in U.S. policy? In what ways did it maintain continuity from the policies of previous administration?
5. In what ways can dependency theory contribute to an understanding of U.S. intervention in the first third of the twentieth century?
6. What combination of factors led to U.S. support for personalistic dictatorships in the 1930s?

Further Sources

Books

GILDERHUS, MARK T. *The Second Century: U.S.–Latin American Relations since 1889* (Wilmington, Del.: Scholarly Resources, 2000). A good overview and historiography of U.S.–Latin American relations that covers the first third of the twentieth century in detail.

MARICHAL, CARLOS. *A Century of Debt Crises in Latin America* (Princeton, N.J.: Princeton University Press, 1989). A historical examination of the politics of debt in the region, from the time of independence until the depression of the 1930s. The author blames creditor countries for the instability that ensued in the debtor countries.

WOOD, BRYCE. *The Making of the Good Neighbor Policy* (New York: Columbia University Press, 1961). A detailed analysis of the political origins and rationale of the Good Neighbor Policy and what "good neighbor" came to mean in practice in specific chapters on Bolivia, Cuba, Mexico, Nicaragua, and Venezuela.

Web Sites

Augusto C. Sandino This Web site, created as part of the graduate work of a student at the University of Calgary, is dedicated to the Nicaraguan rebel Augusto Sandino and openly admiring of him. It includes a bibliography, a biography, documents (mostly correspondence), and other links related to Sandino (in both Spanish and English). http://www.sandino.org.

Franklin D. Roosevelt Presidential Library. The library's Web site has access to more than 13,000 pages of documents. A search engine makes it possible to find documents according to region or country. The site also offers a bibliography and other means to find more information on Roosevelt's policies. http://www.fdrlibrary.marist.edu/.

Notes

1. Acereda and Derusha 2001, 169.
2. Quoted in Gilderhus 2000, 30.
3. Quoted in Bermann 1986, 146.

4. Quoted in Schoultz 1998, 219.
5. Quoted in Pastor 1987, 27.
6. Quoted in Pastor 1987, 22.
7. Pérez 1990, 149.
8. Quoted in Holden and Zolov 2000, 111.
9. Quoted in Schoultz 1998, 242.
10. Quoted in Tuchman 1958, 202.
11. Quoted in Raat 1996, 143.
12. Quoted in Gilderhus 2000, 48.
13. Quoted in Gilderhus 2000, 48.
14. Gil 1971, 157.
15. Conniff 2001, 89.

CHAPTER 5

The Early Cold War Period

TIMELINE	
1939–1945	World War II
1947	Rio Treaty signed
1948	Organization of American States formed
1949	Creation of the Economic Commission for Latin America
1951	Mutual Security Act signed
1954	Invasion of Guatemala and overthrow of Jacobo Arbenz
1958	Vice President Nixon attacked in Venezuela
1959	Creation of Inter-American Development Bank
1959	Cuban revolution; Batista flees Cuba

The relationship between the United States and Latin America took a significant turn in the 1920s and 1930s. Economic and political dependence remained in place, but Franklin Roosevelt's Good Neighbor Policy gave U.S.–Latin American relations a new hue, one based more on respect for sovereignty and acknowledgment of equality. But it was a difficult time. The Great Depression had led to economic disasters, and Latin American political leaders found themselves ever deeper in debt and unable to contain the rising demands of their impoverished populations. Many countries succumbed to dictatorships during the 1930s, and in some cases the United States either accepted them or had played an active role in creating them. As discussed in Chapter 4, Roosevelt's policy did not mean giving up the right to wield U.S. power, even to the point of forcing out a government (as in Cuba). In that sense, being a good neighbor did not entail a rejection of power politics.

Following a realist perspective, this chapter examines how the early Cold War (that is, prior to the Cuban revolution) brought national security and self-interest once again squarely to the fore. During this time, U.S. policy makers took for granted that Latin American politics were intimately related to the overall struggle between the United States and the Soviet Union. Latin American leaders were acutely aware of that fact and made strategic choices about the direction their countries would take. This might mean allying with the United States, opposing it, or simply seeking to extract as many benefits as possible from the situation without explicitly taking sides.

The Effects of World War II

As the 1930s progressed, the United States began to view Latin America increasingly in security terms. Economic factors had certainly not disappeared, but foreign policy reflected preoccupation with European politics. German aggression and imperial aspirations represented a potential threat to the Western Hemisphere. At the Eighth Pan-American Conference in 1938, the United States pushed for an accord to counter any European-inspired belligerence. Two agreements came from the meeting. The first was the Declaration of Lima, which stipulated that if the security of any American state were threatened, the foreign ministers of all countries would meet to determine a hemispheric response. The second was the Declaration of American Principles, which reaffirmed the ideals of "nonintervention, peaceful settlement of disputes, proscription of the use of force as an instrument of national or international policy, respect for the precepts of international law and faithful observance of treaties, intellectual interchange among peoples, and satisfactory economic relations."[1] For the time being, these agreements meant that the United States had been successful in convincing Latin Americans that its chronic habit of intervention was being cured.

World War II made South America a much greater foreign policy priority for the United States, and the threat posed by Germany was real. Soon after the outbreak of war in 1939, German ships began coming close to the eastern shores of South America, and one was chased and sunk by the British navy. Their intent was not invasion but rather harassment of ships carrying munitions and supplies to the Allies. In 1940, the nations of the Americas signed several new agreements. At the second meeting of foreign ministers in Havana, delegates agreed to a new "no transfer" policy (known as the Act of Havana), whereby no territory controlled by a non-American country could transfer ownership to another non-American country. In other words, Germany could not take possession of territory in the hemisphere, specifically Dutch, French, or British colonies in the Caribbean. There was also a Declaration of Reciprocal Assistance and Cooperation, asserting that an act of aggression against one American state would be considered aggression against all.

During the war, the United States needed Latin American support more than ever before, and the attack on Pearl Harbor in 1941 made that even more apparent. The United States formally entered the war and immediately required assistance in maintaining the security of supply lines, which were endangered by German U-boats that sank their first U.S. ship in 1942. The United States therefore worked to establish naval bases in several Latin American countries to make patrols easier. The United States also needed access to a number of raw materials that were integral to the war effort. In addition to the obvious example of oil, there was also demand for rubber, asbestos, tin, manganese, zinc, and tungsten. Such a pressing demand gave the United States incentive to cultivate friendlier relations.

Countries like Argentina, Brazil, Bolivia, Chile, and Paraguay had significant sympathy for Germany and the Axis powers in general, which sometimes complicated efforts at hemispheric unity. Sympathies were due in part to the popularity of **fascism** (or at least its Latin American variant) and partly related to national self-interest. There was much to be gained by remaining neutral and attempting to trade with all sides. During World War I, that strategy had often proved lucrative. Argentina was especially reluctant to declare war and did not do so until March 1945, when the outcome was already clear. This frustrated U.S. policy makers and would lead in 1946 to a tactical error. Hoping to prevent the election of Juan Perón as president, U.S. Assistant Secretary of State Spruille Braden wrote the "Blue Book on Argentina," denouncing Argentina's position on the war and by extension Perón's role in it (although not president during the war, he wielded tremendous influence), and had it distributed in Argentina. Perón used the report to his advantage with the campaign slogan "Perón or Braden?" and won.

World War II had another important consequence, the creation of relationships between the U.S. and Latin American militaries. Before the war, such ties did not exist to any significant degree because the U.S. government and its armed forces viewed their counterparts as antiquated, backwards, and lacking professionalism. Even before Pearl Harbor, the United States had signed bilateral lend-lease agreements for war matériel with several countries, and after December 1941 such agreements spread across the hemisphere. (The notable exception was Argentina). During the war, the amount of lend-lease aid reached almost $500 million.

There was not a sudden sprouting of respect for the militaries of the region. In 1943, a U.S. admiral said of them, "They have never served a useful purpose so far as we are concerned. . . . I have wracked my brain for something for them to do. . . . I am willing to give them anything we can with the understanding that they simply make suggestions and that we don't have to pay any attention to them."[2]

Latin American officers, however, often evinced a keen interest in being taught and trained by the United States (not to mention Great Britain, France, and Germany). Simultaneously, they were borrowing and adapting geopolitical doctrines that would lead to "professional militarism," in which the military viewed itself as the central national actor in the struggle against subversion.[3] In the 1950s and 1960s, military journals across the region were filled with articles on that general topic, in which officers proclaimed that the armed forces constituted the last bastion of Western civilization. Cooperation with the United States was not only useful but also necessary to preserve all that was orderly and good.

At this time, the policy process in Latin America became more complex than ever. Strong forces pulled in different directions, and all wanted to play a policy role. Politics remained highly presidential, but grassroots movements, embodied by large-scale protests or even riots, forced new voices into the mix. Combined with the growth of electoral democracy, where voting mattered, the demands of the dispossessed and discontent couldn't be ignored.

The Cold War Begins

The alliance between the Soviet Union and the United States established during World War II was based on having a mutual enemy (Germany), and once that enemy lay in ruins, the partnership disintegrated. The ideological bent of both countries fostered deep antagonism, as each believed (often correctly) that the other's main goal was destruction of their political system. The idea that a "cold" war ensued is misleading, because it refers only to the fact that the two countries never engaged in direct combat with each other. For much of the rest of the world, this "cold" war, which would last from the late 1940s until the beginning of the 1990s, was hot and also bitter, destructive, and murderous. Latin America would feel the effects within only a few years.

In particular, the U.S. government became less willing to swallow reforms within Latin American countries that had any socialist flavor, even though the United States itself had been undergoing similar progressive reforms during the Roosevelt administration. Yet such reformist movements were gaining momentum in a number of countries. Although the United States had often been skeptical of reform (the Mexican revolution being a clear example), the Cold War sharpened its suspicion. Many in the U.S. government believed that such reforms were the thin edge of a wedge that would impose a Moscow-controlled Communist dictatorship. It was therefore the duty of the international community, or the United States alone if necessary, to prevent that from happening.

Evidence suggests, however, that the influence of the Soviet Union in the early Cold War period was minimal. It was not able to achieve diplomatic and commercial relations with most Latin American countries until the late 1960s. The Soviets had few historical ties to the region, and most Communist parties—one of the key avenues for Soviet influence—were weak. The exceptions were Argentina and Mexico, where the Soviet Union had established trade relations not long after the Russian revolution (and it is no coincidence that both countries had historically prickly relationships with the United States). Even in Chile, where the Communist (and Socialist) party had existed for decades, the government outlawed the party from 1948 to 1958. Communists rarely found a political toehold. As Chapter 6 will explain, Fidel Castro and the Cuban revolution owed nothing to Moscow.

The perception of imminent threat was therefore largely exaggerated. Nonetheless, the Soviet Union was making a concerted effort to expand its presence in the hemisphere, especially economically. As a newly industrializing power, it required new markets to sell manufactured goods and earn hard currency. It was also encouraging and funding members of individual Communist parties to become more active in political and student organizations, which raised their profile. Very often, however, the overall message was far from revolutionary. In Cuba, for example, during the 1950s the Communist party favored working within the political system for reform instead of going to the mountains to fight. Overall, during this period the Soviet Union did not yet have the diplomatic, military, or economic leverage necessary to establish itself firmly in Latin America, yet the United States insisted it should be viewed as a far-reaching power with its tentacles probing into nearly all aspects of Latin American life.

This new ideological intensity occurred when many Latin American countries were beginning to show signs of serious internal conflict. From the early 1930s until the end of World War II, there were elections and civilian governments in Argentina, Brazil, Chile, Costa Rica, Colombia, Cuba, Guatemala, Peru, and Venezuela. But in the decade after 1945, they would begin succumbing to coups d'état. Reformist movements that had gained ground within a democratic context were labeled "Communist" by domestic political and economic elites, as well as the U.S. government and its diplomatic representatives. A new era had begun.

It was also apparent that the Good Neighbor Policy had not changed the views of U.S. policy makers and diplomats toward their Latin American counterparts. In the 1940s, many embassies wrote reports detailing the "national character" of their host countries.[4] Cubans, for example, were marked by vanity and "are prone to be extremely nervous, which, coupled with a tendency to stomach and liver disorders, frequently make them short-tempered and excitable," while the typical Cuban peasant "has little ambition or drive but in spite of his wretchedness is fairly content with his lot and resists change."[5] Policy after the war would reflect this persisting and prevailing paternalistic attitude. Eisenhower himself spoke to his ambassador to Mexico about Mexicans saying, "You know, they're rascals at heart. You can't trust them and so forth, but they're lovable types."[6]

The issue of hemispheric security very quickly became prominent. Soon after the end of World War II, the nations of the Americas signed two enduring agreements. The first was the Inter-American Treaty of Reciprocal Assistance (the "Rio Treaty") in 1947, and the second was the charter of the Organization of American States (OAS) in 1948. Both of them were aimed directly at the perceived threat of Communism.

The Rio Treaty had its roots in a 1945 conference held in Mexico City's Chapultepec Castle. It reinforced the commitment to regional security and affirmed that the "maintenance of international peace" would be in accord with the United Nations, which was then being formed. Latin American delegates were disappointed, however, that the United States refused to include economic aid as part of any agreement. Security and economics were treated as separate issues. Nonetheless, all parties pursued—albeit with different motives—the completion of a new security pact, because the Act of Chapultepec expired at the end of the war.

 ### Inter-American Treaty of Reciprocal Assistance (Rio Treaty) (1947)

In the name of their Peoples, the Governments represented at the Inter-American Conference for the Maintenance of Continental Peace and Security, desirous of consolidating and strengthening their relations of friendship and good neighborliness, and Considering:

That the High Contracting Parties reaffirm their adherence to the principles of inter-American solidarity and cooperation, and especially to those set forth in the preamble and declarations of the Act of Chapultepec, all of which should be understood to be accepted as standards of their mutual relations and as the juridical basis of the Inter-American System;

That the obligation of mutual assistance and common defense of the American Republics is essentially related to their democratic ideals and to their will to cooperate permanently in the fulfillment of the principles and purposes of a policy of peace;

That the American regional community affirms as a manifest truth that juridical organization is a necessary prerequisite of security and peace, and that peace is founded on justice and moral order and, consequently, on the international recognition and protection of human rights and freedoms, on the indispensable well-being of the people, and on the effectiveness of democracy for the international realization of justice and security,

Have resolved, in conformity with the objectives stated above, to conclude the following Treaty, in order to assure peace, through adequate means, to provide for effective reciprocal assistance to meet armed attacks against any American State, and in order to deal with threats of aggression against any of them:

Article 1

The High Contracting Parties formally condemn war and undertake in their international relations not to resort to the threat or the use of force in any manner inconsistent with the provisions of the Charter of the United Nations or of this Treaty.

Article 2

As a consequence of the principle set forth in the preceding Article, the High Contracting Parties undertake to submit every controversy which may arise between them to methods of peaceful settlement and to endeavor to settle any such controversy among themselves by means of the procedures in force in the Inter-American System before referring it to the General Assembly or the Security Council of the United Nations.

Article 3

1. The High Contracting Parties agree that an armed attack by any State against an American State shall be considered as an attack against all the American States and, consequently, each one of the said Contracting Parties undertakes to assist in meeting the attack in the exercise of the inherent right of individual or collective self-defense recognized by Article 51 of the Charter of the United Nations.

2. On the request of the State or States directly attacked and until the decision of the Organ of Consultation of the Inter-American System, each one of the Contracting Parties may determine the immediate measures which it may individually take in fulfillment of the obligation contained in the preceding paragraph and in accordance with the principle of continental solidarity. The Organ of Consultation shall meet without delay for the purpose of examining those measures and agreeing upon the measures of a collective character that should be taken.

3. The provisions of this Article shall be applied in case of any armed attack which takes place within the region described in Article 4 or within the territory of an American State. When the attack takes place outside of the said areas, the provisions of Article 6 shall be applied.

4. Measures of self-defense provided for under this Article may be taken until the Security Council of the United Nations has taken the measures necessary to maintain international peace and security.

(Continued)

Article 6

If the inviolability or the integrity of the territory or the sovereignty or political independence of any American State should be affected by an aggression which is not an armed attack or by an extra-continental or intra-continental conflict, or by any other fact or situation might endanger the peace of America, the Organ of Consultation shall meet immediately in order to agree on the measures which must be taken in case of aggression to assist the victim of the aggression or, in any case, the measures which should be taken for the common defense and for the maintenance of the peace and security of the Continent.

Article 7

In the case of a conflict between two or more American States, without prejudice to the right of self-defense in conformity with Article 51 of the Charter of the United Nations, the High Contracting Parties, meeting in consultation shall call upon the contending States to suspend hostilities and restore matters to the status quo ante bellum, and shall take in addition all other necessary measures to reestablish or maintain inter-American peace and security and for the solution of the conflict by peaceful means. The rejection of the pacifying action will be considered in the determination of the aggressor and in the application of the measures which the consultative meeting may agree upon.

Article 8

For the purposes of this Treaty, the measures on which the Organ of Consultation may agree will comprise one or more of the following: recall of chiefs of diplomatic missions; breaking of diplomatic relations; breaking of consular relations; partial or complete interruption of economic relations or of rail, sea, air, postal, telegraphic, telephonic, and radiotelephonic or radiotelegraphic communications; and use of armed force.

Online source: http://www.oas.org/juridico/english/Treaties/b-29.html

The interests of the United States were very clear. The Truman administration wanted a mechanism through which Communist aggression could be counteracted. From that perspective, the United States would always play the lead, and the Rio Treaty would provide the necessary cloak of legality. For Latin American delegates, the treaty's appeal was different. Although many were concerned about extrahemispheric threats, an additional goal was to place a barrier to U.S. intervention that was grounded in international law. Latin American governments could then potentially utilize the Rio Treaty to address U.S. actions.

The charter of the Organization of American States emerged from a Bogotá conference in 1948. It has multiple structures for decision making and conflict resolution, the most important of which is the General Assembly, and all member countries sent a delegate. Another key organ is the Meeting of Ministers of Foreign Affairs. The charter members of the OAS were the United States and twenty Latin American countries, though over time membership would be expanded to Caribbean nations whose colonial origin was not Spanish or Portuguese. Over time, the organizational structure of the OAS would branch out considerably to address specific issues, such as the Inter-American Commission on Human Rights (1959), Inter-American Juridical Committee (1972), the Inter-American Drug Abuse Control Commission (1986), and the Inter-American Committee against Terrorism (1999). It is headquartered in Washington, D.C. As Chapter 10 analyzes, the OAS would very gradually become something of a balance to U.S. power.

During those initial meetings, Bogotá itself seethed with unrest and distinctly anti-U.S. sentiments. Violence gripped the Colombian capital for several days, and upwards of 500 people died. Most of the delegates (including retired Gen. George C. Marshall) blamed the Communists, and they were not entirely

Charter of the Organization of American States (1948)

Article 1

The American States establish by this Charter the international organization that they have developed to achieve an order of peace and justice, to promote their solidarity, to strengthen their collaboration, and to defend their sovereignty, their territorial integrity and their independence. Within the United Nations, the Organization of American States is a regional agency.

Article 4

The Organization of American States, in order to put into practice the principles on which it is founded and to fulfill its regional obligations under the *Charter of the United Nations,* proclaims the following essential purposes:

    a. To strengthen the peace and security of the continent;

    b. To prevent possible causes of difficulties and to ensure the pacific settlement of disputes that may arise among the Member States;

    c. To provide for common action on the part of those States in the event of aggression;

    d. To seek the solution of political, juridical and economic problems that may arise among them; and

    e. To promote, by cooperative action, their economic, social and cultural development.

(Continued)

Article 5

The American States reaffirm the following principles:

a. International law is the standard of conduct of States in their reciprocal relations;

b. International order consists essentially of respect for the personality, sovereignty and independence of States, and the faithful fulfillment of obligations derived from treaties and other sources of international law;

c. Good faith shall govern the relations between States;

d. The solidarity of the American States and the high aims which are sought through it require the political organization of those States on the basis of the effective exercise of representative democracy;

e. The American States condemn war of aggression: victory does not give rights;

f. An act of aggression against one American State is an act of aggression against all the other American States;

g. Controversies of an international character arising between two or more American States shall be settled by peaceful procedures;

h. Social justice and social security are bases of lasting peace;

i. Economic cooperation is essential to the common welfare and prosperity of the peoples of the continent;

j. The American States proclaim the fundamental rights of the individual without distinction as to race, nationality, creed or sex;

k. The spiritual unity of the continent is based on respect for the cultural values of the American countries and requires their close cooperation for the high purposes of civilization;

l. The education of peoples should be directed toward justice, freedom and peace.

Article 15

No State or group of States has the right to intervene, directly or indirectly, for any reason whatever, in the internal or external affairs of any other State. The foregoing principle prohibits not only armed force but also any other form of interference or attempted threat against the personality of the State or against its political, economic and cultural elements.

Article 24

Every act of aggression by a State against the territorial integrity or the inviolability of the territory or against the sovereignty or political independence of an American State shall be considered an act of aggression against the other American States.

Article 29

The Member States agree upon the desirability of developing their social legislation on the following bases:

a. All human beings, without distinction as to race, nationality, sex, creed or social condition, have the right to attain material well-being and spiritual growth under circumstances of liberty, dignity, equality of opportunity, and economic security;

b. Work is a right and a social duty; it shall not be considered as an article of commerce; it demands respect for freedom of association and for the dignity of the worker; and it is to be performed under conditions that ensure life, health and a decent standard of living, both during the working years and during old age, or when any circumstance deprives the individual of the possibility of working.

Online Source: http://www.yale.edu/lawweb/avalon/decade/decad062.htm

wrong. But Colombian Communists were only tapping into a deep mine of hostility. The incidents left a strong impression on a young—barely more than twenty years old—Fidel Castro, who had gone with other Cuban students to participate in the protests.

In addition to those diplomatic accords, the U.S. Mutual Security Act of 1951 sought to establish U.S. dominance over the arms trade in Latin America, thus displacing European sellers. It would reinforce the military relationships that had begun during World War II. Before the war, both Great Britain and Germany had served as examples to Latin American militaries and over the years had sent advisors and arms. South American militaries often owed more of their doctrine to Europe than to the United States. World War II, however, had left Germany in rubble and destroyed its historically militaristic tendencies, and Great Britain was too weakened and distracted to play a prominent military role in Latin America. The United States filled this vacuum.

In 1952, Ecuador became the first country to sign a defense pact that would provide "equipment, materials, services, and other military assistance designed to promote the defense and maintain the peace of the Western Hemisphere."[7] These agreements went hand in hand with the development of a U.S. Army training facility in the Panama Canal Zone. Although initially focused solely on professional military issues, after the Cuban revolution in 1959 it would become more ideologically oriented and in 1963 would be renamed the United States Army School of the Americas.

Most Latin American militaries espoused deeply anti-Communist doctrine and at the same time lacked the technical skills and weapons they believed were necessary for an effective twentieth-century fighting force. They were therefore open to the idea of receiving U.S. influence and aid to fill the gap. The U.S. government did not create the anti-Communist views of the armed forces of the region, but it certainly encouraged their continued development.

When voting to approve military agreements, the U.S. Congress was under no illusions about their effects. As Senator Russell Long noted even as he voted in favor, the main result "is to provide some dictators with tanks and planes with which to murder their own people when their people try to throw them out."[8] The agreements continued, however, because no member of Congress wished to be viewed as "soft" on Communism. By the Cuban revolution, this intermestic political reality was evident. Policy toward Latin America was often based largely on whether the U.S. public might view a given decision as caving in to Communism. Political opponents could wave any sign of a failure to fight Communism—even in such small terms such as voting for military aid—as evidence to oust an incumbent.

A similar dilemma held for Latin American presidents as well, as they decried arms buildups while trying to appear tough on Communism. For example, in 1960 Chilean and Peruvian diplomats asked the United States to limit arms sales to Latin America while simultaneously making their own armament requests. The fight against Communism was gaining momentum, and with strong support from the U.S. government, Latin American economic elites, and the armed forces, the military response to the Cold War escalated.

Reactions to Revolutions: Bolivia and Guatemala

Two developments in U.S.–Latin American relations came to a head soon after the Cold War began. The first was an effort on the part of many Latin American political activists to enact reform, especially with regard to land. All over the region—though most notably in Central America—a small elite owned the best land, and the majority of the population remained landless and under the tight control of landowners. Land reform involved breaking large landholdings into smaller pieces that could then be distributed to peasants. Of course, Communist and Socialist parties were not only supportive of such reform but also often spearheaded them. The second development was the belief among U.S. policy makers and many within the Latin American upper classes that reform was simply a Communist Trojan horse in weak states that would eventually lead to a Moscow-controlled dictatorship. As such, very often only the use of U.S. economic and military power would be sufficient to combat such a threat.

In Central America, these issues were combined with a high level of dependence on the United States for exports, because the vast majority of Central American exports went there. In 1948, the numbers were striking: 90 percent of Guatemalan exports were destined to the United States, with El Salvador at 76 percent, Honduras at 70 percent, Nicaragua at 74 percent, and Costa Rica at 78 percent.[9] Across the region, the 1940s and 1950s marked a time of significant dependency because on average 63 percent of exports went to the United

States, compared with 48 percent at the turn of the century. (By the 1980s, the average would be down to 32 percent.)[10]

Bolivia

The first test of breaking that dependency would come in Bolivia, where in 1952 a triumphant revolution led by the Nationalist Revolutionary Movement (MNR) swept the country. It began a series of reforms that included land reform, universal suffrage, and decreasing the status of the army and also the nationalization of three large tin companies that were owned by U.S. citizens. The government had the active support of local Communists, but the U.S. government did not intervene (though it hesitated several months before granting recognition) because Bolivia negotiated a compensation plan to the tin companies and also because it was concerned that interference could possibly lead to an even more radical government assuming power. Simply put, U.S. officials had come to the conclusion that although the MNR was not desirable, there was no viable alternative. Over time, the U.S. government would successfully pressure the MNR to purge Communists from the government. Economic aid then flowed in.

Bolivia's president Víctor Paz Estenssoro and his successor, Hernán Siles Zuazo, managed to pursue their own policies but at the same time accept conditions. For example, during the Siles administration, a Communist named Francisco Lluch was in the government, and the U.S. ambassador wrote back to Washington, "The Foreign Minister has stated that if the Embassy really feels that Lluch's presence is an embarrassment, that he can be removed. The Embassy has so indicated."[11] In the face of resistance, the U.S. response would be different.

The Invasion of Guatemala

The second and more stringent test would be Guatemala, where the outcome was less peaceful. Guatemala was among the poorest countries in the hemisphere and had long suffered dictatorial rule. In addition, in a country dominated by agriculture, the United Fruit Company was a fixture in the economy. It was the largest employer in the country with 10,000 employees, owned hundreds of thousands of acres (most of it uncultivated at any given moment), and also enjoyed a near monopoly on transportation. This, in turn, meant that United Fruit controlled the means by which all Guatemalan goods could reach the coasts or highways to be exported.

In 1944, a broad coalition (including junior officers in the military) forced the U.S.-supported dictator Jorge Ubico out of power, and elections were held the next year. In largely free and fair elections, Juan José Arévalo won with a reformist platform he called "spiritual socialism," which included a call to end foreign domination. His policies included wage increases and collective bargaining, public works (such as school and hospitals), efforts to reduce illiteracy (which at the time was 75 percent), disease control, and even a cautious move to expropriate and redistribute land.

These reforms brought Guatemala to the attention of the U.S. government, which began hearing complaints from investors and prominent Guatemalans. Not only were their interests threatened but also the Communists were very involved in the labor movement and formed a national Communist Party in 1949. Such developments did not go unnoticed within Guatemala (during Arévalo's five years in office, there were twenty-two military revolts), but Arévalo was careful to not push his reforms too quickly and, in particular, to encroach as little as possible on United Fruit. Nonetheless, the U.S. State Department issued numerous reports warning of Communist infiltration, including concern that in Arévalo's literacy program, "at the same time these backward Indians get their A.B.C.'s, they get a shot of communism."[12] For the 1950 elections, the Communists supported the government's chosen candidate, Jacobo Arbenz, who leaned even more to the left.

The U.S. reaction to Arbenz would represent the demise of the Good Neighbor Policy. The strong contrast between U.S. and Latin American views of the situation are apparent through the words of two important figures of the time. President Arévalo published a book called *The Shark and the Sardines* in 1956, a harsh critique of U.S. policy. Asserting that the United States needed a war as an excuse to demand primary products at low prices, Arévalo wrote that out of the minds of Wall Street came "the mythical and scheming idea of the danger of war. Stalin the terrible: Russia, the ravenous."[13] In this manner, the United States as shark could continue to devour the sardines to its south.

The view of prominent U.S. policy makers could not have been more different. George Kennan, an influential intellectual and former State Department official, traveled to Latin America and wrote a report on his observations. Beginning with the assertion "It seems to me unlikely that there could be any region of the earth in which nature and human behavior could have combined to produce a more unhappy and hopeless background for the conduct of human life than in Latin America," he went on to argue that, given the inability of Latin Americans to govern themselves effectively and protect themselves from Communism, "then we must concede that harsh governmental measures of repression may be the only answer."[14]

Within the U.S. government, Kennan's appraisal was not much disputed, and events outside the hemisphere gave it even more credence. In the late 1940s, the global struggle between Communism and capitalism had begun with stunning losses for the United States. The Soviet Union proved that it had nuclear weapons and consolidated its power over Eastern Europe, including a blockade of Berlin. The communist Mao Zedong defeated a friendly government in China, the most populous country on earth. Soviet-occupied North Korea became an independent Communist state. Guatemala, small and poor, thus took on a much more prominent position in U.S. policy. If the overall war against Communism was to be won, then every battle must be taken seriously.

Arbenz was a retired army colonel who had been minister of defense in the Arévalo administration. He promised further reforms and, by 1952, was embarking on an ambitious plan to restructure the entire economy. The centerpiece was the expropriation of unused land, especially the large tracts owned by United Fruit. Arbenz claimed that if the land was not being used, then it should belong to the nation. United Fruit countered with the argument that such land was necessary in case of natural disaster on other properties and also to preserve the soil.

In the U.S. State Department, an official named Louis Halle was called upon in May 1954 to analyze the situation and justify U.S. action. Using the "Communism as disease" metaphor that was ubiquitous across the hemisphere, he wrote that the "Communist infection is not going to spread to the U.S. but if it should in the fullness of time spread over much of Latin America it would impair the military security of the Hemisphere and thus of the U.S." An aggressive response was the only cure.

Our Guatemala Policy (1954)

Major decisions affecting our Latin American policy are being made in an atmosphere of urgency generated by (a) the outbreak of a strike among United Fruit Company and Standard Fruit Company workers in Honduras, and (b) the delivery at a Guatemalan port of a cargo of arms from behind the Iron Curtain. . . .

In Guatemala historic conditions provide substantial fuel to fire the revolution. Foreign ownership of the elements of Guatemala's economic life, together with the pattern of its international trade, gives the Guatemalans a vivid and unwelcome sense of dependence on foreigners. . . . Today the United Fruit is. . . an agent of social betterment; but its past is not forgotten and what really counts is that, whether beneficent or maleficent in its practices, it remains the expression of Guatemala's economic colonialism.

The international Communist movement is certainly not the cause of the social revolution in Guatemala, but it has made the same effort there that it has made everywhere else to harness the revolutionary impulses—nationalism and social reform alike—and exploit them for its own purposes. . . . It has achieved a high degree of covert control over the reformist regime of President Arbenz and is dominant in the national labor movement. . . .

More serious in its implications is the use that the international Communist movement might make (or be making) of Guatemala as a base from which to operate against the political and social structures of other Latin American states, and from which to organize sabotage of physical installations that contribute to the defense of the Hemisphere. It is the projection of the Communist will from Guatemala across its borders that properly gives us the chief cause for concern.

(Continued)

The real and direct threat that Guatemala poses for her neighbors is that of political subversion through the kind of across-the-borders intrigue that is a normal feature of the Central American scene. The danger is of Communist contagion and is most immediate with respect to Guatemala's immediate neighbors. The Communist infection is not going to spread to the U.S. but if it should in the fullness of time spread over much of Latin America it would impair the military security of the Hemisphere and thus of the U.S.

The infection could spread by intrigue supplemented by the smuggling of arms. . . . It could also spread through the example of independence of the U.S. that Guatemala might offer to nationalists throughout Latin America. It might spread through the example of nationalism and social reform. Finally and above all, it might spread through the disposition the Latin Americans would have to identify themselves with little Guatemala if the issue should be drawn for them (as it is being drawn for them) not as that of their own security but as a contest between David Guatemala and Uncle Sam Goliath. This latter, I think, is the danger we have most to fear and to guard against.

Source: United States Department of State, *Papers Relating to the Foreign Relations of the United States, 1952-1954,* vol. 4 (American Republics): http://www.state.gov/r/pa/ho/frus/ike/iv/20211.htm.

The Eisenhower administration had already cut foreign aid and blocked Guatemalan attempts to purchase weapons and military supplies in Europe, and so it listened sympathetically to United Fruit's complaints. Many members of the Eisenhower administration (including his Secretary of State John Foster Dulles and CIA Director Allen Dulles) had ties of one kind or another to the company. Irrespective of United Fruit's influence, however, there remained the issue of Communist infiltration and expansion. As the leader of Guatemala's Communist Party said, "They would have overthrown us even if we had grown no bananas."[15] Unlike the Bolivian case, Arbenz refused to renounce his socialist goals or to assure the United States of Guatemala's willingness to accept U.S. demands.

With economic pressure already in place, the next step was a trip by Secretary of State Dulles to the tenth Inter-American Conference in Caracas, Venezuela, with the goal of promoting a multilateral solution to the problem. What he wanted was a resolution that would proclaim Communism as an external threat to the hemisphere, which would allow for immediate action in Guatemala based on the Rio Treaty. What he got instead was a much-diluted version that had no effect on the situation. Approved by a 17-1 vote (Guatemala voted against it; Argentina and Mexico abstained), it called only for future discussion regarding treaty obligations. There would be no Latin American support for intervention, as the delegates were more concerned about the United States than they were about the threat of Communism spreading outward from Guatemala.

Immediately after Arbenz's election, there was debate between the CIA and the State Department about whether covert operations would be effective. State

Department officials favored a "wait and see" approach, but when Arbenz's reforms widened in 1952, covert action planning began. Although domestic opposition to Arbenz did exist—especially the army (despite his army origins, Arbenz failed to convince the institution as a whole), landowners, and the Catholic Church—it was not organized or united enough for the CIA's taste. It was therefore necessary for the United States to finance and organize the operation. The planning also involved neighboring dictatorships in El Salvador, Honduras, and Nicaragua that feared the spread of reformist movements.

The operation, called PBSUCCESS (PB was a CIA code name for Guatemala), was unlike anything the U.S. had done before in Latin America, employing techniques developed during World War II. For example, psychological warfare was introduced long before armed intervention and was intended to make the invasion easier. This effort included spreading rumors about the ominous Communist designs of the Arbenz government (aimed both at peasants and the military) and then, in the last moments, warning of an impending large invasion. Radio broadcasts beamed anti-Arbenz rhetoric (although the CIA relied more heavily on word of mouth because few Guatemalans outside urban areas owned a radio). But it also reached a U.S. market. A 1954 NBC news documentary titled "Red Rule in Guatemala" emphasized to the U.S. public that Arbenz posed a threat to the Panama Canal, which readied the United States for the invasion itself.

In 1954, President Eisenhower had referred to countries as "dominoes," such that if one country—no matter how far away from the United States—fell to Communism, then its neighbors would be next, like dominoes in a row. Guatemala, just like Vietnam and Iran in the 1950s, was a potential domino that must be stopped before it had the chance to fall. This argument of connections between Communist countries appeared to be vindicated when a Swedish ship was discovered carrying Czechoslovakian weapons that Arbenz had purchased. In June 1954, the invasion began, and it would prove strikingly easy. Despite having only approximately 250 troops, the CIA's chosen rebel leader, Col. Carlos Castillo Armas, had the advantage of U.S.-supplied planes and propaganda. Unnerved and already wavering, after several days of fighting, the Guatemalan army turned against Arbenz and ordered him to resign. He complied and fled the country. (He died in Mexico in 1971.)

The overthrow of Jacobo Arbenz had enormous consequences. The return of dictatorship to Guatemala—even more repressive than before—would soon plunge the country into a civil war of apocalyptic proportions. The country, battered and torn, would not emerge from that war until 1996, and not until 200,000 Guatemalans, many of them indigenous and uninterested in the ideological battle, had been killed.

The effects of the invasion would also later bear directly on U.S.–Cuban relations and the politics of guerrilla warfare. For example, the future guerrilla and revolutionary Ernesto "Che" Guevara was in Guatemala and saw firsthand the U.S. use of power. From that experience, he believed that Arbenz had made a serious mistake by allowing foreign investors and political opposition to remain unmolested in the country. Real reform, he felt, was possible only in a socialist revolution that excluded the old oligarchic elite and rejected the façade of "democracy" so heralded in the United States.

Finally, many within the U.S. government—especially the CIA—also felt they had learned a lesson from Guatemala. Domestic support for Arbenz had been disorganized and easy to overcome, and the CIA was convinced that this support was also minimal outside leftist political activists. Therefore, if another similar situation occurred, the same tactics could be successfully employed. Psychological warfare, for example, had proved highly successful. The Guatemalan military and much of the public had been influenced by the CIA's radio broadcasts.

As a member of the U.S. National Security Council argued in 1953, "We should regard Guatemala as a prototype area for testing means and methods of combating Communism."[16] A relatively small group of soldiers under the direction of the CIA could overthrow a government without an overt U.S. presence. The idea that there might be widespread support for reformist or even Communist governments was, they believed, pure propaganda.

Cuba after the Platt Amendment

While the CIA organized the Guatemalan invasion, Cubans watched in 1952 as Fulgencio Batista canceled elections and established dictatorial rule. Buoyed by U.S. support, Batista embodied everything that had gone wrong in Cuba. Organized crime flourished and lined the pockets of Cuban politicians and bureaucrats. Corruption was rampant, and the brief Cuban experience with democracy had withered away.

Plus, economic stagnation in the 1950s fueled discontent. As historian Louis Pérez writes, "Cubans participated in and depended largely on the U.S. economic system, in very much the same fashion as North Americans but without access to comparable U.S. social service and public assistance programs and at employment and wage levels substantially lower and prices higher than their North American counterparts."[17] The Cuban middle class was becoming frustrated as it lost economic ground.

One such member of the middle class was Fidel Castro. He became famous for a 1953 attack on the Moncada army barracks, for which he was imprisoned. His popularity—bolstered considerably by his personal charisma—grew, and after being released in a general amnesty (intended by Batista to demonstrate his fairness and democratic principles), he went to Mexico to begin planning a revolution through guerrilla war. The amnesty was disastrous for Batista because it freed the man who would overthrow him, and in Mexico, Castro would meet Che Guevara. Together with a small group, they launched their guerrilla war in 1956, sailing to Cuba (on a boat named Granma, which after the revolution became the name of Cuba's state newspaper) and only narrowly avoiding annihilation.

Although Guevara and many of Castro's other acquaintances were either Communists or sympathetic to Communist goals, Castro himself advocated radical reforms but not yet full-fledged socialism. He denied that his intentions were anything but democratic and was very careful to preserve a clean image as a champion of the poor and not as a Communist revolutionary. A *New York Times* reporter traveled into the Cuban mountains to interview him, and the subsequent press accounts were highly flattering. Castro emphasized the domestic nature of his mission: "You can be sure that we have no animosity towards the United States and the American people."[18]

The U.S. government had been perfectly willing to support Batista as long as he managed to keep order on the island, but toward the end of the 1950s, it was obvious that he no longer could. The Eisenhower administration decided that Batista, whose political support had dwindled to dangerously low levels, had to go so that a new leader could restore confidence and take the steam out of Fidel Castro's movement. To that end, the United States enacted a trade embargo against Batista in 1958, and several months later the U.S. ambassador was recalled. The symbolic effect was perhaps the most devastating: by its actions the United States had announced that it no longer supported the dictator, so his days were numbered. Later Batista would lament the "technique of the big lie" used against him, claiming that all charges were false. According to him, a completely false image of Cuba "was achieved by repetition, by the planned utilization of the gullible, the ignorant, the naïve, the unscrupulous, the perennial sympathizers with leftwing causes, the thwarted, the psychic and physical cripples, the men of resentment."[19] But by 1959, few outside Batista's small circle of loyalists believed his rhetoric anymore.

The Nixon Trip and Its Consequences

Reformist movements, heavily infused with resentment toward the United States, were evident throughout the region. Vice President Richard Nixon discovered that firsthand in 1958, when he undertook a quick "good will" trip to Latin America. The popular response in the streets was often negative and became violent when he reached Caracas, to the point that his car was attacked. Venezuelans had recently ousted a U.S.-supported dictator, Marcos Pérez Jimenez, and Nixon treated the interim government with "deliberate coolness" because "They had welcomed Communist support in the revolution against Pérez Jimenez and now they did not know how to handle their Communist allies in the government."[20]

The attacks were an outrage to the U.S. government, which launched a variety of investigations and analyses. In Congress, the State Department, and the White House, the conclusions varied little from Halle'e analysis in 1954. There was consensus that domestic, grassroots reformist movements existed and were viewed as legitimate by the general population but that inevitably they were infiltrated and controlled by Communists, which in turn were receiving orders directly from Moscow. Such movements, therefore, had to be watched very carefully and required a rapid response if the threat of Communist takeover appeared imminent.

After Nixon's trip, Brazilian President Juscelino Kubitschek wrote to Eisenhower to ask that U.S.–Latin American economic relations be rethought completely. He advocated an "Operation Pan America" involving an influx of U.S. capital along the lines of the Marshall Plan in Europe. U.S. policy makers were opposed to a project on that scale, but the OAS began discussions about economic cooperation, and soon Eisenhower would announce U.S. support for new economic institutions.

Nonetheless, there was still considerable wariness about the expansion of Communism. President Eisenhower's own brother reinforced previous conclusions. Milton Eisenhower became a sort of roaming advisor, traveling throughout Latin America and offering his opinions. He argued that democratic reformists should be applauded but that Communists were "using tried techniques of subversion and economic influence in an atmosphere of poverty, misery, and social turbulence that is ideal for the breeding of violent revolutions."[21] There was therefore always the danger that any movement would be infiltrated. His reports, however, also demonstrated the growing consensus that Communism fed off poverty and consequently only economic growth could be a bulwark against Communist aggression. That idea would not reach fruition until President John F. Kennedy took office.

The Political Economy of the Early Cold War

From the end of World War II until the rise to power of Fidel Castro in 1959, Latin America remained a center for U.S. investment but not for foreign aid. The fiscally conservative Eisenhower administration did disburse aid to developing countries throughout the world, but the majority went to areas considered more susceptible to Communist influence. As usual, the primary attention of U.S. policy makers was elsewhere, such as Europe, the Middle East, and Asia. From the U.S. strategic point of view, Latin America mattered far less.

So instead of aid, there came only admonitions. In 1953, Latin Americans were told that their best strategy was to follow free market principles and to attract private foreign investment to supply the necessary capital. In developing countries, this advice usually fell on deaf ears. The United States itself, in fact, had not followed free market principles as it developed in the nineteenth century, which was not lost in the minds of Latin American leaders. These leaders were openly disappointed that, despite their nearly unanimous unity against the Axis powers and protection of U.S. access to their natural resources, their concerns were not considered.

The shock of Richard Nixon's reception in Venezuela had a moderate effect on economic policy that would be a precursor to a much more ambitious program—the Alliance for Progress—during the Kennedy administration. Nixon himself claimed to advocate increasing economic aid, though he did not appear to push too hard to find support for the idea, which did not materialize.

The idea of a regional development bank had been around for several decades but had never gone beyond the conceptual stage. In 1959, the Eisenhower administration announced its support for the creation of the Inter-American Development Bank (IADB). It came into being the following year, and the United States provided $500 million for development projects in the region. The IADB's purpose was to loan money to public institutions for specific projects, especially those related to infrastructure, such as housing, electricity, road building, and education. By the twenty-first century, it would have capital exceeding $100 billion.

The IADB was, from the outset, funded in large part by the United States and often viewed in Latin America as yet another instrument of U.S. policy. Even earlier, another organization had been created, inspired entirely by Latin America. The Economic Commission for Latin America (ECLA), founded in 1948, was part of the United Nations and therefore not dependent upon the United States. It would later include the Caribbean and in Latin America would be more widely known by its Spanish acronym, CEPAL.

The founding principles of CEPAL revolved around an early version of dependency theory.[22] Its first director, the Argentine Raúl Prebisch, argued that Latin America suffered as a result of its place in the global economy. More specifically, its countries exported primary products (such as agricultural goods), the prices of which did not rise significantly (or often fell) as they imported manufactured goods from the wealthier countries, paying increasingly higher prices for them. In addition, a surplus of Latin American labor kept wages low. Given those realities, it was impossible for Latin American countries to improve their economic situations without significant change. Unemployment and economic stagnation were in part a function of Latin America's place in the international division of labor. To make matters worse, according to CEPAL, U.S. investment was not even having a positive economic effect because it ended up taking more wealth out of the region than it contributed. On account of its criticisms of the United States, the Truman administration tried unsuccessfully to have CEPAL disbanded.

Prebisch's proposed solution to this dilemma was industrialization, but his vision included a prominent role for the state instead of the primacy of a free market system. During World War II, many Latin American countries had begun a process called **import-substitution industrialization** (ISI), which fit well in CEPAL's model of economic development. The idea was that to reduce dependency on imports, the state would direct, encourage, and subsidize targeted domestic industries, whose production would substitute for foreign goods.

As this Latin America–based model developed, however, it relied more on foreign direct investment than on public money, such that dependence on foreign (especially U.S.) capital remained. In many countries, it also tended to deepen the relationship between U.S. investors and policy makers, Latin American economic elites, and Latin American militaries. If foreign investors were to feel secure about putting their money in a country, then the state—through the military and police—needed to ensure that labor militancy was kept to a minimum. Repression of labor was therefore an unintended consequence. At the very least, however, CEPAL's vision represented a counter to the hegemonic economic policies of the United States.

Summary and Conclusion

During World War II, U.S. security interests represented the primary motivating factors for U.S. policy and would intensify when the Cold War began soon after the war's end. Within Latin America, the predominance of security over all else bred dissatisfaction. While the United States rebuilt and/or poured aid into other parts of the world, Latin America received relatively little. At the same time, the high ideals of the Good Neighbor Policy were rapidly disappearing, and after the 1954 invasion of Guatemala, U.S. policy makers could not credibly claim to reject armed intervention. Power was once again central.

In part to counter U.S. influence, Latin America supported the creation of hemispheric pacts and organizations such as the Rio Treaty, the Organization of American States, and the Economic Commission for Latin America. On the streets of Latin America, protests and riots marked a swell of resentment against poverty and U.S. domination of economies in the region. In Cuba, however, another response to U.S. influence was brewing under the direction of Fidel Castro as he led a ragtag but growing (and determined) revolutionary army in the Cuban mountains with the intent of overthrowing a corrupt dictator who owed his continued existence to U.S. support. Revolutionary fervor with a distinctly anti-U.S. bent was developing during the early Cold War, though it would not fully flower until after Castro and the Cuban revolution triumphed.

Especially during the Eisenhower administration, the United States became more openly supportive of dictatorships and authoritarian governance in order to fight against Communist infiltration. The era of good will under Roosevelt collapsed under the weight of ideological struggle. Reformist movements in Latin America faced an uphill battle because not only did they threaten business interests but also U.S. policy makers assumed that they were too weak to resist Communist domination and therefore targeted them as threats to national security. In a book based on his travels to Latin America in the 1950s, Milton Eisenhower correctly noted that "Our present declarations of honorable intentions as we seek to help Latin Americans achieve a better life are often obscured in their minds by the grim echoes of history."[23]

The divergence between the interests and concerns of the masses in Latin America and U.S. policy could not have been more striking. Demands for land reform, higher wages, better working conditions, expanded political rights, and the nationalization of prominent agricultural or extractive industries collided violently with the traditional and entrenched interests of the U.S. government and investors. Fidel Castro's revolution in Cuba was a stark reminder of that divergence. Chapter 6 addresses how the United States and groups within Latin

America dealt with that divergence of interests and how the struggle against a hegemonic power engulfed the entire region.

Research Questions

1. Compare the expropriation of land in Guatemala under Arbenz to expropriations in other countries during the same period (such as Bolivia and Mexico). Why did the United States respond to them in different ways?
2. What lessons did the CIA learn from the Guatemalan invasion? In what ways did errors in those lessons later contribute to the Bay of Pigs disaster in Cuba?
3. What were the main contrasts between the views of the U.S. government and Latin Americans regarding strategies for economic development? What differences of opinion existed within Latin America as well?
4. How significant was the threat of Soviet domination in Latin America before the Cuban revolution? To what degree (if at all) did U.S. policy makers misjudge Soviet strength and political goals in the region?
5. Given that the United States deemed security an essential factor in its policy toward Latin America during World War II, what were the causes of the drastic shift in policy after the war that served to dismantle the Good Neighbor Policy?

Further Sources

Books

GLEIJESES, PIERO. *Shattered Hope: The Guatemalan Revolution and the United States, 1944–1954* (Princeton, N.J.: Princeton University Press, 1991). Based on a close analysis of archival documents, this classic work details the political, economic, and ideological factors that led to the Guatemalan invasion.

LAFEBER, WALTER. *Inevitable Revolutions: The United States in Central America* (New York: W. W. Norton, 1984). A widely cited work arguing that Central American dependency—political, economic, and military—created conditions that made later revolutions inevitable. More than half the book analyzes the period leading up to the early Cold War.

RABE, STEPHEN G., *Eisenhower and Latin America: The Foreign Policy of Anticommunism* (Chapel Hill: University of North Carolina Press, 1988). Based on archival sources, the book reappraises the role the Eisenhower administration played in Latin America, especially in terms of the construction of a new Cold War policy.

SCHLESINGER, STEPHEN, and STEPHEN KINZER, *Bitter Fruit: The Story of the American Coup in Guatemala* (Cambridge: Harvard University Press, 1999). A well-written analysis of the factors that eventually led to the U.S.-initiated coup against Jacobo Arbenz in 1954. Its thesis is that the expropriation of United Fruit property was the primary reason the U.S. government reacted to Arbenz so strongly.

WOOD, BRYCE. *The Dismantling of the Good Neighbor Policy* (Austin: University of Texas Press, 1985). The sequel to Wood's book on the creation of the Good Neighbor Policy, this book describes how the administrations after Roosevelt began to utilize other strategies as the Cold War progressed, which would result in the disintegration of the policy itself. It pays particular attention to the cases of Argentina, Bolivia, and Guatemala.

Web Sites

Economic Commission for Latin America and the Caribbean (ECLAC, or CEPAL in Spanish). This official Web site has an extensive collection of documents and economic reports, including the social aspects of development, international insertion, macroeconomics, economic governance, the environment and development, and productive and managerial development. There is also a free email subscription for a monthly publication called *Cepal News.* http://www.eclac.cl.

The Inter-American Development Bank. The official Web site of the bank, which includes a great deal of information on investment, economic policies, reports on specific countries, status reports on development projects, and a wide array of related topics. It is a useful source for studying either individual countries or the region as a whole. http://www.iadb.org/.

The National Security Archive, Guatemala Documentation Project. The National Security Archive has links to previously classified U.S. government documents related to the 1954 invasion, as well as the civil war that began not long afterward. It includes instructions on assassination and lists of those targeted for murder. http://www.gwu.edu/~nsarchiv/latin_america/guatemala.html.

The Organization of American States. This is the official website of the OAS, which has a large number of documents, publications, and general information on its activities and its organizational structure. http://www.oas.org.

Notes

1. Quoted in Gil 1971, 169.
2. Quoted in Schoultz 1998, 314.
3. Nunn 1992.
4. Schoultz 1998, 329.
5. Schoultz 1998, 329–30.
6. Quoted in Rabe 1988, 27.
7. Gilderhus 2000, 138.
8. Quoted in Rabe 1988, 108.
9. LaFeber 1984, 91.
10. Thorp 1998, 349.
11. Quoted in Wood 1985, 149.
12. Quoted in Schoultz 1998, 339.
13. Arévalo 1980, 147.
14. Quoted in LaRosa and Mora 1999, 178; 182.
15. Quoted in Gleijeses 1991, 7.
16. Quoted in Cullather 1999, 35.
17. Pérez 1990, 230.
18. Quoted in Thomas 1998, 921.
19. Batista 1964, xi.
20. Nixon 1962, 222.
21. Eisenhower 1963, 316.
22. Klarén 1986.
23. Eisenhower 1963, 167.

CHAPTER 6

The Cuban Revolution

TIMELINE	
1959	Cuban revolution succeeds
1960	Cuba signs trade deals with USSR; United States begins trade embargo
1961	United States cuts diplomatic relations with Cuba (January); Alliance for Progress announced (March); Bay of Pigs invasion (April 17); Castro declares the revolution is socialist
1962	Cuban missile crisis; Hickenlooper Amendment
1963	President John F. Kennedy assassinated
1964	Mann Doctrine outlined; United States supports overthrow of Goulart in Brazil
1965	Invasion of Dominican Republic
1966	"Tricontinental" meetings

After New Year's Day 1959, U.S.–Latin American relations experienced a drastic shift. During the 1950s, there had already been a clash between Latin American reformist movements and a U.S. policy based largely on security. In addition, although fear of Communist advances had already begun to color the attitudes of U.S. policy makers and many Latin American economic and political elites, the Cuban revolution intensified that factor and brought it to the forefront. In the eyes of U.S. policy makers, the mere existence of a socialist Cuba put into jeopardy the very stability of the hemisphere; it posed a direct challenge to U.S. hegemony, and its destruction became an obsession.

From a realist perspective, U.S.–Cuban relations boil down to power politics. In an international system characterized by anarchy, countries with competing ideologies will use whatever means possible to pursue their own interests. For the United States, this meant trying to assassinate, overthrow, and isolate the regime of Fidel Castro. Cuba, meanwhile, would seek to spread revolution not only across Latin America but also to the rest of the world, attacking governments friendly to the United States.

Yet dependency theory also has something useful to say about the relationship or, to be more specific, the rupture of the relationship. The revolution severed ties of economic dependency on the United States, thus fulfilling the aspirations of more radical dependency theorists by breaking free of the chains imposed by the core. Although Cuba would ultimately become heavily dependent on the Soviet Union, it accomplished something unique. Through determination and sacrifice, the revolutionary government of Fidel Castro survived despite all the efforts of the United States to destroy it. In their classic work on dependency, Cardoso and Faletto discuss the conditions of dependency and conclude, "The important question, then, is how to construct paths toward socialism."[1]

It is very difficult, if not downright impossible, to overstate the importance of the Cuban revolution for U.S.–Latin American relations. The relationship between the two countries, dominated by the United States for sixty years, would be turned on its head. The revolution, with its strong anti-U.S. overtones, was a rallying cry for many in the region who desired to shed what they believed was an economic and political chokehold by the United States.

The revolution riveted the Eisenhower administration's attention because it suddenly seemed possible that the United States could lose the Cold War in Latin America. For the first time since 1898, the U.S. government had no control over Cuban political developments. Castro himself usually avoided mentioning the United States in his initial speeches and was cagey, even humorous, when asked directly about his northern neighbor. When told that the United States might withdraw its military mission in Cuba, Castro said he wasn't sure what purpose it served anyway; had it taught Batista how to lose a war?[2] He used nationalist rhetoric to boost support for his reforms but did not yet use these reforms as an opportunity to lambaste the United States.

The New York Times

Photo 6.1 Castro and Guevara.

Fidel Castro was unpredictable and initially was hard to pinpoint ideologically. Although he had claimed not to be a Communist, his tendencies were clearly leftist and radically reformist. In April 1959, he even traveled to the United States, invited by a conference of newspaper editors, and met with Vice President Richard Nixon. (President Eisenhower refused to see him.) Nixon's appraisal was that Castro was "either incredibly naïve about Communism or under Communist discipline—my guess is the former."[3]

On his return, Castro soon enacted reforms that were wildly popular with much of his domestic audience, including deep cuts in monthly rents, wage increases, unemployment insurance, health and education reforms, reduction of telephone and electricity rates, renegotiation of labor contracts, and nationalization of large landholdings. Not all Cubans, however, felt like celebrating, especially as Castro became more autocratic. Large public trials and subsequent executions revealed what could happen to "counterrevolutionaries." Repression became more widespread. Many middle-class Cubans felt threatened and began leaving for the United States, especially Florida and more specifically Miami.

Through 1959, U.S. officials and businesses watched as **nationalizations** occurred and members of the Cuban Communist Party took a greater number of government positions, displacing moderates who had initially supported the revolution but were growing disillusioned by Castro's centralization of power.

By the middle of the year, there was already talk within the U.S. government of cutting the sugar quota as a means of economic retaliation. In September 1959, Castro became more openly against the United States in a speech at the United Nations in which he denounced U.S. imperialism. The issue of sugar became moot in early 1960, when the first Soviet trade delegation arrived in Havana and soon reached an agreement to guarantee sugar purchases and lend money to the Castro government.

The Cuban revolution was a welcome surprise to Soviet Premier Nikita Khrushchev. The Moscow-affiliated Cuban Communist party had argued against struggle in the countryside, and only near the end did it join Fidel Castro's rebellion. For the Soviet Union, Cuba couldn't have been a better placed ally. Ninety miles from Florida, in the very heart of a geographic area long controlled by the United States, Cuba was a strategic pearl. Khrushchev poured aid Castro's way, which would soon have the effect of shifting Cuba's economic dependence from the United States to the Soviet Union.

For the Eisenhower administration, these new ties to the USSR represented proof that Castro was Communist. Policy decisions were based on unease about the designs of the Soviet Union on the Western Hemisphere. Just as in 1898, Cuba itself was almost peripheral to the debate. Within a month of the arrival of the Soviet officials, Eisenhower signed an order for the CIA to begin planning for Castro's ouster. Using lessons it learned from Guatemala in 1954, the CIA recruited Cuban exiles and began training them (ironically, in Guatemala) and making preparations for the psychological warfare that would accompany an eventual invasion of the island. The precise timetable and strategies were not yet defined.

Another aspect of the deals that Cuba made with the Soviet Union involved subsidized oil. When crude oil began arriving in 1960, President Eisenhower ordered U.S. oil companies not to refine it. In response, Castro nationalized the refineries and then every other remaining U.S.-owned business. The U.S. Congress also voted to cut the Cuban sugar quota drastically. Later in 1960, Eisenhower would take economic sanctions to a new level by imposing a trade **embargo,** which has never been lifted. Its purpose was to strangle Cuba economically to the point that Castro would be unable to maintain popularity and that the Cuban people, tired of deprivation, would overthrow Castro. As one U.S. member of Congress said at the time, "If Cuba's splendid people understand that they must sell their sugar or their economy will be destroyed, they will themselves find a way to deal with the present misleaders and fomenters of hatred."[4] For more than forty years, U.S. presidents would employ similar strategies and language to justify continuing the embargo. Economic sanctions and similar measures such as travel restrictions are always supposedly on the brink of succeeding. By the 1990s, the United States would open up to China and Vietnam, arguing that an injection of capitalism would erode Communism from within—and, in fact, both countries became more capitalistic, if not much more democratic—but with Cuba the ironclad rule of isolation held.

To further codify these policies, in 1962 the U.S. Congress passed a bill with an amendment by Iowa Senator Bourke Hickenlooper. The Hickenlooper Amendment cut off all assistance to any country that nationalized property owned by U.S. citizens or imposed taxes or conditions deemed discriminatory enough to have the effect of seizing control of that property. The law was intended to compel any administration to act immediately if Castro-style socialism took hold anywhere in the world.

Latin American View: The OAS

The Organization of American States also reacted to these revolutionary developments, although the United States still was not viewing the group as very relevant in terms of contributing to security, and it had yet to provide much counterbalance to U.S. hegemony. In August 1960, the OAS approved the Declaration of San José, which proclaimed that intervention from outside the hemisphere—meaning Soviet Communism—represented a security threat. In a reaffirmation of the

The Hickenlooper Amendment (1962)

The President shall suspend assistance to the government of any country to which assistance is provided under this Act when the government of such country or any governmental agency or subdivision within such country on or after January 1, 1962—

1. has nationalized or expropriated or seized ownership or control of property owned by any United States citizen or by any corporation, partnership, or association not less than 50 per centum beneficially owned by United States citizens, or

2. has imposed or enforced discriminatory taxes or other exactions, or restrictive maintenance or operational conditions, which have the effect of nationalizing, expropriating, or otherwise seizing ownership or control of property so owned, and such country, government agency or government subdivision fails within a reasonable time (not more than six months after such action or after the date of enactment of this subsection, which is later) to take appropriate steps, which may include arbitration, to discharge its obligations under international law toward such citizen or entity, including equitable and speedy compensation for such property in convertible foreign exchange, as required by international law, or fails to take steps designed to provide relief from such taxes, exactions, or conditions, as the case may be, and such suspension shall continue until he is satisfied that appropriate steps are being taken.

Source: United States Statutes at Large, vol. 76 (Washington, D.C.: Government Printing Office, 1963): 260–61.

Monroe Doctrine, the declaration resolved "the acceptance of a threat of extra-continental intervention by any American state endangers American solidarity and security, and that this obliges the Organization of American States to disapprove it and reject it with equal vigor."[5] The vote was approved 19-0; the Dominican Republic did not attend, and Cuba withdrew before the voting took place.

Many Latin American delegates, however, were hesitant to be party to U.S. aggression toward Cuba in a situation they generally did not view as a hemispheric threat. Mexico, in fact, added its own statement reaffirming the inviolability of sovereignty, stating that "in no way is it a condemnation or a threat against Cuba, whose aspirations for economic improvement and social justice have the fullest support of the Government and the people of Mexico."[6] Castro called the OAS a tool of U.S. imperialism and later that year announced his support for Soviet foreign policy and its efforts to provide assistance to developing countries.

Eisenhower's last measure, taken just before he left office in 1961, was to break off diplomatic relations. The battle for Cuba was in full swing, and the perceived stakes were high. According to U.S. officials, it was nothing less than the protection of civilization itself.

President John F. Kennedy and Cuba

The sense in the United States that Cuba was a test case for the civilized world stemmed in part from the rhetoric of the 1960 presidential elections in the United States. Senator John F. Kennedy and Vice President Richard Nixon each tried to outdo the other in assuring the U.S. public that their anti-Communist credentials were better than the other candidate's. Kennedy accused the Eisenhower administration (and by extension Nixon) of "losing" Cuba to Communism and, unaware of covert plans already underway, criticized it for not doing more to get Cuba back into the U.S. orbit. For his part, Nixon hammered away at Kennedy's inexperience.

Kennedy barely won the election and came to office needing not only to prove himself in foreign policy but also to demonstrate his anti-Communist credentials. During a presidential debate with Nixon, he had said, "The big struggle will be to prevent the influence of Castro spreading to other countries—Mexico, Panama, Brazil, Bolivia, Colombia."[7] By making Castro a prominent campaign issue, Kennedy felt he had no choice but to act tough on Communism.

The Alliance for Progress

In 1960, Eisenhower provided $500 million in loans, the so-called Social Progress Trust Fund, to be used for improving social conditions in Latin America. Belatedly, his administration had come to the conclusion that anti-U.S. sentiment and support for Communist movements were in part fueled by terrible living conditions, misery, and hopelessness. But Eisenhower's commitment to expenditures for economic development had always been halfhearted and did not amount to a coherent, large-scale program. In March 1961, Kennedy announced that the 1960s would be a "decade of development," and to that end, he laid plans for the Alliance for Progress. The program's goals would be to provide "homes, work and land, health and schools" and generally reduce poverty. The United States put in an initial $500 million, and during the 1960s, the total amount from all sources reached $18 billion.

Later in 1961, delegates from around the hemisphere met at Punta del Este, a beach town in Uruguay, to determine the nature and scope of the Alliance's activities. On paper it was vast, with the goals of promoting democracy, socio-economic development, education, fair wages and working conditions, health care, tax reform, reduced inflation, and private enterprise. A combination of U.S. funding and Latin American efforts would bring the region closer to those goals. The OAS, the Inter-American Development Bank, and the United Nations Economic Commission for Latin America all worked together to put programs into place. The U.S. delegation promised $1 billion the first year and $20 billion over the decade from all international sources. Che Guevara, who had come as Cuba's delegate, challenged the U.S. commitment to reform and dismissed the Alliance as economic imperialism.

The Alliance's founding principle was that poverty spawned Communism, and therefore one way to combat Communism was to eliminate, or at least reduce, that source of support. It was based on "modernization theory," which emerged from political science and economics and held that nations went through phases of development as they made their way from "traditional" to "modern." Becoming "modern" (which, in the eyes of modernization theorists, meant copying U.S. institutions) would lead to economic growth and democracy, while traditional societies remained mired in dictatorship and "backwardness." The argument went that the more the United States offered itself as a model and provided aid as a starting point, the more Latin America could become modern and therefore more immune to the siren song of Communism. Such a U.S.-centric vision, however, was perhaps doomed it before it could even start; like the Alliance for Progress itself, it did not fully address Latin American realities.

A number of organizations grew out of the Alliance of Progress, such as the Agency for International Development (which helped to administer funds) and the Peace Corps, which sent idealistic young U.S. citizens to remote parts of Latin America, as well as the rest of the world, to act as teachers and builders. Capitalism could thus offer a viable alternative to people who might otherwise view socialist revolution as their only solution.

Throughout the Kennedy and Johnson administrations, billions of dollars of public and private investment would flow into Latin America, but the scale of poverty was so immense that the Alliance's founders could never hope to achieve their goals. However, a host of other problems were associated with the Alliance. One serious issue was that the Alliance contained within it a contradiction because it included the promise of reform to a region largely dominated by oligarchs. The United States did not wish to alienate these large landowners, and so the promise of substantive change could not be fulfilled. Another problem was the unilateral nature of the development projects, which were often not fitted well to local customs and conditions. In addition, neither the U.S. nor the Latin American governments were able to generate much enthusiasm in their populations for the programs. Many in the U.S. government, including Vice President Lyndon Johnson, viewed the Alliance with skepticism.

Despite the flow of public and private capital into Latin America, over the course of the 1960s the Alliance failed to achieve its objectives. The balance of trade worsened; from 1960 to 1968, U.S. exports to Latin America increased from $3.8 billion to $5.3 billion, and U.S. imports of Latin American goods rose only from $4 billion to $5.2 billion.[8] The debt burden also increased, which meant that a higher percentage of export earnings disappeared immediately to service it. The Alliance for Progress did not stimulate economic growth or alleviate the crushing weight of unemployment and poverty.

Furthermore, this emphasis on development did not mean that the United States had eschewed more traditional means of pursuing foreign policy. The policy response to events in Cuba revealed that pure power calculations and the use of force were still prominent foreign policy tools. Realist theory would not consider development projects as an essential element in foreign policy, and clearly many U.S. policy makers didn't either.

The Struggle to Maintain Hegemony: 1960–1962

After the 1960 U.S. election, President-elect Kennedy learned of the CIA operation to overthrow Fidel Castro. The CIA had assembled a group of Cuban exiles who were training in Guatemala (moving later to Nicaragua) to invade the island. Kennedy had misgivings about the entire plan but was boxed in. If he scuttled it, for example, the exiles would become angry, blow the cover of the secret plans, humiliate Kennedy, and leave him wide open to Republican critics who would label him as weak.

Instead, Kennedy chose to allow the operation to develop but not to give it his full support. Most important, this meant a refusal to allow any air cover by U.S. planes. Although the CIA was still enthusiastic, many skeptics within the administration, questioned some of the main assumptions of the invasion plan. The CIA believed that a majority of Cubans opposed Castro and would join a rebellion if the initial landing were successful, an assumption that rested further on the assumption that the revolution had been Moscow-inspired instead of homegrown. In addition, despite the size of Castro's military (estimated at 225,000), the plotters were certain that once they reached Cuba's shores, they could overwhelm whatever force was present.

The plan had originally conceived the city of Trinidad to be the landing location, but Kennedy rejected it as too prominent. The CIA suggested a new area, the Bahía de Cochinos, or Bay of Pigs. Without adequate checks regarding suitability, the final approval was made to launch the attack in an entirely inappropriate area, marked by shallow, rocky water and swamps. Poor planning, along with Kennedy's refusal to allow U.S. military assistance—though the CIA and the exiles themselves believed erroneously that, if push came to shove, Kennedy would come to their aid—doomed the invasion force of about 1,400, which landed in April 1961. Boats ran aground, and the terrain was so treacherous that they were easy targets for the Cuban army, which had been on alert for some time as a result of the many rumors coming out of Central America about Cuban exiles who had come to train. Those who survived were captured, and later Castro traded them to the United States for money and supplies.

The U.S. government's participation in the affair was immediately obvious, and it was a public relations disaster for Kennedy. In a speech a month later, he acknowledged the U.S. role and framed the attempted invasion in terms of the global struggle against Communism: "The message of Cuba, of Laos, of the rising din of Communist voices in Asia and Latin America—these messages are all the same. The complacent, the self-indulgent, the soft societies are about to be swept away with the debris of history."[9]

The CIA, meanwhile, studied its own obvious failures, a review that was not declassified until the 1990s. It came to the conclusion that the CIA had no evidence that an internal opposition would rise up against Castro, that plausible deniability of being tied to the invasion was "a pathetic illusion," and even that CIA agents treated their Cuban counterparts "like dirt."[10] Ever since independence, U.S. policy makers, diplomats, and soldiers had viewed Latin Americans as inferior. The report asserted that the CIA "was not likely to win many people away from Communism if the Americans treat other nationals with condescension or contempt . . . [or] as incompetent children whom the Americans are going to rescue for reasons of their own."[11]

Castro, on the other hand, emerged a hero and as a result was able to consolidate his hold on the country even further; in the aftermath, he arrested up to 100,000 people. He had stood firm against the United States, thus achieving a rare feat—especially for a small country—in the history of U.S.–Latin American relations. At that point, Castro announced what by then everyone knew, namely, that his revolution was socialist. Pro-Castro demonstrations appeared throughout the region. The invasion also provided undeniable proof that Castro was right when he claimed that the United States was trying to undermine his government. It would also lead to the Soviet decision to send nuclear missiles to Cuba.

During the summer of 1962, the U.S. government was aware that the Soviet Union was transporting weapons and even troops to Cuba, ostensibly to serve as a deterrent to a U.S. attack. The Soviets repeatedly assured the Kennedy administration that all such weapons were strictly defensive, and in turn they received warnings that no offensive armaments would be tolerated. The administration debated the possibility that nuclear weapons might be included, but to most advisors it seemed far-fetched that Nikita Khrushchev, knowing how the U.S. would probably react, would risk war. Yet he had.

On October 15, President Kennedy was informed that photos had been taken proving the existence of Soviet ballistic missiles. From White House tapes, Kennedy can be heard wondering in vain why Khrushchev had done so. At least four times, he comes only to the conclusion that "it's a goddamn mystery to me."[12] Recent analyses suggest that although Khrushchev valued the missiles from a strategic perspective, he was intent on protecting Cuba and its socialist experiment from U.S. invasion. In 1960, he met Castro in the United States for a meeting of the UN General Assembly, and he "came away emotionally committed to the new Cuban regime and its youthful, powerful leaders."[13] What followed were thirteen of the most dangerous days of the Cold War. Accounts of decision making within the Kennedy administration have yielded fascinating insights into the process of crisis management.

Although Cuba was the physical location of the crisis, the true focal point was not Latin America. The view of the Kennedy administration was that the entire "free world" was at stake, but individual cabinet members and advisors disagreed intensely about the best course of action. Knowing that the outbreak of nuclear war was entirely possible, Kennedy ordered U.S. ships to patrol around Cuba to be certain that no more missiles could arrive. He went on national television to explain the situation, which had the effect of putting public pressure on the Soviets to withdraw the missiles. The tension escalated further when a U.S. U-2 spy plane was shot down over Cuba.

Using both public and private channels, Kennedy and Khrushchev entered into delicate and difficult negotiations. Finally, the Soviet leader capitulated. He would remove the missiles if the United States accepted two conditions: first, it would pledge not to invade Cuba. Second, it would remove missiles it currently had in Turkey. Kennedy agreed, especially between he had already planned to remove the missiles, though he refused to make the second part of the agreement public. With that, the Cuban missile crisis concluded.

From Fidel Castro's perspective, the affair was a disaster. He was never consulted and had no say in the agreement. Angry and insulted, he was reduced to sending a plaintive letter to Khrushchev. He did receive the promise that the United States would not invade, but that was certainly cold comfort. The CIA continued its efforts to assassinate the Cuban leader, and he was well aware that U.S.–Cuban relations were unlikely to improve. The crisis had demonstrated that the Cold War was about the strategic relationship between the United States and the Soviet Union and that Latin America was viewed largely in terms of its effect on that relationship.

The Administration of Lyndon Johnson

Upon the assassination of President Kennedy, Vice President Lyndon Baines Johnson moved into the White House. Like Kennedy, Johnson needed to prove that he and the Democratic party had a strong and anti-Communist foreign policy. Unlike Kennedy, Johnson already had firm anti-Communist credentials. As a member of the Senate in 1949, he had destroyed the political career of the chairman of the Federal Power Commission, who needed Johnson's committee to approve him for another term. Using dubious evidence and tactics that were becoming all too common, Johnson accused him of being Communist and intimidated other senators at a time when Communist paranoia was widespread. This attitude would recur in policy toward Latin America.

Johnson's commitment to the Alliance for Progress was shaky, and his belief in the use of U.S. power to attack perceived national security threats was firm. In his own words, "we've got Alliance for Progress, but it is being run by an alliance of misfits."[14] He was even more inclined than Kennedy to forge ties with Latin American militaries and to use covert action. His choice of advisor on Latin American affairs showed that commitment. Thomas Mann was one of the first appointments that President Johnson made after Kennedy's assassination. Mann was often an outspoken critic of U.S.-led invasions but took a hard line about the need to maintain stable and friendly governments. He also believed that the Alliance for Progress was unrealistic and the notion that a decade of development would solve the region's problems was "patently absurd."[15] In particular, he opposed land reform, which he believed put too much land in the hands of small farmers who lacked the ability to produce crops on a large scale, thus weakening the overall economy.

As a senior advisor to the president, Mann's statements carried tremendous weight, and he argued against state-led industrialization and redistribution of wealth. His ideas all came together in a March 1964 address to senior officials (such as ambassadors) who worked in Latin America, which would be dubbed the Mann Doctrine. Interestingly, this "doctrine" was never made official in any document, but rather consisted of leaks of his address to reporters (in particular the *New York Times,* which ran a front-page article) and members of Congress. The administration, however, did not disavow its contents.

Mann said U.S. policy had four goals: economic growth, protection of U.S. investments, noninterference "in the internal political affairs" of the hemisphere's republics, and opposition to Communism. The promotion of democracy was explicitly not part of the equation, because it was futile to try to "force" democracy on Latin American countries.

The Mann Doctrine emphasized stability over democracy. The policy of noninterference meant that if stable nondemocratic governments came to power, the United States would not try to "teach" them how to achieve democracy. According to Mann, the "antidictatorship policy" had failed to achieve any foreign policy goals. The clear implication was that the only rationale for intervention would be a Communist presence, where hemispheric stability would trump noninterference. The Alliance for Progress was never mentioned.

The New Guerrillas

And just who were these Communists who led the Johnson administration to openly reject the policy goal of promoting democracy? The U.S. government

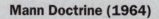

Mann Doctrine (1964)

The United States was reported today to be considering modification of its policy of actively opposing rightist and military dictatorships that might emerge in the future in Latin America.

It will continue to oppose forcefully Communist dictatorships, such as Cuba.

The reported shift in policy, under which the United States would no longer seek to punish military juntas for overthrowing democratic regimes, was outlined last night by Thomas C. Mann, Assistant Secretary of State for Inter-American Affairs.

The suggested policy change, it was said, is not designed to display any United States sympathies for dictatorships, but rather to avoid involvement in domestic political crises in the Latin-American republics.

Its immediate effect would be to eliminate such deterrents as were used by the Kennedy Administration. Policy under the previous Administration was to deny diplomatic relations and economic aid to newly created military regimes, unless they offered firm assurances of restoring democratic rule within the foreseeable future.

That policy was applied only to military coups that emerged during the Kennedy Administration. It did not retroactively affect established authoritarian regimes.

Mr. Mann, who is President Johnson's chief Latin-American policy-maker, discussed his views on dictatorships and democracy in the Western Hemisphere in an address to a group of high-ranking United States officials serving in Latin America.

Mr. Mann was quoted as having said that going back to the nineteen-thirties, when Sumner Welles was Under-Secretary of State, the United States had not succeeded by its opposition in unseating a dictator. He cited Juan D. Perón of Argentina and the late Gen. Anastasio Somoza of Nicaragua.

Therefore, he was said to have concluded, the United States should stop trying to distinguish among such regimes. John O. Bell, Ambassador to Guatemala, asked whether the new policy meant that there would no longer be "good guys or bad guys" as far as United States policy was concerned. Mann was reported to have replied that that was correct.

He recalled that Mexico traditionally invoked the so-called Estrada doctrine in recognizing new Latin-American governments following coups d'état. This doctrine proclaims, in brief, that the criterion for recognition should be the effective control of the country by the new government.

The group the Assistant Secretary addressed included all the United States Ambassadors, charges d'affaires and chiefs of aid missions in Latin America, who were summoned here by President Johnson for a three-day review conference. They met with the President this afternoon.

Mr. Mann spoke at a closed session at the State Department and no transcript of his remarks was available. The essence of his comments, and numerous details, were conveyed today to key members of Congress. Mr. Mann is said to have emphasized four purposes United States policy in Latin America should serve.

(Continued)

They are the fostering of economic growth in the area, the protection of $9 billion in United States investments there, non-intervention in the internal political affairs of the hemisphere's republics, and opposition to Communism.

Mr. Mann was said to have told the ambassadors that while the United States believed in democracy and should advocate its development, it could not impose this system on Latin-American countries.

Therefore, he indicated, the United States should not become involved in domestic political situations in Latin America.

Mr. Mann's views were considered as representing a radical modification of the policies followed by the Kennedy Administration under the Alliance for Progress.

President Kennedy believed that economic and social development under the Alliance must move hand-in-hand with the development of democracy and that, therefore, the United States had the duty actively to encourage the practice of democracy and refuse its help to regimes that had overturned representative democracies. . . .

The impression made by Mr. Mann's remarks was that the United States would no longer embark on such policies.

In his criticism of the asserted failure of the anti-dictatorship policy, Mr. Mann was reported to have said that, while the United States must not identify itself with dictators or award them medals, it should likewise avoid identification with other political groups in the Latin American countries.

Mr. Mann was reported to have remarked that it was very difficult to classify rulers as dictators or democrats in Latin America.

He was quoted as having said he had difficulties in distinguishing politically between Presidents Adolfo Lopez Mateos of Mexico, Victor Paz Estenssoro of Bolivia, and Alfred Stroessner of Paraguay. . . .

Diplomats who attended least [sic] night's session said that in his entire presentation Mr. Mann made no mention of the Alliance for Progress.

Source: Tad Szulc, "U.S. May Abandon Effort to Deter Latin Dictators." New York Times, March 19, 1964.

had been suspicious of leftists, but the emergence of guerrilla groups posed a threat to the socioeconomic status quo in Latin America. To achieve their goals, these groups advocated the use of violence against anyone they believed to be allied with capitalist forces. Guerrilla war was not new to Latin America; it had already been utilized against the United States, such as Pancho Villa's forces in Mexico or Augusto Sandino's in Nicaragua. Castro's success, however, transformed guerrilla warfare from a way to make isolated attacks to a internationally coordinated strategy to overthrow a government and remake the economic, political, and social structures of a country. Che Guevara, whose intellectual influence was soon to be global, wrote his own theories of guerrilla war, which were published and disseminated widely. Being a Latin American guerrilla now meant becoming a Marxist revolutionary.

In the first chapter of his book *Guerrilla War,* Guevara stated that the Cuban Revolution taught three lessons:

1. Popular forces can win a war against the army.
2. It is not necessary to wait until all conditions for making revolution exist; the insurrection can create them.
3. In underdeveloped America the countryside is the basic area for armed fighting.[16]

Although Guevara also argued that guerrillas alone cannot create all the conditions necessary for successful guerrilla warfare—he noted that "people must see clearly the futility of maintaining the fight for social goals within the framework of civil debate"—he clearly advocated the sparking of revolutionary wars wherever possible in the hemisphere.[17] The fight required using favorable terrain, winning the hearts and minds of the peasants and workers, and refusing to attack the enemy military head-on. Guerrilla warfare was protracted and arduous because it did not allow for large-scale victories. Wearing down the enemy was the only means of victory.

Fidel Castro's triumph thus became an example to other aspiring revolutionaries, and he actively cultivated their friendship. The Cuban example would be the guide for dozens of revolutionary groups organized in the 1960s across the region. Most would fail in their quest for political power, crushed by national armies (which received financial, technical, and logistical assistance from the United States). Sometimes they were even betrayed by the peasants they sought to help, who viewed the revolutionaries with suspicion, knowing that the army would always eventually arrive and begin indiscriminately killing anyone it decided had been an accessory to the guerrillas. In fact, in 1967 Bolivian peasants helped the military find Guevara himself, where he had traveled to re-create the Cuban experience. He was executed, and then photographed for the world to see, and he passed immediately into martyrdom.

In 1966, Guevara gave a famous speech in Havana at the first meeting of the Organization of Solidarity with the Peoples of Asia, Africa and Latin America, also called the Tricontinental. He proclaimed his hope for "two, three, many Vietnams" because U.S. action there was draining its economy and causing domestic unrest for the Johnson administration. The time was nigh; the United States could be defeated and overwhelmed from all directions.

Many would-be rebels found great inspiration in Che's words, and guerrilla movements—generally founded on some variant of Marxism—sprang up quickly. Most were very small and/or short-lived; others managed to survive (See Table 6.1). Violence was ever present, including kidnappings as a way to extract ransom for funding. Guerrilla organizations in Colombia have persisted for forty years. Some also received concrete assistance from the Cuban state. For U.S. policy makers, every guerrilla movement was Communist, directed by the USSR and aided by Cuba. This meant acceptance not only of a military response but

Table 6.1 Major Guerrilla Movements in Latin America, 1960s–1980s
(and Year of Creation)

Argentina – Montoneros 1970
Chile – Left Revolutionary Movement (MIR) 1966; Manuel Rodríguez Patriotic
  Front (FPMR) 1983
Colombia – Revolutionary Armed Forces of Colombia (FARC) 1966;
  Army of National Liberation (ELN) 1964
El Salvador – Farabundo Martí National Liberation Front (FMLN) 1980
Guatemala – Rebel Armed Forces (FAR) 1962
Nicaragua – Sandinista Front of National Liberation (FSLN) 1961
Peru – Shining Path 1980; Tupac Amaru Revolutionary Movement 1983
Uruguay – Tupamaros 1963
Venezuela – Armed Forces of National Liberation (FALN) 1963

Che Guevara's Message to the Tricontinental (1966)

Twenty-one years without a world war, in these times of maximum confrontations, of violent clashes and sudden changes, appears to be a very high figure. However, without analyzing the practical results of this peace (poverty, degradation, increasingly larger exploitation of enormous sectors of humanity) for which all of us stated that we are willing to fight, we would do well to inquire if this peace is real. . . .

There were limited confrontations in every continent although in Our America, for a long time, there were only incipient liberation struggles and military coups d'etat until the Cuban revolution resounded the alert, signaling the importance of this region. This action attracted the wrath of the imperialists and Cuba was finally obligated to defend its coasts, first in Playa Girón, and again during the Missile Crisis. . . .

But, evidently, the focal point of all contradictions is at present the territory of the peninsula of Indo-China and the adjacent areas. Laos and Vietnam are torn by a civil war which has ceased being such by the entry into the conflict of U.S. imperialism with all its might, thus transforming the whole zone into a dangerous detonator ready at any moment to explode. . . .

The largest of all imperialist powers feels in its own guts the bleeding inflicted by a poor and underdeveloped country; its fabulous economy feels the strain of the war effort. Murder is ceasing to be the most convenient business for its monopolies. Defensive weapons, and never in adequate number, is all these extraordinary soldiers have—besides love for their homeland, their society, and unsurpassed courage. But imperialism is bogging down in Vietnam, is unable to find a way out and desperately seeks one that will overcome with dignity this dangerous situation in which it now finds itself. . . .

(Continued)

What role shall we, the exploited people of the world, play? The peoples of the three continents focus their attention on Vietnam and learn their lesson. Since imperialists blackmail humanity by threatening it with war, the wise reaction is not to fear war. The general tactics of the people should be to launch a constant and firm attack in all fronts where the confrontation is taking place.

In those places where this meager peace we have has been violated, which is our duty? To liberate ourselves at any price. . . .

Our America is integrated by a group of more or less homogeneous countries and in most parts of its territory U.S. monopolist capitals maintain an absolute supremacy. Puppet governments or, in the best of cases, weak and fearful local rulers, are incapable of contradicting orders from their Yankee master. The United States has nearly reached the climax of its political and economic domination; it could hardly advance much more; any change in the situation could bring about a setback. Their policy is to maintain that which has already been conquered. The line of action, at the present time, is limited to the brute use of force with the purpose of thwarting the liberation movements, no matter of what type they might happen to be.

The slogan "we will not allow another Cuba" hides the possibility of perpetrating aggressions without fear of reprisal, such as the one carried out against the Dominican Republic or before that the massacre in Panama—and the clear warning stating that Yankee troops are ready to intervene anywhere in America where the ruling regime may be altered, thus endangering their interests. This policy enjoys an almost absolute impunity: the OAS is a suitable mask, in spite of its unpopularity; the inefficiency of the UN is ridiculous as well as tragic; the armies of all American countries are ready to intervene to smash their peoples. . . .

America, a forgotten continent in the last liberation struggles, is now beginning to make itself heard through the Tricontinental and, in the voice of the vanguard of its peoples, the Cuban Revolution, will today have a task of much greater relevance: creating a Second or a Third Vietnam, or the Second *and* Third Vietnam of the world.

Source: Marxists Internet Archive http://www.marxists.org/archive/guevara/1967/04/16.htm.

also of harsh measures intended to intimidate local populations, extract information, and have wide latitude in deciding who deserved to die.

In the 1960s and 1970s, Cuba had an active policy of exporting revolution to other developing countries that served several foreign policy objectives: it deterred Cuba's enemies, raised the cost for the United States to pursue hostile relations, at times brought gratitude from the Soviet Union, and more generally fostered friendlier governments that would "make a world safer for Cuba's brand of socialism."[18] Over the years, Cuba aided the cause of Marxist revolution in both Latin America and Africa, including Algeria, Angola, Bolivia, Colombia, the Congo, the Dominican Republic, El Salvador, Guatemala, Guinea-Bissau, Morocco, Namibia, Nicaragua, and Venezuela. The level of support for rebels in each country varied, but all received some degree of assistance, especially in terms of military training from the highly skilled Cuban military advisors.

This proclivity to help fellow revolutionaries did not originate in orders from the Soviet Union—though the Soviets certainly welcomed any enlargement of the socialist camp—but rather reflected Castro's own commitment to the global struggle against capitalism. From the U.S. perspective, the distinction did not necessarily matter much because, regardless of the origins of these movements, they posed a real threat to U.S. strategic interests and private investment. Led by Fidel Castro, the small island, which at the time of the revolution had a population of only about 7 million (by contrast, in 1960 New York City had 7.8 million inhabitants), had managed to become the greatest intrahemispheric rival in the history of U.S.–Latin American relations.

Nonetheless, not everyone who desired change was a guerrilla. Presidents such as Arturo Frondizi in Argentina, José Figueres in Costa Rica, Victor Haya de la Torre in Peru, and Rómulo Betancourt in Venezuela sought to redistribute national income through democratic means. Such reformers found themselves precariously balancing the needs of their own people and the international pressures of the Cold War. What they asked from the United States was flexibility. In 1962, President Adolfo López Mateos of Mexico told President Kennedy that improving social and economic conditions should be a central policy priority and that "the Alliance for Progress is the best way to combat Communism."[19]

There was thus a middle ground between Communist and capitalist dictatorships, but its proponents often found themselves drowned out. They would also risk isolation if they deviated from U.S. Cold War policies, especially with regard to Castro's Cuba. For example, President Frondizi of Argentina (1958–1962) refused to break diplomatic relations with Cuba, and although he was a moderate, the Kennedy administration made overtures to the Argentine military to help convince Frondizi to denounce Cuba publicly. He eventually did so, but the military overthrew him anyway, and the U.S. government quickly recognized the new regime.

The U.S. Crusade against Communism

The pressing need to prevent another Cuba brought the word "counterinsurgency" to the popular lexicon. For the United States, the presence of guerrilla fighters, or insurgents, required a coherent, well-organized, and decisive response. Latin American militaries, which had already been forging ties to the United States in the 1950s, became natural allies. For the armed forces, Communism represented a cancer eating away at the nation itself. As with a cancer in the human body, the only way to achieve victory was by killing it off. Civilian and military governments alike passed new national security legislation expanding the internal missions of the armed forces. Militaries were given domestic law enforcement functions and put in charge of controlling the population with regard to strikes, protests, riots, and land seizures.[20] They were also put in charge of many civic projects, such as natural disaster response and building roads. In short, they became even more deeply involved at virtually every level of government and society.

The United States supported the expansion of Latin American military activities. In countries beset by chronic instability, the armed forces often constituted the best organized institution. That fact, combined with their training and weapons, led U.S. policy makers to view them as an ally against Communist subversion. Latin American militaries were not given any more respect than in the past—over time, intelligence reports were open about the brutality and crudeness of military governments and counterinsurgency operations—but were viewed simply as a necessary actor in a global war.

To help the armed forces, the United States revamped its military school in the Panama Canal Zone (founded in 1946) and in 1963 renamed it the United States Army School of the Americas. The changes in curriculum reflected the impact of the Cuban revolution. A new counterinsurgency course taught officers how to weed out subversive elements in the population, gather intelligence, and employ psychological warfare. By the late 1960s, lessons on the "fallacies of the Communist theory" were integrated into every course, even motor pool operations.[21] Very quickly, there were new courses in jungle operations, military intelligence, and counterinsurgency.

Covert Action and Chile

Covert action was utilized even in situations where a guerrilla force was not yet a threat. In Chile, one of the most stable countries in the hemisphere, democratic elections had advanced the cause of Senator Salvador Allende, a member of the Socialist party. He had first run for president in 1952 and then ran in each subsequent presidential election, gradually gaining a greater share of votes. His platform called for sweeping reforms that challenged the socioeconomic status quo and capitalism itself, but all within the context of democracy, which had deeper roots in Chile than in many other Latin American countries.

Allende's electoral gains brought Chile into the foreign policy radar of the Johnson administration, which viewed him as politically dangerous by virtue of his socialist views. Chilean elections were scheduled for 1964, and the CIA was instructed to do whatever necessary to prevent Allende from winning. Chile quickly became the largest single recipient of Alliance for Progress funds, and moderate Christian Democrat Eduardo Frei's campaign became flush, as half of its assets had been funneled through the CIA. The operation was deemed a success when Frei won handily and Allende returned to the senate. Covert action, it seemed, could achieve anything.

Covert Action and Brazil

Another test for the Johnson administration and the Mann Doctrine was in Brazil. In the 1950s, President Juscelino Kubitschek had tried in vain to get Washington's attention on economic issues, and by the end of the decade much of the country was moving leftward. The 1960 election brought state governor Janio Quadros to office. Quadros's rhetoric, which combined nationalism, solidarity with the developing world, and support for state-led development (and even with Fidel Castro), made U.S. officials believe he was too soft on Communism for comfort. Quadros resigned in 1961, in a strange gambit seemingly intended to compel elites to woo him back. No one did so, however, and Vice President João Goulart took power. Goulart's rhetoric was similarly alarming to the United States and, in conjunction with economic crisis, unrest, and political conflict, led the Kennedy administration to fear a Communist takeover. It therefore made contacts with the Brazilian military to communicate U.S. support for a coup. The Johnson administration did the same and, by early 1964, had sent signals, including an aircraft carrier off the coast.

The coup occurred in March 1964, a mere two weeks after the Mann Doctrine was announced. In a sign of the new times, the military did not hand back power to civilians but instead began a campaign of terror to eliminate all "subversive" elements in the country. It provided no timetable for elections or for military withdrawal from the government. However, U.S. policy makers, were content with the outcome. The military had saved Brazil from Communism and made it more appealing for investors who, they believed, would foster economic growth and create jobs and stability.

After the coup, Johnson called Mann to mention how pleased he was with the change of government in Brazil:

MANN: I hope you're as happy about Brazil as I am.

LBJ: I am.

MANN: I think that's the most important thing that's happened in the hemisphere in three years.

LBJ: I hope they give us *some* credit, instead of hell.[22]

The event was indeed important, although only with hindsight is it evident how much. The overthrow of a democratic government in Brazil, the largest country in Latin America, was a sign of things to come. U.S. presidents had become accustomed to overthrowing governments but had limited themselves to small nations in the Caribbean and Central America. The overt moral support for toppling the government of a large South American country took the Cold War to a new level.

The United States also continued to work with the OAS to isolate the Castro regime. In a meeting of foreign ministers in 1964 (four months after the Brazilian coup), the United States invoked the Rio Treaty in an effort to condemn Cuba for supplying arms to rebels in Venezuela. In a fifteen-to-four vote (Bolivia, Chile, Mexico, and Uruguay voted against, while Argentina abstained), the countries of the region agreed not to maintain diplomatic or consular relations and even to suspend all trade with Cuba except for humanitarian reasons. Such measures, however, never held. Although the United States placed increasing pressure on Latin American leaders to accept the idea that Cuba posed an imminent threat, it was never fully successful in doing so. As U.S. efforts to topple governments continued, the Castro government remained defiant.

Hegemony and Invasion: The Case of the Dominican Republic

Johnson also inherited a long-running debate about how to address events in the Dominican Republic. Support for Rafael Trujillo remained significant; he was, after all, an ardent anti-Communist. Many policy makers agreed with Louisiana Senator Russell Long, who in 1956 argued Trujillo was no dictator because he held elections, and it didn't even matter what kind of regime he had "so long as it is not an atheistic Communist government which would endanger our own safety and security."[23] Trujillo, however, was demonstrating such greed and venality that members of the U.S. Congress began to call for cutting off aid. For example, a Spanish exile who had just written an anti-Trujillo doctoral dissertation in the United States was kidnapped and taken to the Dominican Republic, where he was killed. To cover it up, Trujillo also killed the U.S. pilot who had unwittingly flown the victim to this death. From the perspective of U.S. policy, repressing one's own citizens was not necessarily a problem, but operating on U.S. soil was a different matter, and several members of Congress took great interest in the case. Meanwhile Trujillo's son—an air force general—lived lavishly in Hollywood while ostensibly training with the help of U.S. foreign aid.

Trujillo was becoming an embarrassment, but for the Eisenhower administration, the situation in his country was bearing a close resemblance to Batista's Cuba, and after the Cuban revolution, U.S. support for the dictator disappeared. Trujillo also posed a challenge to gathering hemispheric opposition to Castro. The State Department noted that Trujillo's presence "makes more difficult the achievement of U.S. objectives with respect to Cuba because of the tendency of many Latin Americans to place hatred of Trujillo higher than concern of Castro."[24] It was evident that Latin American moderates, who were both open to reform and anti-Communist, were not interested in supporting the U.S. position on Castro as long as it continued to tolerate Trujillo's regime. Trujillo, then, was an obstacle to U.S. influence.

The administration tried to persuade him to step down, but he refused, so Eisenhower gave the CIA an order to assist Dominican dissidents in assassinating him. As that was being planned in 1960, Eisenhower broke off diplomatic relations and imposed new taxes on imported Dominican sugar. In May 1961, CIA-supported Dominicans shot Trujillo to death. Unfortunately, assassinating the president did not serve to stabilize Dominican politics. Instead, it stirred the cauldron of political conflict. His sons managed to maintain control of the armed forces, and his hand-picked successor, Joaquín Balaguer, fought off rebellions.

An election in 1962 brought Juan Bosch, a longtime Trujillo foe, to office. But the perception among conservatives and the armed forces that he was dangerously leftist led to his overthrow a year later. His replacement, Donald Reid Cabral, suffered the same fate in April 1965. The military had split into two factions. The pro-Bosch group referred to themselves as "Constitutionalists" because they wished to put Bosch back into the presidency (their opponents called them the "Rebel" group); the latter called themselves "Loyalists" referring to support of the fallen Reid government (their opposition labeled them "Military" of its armed forces and police members). In an increasingly violent atmosphere, the "Loyalists" requested U.S. intervention.

The country moved toward civil war as the Constitutionalists armed themselves with weapons captured from police arsenals. When it became clear that the Loyalists were beginning to lose, the Johnson administration decided to send U.S. Marines. President Johnson was convinced that the Constitutionalists were being directed from Moscow and that events in disparate parts of the world were all interconnected. As he told his national security advisor, "I am seeing the pattern and I can't be silent. . . . What they are doing in La Paz, Bolivia, what they are doing in Mexico City and what they are doing in Vietnam and the Dominican Republic is not totally unrelated."[25] He was also constantly concerned about public opinion. For Johnson, Latin America policy was periodically intermestic, driven in large part by domestic political concerns. At the same time, however, Johnson remained concerned about the potential expansion of Communism around the world. After deciding to invade, he summoned two high-ranking Republicans (including future president Gerald Ford) to say that he had "just taken an action that will prove that Democratic presidents can deal with Communists as strongly as Republicans."[26]

The invasion prompted global outcries of opposition. The OAS had been bypassed, with Johnson stating that there had been no time for consultation. In a phone conversation to Senate Majority Leader Mike Mansfield, Johnson explained his view of the OAS:

> They're just the damndest fraud I ever saw. . . . These international organizations ain't worth a damn, except window dressing. . . . It looks to me like I'm in a hell of a shape. . . . They're going to eat us up if I let another Cuba come in there. They'll say, "Why did you sit on your big fat tail?"[27]

Instead, the United States sought OAS approval after the fact to provide the proper window dressing. With the bare minimum of votes necessary, the OAS created the Inter-American Peace Force, which would replace U.S. soldiers. In fact, the overall number of IAPF troops remained small. In contrast, the U.S. public was firmly in favor, because the action was framed in terms of preventing another Cuba. Despite sometimes acrimonious debate, the U.S. House of Representatives voted 213–52 in favor of a resolution supporting the president's use of force.

With the support of the OAS, the United States worked to find a provisional president, someone relatively moderate and acceptable. That person was Héctor García Godoy. Elections were then held in 1966, pitting Bosch against Balaguer. Balaguer, the former supporter of Trujillo, became president, and the Dominican Republic again disappeared as a central U.S. policy priority. What remained was a renewed willingness of the U.S. government to invade and occupy a small Latin American country.

Summary and Conclusion

The Cuban Revolution had a truly massive impact on U.S. policy and Latin American elites, on the one hand, and on the attitude of the Latin American left, on the other. To the former, the revolution was a sign of the spread of Soviet-directed Communist movements and the pressing need to stop it in any way possible. To the latter, Castro's success was a symbol of hope; the United States was not all-powerful, and so radical reform was within the realm of possibility. Understanding the dynamics of post–Cuban revolution relations requires a close look at power.

The use of power to advance national interests was all too evident, as was the utter U.S. disdain for international institutions such as the OAS. Such institutions were useful only to the extent that they might legitimate actions the United States already planned on launching. Cuba represented a threat to U.S. hegemony in the region, so any and all manifestations of military and economic power were on the table.

The Alliance for Progress seemed to represent a new approach, centered on the notion that economic development could decrease the appeal of Communism in countries beset by poverty. Its ambitious goals could not be met, however, and never implied the reduction of U.S. covert and overt actions to destabilize "unfriendly" governments. When Lyndon Johnson assumed office after Kennedy's assassination, he and his advisors paid only lip service to the Alliance.

The Mann Doctrine enunciated in 1964 outlined the future trajectory of U.S. policy, which involved a much more open encouragement of military action against governments considered either too leftist or just too soft on Communism. The 1964 Brazilian coup, which ushered in more than twenty years of dictatorship, was one of the first signs of this policy shift. The 1965 invasion of the Dominican Republic demonstrated the lengths the United States was willing to go when a Communist threat had been identified. Unlike the invasions of Guatemala (1954) and Cuba (1961), in the Dominican Republic the United States did not resort to potentially unreliable national dissidents and did not hide U.S. participation in any way. By that time, the war in Vietnam was rapidly widening, and the Johnson Administration believed the global stakes were so high that U.S. troops were necessary. Interestingly, U.S. policy makers and Latin American guerrillas alike believed that the example of Vietnam was connected to U.S.–Latin American relations.

In Latin America, conflict arose as leftists, inspired by Fidel Castro's example, struggled to reform or even to overturn long-held elite control over politics and the economy. Dependency theory would assert that the revolution was about breaking the economic chains that had bound Cuba to the United

States since 1898. These counterhegemonic movements were instilled with a nationalistic and anti-imperialist fervor that stood in direct contrast to almost all U.S. interests. Some of them would sputter; others would last for decades (and, in the case of the Sandinistas, would successfully overthrow a government). The U.S. hegemony in the Latin America was no longer complete. The resulting clashes led to one of the darkest periods of U.S.–Latin American relations. Chapter 7 will turn to the era of anti-Communist military dictatorships.

Research Questions

1. Compare the U.S. invasions of Guatemala (1954) and the Dominican Republic (1965). What were the key factors that led to very different strategies?
2. To what degree did the Mann Doctrine represent a radical shift in U.S. policy toward Latin America?
3. What were the effects of the Bay of Pigs and the Cuban missile crisis on Cuban domestic politics? How did they affect Castro's hold on power in Cuba?
4. How well does dependency theory explain Cuba's policy toward the United States in the postrevolutionary era?
5. What was the Latin American reaction to the invasion of the Dominican Republic? How did OAS involvement affect the credibility of that institution?
6. How did the role of the military in Latin America change after the Cuban revolution, and to what degree did the United States contribute to this change?

Further Sources

Books

ALLISON, GRAHAM, and PHILIP ZELIKOW. *Essence of Decision: Explaining the Cuban Missile Crisis,* 2nd ed. (New York: Longman, 1999). A new edition of a classic work on the crisis, which uses organizational behavior and a governmental politics model to augment a rational choice approach to the evolution and conclusion of the crisis. It includes new documents declassified in the 1990s.

BARBER, WILLARD F., and C. NEALE RONNING. *Internal Security and Military Power: Counterinsurgency and Civic Action in Latin America* (Columbus: Ohio State University Press, 1966). A classic work analyzing the U.S. encouragement of increased military action in Latin America during the 1960s. In particular, it focuses on the dangers to democracy of expanding the military's role.

GUEVARA, CHE. *Guerrilla Warfare, with an Introduction and Case Studies by Brian Loveman and Thomas M. Davies Jr.* (Lincoln: University of Nebraska Press, 1985). In addition to the full text of Che Guevara's work, the book offers a clear introduction and case studies to provide political and historical perspective on the application (both successful and unsuccessful) of Che's theories.

KORNBLUH, PETER. *Bay of Pigs Declassified: The Secret CIA Report on the Invasion of Cuba* (New York: New Press, 1998). A fascinating edited collection of declassified CIA documents. It is, the author argues, "the most brutally honest self-examination ever conducted inside the agency" in discussing why the operation was such a failure.

Web Sites

Foreign Relations of the United States, 1961–1963, Cuban Missile Crisis and Aftermath. As part of the FRUS series online, this site offers detailed memoranda of meetings, telegrams, telephone conversations, and other interactions between the key members of the U.S. government. http://www.state.gov/www/about_state/history/frusXI/index.htm/.

Cuban Missile Crisis. A site developed by Harvard College that provides primary documents, commentary, and analyses about the crisis itself and crisis decision making in general, links to other sites on the topic, and a bibliography on further sources (including those by Soviet officials). http://www.cubanmissilecrisis.org/.

School of the Americas Watch. The Web site of a nonprofit organization dedicated to closing the School of the Americas (in 2001, renamed the Western Hemisphere Institute of Security Cooperation). It contains detailed descriptions of the school's graduates, especially those involved in human rights abuses, copies of press articles about the school, and other information about military abuses of power. http://www.soaw.org.

CIA Electronic Reading Room, Bay of Pigs. As a result of the Freedom of Information Act, the Central Intelligence Agency has placed online its own assessment of the failure of the Bay of Pigs. It consists of two volumes and approximately 400 pages in PDF format. http://www.foia.cia.gov/bay_of_pigs.asp.

Notes

1. Cardoso and Faletto 1979, xxiv.
2. Thomas 1998, 1075.
3. Quoted in Schoultz 1998, 355.
4. Quoted in Blasier 1976, 194.
5. Avalon Project Web site.
6. Avalon project Web site.
7. Quoted in Holden and Zolov 2000, 222.
8. Levinson and de Onís 1970, 134.
9. Holden and Zolov 2000, 231.
10. Kornbluh 1998, 12.
11. Kornbluh 1998, 12.
12. Allison and Zelikow 1999, 81.
13. Zubok and Pleshakov 1996, 207.
14. Quoted in Beschloss 1997, 74.
15. Quoted in LaFeber 1993, 182.
16. Quoted in Loveman and Davies 1985, 47.
17. Quoted in Loveman 1985, 48.
18. Domínguez 1989, 114.
19. Quoted in Rabe 1999, 19.
20. Loveman 1999, 181.
21. Weeks 2003.
22. Quoted in Beschloss 1997, 306.
23. Quoted in Atkins and Wilson 1997, 113.
24. Quoted in Rabe 1988, 155.
25. Quoted in McPherson 2003, 126.
26. Quoted in Chester 2001, 262.
27. Quoted in Beschloss 2001, 297.

CHAPTER 7

The Communist Threat and U.S. Intervention

	TIMELINE
1973	United States supports coup in Chile
1975	Church Committee report released
1977	Panama Canal treaties signed
1979	Sandinistas overthrow Anastasio Somoza
1980	Ronald Reagan elected president
1981	The Contras receive U.S. funding
1983	United States invades Grenada
1987	Esquipulas II Accords signed
1988	George H. W. Bush elected president
1989	United States invades Panama
1992	Peace agreements implemented in El Salvador and Nicaragua
1999	Panama Canal treaties go into force

During the 1960s, the effects of the Cuban revolution—especially in terms of support for guerrilla warfare against U.S. allies—became all too evident, and the United States pursued interventionism with a new vigor. This renewed use of power included economic and diplomatic pressures, covert operations, and even invasion. The Cold War was framed as a valiant struggle to protect freedom in the hemisphere, and the cases of Cuba and Guatemala epitomized the lengths to which the United States would go to fight what it considered to be security threats. In Latin America, many elites supported U.S. policy, but a growing undercurrent of discontent also emerged, which pushed for negotiated conclusions to war and protested against the treatment of so many citizens caught in the middle. They did not share the notion that leftist or even Marxist governments automatically constituted a threat to national security and global order. This chapter examines how the Mann Doctrine and the 1964 coup in Brazil marked a new intensification of the Cold War in Latin America.

In theoretical terms, this era conforms well in many ways to the expectations of realism. The rationale for the use of force was self-preservation, expressed in almost apocalyptic terms, and power was employed in manners wholly divorced from international law. Although international institutions and even specific Latin American leaders did become more prominent actors, given the preponderance of U.S. power, they were not able to block U.S. actions. Nonetheless, both U.S. and Latin American voices, raised against these dictatorships, were heard as never before and did eventually play a part in finding solutions to problems to which the United States had greatly contributed.

Dependency theorists, however, would not agree. From that view, in the context of the Cold War, the United States was seeking to ensure its continued and privileged access to important primary goods, which was threatened by the possibility of nationalization associated with socialist movements. Intervention, therefore, was related less to security than to the needs of the capitalism.

Strategies for Fighting "Subversion"

The military overthrow of Brazilian President João Goulart in 1964 demonstrated that the United States was willing to support coups if they were aimed at ousting governments deemed too leftist. Unlike Cuba, Nicaragua, or the Dominican Republic, which were small countries that had been within the U.S. sphere of influence for many years, Brazil was a large, economically dynamic country with leaders who refused to kowtow to the United States. The Brazilian coup would soon be repeated in other Latin American countries, even some (like Chile and Uruguay) where such overthrows were historically fewer and further between. Although the circumstances would vary, they would share certain characteristics. In some manner, the left would either gain power or threaten to do so, which would be marked by socioeconomic conflict. The opposition, with the support of the majority of the military leadership, would label leftist movements as Communist. The United States, often through its extensive CIA contacts, would assure the country's armed forces that a new military government would receive U.S support.

Coups and military actions were not the only means of dispensing with "undesirable" governments. Into the 1970s, assassination—in some cases approved by the U.S. president himself—was another policy option. In 1975, Senator Frank Church chaired Senate committees that investigated and reported on covert operations and political assassinations. In addition to a report on Chile, the Select Committee to Study Government Operations with Respect to Intelligence Activities released a long report entitled "Alleged Assassination Plots Involving Foreign Leaders." It had a distinctly Latin American emphasis, including plots against Fidel Castro, Rafael Trujillo, and Chilean Army Commander in Chief René Schneider. (The other two specific cases were Patrice Lumumba of the Congo and President Ngo Dinh Diem of South Vietnam, both of whom were killed.)

The report detailed extensive U.S. involvement in murdering (or, in the case of Castro, attempting to murder) foreign leaders. With regard to Castro, the plots reflected covert operations rum amok, with references to poisoned cigars, mafia contacts, and chemicals to make his beard fall out. To kill Trujillo and Schneider, the CIA worked closely with opposition groups, even providing weapons intended to carry out the job (though it wasn't clear whether those exact weapons were used). As a result of the study, in 1976 President Gerald Ford issued Executive Order 11905, which outlawed political assassinations by employees of the U.S. government.

The debate over U.S. policy during the Cold War rages unabated. Supporters argue that, when all was said and done, the United States helped to win the overall war against Communist aggression and that its aggressive tactics had served a noble overall purpose. The Soviet Union, often working through Fidel Castro, was a real threat to countries very close to the United States. From that perspective, since by the early 1990s, Latin American countries were having elections, all previous actions—even violent—were worthwhile. Much of the violence, it is argued, was initiated not by the United States but by armed groups seeking to overthrow legitimate governments. The abuses of human rights that did occur were regrettable but should not deter from the regional victory.

Opponents have a different argument, one that emphasizes the exaggeration of the Communist threat, especially in terms of the U.S. viewing local demands for justice as a global Communist plot. Although the Soviet Union was certainly interested in the region, it was not directing events and was used by policy makers as a boogeyman to continue both overt and covert operations. The deaths of so many thousands could not ever be rationalized, regardless of the Cold War's outcome, because none of them needed to die. The United States used its hegemonic position to reinforce its political grip on Latin America and refused to allow any radical changes that might loosen it.

Alleged Assassination Plots Involving Foreign Leaders, an Interim Report of the Select Committee to Study Governmental Operations with Respect to Intelligence Operations (Church Report) (1975)

The evidence establishes that the United States was implicated in several assassination plots. The Committee believes that, short of war, assassination is incompatible with American principles, international order, and morality. It should be rejected as a tool of foreign policy. . . .

CUBA

We have found concrete evidence of at least eight plots involving the CIA to assassinate Fidel Castro from 1960 to 1965. Although some of the assassination plots did not advance beyond the stage of planning and preparation, one plot, involving the use of underworld figures, reportedly twice progressed to the point of sending poison pills to Cuba and dispatching teams to commit the deed. Another plot involved furnishing weapons and other assassination devices to a Cuban dissident. The proposed assassination devices ran the gamut from high-powered rifles to poison pills, poison pens, deadly bacterial powders, and other devices which strain the imagination. . . .

Efforts against Castro did not begin with assassination attempts. From March through August 1960, during the last year of the Eisenhower Administration, the CIA considered plans to undermine Castro's charismatic appeal by sabotaging his speeches. According to the 1967 Report of the CIA's Inspector General, an official in the Technical Services Division (TSD) recalled discussing a scheme to spray Castro's broadcasting studio with a chemical which produced effects similar to LSD, but the scheme was rejected because the chemical was unreliable. During this period, TSD impregnated a box of cigars with a chemical which produced temporary disorientation, hoping to induce Castro to smoke one of the cigars before delivering a speech. The Inspector General also reported a plan to destroy Castro's image as "The Beard" by dusting his shoes with thallium salts, a strong depilatory that would cause his beard to fall out. The depilatory was to be administered during a trip outside Cuba, when it was anticipated Castro would leave his shoes outside the door of his hotel room to be shined. TSD procured the chemical and tested it on animals, but apparently abandoned the scheme because Castro cancelled his trip. . . .

[A]n official was given a box of Castro's favorite cigars with instructions to treat them with lethal poison. The cigars were contaminated with a botulinum toxin so potent that a person would die after putting one in his mouth. The official reported that the cigars were ready on October 7, 1960; TSD notes indicated that they were delivered to an unidentified person on February 13, 1961. The record does not disclose whether an attempt was made to pass the cigars to Castro. . . .

TRUJILLO

Trujillo was a brutal dictator, and both the Eisenhower and Kennedy Administrations encouraged the overthrow of his regime by Dominican dissidents. Toward that end the highest policy levels of both Administrations approved or condoned supplying arms to the dissidents. Although there is no evidence that the United States instigated any assassination activity, certain evidence tends to link United States officials to the assassination plans.

Material support, consisting of three pistols and three carbines, was supplied to various dissidents. While United States' officials knew that the dissidents intended to overthrow Trujillo, probably by assassination, there is no direct evidence that the weapons which were passed were used in the assassination. . . .

Late in the evening of May 30, 1961, Trujillo was ambushed and assassinated near San Cristobal, Dominican Republic. The assassination closely paralleled the plan disclosed by the action group to American representatives in the Dominican Republic and passed on to officials in Washington at both the CIA and the State Department.

There is no indication or suggestion contained in the record of those post-assassination meetings, or in the Robert Kennedy notes, of concern as to the propriety of the known United States involvement in the assassination. Nor is there is any record that anyone took steps following Trujillo's assassination to reprimand or censure any of the American officials involved either on the scene or in Washington, or to otherwise make known any objections or displeasure as to the degree of United States involvement in the events which had transpired.

SCHNEIDER

On September 15, 1970, President Richard Nixon informed CIA Director Richard Helms that an Allende regime in Chile would not be acceptable to the United States. The CIA was instructed by President Nixon to play a direct role in organizing a military coup d'etat in Chile to prevent Allende's accession to the presidency. . . .

One of the major obstacles faced by all the military conspirators in Chile was the strong opposition to the coup by the Commander-in-Chief of the Army, General Rene Schneider, who insisted the constitutional process be followed. As a result of his strong constitutional stand, the removal of General Schneider became a necessary ingredient in the coup plans of all the Chilean conspirators. Unable to have General Schneider retired or reassigned, the conspirators decided to kidnap him. An unsuccessful abduction attempt was made on October 19, 1970, by a group of Chilean military officers whom the CIA was actively supporting. A second kidnap attempt was made the following day, again unsuccessfully. In the early morning hours of October 22, 1970, machine guns and ammunition were passed by the CIA to the group that had failed on October 19. That same day General Schneider was mortally wounded in an attempted kidnap on his way to work.

By the end of September 1970, it appeared that the only feasible way for the CIA to implement the Presidential order to prevent Allende from coming to power was to foment a coup d'etat. All of the known coup plots developed within the Chilean military entailed the removal of General Schneider by one means or another.

Source: Church Report, pp. 71–73, 191, 213, 215, 225–226. www.aarclibrary.Org/publib/church/reports/ir/contents.htm

The Nixon Administration and South America

In 1968, Lyndon Johnson made his surprise announcement that he would not run for reelection as president, and Richard Nixon won the November election. Like Johnson, Nixon had a history of using the perceived threat of Communism to attack political opponents, which became manifest in policy toward Latin America. He also had personal experience in the 1958 incident in Venezuela, when angry protesters mobbed his car. Nixon viewed Latin America almost strictly in security terms, with the dangers of Communism always paramount; his attention was often elsewhere, and he looked at the region largely in terms of its effect on U.S. global interests. For the White House, that danger was rapidly becoming evident in South America.

South America had become more prominent for the United States during World War II, as it sought hemispheric unity against an external enemy. After Castro's victory, the same happened again. Many countries in South America had long histories of socialist and Communist parties, worker's movements, and democracy, and these very combinations made them ideological battlefields. The United States looked to South America as a region that would help decide the Cold War.

The Case of Chile

The violent military overthrow of the democratically elected socialist president Salvador Allende in Chile provides the perfect example of the complex relationships between the U.S. government, Latin American militaries, reformist efforts, and democracy and of the ways in which the power imbalance had a direct impact on the future of a country. The U.S. goal of promoting democracy had withered under the relentless logic of the Cold War. In Latin America, even presidents who came to office through free and fair elections could find themselves targets if they were on the wrong side of the ideological divide.

Despite the concerted effort of Chilean conservatives and the U.S. government, Allende was elected president in 1970. The CIA had even been involved in a plot to assassinate Army Commander in Chief René Schneider and then blame it on leftists. Two days after he was inaugurated, President Nixon told his National Security Council, "We want to do it right and bring him down. . . . We have to do everything we can to hurt [Allende] and bring him down."[1] It was unthinkable that a socialist president be allowed to prosper while the Cold War raged on. In the eyes of the Nixon administration, acceptance would just be an invitation for other leftists to seek power, all of whom would eventually become like Cuba—Communist puppets of the Soviet Union.

President Nixon and National Security Advisor Henry Kissinger decided against an overt policy of hostility, which could backfire by making Allende more popular. Instead, they chose a less direct strategy, such as using U.S. leverage at the International Development Bank and the World Bank to block new loans to Chile, while also drastically cutting bilateral aid through the Agency for International Development and the U.S. Export-Import Bank. It was in this context that Nixon made his famous statement that he wanted to make the Chilean economy "scream."[2] The idea was that a sharp economic downturn would reduce popular support for the Allende government and accelerate his downfall. The only aid that continued—and in fact increased—was military, which was intended to curry favor with anti-Allende officers.

These efforts by the United States did not take place in a political vacuum. Allende's election had polarized Chile. The constitution stipulated that if no candidate won a majority of the popular vote, then Congress would decide between the two who had won the most. Allende received a plurality of the vote, but only 36 percent of the total. Congress, following its tradition of approving the election of whichever candidate had received the most votes, did finally vote to elect Allende, but only after a bitter debate that included forcing him to sign an agreement supporting a number of constitutional guarantees before allowing him to assume the presidency.

Allende's platform was a "peaceful road to socialism" and entailed a far greater role of the state, nationalization of land, increased wages, and other measures intended to redistribute income. The policy of the U.S. government thus received support from certain sectors in Chile: business leaders, conservatives, many military officers, and even right-wing terrorists began to receive both encouragement and financial aid in the quest to "cleanse" Chile and prevent it from becoming "another Cuba." Strikes and other disruptive measures contributed to the crisis atmosphere and led to shortages of basic goods.

Meanwhile, under Kissinger's personal direction, the CIA began a coordinated effort to have Allende overthrown.[3] In 1971, one CIA cable explicitly noted, "We conceive our mission as one in which we work consciously and deliberately in the direction of a coup."[4] On September 11, 1973, the military initiated its coup plans, which included bombing the presidential palace and imprisoning thousands of Chileans. The government was overthrown, Allende killed (although rumored to have been murdered, most evidence suggests he committed suicide rather than be taken prisoner), and a military government under the direction of General Augusto Pinochet settled in.

The debate over U.S. culpability in the coup began immediately and has continued over time as more U.S. government documents are declassified and released. The Nixon administration, with the personal attention of Henry Kissinger, went to great lengths to have Allende removed from power. It made very clear to the Chilean armed forces that the United States would immediately recognize a military government and would restore all the credits and loans that were being blocked. After the coup, the United States also worked closely with the Pinochet government to ensure its long-term survival. In addition to providing all the financial aid denied to Allende, the U.S. government was quick to tell the Chilean military, just as it would military governments throughout the region, that they were allies against a widespread Communist invasion. Only gradually would the human rights abuses of the Chilean dictatorship create significant opposition within the U.S. executive and legislative branches.

The Spread of Military Governments in Latin America

The period beginning with the Cuban Revolution (1959) and ending with the dissolution of the Soviet Union (1990–1991) saw the proliferation of U.S.-supported military governments. As already mentioned, South America had become a Cold War battleground, with its militaries working to erase all traces of the left, reformers, or anyone else labeled "subversive." In Paraguay, dictator Alfredo Stroessner was already in power at the time of Castro's revolution, but by the mid-1970s there were also dictatorships in Argentina, Bolivia, Brazil, Chile, Ecuador, Peru, and Uruguay (of South American countries, only Colombia and Venezuela retained civilian governments, largely because of strong elite-based agreements to share power).

Reports of brutal human rights abuses poured into U.S. embassies and were picked up by the U.S. press, and the State Department was peppered with similar confidential messages. People, even U.S. citizens, were being arrested without warrants, held incommunicado, interrogated, tortured, and sometimes executed and/or **disappeared** (referring to the disappearance of an individual, who would eventually be presumed dead with no body found).

Similar events were playing out around South America. In Argentina, a military government came to power in 1976 and quickly established itself as even more repressive than its Chilean counterpart. The generals viewed themselves, however, as on the U.S. side in the Cold War and consequently put out diplomatic feelers for support. Kissinger, who had become secretary of state, met with the Argentine foreign minister and Argentina's ambassador to the United States. They were concerned about the negative press the military government was receiving and sought assurances that U.S. policy would not be affected by it. Kissinger quickly reassured him:

> Look, our basic attitude is that we would like you to succeed. I have an old-fashioned view that friends ought to be supported. What is not understood in the United States is that you have a civil war. We read about human rights problems but not the context. The quicker you succeed the better.[5]

At the time, the Argentine military was actively attacking its political opposition, labeling all opponents Communist. Its actions would become known as the Dirty War for the tactics used.

Upwards of 20,000 people were killed in Argentina. As in Chile, the logistical problem of dealing with bodies was resolved in part by throwing them into the ocean (with their bodies either slit open to prevent floating or tied to railroad ties to weigh them down). Over time, more evidence has come to light that demonstrates U.S. contribution to Operation Condor, an organization created by the Chilean dictatorship to enable cooperation between military governments in their efforts to track down their political enemies. As Patrice McSherry writes, "U.S. military and intelligence officials, operating from the Canal Zone headquarters and U.S. embassies, provided vital resources and support to upgrade, modernize, and make more efficient the program of coordinated repression."[6] The full implications of human rights policy will be addressed in more detail in Chapter 10.

Latin American Reactions

The sheer brutality of military dictatorships in Latin America gave rise to new actors in U.S.–Latin American relations who had no ties to governments. Nongovernmental organizations (NGOs) became more prominent in response to political violence. They included religious groups, academic think tanks, international social movements and organizations, and individual activists. They grew out of disillusionment, because their members had come to believe that governments—both in Latin America and in the United States—would not willingly support democratic change. Especially in the 1980s, they organized protests against U.S. policy in Central America that would define even more explicitly the political differences in the United States over the Reagan administration's handling of Central American crises and human rights abuses. In the context of liberal institutional theory, they represented a new way to prevent the United States and its allies from ignoring human rights concerns. By providing information and testimony to organization like the OAS, they could effectively contradict the message that the abuses of military governments were minimal or solely the work of rogue elements within the armed forces.

Although anti-Communist dictatorships in Latin America generally turned to the United States for aid, trade, and political support, there were other alliances as well. For example, the Nonaligned Movement formed in the 1950s as a counterweight to both U.S. and Soviet influence. Many countries, some of which were newly independent, wanted to avoid being cornered ideologically and also wanted to support movements intended to break the chains of colonization (especially French and Portuguese colonies in Africa). Fidel Castro became an enthusiastic supporter of the Nonaligned Movement and used it to great effect in the United Nations, where he could often rely on votes from nonaligned countries to overcome U.S. opposition to Cuban participation in various U.N. committees. Many other Latin American countries joined as well, although both Brazil and Mexico chose to remain only observers, as their governments decided to remain as flexible as possible.

Given the Nonaligned Movement's emphasis on economic independence, it heartily endorsed the notion that Latin American countries should have the right to pursue economic policies autonomously, without pressure from the United States. The same message emerged through the Group of 77, a collection of developing countries that came together in 1964 as a result of the first United Nations Conference on Trade and Development (UNCTAD). Its goal was to provide developing countries a collective voice that could offset the hegemonic position of the wealthiest countries. It worked as a coalition within the United Nations and called for increased cooperation and assistance from developed countries in terms of access to capital, aid, technology transfers, and control over foreign investment.

The Organization of American States proved not to be an effective brake on U.S. policies. In some cases, U.S. policy makers evinced barely disguised contempt. For example, when talking privately to President Johnson about Panama, Senator Richard Russell told him, "You've got all the cards, and this damn yapping over here by this OAS doesn't amount to a thing. Just because they feel like they've got to stick together."[7] Yet it did remain an important vehicle for Latin American voices of dissent with U.S. policies, and so the United States could not simply ignore it.

Taken together, these efforts at contradicting or protesting U.S. policy reflected broad and diverse disillusionment with the rigidities of Cold War politics and raised potent questions about its human costs. Public consciousness in many different countries was raised through their actions, and many lives saved. However, given the sheer economic and military strength of the United States, they could not fundamentally negate the effects of the ideological war.

Political Turmoil in Central America

Despite efforts in the 1960s to spur economic growth, Central American countries suffered as prices for their primary products—especially bananas and coffee—declined. With the exception of Costa Rica, which avoided military adventurism by virtue of having dismantled the institution entirely in 1949, socioeconomic conflict was intense in the 1960s and 1970s, made worse by an oil shock and a drastic rise in prices in 1973. As had always been the case, the wealth of the region was in land, which in turn was owned by a relatively small but very powerful oligarchy that allied itself with the armed forces. In his history of Central America, Woodward notes, "Widespread corruption, the heritage of an underpaid and poorly trained bureaucracy, resistance to structural change, and protection of position and wealth characterized the elites everywhere."[8]

The economic and political might of United Fruit was no longer an issue because the company had ceased to exist. An antitrust lawsuit filed in 1954 was used by the U.S. government to begin breaking it up in 1958. For example, it sold off parts of its Guatemala operation to Standard Fruit. As it divested, the company changed its name to United Brands, which in 1990 became Chiquita (named after a cartoon banana dressed as a woman launched as an ad campaign in 1944). To this day, it continues to operate under the Chiquita brand name. Even as United Fruit was taken apart, the U.S. government's policy emphasis shifted clearly away from economic factors. The proximity of Cuba, combined with societies in a state of upheaval, brought national security front and center.

The militaries in El Salvador, Guatemala, and Honduras were firmly in power, and in Nicaragua the dictatorship of Anastasio Somoza (his father had originally been hand-picked by the United States to head the country's National Guard), though unpopular, survived with U.S. economic assistance.

Guerrilla organizations in Nicaragua had appeared after the Cuban Revolution, but by the time President Jimmy Carter took office in January 1977 there was an armed opposition movement making real progress in its efforts to topple the incumbent regime. The Frente Sandinista de Liberación Nacional (FSLN), which had been active but not very successful in the 1960s, saw resurgence after 1972. That year, a massive earthquake hit the capital of Managua, and Somoza siphoned off millions of dollars of international aid. The egregious corruption, which now came at the expense of people who were suffering from the earthquake, sickened all but the hardest pro-Somoza population. The Sandinistas became strong enough in 1974 to stage a bold raid of a Christmas party being held for the U.S. ambassador. Although he had already left the party, the Sandinistas held other guests hostage, including Somoza's brother-in-law. They held out for more than three days, demanding as ransom the release of fourteen political prisoners (including future Sandinista president Daniel Ortega), $1 million, and the reading of an antigovernment message on radio and television. Somoza accepted the demands but subsequently responded with harsher repression. The Sandinistas, however, had proven they were a force to be reckoned with.

Between 1974 and 1979, Somoza's moderate opposition was pushed ever closer to support for the Sandinistas, despite the latter's more avowedly radical stance. Anti-Somoza sentiment increased further in 1978 with the assassination of Pedro Joaquín Chamorro, a prominent Nicaraguan newspaper editor. Chamorro had been vocal in criticizing Somoza but was moderate compared with the Sandinistas, and his murder demonstrated that Somoza was unwilling to allow any opposition at all.

The Carter administration underestimated the political deterioration in both Nicaragua and El Salvador. Shortly after President Carter took office, the State Department held a meeting to analyze Central America, inviting members of the academic community. They predicted that Somoza would be able to withstand the Sandinistas and that the guerrilla movement in El Salvador would not be a major problem. Robert Pastor, who was Carter's Latin America expert on the U.S. National Security Council, writes that the FSLN appeared so weak that Somoza's main problem seemed to be his obesity, as he weighed 267 pounds when Carter took office.[9] As the guerrillas gained momentum, the administration scrambled to respond to events. Although Carter would admonish Somoza for human rights violations, the FSLN charged that it did so only when Somoza appeared stronger, in order to minimize the weakening of the regime.

Ultimately, U.S. policy toward Nicaragua in the late 1970s bore a striking resemblance to U.S. policy toward Cuba in the late 1950s. In both cases, the regime of a corrupt dictator with a history of U.S. support began to collapse under its own bloated weight of repression and greed. Both Somoza and Batista faced revolutionary forces with a distinctly anti-U.S. ideology (openly Marxist-Leninist for the Sandinistas), and as a result, U.S. policy makers, hoping to control the flow of events, sought a negotiated solution whereby the dictator would step aside but the rebels would not assume power. In both Cuba and Nicaragua, that solution was unworkable in practice and therefore rejected by all sides. As the revolutions moved closer to success, the Carter and Eisenhower administrations both placed pressure on the dictators, hoping to force them out and maintain some influence in the formation of a new regime. In both countries, the United States was ultimately compelled to accept the demands of the revolutionary forces, and then it would soon turn to new measures to undermine those new governments. As Pastor writes, "The ghost of Cuba past, which had haunted U.S. policy makers as Somoza was falling, continued to taunt them after the Sandinistas marched into Managua."[10]

Facing the inevitable, the Carter administration instructed Ambassador Lawrence Pezzullo to arrange Somoza's resignation and to fly him to Miami. (He would later be forced to seek sanctuary in Paraguay, where he was killed by a car bomb the following year.) The Sandinistas took power with wide support, and their coalition proclaimed a "Plan to Achieve Peace" that on paper was the very model of moderation. The plan would reconstruct the Nicaraguan political system without vengeance and would include "all sectors of Nicaraguan politics." Initial relations with the United States proved laden with suspicion, no surprise given the long-time U.S. support for the Somoza dictatorship. During 1980, the U.S. Congress debated and finally approved an aid package, but the Marxist leanings of the Nicaraguan revolution, which included relationships with Cuba and the Soviet Union, created steadfast political enemies not only in the United States but also in Nicaragua. Many within the Nicaraguan government, however, continued to hope that a modus vivendi could somehow be worked out, so that socioeconomic reforms (including nationalizations) could be made without making an enemy of the United States. The 1980 election of Ronald Reagan, however, made any such arrangement impossible. Power, which President Carter had often worked (often unsuccessfully) to keep secondary in policy, once again took center stage.

"Plan to Achieve Peace" of the Nicaraguan Junta of National Reconstruction (1979)

Our premise is that while it is true that the solution to Nicaragua's serious problem, is the exclusive competence of the Nicaraguan People. Hemispheric solidarity, essential for this plan to take hold, will be accorded in fulfillment of the Resolution of the Seventeenth Meeting of consultation of Ministers of Foreign Affairs of the OAS, approved on June 23, 1979.

The following steps will ensure the immediate and definitive replacement of the Somoza regime. Already destroyed by the heroic and combative people of

Nicaragua and their vanguard, the Sandinista national Liberation Front. Rejection of this plan in favor of a political solution would leave military destruction of Somocismo as the only recourse; this could go on for weeks and would lead, unnecessarily, to many more deaths and destruction.

STAGES OF THE PLAN:

I. Somoza submits his resignation to his Congress, which in turn accepts it and turns over the reins of power to the Government of National Reconstruction in recognition of the backing it has received from all sector of Nicaraguan society.

II. Installation of the Government of National Reconstruction. This Government is made up of representatives of all sectors of Nicaraguan politics and has received the official support of all.

III. Immediately after the Government of National Reconstruction has installed itself in Nicaragua, the member countries of the OAS, especially those that sponsored or voted in favor of the Resolution, will then recognize it officially as the legitimate Government of Nicaragua.

IV. The Government of National Reconstruction will immediately do the following:

1. Repeal the Somoza Constitution.
2. Decree the Fundamental Statute, which shall provisionally govern the Government of National Reconstruction.
3. Dissolve the National Congress.
4. Order the National Guard to cease hostilities and immediately confine them to barracks with the guarantees that their lives and other rights will be respected. The officials, noncommissioned officers and soldiers of the National Guard that so desire may joint the new national army or civilian life.

    The Sandinista Army will enforce the cease-fire to facilitate fulfillment of these agreements by maintaining the positions won as of the time of the Decree.
5. Maintain order by means of those sectors of the National Guard which have honored the cease-fire and were appointed to these functions by the Government of National Reconstruction, a task that they will carry out in coordination with the combatants of the Sandinista Army.
6. Decree the organic law that will govern the institutions of the State.
7. Implement the program of the Government of National Reconstruction.
8. Guarantee the departure from the county of all those military personnel, Somoza's functionaries who wish to leave and who are found not to have been involved in serious crimes against the people.

Source: http://www.cidh.oas.org/countryrep/Nica81eng/intro.htm.

President Reagan and Central America

President Reagan took office in January 1981, and criticisms of President Carter's Central America policy had been an important part of his campaign. The most important issues were the perception that Carter had allowed a pro-U.S., anti-Communist ally (Somoza) to fall to Communist rebels; that he was not active enough in countering similar rebels in El Salvador; and that the president had given away the Panama Canal. A new "get tough" attitude was immediately apparent, and it resonated with many U.S. voters. Carter had noted in a speech that the United States suffered from a "malaise," and many people responded—especially in the wake of defeat in Vietnam—to Reagan's call for an invigorated foreign policy. The Cold War raged on, and given Central America's proximity, it became prominent in Reagan's speeches.

The new administration's view of foreign policy was perhaps best summed up by an article written by Jeane Kirkpatrick, a conservative Republican whom Reagan appointed U.S. Ambassador to the United Nations. She wrote a much-cited article criticizing the Carter administration for its bungling of the Nicaraguan crisis, and she also addressed Iran, where an Islamic revolution overthrew the U.S.-backed Shah).[11] Her main argument was that in some countries there is no alternative to dictatorship and therefore the United States should not aim or claim to produce one. She asserted there are two types of dictatorships: authoritarian and totalitarian. The former includes autocrats like Somoza, who are repressive but friendly to the United States. The latter often represent Communism, which is not only hostile to the United States but also worse for its own citizens because it is more repressive. She wrote that Carter and his supporters were duped into believing Sandinista claims about being a popular voice, when in fact they were the leading edge of a Communist wave. The answer, then, was to support even distasteful dictatorships if they found themselves under attack by guerrillas and to take decisive action against so-called revolutionary governments.

Within two months, Reagan ended the aid program to Nicaragua and also approved a covert plan to fight the Sandinistas. His rationale was that Nicaragua, with the help of Cuba, was funding a revolutionary guerrilla movement in El Salvador, the Farabundo Martí Liberation Front, or FMLN (like the FSLN, it was named for the leader of a past uprising, in this case 1932). The FMLN was fighting a U.S.-supported government in El Salvador that was becoming notorious for its violence. From the U.S. perspective, both movements represented dominoes falling to Marxism-Leninism and, by extension, Soviet domination. Under this new policy shift, the fact that both were the result of long-standing socioeconomic divisions and political alienation tended not to register. At the very least, conventional wisdom was that Communists were taking advantage of difficult situations that otherwise would have peaceful solutions.

El Salvador had been controlled for many years by a civilian-military coalition of elites, which became more militarized in the 1970s in response to guerrilla activities. In 1980, government agents murdered Salvadoran Archbishop Oscar Romero as he said Mass, and later the same year four U.S. nuns were also killed. One militia group had even issued pamphlets saying, "Be a patriot! Kill a priest!"[12] Throughout the 1980s, the human rights record of the government was abysmal, but the U.S. government insisted it was making progress and, at the same time, was dealing with the challenge of fighting Communists. Approximately $5 billion in aid would flow into El Salvador, accompanied by the assertion that if the FMLN were to win, human rights would be abused even more, so support for the military government could be viewed as the "least bad" policy.

The U.S. answer for Nicaragua was the formation of an anti-Communist rebel army, popularly known as the Contras (a shortened version of the Spanish word for counterrevolutionary; "contra" means "against"). The Contras began as a ragtag force (receiving some money from the approving Argentine dictatorship) of former national guard officials, but ample funding and CIA training made it into an effective force. In 1981, Reagan approved $19 million to support approximately 1,000 soldiers, and then in 1982 the Contras blew up two bridges in northern Nicaragua, which was the first major assault. From then on, the Reagan administration committed itself to the cause, while the Sandinistas were pushed even more firmly into the arms of Cuba and the Soviet Union as they pursued aid and arms deals.

The revolution had not begun in the same radical manner as in Cuba, but after Reagan took office the incipient signs of hardening became increasingly evident. This included a larger security force, the arrests of members of the opposition and censorship of their publications, alienation and resettlement of indigenous groups (who were believed to be potential counterrevolutionaries), and more strident rhetoric against the United States. The Sandinistas were, however, also trying to follow the Cuban model of fostering greater equality and social justice in a country where such ideals had never existed. With Cuban help, literacy rates increased, and for those "within the revolution" there existed the continued hope that Nicaragua could raise itself out of the mire of poverty and dependence, made worse by the destruction and rubble in Managua and elsewhere, a daily reminder of a bitter past.

The revolutionary government embarked on a series of reforms, with the state taking immediate control of Somoza's vast holdings. Agrarian reform provided land to peasants, while new health and education policies were launched to address the dire needs of the poor. The Sandinistas immediately received aid from Cuba, which included teachers (1,500 arrived in 1979, with more to come), construction workers, and military advisors (Cuba claimed in the mid-1980s that there were 200, the United States believed it to be around 2,000, and a Cuban army general who defected said it was 300 to 400), and nonmilitary aid reached almost $300 million by 1982.[13] The Cuban presence was therefore significant, while Soviet-Nicaraguan relations remained relatively cool. In general, the USSR was wary of entangling itself in risky revolutionary wars so close to the United States, and so the Sandinista leadership did not develop friendly ties with the Soviets.

The Reagan administration's insistence that the Sandinista government be toppled led to one of the most famous U.S. political scandals of the twentieth century, the so-called **Iran-Contra** affair. The scandal erupted because many members of the U.S. Congress were becoming concerned about reports filtering in from Nicaragua that detailed corruption, drug trafficking, and terrorism by the Contras. In response, in 1982 the Boland Amendment passed (its sponsor was Massachusetts Democratic Representative Edward Boland), which cut off all funding intended to overthrow the Sandinistas. However, this prohibition was easy to evade, as the Reagan administration simply asserted that money was being used to stop the flow of arms to El Salvador and not to topple the Sandinista regime. To close the loophole, Congress passed a second Boland Amendment in 1984, which forbade providing any military aid at all to the Contras.

Intent on keeping the military aid spigot open, officials in the administration, led by National Security Council staff member Lt. Col. Oliver North, devised schemes to have other countries send funds. Contributors were both private donors and governments, including El Salvador, Guatemala, Honduras, Israel, Panama, Saudi Arabia, and Taiwan. Already skirting the law, North bounded well over it when he approached Iran, offering U.S. weapons (at inflated prices) with the proceeds going to the Contras. Iran was one of the most vocal enemies of the United States, and indeed part of Jimmy Carter's defeat in 1980 was due to criticism surrounding the U.S. hostages taken by the revolutionary and militant Muslim government in 1979. Nonetheless, the Reagan administration had already been involved in trading arms for hostages with Iran, so the Contra deal was just a new step in the same direction.

Latin American Opponents to the War

As fighting in Central America raged, a number of Latin American leaders came together to find peaceful solutions. In 1982, Mexican President Miguel de la Madrid brought together officials from Colombia, Panama, and Venezuela to Contadora Island, off Panama. This Contadora group would eventually also include Argentina, Brazil, Peru, and Uruguay and was intended to demilitarize the conflicts while acknowledging the concerns of all sides. Although it offered a peace plan in 1983, the United States rejected it, and so did the Sandinistas. Nicaragua's foreign minister refused to negotiate with the Contadora group, saying, "We don't talk to puppets, only to puppeteers."[14] The Reagan administration claimed that no such agreement was possible in practice, because the Sandinistas could not be trusted to hold up their side of any bargain.

Nonetheless, opponents of the wars did not give in easily. The most notable was Costa Rican president Oscar Arias Sánchez, who worked assiduously through the 1980s to end the fighting; for his efforts, he would eventually be awarded the Nobel Peace Prize. His desire to end the war did not mean he supported the Sandinistas themselves; as he bluntly told Sandinista President Daniel Ortega in 1986, "What you call democracy isn't called democracy here nor in any part of the world."[15] But he also believed that because there was no chance the Contras could ever become a legitimate government, then the war itself did nothing more than destroy the country.

Arias took the basic model of the Contadora plan and in 1987 presented a new peace plan that was signed by the presidents of Guatemala, El Salvador, Honduras, and Nicaragua. This was known as the Esquipulas II Accords, named for the Guatemalan town where the accords were signed. ("Esquipulas I" referred to a summit meeting of Central American presidents the year before.) It called for cease-fires, amnesties for political prisoners, and free and fair elections. The Esquipulas II Accords would provide the necessary framework for a workable peace process.

The Reagan administration did not support any of those negotiations, as it insisted that only military action could counter the Communist surge. In 1983, the president created a commission to analyze the situation in Central America, chaired by former Secretary of State Kissinger. Not surprisingly, this U.S. National Bipartisan Commission on Central America issued a report the next year supporting the president's current plans of action. Although it acknowledged the dire need for economic assistance and alleviation of poverty and for protecting human rights, its main policy suggestion was to increase military aid. It did not specify how the former goals could be pursued with the latter solution.

U.S. National Bipartisan Commission on Central America (Kissinger Commission) (1984)

Perhaps the United States should have paid more attention to Central America sooner. Perhaps, over the years, we should have intervened less, or intervened more, or intervened differently. But all these are questions of what might have been. What confronts us now is a question of what might become. Whatever its roots in the past, the crisis in Central America exists urgently in the present, and its successful resolution is vital to the future. . . .

The international purposes of the United States in the late twentieth century are cooperation, not hegemony or domination; partnership, not confrontation; a decent life for all, not exploitation. Those objectives must achievable in this hemisphere if they can be realized anywhere. . . .

First, the commanding economic issue in all of Latin America is the impoverishment of its people. The nations of the hemisphere—not least those of Central America—advanced remarkably throughout the 1960's and 1970's. Growth was strong, though not nearly enough was done to close the gap between the rich and the poor, the product of longstanding economic, social and political structures. . . .

Second, the political challenge in the hemisphere centers on the legitimacy of government. Once again, this takes a particularly acute form in Central America. . . .

A comprehensive effort to promote democracy and prosperity among the Central American nations must have as its cornerstone accelerated "human development."

(Continued)

Widespread hunger and nutrition, illiteracy, poor educational and training opportunities, poor health conditions, and inadequate housing are unstable foundations on which to encourage the growth of viable democratic institutions. . . .

We ardently wish that there was no need for a security chapter in a report on Central America. But there is. . . . We have stressed before, and we repeat here: indigenous reform movements, even indigenous revolutions, are not themselves a security concern of the United States. History holds examples of genuine popular revolutions, springing wholly from native roots. In this hemisphere Mexico is a clear example. But during the past two decades we have faced a new phenomenon. The concerting of the power of the Soviet Union and Cuba to extend their presence and influence into vulnerable areas of the Western Hemisphere is a direct threat to U.S. security interests. This type of insurgency is present in Central America today.

Soviet policy in this hemisphere has followed the pattern of Soviet policy elsewhere in the world: Moscow has exploited opportunities for the expansion of Soviet influence. In the aftermath of the Cuban Missile Crisis, the Soviets concentrated on expanding their diplomatic, economic and cultural ties in Latin America and on strengthening the influence of local Communist parties in broad electoral fronts, trade unions and the universities. In this respect they differed from Castro, who continued to support a course of armed struggle in Venezuela, Colombia, Guatemala, and several other countries. But later the fall of Allende in Chile and the subsequent right wing takeovers in Uruguay, Argentina and Bolivia discredited the Soviet expectation of the "peaceful path" to communism in Latin America.

Beyond the issue of U.S. security interests in the Central American–Caribbean region, our credibility worldwide is engaged. The triumph of hostile forces in what the Soviet call the "strategic rear" of the United States would be read as a sign of U.S. impotence.

The commission has concluded that the security interests are importantly engaged in Central America; that these interests require a significantly larger program of military assistance, as well as greatly expanded support for economic growth and social reform; that there must be an end to the massive violation of human rights if security is to be achieved in Central America; and that external support for the insurgency must be neutralized for the same purpose. . . .

Source: The Report of the President's National Bipartisan Commission on Central America (New York: Macmillan, 1984): 2, 11, 12, 81, 100–101, 105–106, 111, 125.

The conclusions of the Kissinger Commission's report stood in contrast to the opinions of many Central Americans. Aside from the efforts of Oscar Arias, there was other opposition to a continuation of the military solution, especially from the religious community. Catholic priests spread the news of Contra-sponsored violence, which included murder, rape, and destruction of property. As one Spanish priest wrote, "The innocent blood of Christ's sisters and brothers cries out from the earth of Nicaragua."[16] Many Catholic clergy contradicted the more conservative Vatican view and became advocates for the lower classes, especially in El Salvador. The ideas of **liberation theology,** which exhorted Christians to fight against injustices and to become more active in politics, became very prominent. In El Salvador, the murder of Archbishop Romero underlined the tension between repressive governments and the clergy. Priests were often labeled as either subversives or Communist dupes as they worked to advance the cause of the poor.

Within the United States itself, there was also movement at the grassroots, especially through the religious communities of numerous denominations that protested U.S. policy toward Central America. The movement reached upwards of 100,000 people in the 1980s, and they were able to mobilize effectively because they tapped into existing church resources and infrastructure. As one analyst of the movement argues, "President Reagan's Central American policy so deeply violated the sense of right, of justice, of decency of so many U.S. citizens, that they believed they had no choice but to do whatever they could to defeat it."[17] These groups had an independent impact on congressional voting, and their lobbying efforts forced the Reagan administration to expend more political capital to maintain aid.

The Future of the Panama Canal

In addition to the civil wars in Central America, there was also the tangle of relations with Panama and the future of the canal. Although Carter bore the brunt of criticism for "losing" the canal, the idea of negotiating an end to the 1903 Panama Canal Treaty had, in fact, already been accepted during the more conservative Nixon administration. In 1974, the U.S. secretary of state and the Panamanian foreign minister had agreed to a set of principles that would recognize Panamanian sovereignty and jurisdiction, while the United States would continue to manage and protect the canal. Reagan (at the time governor of California) allied with other Republican conservatives such as North Carolina Senator Jesse Helms to denounce any such talks. In the 1976 presidential primaries, Reagan would repeat the line, "We bought it, we paid for it, it's ours and we're going to keep it."[18]

Panama's president, Gen. Omar Torrijos, was persistent. For him, the matter revolved around sovereignty or, more specifically, absence of the same. Nationalist and leftist, Torrijos used the canal issue to consolidate support at home and to pressure the United States. The specter of riots in Panama hovered over the Nixon and Ford administrations and prompted them to take Torrijos seriously. In 1973, when Panama had a temporary seat on the Security Council, Torrijos himself had worked at the United Nations to bring international attention to the canal, though the United States eventually vetoed the effort to force a U.S.–Panama meeting. Torrijos also threatened to expand Panama's relationship with Cuba. As a result, Panama, despite its dependence on the United States, forced the larger country to the negotiating table.

President Carter was sympathetic and set up a team to work with the Panamanians. By mid-1977, two separate treaty drafts were completed and signed. The first set December 31, 1999, as the last day of U.S. control over the canal,

with joint control of operations (and profits) in the meantime. The second stipulated that, even after 1999, the United States would have the right to "guarantee
the neutrality" of the canal, meaning use military force if any country tried to
seize it. Torrijos resisted the second treaty, but the agreement would not gain the
necessary two-thirds vote in the U.S. Senate without it. In March and April
1978, both treaties successfully passed the Senate by a vote of 68–32, and a generation later, the canal would be more firmly in Panamanian hands.

For Reagan, the treaties symbolized everything wrong with Democrats and
the Carter administration in terms of being soft in foreign affairs, but they were
signed, sealed, and delivered. In 1981, U.S.–Panamanian relations became even
more complicated when Torrijos was killed in a mysterious plane crash and his
former head of intelligence, Gen. Manuel Noriega, took over. Noriega was well
known to the United States as an ally in the fight against the Sandinista government in Nicaragua. The serious drawback was that the U.S. government had
known from the early 1970s that he trafficked in drugs, especially cocaine. As
long as the Contra war raged, it was easy to look the other way, but by the mid-
1980s President Reagan had announced a domestic "war on drugs," and the
Boland amendments meant that Noriega's services were no longer needed. Congressional attention—even by conservatives who approved of his participation
in the Contra war—turned to his drug trafficking. The consequences of that
shift would lead to invasion during the administration of George H. W. Bush.

The Reagan administration viewed Central America as a primary battleground of the Cold War, where every effort should be made to counter Soviet
and Cuban influence. As Reagan pointed out in a 1983 address before a joint
session of Congress, U.S. influence globally was at stake in Central America:

> If Central America were to fall, what would the consequences be for our position
> in Asia, Europe, and for alliances such as NATO? If the United States cannot
> respond to a threat near our own borders, why should Europeans or Asians
> believe that we're seriously concerned about threats to them? If the Soviets can
> assume that nothing short of an actual attack on the United States will provoke an
> American response, which ally, which friend will trust us then?[19]

The **domino effect** had thus taken on a new hue. Not only could Communism spread northward but also failure to take action would lead to consequences
with friend and foe alike.

A report issued jointly by the Departments of State and Defense in 1985
echoed the same sentiments but focused more directly on the Soviet desire to
take advantage of Central American political turmoil:

> The Soviet Union sees in the region an excellent and low-cost opportunity to
> preoccupy the United States—the "main adversary" of Soviet strategy—thus
> gaining greater global freedom of action for the USSR. . . . Working through its
> key proxy in the region, Cuba, the Soviet Union hopes to force the United
> States to divert attention and military resources to an area that has not been a
> serious security concern to the United States in the past.[20]

The Reagan administration used the domino theory as a rationale to invade the tiny Caribbean island of Grenada in 1983. Although not part of Latin America—given its British roots—the invasion's purpose was to counter Cuban influence. Operation Urgent Fury sought to overthrow a leftist government that was openly friendly with Fidel Castro, a relationship that deepened as the government came to see that U.S. invasion was a serious threat. One justification for the invasion was the construction of an air strip, which the U.S. claimed was being built to accommodate Soviet jets. The government responded that it was being built to accommodate large planes carrying tourists, and indeed it would later be used for that purpose. A second justifation was the perceived need to protect U.S. medical students there. The United States easily overthrew the government and thereby sent a clear signal to other small countries that might seek to ally themselves with Cuba.

The End of the Cold War and the Bush Administration

Reagan's vice president, George H. W. Bush, was elected easily in 1988, riding the wave of the president's popularity. The U.S. foreign policy toward Central America in the 1980s had been disastrous for that region and very divisive within the United States, and Bush came to office with the goal of resolving longstanding issues, especially with regard to guerrilla war and revolution. Because the Cold War was winding down, there was less of an ideological charge to his rhetoric and policy toward the region. From a realist perspective, the demise of the primary adversary suddenly meant that military force was no longer necessary.

Almost immediately, Bush sent his new Secretary of State James Baker to Congress to discuss ways to pull out of Central America. He told Speaker of the House Jim Wright, "We want to wind this thing down. . . . We are willing to substitute negotiations for military action."[21] This "winding down" was intended to be gradual, with nonmilitary aid to the Contras continuing. By providing such aid, the Bush administration felt it could appease hardliners within the Republican Party while pressuring the Sandinistas to keep up its side of the Esquipulas agreements.

In 1990, the Sandinistas agreed to free elections, and their candidate, Daniel Ortega, was voted out, a surprise for the FSLN, which believed it would win a majority. The winner was Violeta Chamorro, widow of a newspaper editor murdered by Somoza's forces twelve years earlier. The FSLN integrated itself into democratic politics, fielded candidates, and articulated its positions vis-à-vis the political opposition. Thus, by the early 1990s procedural democracy, whereby elections and not coups bring leaders to power, was appearing in Central America after decades of war.

The civil wars in El Salvador and Guatemala were also winding down, with all sides exhausted. Despite elections in El Salvador during the 1980s, the military trumped civilian power behind the scenes. In 1989, the FMLN guerrillas launched what would be their final offensive, and the government retaliated with a new wave of repression, even killing six Jesuit priests and two women on a university campus, which shocked even the most ardent anti-Communists in the U.S. government. The priests were well known to some members of Congress, which, combined with the disintegration of the Soviet Union, created new support for a negotiated solution, though the Bush administration was slow to pursue that option. Eventually, the U.S. Congress began to cut El Salvador's aid, and the United Nations sponsored peace talks. In December 1991, those discussions yielded an agreement whereby a formal cease-fire would go into effect in early 1992. As in Nicaragua, the FMLN positioned itself as a political party in the new democratic political system.

In Guatemala, the aftermath of Arbenz's overthrow had been political violence that by early 1960 became full-fledged civil war, with military-dominated governments supported by the United States fighting guerrillas. Facing serious economic problems, the military agreed to allow elections in 1984, which restored civilian rule. Democracy got a boost in 1993, when the president attempted to dissolve Congress and seize dictatorial power (in a so-called **autogolpe** or "self-coup"), but widespread opposition prompted the army to force his resignation. With the Cold War fading into the past, new peace talks were encouraged by the United States and even more vigorously by the United Nations and Mexico, and in 1996 a peace agreement was finally signed with the rebels, ending thirty-six years of horror. By official counts, the war had left 200,000 dead.

However, one Central American leader did not benefit from the resolution of Cold War hostilities. Ironically, despite his avowed interest in ratcheting down U.S. policy, President Bush did invade a Central American country, something President Reagan had never done (at least not with U.S. soldiers). The target was Panamanian dictator Manuel Noriega, who had outlived his usefulness to the United States. He had supported the Contra cause, but once his services were no longer required, he became a liability. His ties to drug trafficking were well known, as were his violations of human rights. In addition, candidate Bush had been dogged during the campaign by what came to be called the "wimp factor" in the U.S. press, and the use of force was perhaps one means of putting that image to rest.

Even late in the Reagan administration, the U.S. Department of Justice filed indictments against Noriega in federal courts that accused him of allowing Panama to be a transshipment area for drugs. That would be followed by calls to Noriega to resign, economic sanctions, and covert operations with his opposition to launch a coup.[22] Despite an attempted coup, all these efforts failed to force him out, thus pumping life into the "wimp factor." Drug trafficking constituted a threat to the United States, and protection of the Panama Canal was also important; although it was not as central to global trade as in the past, many U.S. policy makers preferred not to risk dealing with a hostile Panamanian president. In that sense, realist theory offers a useful guide to understanding the invasion. But the decision to intervene was also very much an intermestic issue based on Bush's desire to avoid looking weak domestically and concerns about the advancement of the "drug war." If, as the administration had claimed, this dictator was a drug smuggler, then why was the U.S. not taking immediate steps to deal with the problem? What finally precipitated invasion, however, was the time-honored justification of the protection of U.S. citizens. In December 1989, a jeep carrying U.S. soldiers was fired on, leaving one dead. That was the final straw, and Operation Just Cause was launched.

There was little resistance, and U.S. troops quickly secured the country. Noriega managed to escape to the papal grounds, where he hoped to be protected by the Vatican's neutrality. For nine days he was surrounded, while the U.S. soldiers used various means to convince Vatican officials to hand him over, which included not only diplomatic entreaties but also loud rock music in his direction (such as "I Fought the Law and the Law Won"). In January 1990, negotiations finally yielded Noriega, who was sent to Florida to face trial. Ultimately he was convicted and sentenced to forty years without possibility of parole in a federal prison. The invasion was deeply unpopular internationally, viewed as yet another example of unilateral and indiscriminate use of force.

Through the 1990s, Panama's economy grew at a steady pace, though entrenched poverty, income inequality, and unemployment remained unresolved. Free elections did become the norm, yet the trafficking of drugs—which was, after all, the stated justification for the invasion—soon resumed unabated or even increased, undeterred by the absence of Noriega himself. Conspiracy theorists had argued that the invasion was a way for the United States to reverse the canal treaties, but in 1999 they were put into effect as planned. The U.S. presence was scaled back dramatically, and although Panama had expanded sovereignty, its economy suffered as a result because the stream of dollars, both from the U.S. government and from U.S. citizens, dwindled.

Summary and Conclusion

The Cold War proved to be very hot in Latin America, and it dominated U.S.–Latin American relations. It was very destructive, and tens of thousands of Latin Americans died, often in almost unimaginably horrible ways, as the wars raged. Many were killed at the hands of their own security forces, which were intent on eradicating anything and anyone resembling "Communism," a nebulous term that could be used as a rallying cry to target even proponents of mild economic or political reform. For those dedicated to the cause of anti-Communism, the deaths were an inevitable and perhaps necessary part of achieving "victory." War involves casualties, the argument went, and paradoxically, the dictatorships supposedly protected democracy. Their proof was that by the 1990s every country except Cuba had experienced elections, and Communism was in utter disarray. They could proclaim "mission accomplished," just as Chilean General Pinochet did when he left power in 1990. When all was said and done, the forces of "good" had won.

The use of power for the stated goal of protecting the state loomed large in U.S. policy. Relations with Latin American countries were viewed largely in terms of security, which lent a convenient rationale to virtually any policy, covert or overt.

For opponents of the wars, there could be no justification for the damage they caused. Many of the dictatorships used Communism as an excuse to kill political enemies and left in their wake a legacy of fear and national psychological scarring. But in the face of the U.S. military strength, international actors were able only to blunt some of its worse effects, not eliminate them. Meanwhile, the living victims and the families of the dead were hurt beyond repair, while U.S. governments had looked the other way or even encouraged the violence. South American dictatorships had been egregious violators of human rights, but the worst damage was in Central America, where civil wars had not only killed hundreds of thousands but also left already weak economies in a state of collapse.

The end of the Cold War did convince many U.S. policy makers that negotiated settlements—especially in Central America—were finally palatable, but it did not mean an end to conflict in Latin America, as other issues jumped to the fore. Fidel Castro remained in power, the legacies of human rights violations remained highly salient, the drug trade was booming, the quest for markets and trade was stronger than ever, Latin American immigrants still streamed to the United States, and even later the attacks of September 11, 2001, raised the stakes of terrorism even higher. It is to these topics that this book now turns.

Research Questions

1. To what degree were Central American revolutions foreign-inspired versus home-grown?
2. To what degree was Cuba involved in promoting revolution in Latin America during the Cold War?
3. Compare and contrast different explanations for the rationale behind the 1989 invasion of Panama. Does realist theory offer the most useful lens to understand it?
4. Analyze the effects of U.S. intervention in a Latin American country. What effect did intervention have on democracy in that country?
5. Discuss the different groups that emerged in both the United States and Latin America to oppose U.S. policy. How well did they work together? How effective did their strategies appear to be?

Further Sources

Books

KORNBLUH, PETER. *The Pinochet File: A Declassified Dossier on Atrocity and Accountability* (New York: New Press, 2003). Based on newly declassified documents (many of which are reprinted after each chapter), the book is a riveting account of the U.S. role in promoting the 1973 coup in Chile and then supporting the military dictatorship of Augusto Pinochet.

LEOGRANDE, WILLIAM. *Our Own Backyard: The United States in Central America, 1977–1992* (Chapel Hill: University of North Carolina Press, 1998). A well-researched and lengthy account of the formation of U.S. policy toward Central America, written by an academic who also served on the staffs of the Democratic leadership in the Senate and House of Representatives in the mid-1980s.

MCSHERRY, J. PATRICE. *Predatory States: Operation Condor and Covert War in Latin America* (Lanham, Md.: Rowman and Littlefield, 2005). Based on archival research, declassified documents, and interviews, this book is a comprehensive examination of Operation Condor and how the U.S. government contributed to its development.

PASTOR, ROBERT. *Not Condemned to Repetition: The United States and Nicaragua, 2nd ed.* (Boulder, Colo.: Westview Press, 2002). An analysis of U.S.–Nicaraguan relations by a former senior policy maker in the Carter administration. It argues that the two countries have finally learned from the past to develop a positive relationship.

SCHOULTZ, LARS. *National Security and United States Policy toward Latin America* (Princeton, N.J.: Princeton University Press, 1987). A detailed analysis of U.S. policy makers' perceptions of the nature of national security threats in Latin America, based on archival research and nearly 300 interviews. In particular, it focuses on how those policy makers viewed the roots of instability in the region.

Web Sites

CNN Cold War Series, Episode 18: Backyard, 1954–1990. This Web site accompanies a CNN video series on the Cold War and focuses on Central America. It includes interviews with key figures, copies of Oliver North's emails, interactive multimedia and maps, and several CIA documents. http://www.cnn.com/SPECIALS/cold.war/episode/18/.

Frente Sandinista de Liberación Nacional. The official Web site of the FSLN. It contains many documents (including some dating prior to the revolution), press releases, official statements, photos, and other links. All of it, however, is in Spanish. http://www. fsln-nicaragua.com/index.htm.

Group of 77 at the United Nations. The official Web site of the Group of 77. The site contains documents such as key declarations (dating back to its creation in 1964), public statements, speeches, and other links that highlight its ongoing economic programs. http://www.g77.org/.

The Public Papers of President Ronald W. Reagan. The Reagan Presidential Library is located at the University of Texas, and its Web site contains a large number of speeches and papers from his administration. They are arranged chronologically, though a search engine is being installed. http://www.reagan.utexas.edu/.

Notes

1. Quoted in Kornbluh 2003, 79.
2. Kornbluh 2003, 82.
3. Haslam 2005, 68–69.
4. Kornbluh 2003, 94.
5. National Security Archive Web site.
6. McSherry 2005, 97.
7. Quoted in Beschloss 1997, 174.
8. Woodward 1999, 206.

9. Pastor 1987, 49.

10. Pastor 1987, 192.

11. Kirkpatrick 1979.

12. LaFeber 1984, 222.

13. Dominguez 1989, 176–77.

14. Quoted in Woodward 1999, 282.

15. Quoted in LeoGrande 1998, 508.

16. Quoted in Cabestrero 1985, 4.

17. Smith 1996, 168.

18. Quoted in Gilderhus 2000, 204.

19. Reagan 1989, 155.

20. Quoted in Bermann 1986, 283.

21. Quoted in LeoGrande 1998, 554.

22. Crandall 2006.

CURRENT ISSUES

CHAPTER **8**

Free Trade and Neoliberal Reform

TIMELINE	
1982	Mexico announces default; beginning of "debt crisis"
1985	Baker Plan announced
1989	Brady Plan announced
1994	NAFTA goes into effect
1994	First Summit of the Americas held in Miami
1995	MERCOSUR goes into effect
2001	Argentina announces default
2003	Chile joins NAFTA
2005	Hemispheric summit rejects the FTAA

After the U.S. Civil War, Latin American economies became increasingly tied to the United States. Latin American exports to the U.S. increased, as did the number of U.S. businesses looking southward for profit. Dollar diplomacy referred to the strong links between the foreign policy interests of the U.S. government and the interests of U.S. investors. Theodore Roosevelt's corollary to the Monroe Doctrine asserted that U.S. troops could be sent as a police force to take over Latin American finances when international debts required payment. Especially in the first third of the twentieth century, Central America and the Caribbean experienced various forms of occupation that involved U.S. control over finances. Despite President Franklin Roosevelt's era of the "good neighbor" in the 1930s and early 1940s, certain realities were settling in.

First, U.S. investment increased dramatically, with U.S. businesses operating many different types of industries, especially the primary products essential to Latin American economies, such as oil, copper, fruit, sugar, coffee, tin, and rubber. Second, as the twentieth century progressed, Latin American countries depended on U.S. markets for their exports. For dependency theorists, this was an era during which core-periphery relationships became firmly established. Third, when those countries took on debt, it was often through either the U.S. government or private banks in the United States.

Through a realist lens, power was manifesting itself in different ways. As in the past, the United States viewed Latin American economic stability in security terms. Instability bred revolt and invited foreign intervention, both of which were anathema to U.S. interests. However, the days of simply sending troops to deal with debt were ending, to be replaced over time by a new era of economic restructuring under the watchful eye of the United States and international monetary institutions. By the twenty-first century, Latin American policy makers would find few alternatives to the dominant neoliberal economic model being promoted by the United States. However, they did not remain docile in seeking such alternatives.

Crisis of the Import Substitution Industrialization Model

As discussed in Chapter 4, beginning in the mid-twentieth century, most Latin American countries experienced significant state intervention in the economy, pursuing some version of import substitution industrialization (ISI). The state played an integral role, joining businesses in joint ventures or in some cases creating fully state-run industries. These ventures were intended to respond to the failures of the free market, and in many cases state-owned enterprises were in fact formerly failed private investments.[1] High tariffs protected these industries from foreign competition.

By the early 1970s, however, the model was in crisis. The tariff walls had protected domestic enterprises but reduced the incentives to compete globally because the state would shield them from competition. That combination fostered inefficiencies. It also had no effect on poverty and income inequality; if any-thing, they became worse. The ISI model was aimed at increasing the internal consumption of domestic goods, but a large majority of the population of Latin American countries simply did not have the income to participate. In addition, the agricultural sector was neglected. Investment was shifted toward industry, sometimes to such a degree that countries became net food importers, relying on foreign trade to feed their populations.

Latin American governments were, of course, acutely aware of poverty. To address it, they increased social spending and also embarked on infrastructure projects. "Economic populism" refers to political leaders redistributing wealth to targeted populations with the ultimate goal of shoring up political support. Although such programs did provide much-needed services to the poor, the increase in government spending also fueled inflation because the largely uncontrolled influx of money into the economy had the effect of raising prices.

The Debt Crisis

Yet even more problematic was ISI's contribution to Latin American debt. Because the state continued to shore up failing businesses while also funding social programs, it borrowed to make up the shortfall, and the 1970s was a pro-pitious decade for borrowing. The key actor was the Organization of the Petro-leum Exporting Countries (OPEC), an eleven-member organization of oil exporters, one of which (Venezuela) is in Latin America. (Most are in the Middle East and North Africa.) OPEC had worked to raise oil prices, which brought enormous profits. Seeking investment opportunities for these profits, many OPEC countries put money into banks in the developed world—money that became known as **petrodollars.** In turn, these banks (including many large U.S. banks such as Bank of America) needed to find ways to pay back the interest. Lending to Latin American governments appeared to be the perfect solution. Those governments were seeking new loans to continue financing their large state projects, so it seemed an excellent match.

In the mid-1970s, interest rates were low in the United States, so the risk involved in borrowing appeared to be minimal. Beginning in 1978, however, the United States raised the interest rate to fight its own problem with inflation by encouraging U.S. citizens to save rather than spend or borrow. Latin American governments were thus faced with repaying interest at the same time that rev-enues from the ISI model were declining and they were paying very high prices for imported oil. State-led enterprises were not profitable, tax collection was uneven and rife with corruption, and social spending—and often military spending as well—continued to climb. The only way to finance the debt was by borrowing more. As long as the already debt-ridden Latin American countries could continue paying by incurring more debt, the system was safe. But it required the money to continue flowing unabated because national production was insufficient to get out of the debt trap.

As the Cold War wound down and most Latin American dictatorships handed power to civilians in the 1980s and 1990s, there was already a strong focus on free trade, buttressed by the United States and international organizations such as the International Monetary Fund and the World Bank. Proponents argued that strong links existed between free trade, prosperity, and democracy. Free market capitalism would promote investment, eliminate wasteful government spending, reduce corruption, increase transparency, and expand individual freedoms. Many Latin Americans, however, were skeptical. Was free trade the answer to the region's problems?

The Debt Crisis and Mexico

In the 1970s, Mexican presidents struggled to combat the simultaneous problems of debt, inflation, poverty, and the exhaustion of the ISI model. President Luis Echevarría (1970–1976) attempted to break away from ISI and open the economy more to foreign investment, but this merely made Mexico depend even more on multinational corporations and did not reduce debt. Only discovery of new oilfields served to postpone the crisis; oil was a commodity that international lenders were happy to finance.

As long as oil prices remained high, the situation remained stable, but in 1981 prices suddenly dropped. The United States and Great Britain had been exploring for new sources of oil, and finally had succeeded in creating a global surplus that prevented OPEC countries from maintaining high prices. At the same time, the United States was experiencing a recession, so U.S. consumers did not buy Latin American goods (or any other goods) as much. The flow of petrodollars slowed, and oil-producing countries could no longer rely on what had seemed like a perpetual source of income. **Capital flight**—an outflow of money from a country as investors try to jump off what they believe is a sinking ship—became rampant in Mexico. The revenue that for years had been constantly financing debt dried up, and in August 1982 the Mexican government announced that it was incapable of paying off $83 billion due that month. It was near bankruptcy.

Of course, the announcement spread like wildfire to international banks, which would also go bankrupt if Mexico did not pay. It was certainly not the first time Latin American countries had faced a debt crisis: the Roosevelt corollary to the Monroe Doctrine had been based on the proclivity of European countries to extract repayment by force in the nineteenth century, and the Great Depression had also been disastrous. One important difference, however, was that until the post–World War II period, most lenders to Latin America were governments, not private banks. The crisis of the 1980s threatened large-scale consequences, and diplomatic negotiations would not suffice.

The Reagan administration's reaction was to arrange for emergency loans, partly from the U.S. Treasury ($1.8 billion) and partly from the International Monetary Fund ($3.85 billion) that could keep the Mexican economy limping along. As part of the deal, the private banks were compelled to continue lending to a certain degree simply to keep Mexico afloat as the repayment schedule was established. The cost of receiving such assistance would eventually become high. In what would become known as **structural adjustment,** the Mexican government was required to make sweeping economic reforms. The term "adjustment" was an understatement, because it entailed cutting government expenditures (including social services), increasing prices for goods the government supplied, doing away with ISI by privatizing many industries in which the state was an investor, promoting an export industry, and inviting greater foreign investment. More fittingly, such austerity measures took on the popular name **shock therapy.** The more precise economic term is "stabilization."

These actions did bring down inflation and improved Mexico's balance of payments, but the overall effect was dismal. Poverty rates increased, because not only did the state cut jobs but also it raised the cost of getting essential goods and services. Throughout the economy, wages decreased while the cost of food rose. More people were unemployed or worked outside the official economy, and more Mexicans also looked to the United States for jobs. The economy stagnated, and periodic crises (such as a devastating earthquake in Mexico City in 1985 and another drop in oil prices the following year) fostered another cycle of borrowing and restructuring.

This scene would be played out in other Latin American countries because the bubble burst everywhere. As banks panicked over Mexico, their decreased willingness and ability to continue lending elsewhere brought the large Latin American economies to their knees, as Argentina, Brazil, Venezuela, and even smaller, more stable countries like Costa Rica and Uruguay also went before the United States and the IMF to work out repayment. Given that each country was on the brink of economic disaster, the leverage of international actors was high, which in turn prevented Latin American leaders from joining together in any type of debtor coalition or union. Separate negotiations tended to favor the banks and left each individual country with little leeway to refuse conditions.

The 1980s are commonly dubbed the **Lost Decade** in Latin America. Economic growth flatlined, the ranks of the poor grew, wages could not keep up with prices, government spending on many social programs evaporated, and domestic businesses went bankrupt. Not until the 1990s would most Latin American countries begin to enjoy renewed economic growth. Meanwhile, the power and influence of the IMF and the World Bank expanded. The IMF in particular would become a clearinghouse for new loans, so that if its demands were not met, Latin American governments could not even receive private loans. Feeling burned by the debt crisis, multinational banks were comfortable having the IMF place certain conditions before the loans would be approved.

The early 1980s reflected a period of "muddling through," as the United States made ad hoc decisions without any coordinated plan. That would change by the mid-1980s. For example, the World Bank's role became more prominent in 1985 as a result of the Baker Plan (named after U.S. Treasury Secretary James Baker), which focused on overseeing the process of moving to an export-led

Table 8.1 Total External Debt in Latin America, 1980–2004 ($ billions)

	1980	1985	1990	1995	2000	2004
Argentina	27.16	50.96	62.23	98.48	147.40	169.25
Bolivia	2.70	4.80	4.28	5.27	5.78	6.10
Brazil	71.53	103.61	119.96	160.52	243.43	222.03
Chile	12.1	20.38	19.23	22.04	37.29	44.06
Colombia	6.94	14.25	17.22	25.05	33.93	37.73
Costa Rica	2.74	4.40	3.76	3.80	4.46	5.70
Dominican Republic	2.00	3.50	4.37	4.45	4.54	6.96
Ecuador	6.00	8.70	12.11	13.99	13.72	16.87
El Salvador	0.91	1.85	2.15	2.61	4.53	7.25
Guatemala	1.18	2.68	2.85	3.28	3.85	5.53
Honduras	1.48	2.73	3.72	4.79	5.57	6.33
Mexico	57.38	96.87	104.44	165.38	150.31	138.69
Nicaragua	2.19	5.77	10.74	10.39	6.85	5.15
Panama	2.96	4.74	6.49	6.10	7.04	9.47
Paraguay	0.95	1.82	2.11	2.57	3.09	3.43
Peru	9.39	12.88	20.04	30.83	28.66	31.30
Uruguay	1.66	3.92	4.42	5.32	8.15	12.38
Venezuela	29.36	35.34	33.17	35.54	38.15	35.57

Source: USAID, Economy Statistics for Latin America and the Carribean http://qesdb.cdie.org/lac/index.html.

economic plan. The World Bank's emphasis was always on development, so it effectively teamed with the IMF to coordinate new projects that would be funded by private investors instead of the state in order to foster long-term "structural adjustments."

This was followed in 1989 by another shift in strategy by Treasury Secretary Nicholas Brady (the Brady Plan), who worked to provide greater options for debt relief, especially through **debt swapping,** enabling Latin American countries to exchange their existing loans for bonds carrying lower interest rates or face values. For Mexico, this reduced debt to U.S. banks by $48.5 billion and cut annual debt payments by $3 billion between 1989 and 1993, whereas under the Baker Plan Mexico's debt had been reduced only by $1.1 billion.[2] Deals worked out under the Brady Plan would continue into the twenty-first century.

The politics of debt also reveals the evolution of Latin American policy processes, particularly as legislatures begin wielding greater influence. El Salvador's constitution, for example, requires two thirds of the legislature to approve new loans. In 2007, the FMLN (which, as discussed in Chapter 6, was previously a guerrilla organization but became a formal political party) had enough votes to block loans the president had negotiated. The head of the country's prison system even resigned after the FMLN refused to vote for a $100 million World Bank loan to fund it.[3]

The Curious Case of Chile

Chile offers a different glimpse into the tension between the ISI model and free market capitalism. It is a critical case because its radical shift away from state-led development offers insights into the benefits and pitfalls of economic reform. After World War II, the Chilean economy was not unlike other Latin American countries. It depended heavily on a primary product—copper—while it attempted ISI, though U.S. firms dominated the copper industry. Also like other countries, it increased government spending, especially on public works projects, financed in part through foreign loans. By the time Salvador Allende was elected president in 1970, the ISI project was exhausted, burdened by debt and inefficiencies. The economy would subsequently be further rocked by U.S. efforts to destabilize it.

Chile is a curious case because of the decisions made by the military government that came to power after Allende was overthrown in 1973. The generals were certainly not economists, and for several years they presented no clear picture of their economic program. The turning point came in 1975, when influential civilian members of the government proposed a radical change. Because some had been educated in the Department of Economics at the University of Chicago, they were dubbed the **Chicago Boys.** Like their mentors, the Chicago Boys believed that free markets were the best way to foster economic development. It reached an almost messianic level: if the state retreated as much as possible from the economy, then prosperity would follow. They shared this vision with U.S. economists and policy makers alike, who applauded their efforts.

General (and soon to be self-proclaimed president) Augusto Pinochet only gradually came to embrace the free market model, which ran counter to the economic policies of previous decades. A year after the coup, the regime's economic policies were not working, and the Chicago Boys were placed in key governmental positions. By 1975, with the increased cost of oil, falling prices for copper, rising inflation and interest rates, and high unemployment, Pinochet agreed to a "shock treatment" for the economy.[4] This entailed deregulation, lower taxes, the removal of price controls, reduction of public employees, suspension of wage increases, privatization of many enterprises nationalized during Allende's presidency, the cutting of tariffs, and the slashing of government spending. The "shock" fell on the poor and even parts of the middle class, who saw their jobs and subsidies disappear. Inflation plummeted, and Chile's budget deficit dropped, but unemployment and poverty rose.

What makes the Chilean case even more curious is that free market reform occurred while Chile's main export—copper—remained in state hands. President Allende had nationalized U.S.-owned copper companies, which had played a role in those firms encouraging and even funding his overthrow. For nationalist reasons, as well as knowing a ready source of cash when it saw one, the military government, for all its orthodoxy, decided to keep it. The Chicago Boys did, however, diversify Chile's exports so that copper no longer represented such a vast share.

The Chilean model would become the blueprint for the **Washington Consensus,** which emerged at the end of the 1980s. In the view of U.S. policy makers, Latin America's economic failures were due in large part to the role of the state, which had been a central aspect of the ISI model. The best strategy, then, was to make permanent the current strategies for debt repayment. In other words, the rest of Latin America should follow the Chilean example by cutting the size of the state, opening up the country to foreign investment, and placing a high priority on exports. It was, in short, an update of classic liberal models, a "neoliberal" economic model paying homage to the economic theories of Adam Smith.

By the early 1990s, most U.S. policy makers agreed that a focus on private enterprise and reduced state presence was the best solution for Latin America. The Latin American reaction was decidedly mixed. There were certainly investors, businesses, and banks that benefited from neoliberal policies. Opponents tended to be unions, grassroots organizations, nationalists (who decried the power of the U.S. dollar), and activists of various stripes who lamented the policies' effects on the poor, women, indigenous groups, and others who found life under neoliberalism to be a daily struggle. All countries also found a similar dilemma when trying to copy some of Chile's policies, which was that Chile had undergone its economic restructuring during a dictatorship; protests were either suppressed or, in the rare moments when they were allowed to occur, were controlled and closely monitored.

The Rise of Free Trade

Reducing the role of state was not the only goal of the Washington Consensus. Part of economic reform would include free trade, meaning the dismantling of protections intended to favor domestic industry over foreign investment. The most visible obstacles to free trade are tariffs, the taxes imposed on foreign goods coming into a country, though there are many others, such as subsidies, whereby a government provides economic assistance to targeted industries. Advocates of economic liberalization argued that free trade would increase productivity (once exposed to foreign competitors, businesses would be forced to work more efficiently) and increase job growth. A rising tide could therefore raise all boats, as the average worker would find more opportunities.

Opponents of free trade used the same arguments that dependency theorists had offered after World War II. Because the global distribution of wealth had not changed, then the wealthier countries would benefit disproportionately from free trade. Latin American countries would suffer as foreign investors, no longer blocked by legal obstacles, would swoop in and take advantage of poor workers, who would have little or no recourse. Import substitution had aimed at building up domestic industries, and free trade would tear it all down because large multinational corporations would dominate the economy. Even if imperfect, ISI had provided certain protections, and free trade would erase them.

For the time being, however, these distress calls were largely ignored. The Cold War was ending, and many politicians and economists were proclaiming the victory of free market capitalism. Those who argued against it were dismissed as naysayers or socialist dinosaurs. Nonetheless, their voices were not drowned out entirely, as the case of NAFTA demonstrates.

The North American Free Trade Agreement was the brainchild of Mexican President Carlos Salinas (1988–1994), a U.S.-educated political leader who had come to the conclusion that there were no other options for economic recovery. Given the strength of the executive branch in PRI-dominated Mexico, where Congress was essentially a rubber stamp, he was able to push the proposal through the legislature. Building on an existing economic agreement between Canada and the United States, formal negotiations between the three countries began in 1991, and the agreement went into effect on January 1, 1994. NAFTA's essential aim was to reduce tariffs over time (with longer periods for more sensitive economic sectors) but it also would reduce restrictions on the sale of agricultural goods, strengthen intellectual property rights, establish rules of origin for goods, and eliminate restrictions on foreign investment. Although side agreements were signed to address the issues of labor and environmental protection, they were not included in the agreement's main text. Importantly, NAFTA did not allow for greater freedom of movement for labor, which would be governed exclusively by U.S. immigration law (which will be discussed in greater detail in Chapter 9).

During the 1992 U.S. presidential campaign, NAFTA was a high-profile issue. Ross Perot, a wealthy third-party candidate with no political experience, warned of a "giant sucking sound" that would be heard as jobs moved from the United States to Mexico, and this view was widely shared. If U.S. businesses could easily relocate to Mexico, where wages were much lower, then they would quickly take advantage of the opportunity. Evidence for this stance could be found in **maquiladoras,** the name for assembly plants set up by U.S. companies just over the border in northern Mexico (but also around the Caribbean, Central America, and in some cases even the northern part of South America). All companies needed to do was to assemble a product cheaply a few miles from the border, then quickly transport it back to the United States, where the low cost of production would yield higher profits.

While the U.S. public feared the departure of companies, many Latin Americans were concerned by their arrival. Large corporations threatened smaller businesses that could not compete. This worry was also tinged with nationalism, because those corporations would be based in the United States, with all net profits flowing back to the country of origin. Even if jobs were produced, how much would Mexico and Latin America benefit?

Opposition to NAFTA took on an even more militant hue with the Zapatista Army for National Liberation (known by its Spanish acronym, EZLN). Naming itself after the indigenous hero of the Mexican revolution, the EZLN appeared in Chiapas, the southern-most Mexican state, which had a large rural

North American Free Trade Agreement (1994)

PREAMBLE

The Government of Canada, the Government of the United Mexican States and the Government of the United States of America, resolved to:

STRENGTHEN the special bonds of friendship and cooperation among their nations;

CONTRIBUTE to the harmonious development and expansion of world trade and provide a catalyst to broader international cooperation;

CREATE an expanded and secure market for the goods and services produced in their territories;

REDUCE distortions to trade;

ESTABLISH clear and mutually advantageous rules governing their trade;

ENSURE a predictable commercial framework for business planning and investment;

BUILD on their respective rights and obligations under the General Agreement on Tariffs and Trade and other multilateral and bilateral instruments of cooperation;

ENHANCE the competitiveness of their firms in global markets;

FOSTER creativity and innovation, and promote trade in goods and services that are the subject of intellectual property rights;

CREATE new employment opportunities and improve working conditions and living standards in their respective territories;

UNDERTAKE each of the preceding in a manner consistent with environmental protection and conservation;

PRESERVE their flexibility to safeguard the public welfare;

PROMOTE sustainable development;

STRENGTHEN the development and enforcement of environmental laws and regulations; and

PROTECT, enhance and enforce basic workers' rights;

HAVE AGREED as follows:

Chapter I—Objectives

Article 102: Objectives

1. The objectives of this Agreement, as elaborated more specifically through its principles and rules, including national treatment, most-favored-nation treatment and transparency, are to:

   a) eliminate barriers to trade in, and facilitate the cross-border movement of, goods and services between the territories of the Parties;

b) promote conditions of fair competition in the free trade area;

c) increase substantially investment opportunities in the territories of the Parties;

d) provide adequate and effective protection and enforcement of intellectual property rights in each Party's territory;

e) create effective procedures for the implementation and application of this Agreement, for its joint administration and for the resolution of disputes; and

f) establish a framework for further trilateral, regional and multilateral cooperation to expand and enhance the benefits of this Agreement.

2. The Parties shall interpret and apply the provisions of this Agreement in the light of its objectives set out in paragraph 1 and in accordance with applicable rules of international law.

Source: OAS Web site http://www.sice.oas.org/trade/nafta/naftatce.asp.

---

indigenous population, was stiflingly poor, and had little to gain from NAFTA. An intellectual who wore a black ski mask and dubbed himself "Subcomandante Marcos" led this army, which in its first communiqué called for a fight against the Mexican government, which, like its predecessors, was composed of "the same ones that today take everything from us, absolutely everything." Its motto was "ya basta!" ("enough is enough!"). A day after NAFTA came into effect, Zapatista soldiers fought and took over five municipalities in Chiapas, while also proclaiming their message via computers and cell phones, which prevented the government from concealing the conflict. As Marcos would later write in the novel *The Uncomfortable Dead,* the Zapatistas were spurred on by "Fear of the long history of defeats. Fear of becoming resigned and getting used to those accounts where we're always on the minus and divide sides and never on the plus and multiply sides."[5]

The government would offer cease-fires and promises of reform, some of which would not be kept, but free trade marched on. The EZLN, however, was a vivid reminder that there were many losers as a result of these reforms. Many Latin Americans did not believe in either free trade or the neoliberal economic model, and many were willing to resort to violent measures if their concerns were ignored.

So has NAFTA been a "success" or a "failure"? The short answer is that it depends on where you look. The U.S. investors have benefited, given that U.S. direct investment in Mexico jumped from $1.3 billion in 1992 to $12.4 billion in 2005.[6] The number of Maquiladora operations rose from 2,114 in 1993 to 2,822 in 2006.[7] But some of that investment came at the expense of U.S. manufacturing jobs, because according to the U.S. Department of Labor, between 1993 and 2003 approximately 500,000 to 800,000 such jobs moved to Mexico. The increase in Mexican exports to the United States has also turned a previous U.S. trade surplus into a deficit.

First Declaration of the Laconda Jungle of the Zapatista Army of National Liberation (EZLN) (1993)

TO THE PEOPLE OF MEXICO: MEXICAN BROTHERS AND SISTERS

We are a product of 500 years of struggle: first against slavery, then during the War of Independence against Spain led by insurgents, then to avoid being absorbed by North American imperialism, then to promulgate our constitution and expel the French empire from our soil, and later the dictatorship of Porfirio Diaz denied us the just application of the Reform laws and the people rebelled and leaders like Villa and Zapata emerged, poor men just like us. We have been denied the most elemental preparation so they can use us as cannon fodder and pillage the wealth of our country. They don't care that we have nothing, absolutely nothing, not even a roof over our heads, no land, no work, no health care, no food nor education. Nor are we able to freely and democratically elect our political representatives, nor is there independence from foreigners, nor is there peace nor justice for ourselves and our children.

But today, we say ENOUGH IS ENOUGH. We are the inheritors of the true builders of our nation. The dispossessed, we are millions and we thereby call upon our brothers and sisters to join this struggle as the only path, so that we will not die of hunger due to the insatiable ambition of a 70 year dictatorship led by a clique of traitors that represent the most conservative and sell-out groups. They are the same ones that opposed Hidalgo and Morelos, the same ones that betrayed Vicente Guerrero, the same ones that sold half our country to the foreign invader, the same ones that imported a European prince to rule our country, the same ones that formed the "scientific" Porfirista dictatorship, the same ones that opposed the Petroleum Expropriation, the same ones that massacred the railroad workers in 1958 and the students in 1968, the same ones at today take everything from us, absolutely everything.

We also ask that international organizations and the International Red Cross watch over and regulate our battles, so that our efforts are carried out while still protecting our civilian population. We declare now and always that we are subject to the Geneva Accord, forming the EZLN as our fighting arm of our liberation struggle. We have the Mexican people on our side, we have the beloved tri-colored flag highly respected by our insurgent fighters. We use black and red in our uniform as our symbol of our working people on strike. Our flag carries the following letters, "EZLN," Zapatista Army of National Liberation, and we always carry our flag into combat.

Beforehand, we refuse any effort to disgrace our just cause by accusing us of being drug traffickers, drug guerrillas, thieves, or other names that might by used by our enemies. Our struggle follows the constitution which is held high by its call for justice and equality.

Therefore, according to this declaration of war, we give our military forces, the EZLN, the following orders:

First: Advance to the capital of the country, overcoming the Mexican federal army, protecting in our advance the civilian population and permitting the people in the liberated area the right to freely and democratically elect their own administrative authorities.

Second: Respect the lives of our prisoners and turn over all wounded to the International Red Cross.

Third: Initiate summary judgements against all soldiers of the Mexican federal army and the political police that have received training or have been paid by foreigners, accused of being traitors to our country, and against all those that have repressed and treated badly the civil population and robbed or stolen from or attempted crimes against the good of the people.

Fourth: Form new troops with all those Mexicans that show their interest in joining our struggle, including those that, being enemy soldiers, turn themselves in without having fought against us, and promise to take orders from the General Command of the Zapatista Army of National Liberation.

Fifth: We ask for the unconditional surrender of the enemy's headquarters before we begin any combat to avoid any loss of lives.

Sixth: Suspend the robbery of our natural resources in the areas controlled by the EZLN.

Source: EZLN Web site, http://www.ezln.org/documentos/1994/199312xx.en.htm.

We might therefore expect that many benefits accrued to Mexico, though again the results are mixed. The agreement certainly solidified the already strong ties of trade; by 2006, 86 percent of Mexican exports went to the United States, and 62 percent of its imports came from the United States. Yet although increased trade with the United States boosted wages in Mexico for more educated workers and those who live in areas with greater international investment (especially in the north), wages for less educated workers, especially in the more rural southern part of the country, have declined. Income inequalities have become worse in the years since NAFTA entered into force, and illegal immigrants keep surging across the border.

Critics have also pointed out that much of the burden of free trade falls on women in Latin America and that no trade negotiators study or even address the impact that such agreements have on women. For example, neither NAFTA nor

Table 8.2 U.S.-Mexico Trade after Ratification of NAFTA, 1994–2003 ($ billions)

	1994	1995	1996	1997	1998	1999	2000	2001	2002	2003
Mexican Exports to U.S.	49.49	61.71	74.29	85.83	94.71	109.71	135.93	131.43	134.62	138.06
U.S. Exports to Mexico	50.84	46.31	56.79	71.38	79.01	86.87	111.35	101.51	97.47	97.40

Source: Bureau of the Census, Foreign Trade Division.

the proposed Free Trade Area of the Americas (FTAA) provides protections for small farmers, and at least 30 million Latin American women are responsible for household farming activities.[8] As prices for crops fall, so will their incomes. The same is true for many women who operate small businesses while simultaneously doing most of the work in their own households.

Increasing numbers of women are taking jobs in maquiladoras, to the point that they are about 70 percent of the workforce. But in the absence of clauses intended specifically to protect women's rights, they consistently receive lower wages and suffer harassment and discrimination. Women's organizations, both in the United States and in Latin America, have protested against poor working conditions and oppose the FTAA, which they argue will institutionalize discrimination.

NAFTA did include a side accord to address labor issues such as nondiscrimination, safety, and collective bargaining. If a member government receives complaints, a trilateral commission can investigate and, through a lengthy process, eventually levy fines or even impose sanctions. Thus far, this hasn't occurred. For example, in 1997 Human Rights Watch reported that women applying for jobs in maquiladoras were being given pregnancy tests so that employers could avoid hiring anyone who might be eligible for maternity benefits.[9] The U.S. government acknowledged the charges were legitimate but chose only to ask the Mexican government to conduct public "outreach sessions" to discuss it, and the practice continues.

According to the U.S. Congressional Budget Office, the impact of NAFTA has been limited but positive; many of the economic effects would have occurred regardless of the agreement.[10] Indeed, one problem with analyzing NAFTA is disentangling the agreement's specific effects from what probably would have happened even in its absence. Certain conclusions, however, can still be drawn. First, NAFTA increased the amount of trade and investment between the United States and Mexico. Second, in each country significant regional differences emerged regarding precisely who benefited. Third, after 1994, income and wage disparities increased in both countries.

The Free Trade Area of the Americas and Latin American Reactions

Bill Clinton won the 1992 election and proved himself a champion of free trade, as he helped to begin laying the groundwork for an expansion of hemispheric trade. In 1990, President Bush had announced the "Enterprise for the Americas Initiative," which envisioned a large trading bloc. In 1994, President Clinton made the vision even more specific when he hosted the Summit of the Americas, a meeting of the heads of state of thirty-four countries (excluding, of course, Fidel Castro) intended to assure Latin America that its economic needs would not be forgotten. The centerpiece of the meeting was the announcement of a "Free Trade Area of the Americas" (FTAA, or ALCA in Spanish). Initially slated to go into effect by 2005, the FTAA's aim was to lower tariffs across the entire hemisphere.

Since its conception, the FTAA has faced stiff resistance both in the United States and in Latin America. Although President Clinton and his successor, George W. Bush, have often cited it as a positive development for the U.S. economy, no broad consensus has emerged. In fact, Latin American enthusiasm for neoliberal reform and free trade has continued to be mixed—from mild reactions, such as Costa Rican reticence to enact reforms that might endanger its relatively well-developed welfare policies, to more extreme, such as riots in Bolivia and the Dominican Republic, leaving many people dead or injured. Many in Latin America argue that the FTAA is simply a recurrence of a long-used U.S. policy of proclaiming Pan-Americanism as a way of advancing its own interests as it faces global challenges. In other words, as realist theory would posit, the United States wields power to achieve its strategic goals.

A hemispheric summit meeting in November 2005 left no doubt that the FTAA would not be implemented for the foreseeable future. Some (especially in Central America) were supportive, but others (like in Argentina and Brazil) believed that although free trade per se was acceptable, the U.S. version was not. There were also insistent calls for free trade to be shelved forever. This last view came most vehemently from Venezuelan President Hugo Chávez, who led a large rally in opposition, saying, "The FTAA is dead and we are going to bury it here."[11] Yet President Fox of Mexico countered that the dissenting countries weren't needed and that the agreement should move forward regardless. As of early 2007, the FTAA had yet to show signs of resuscitation, but its supporters continued to insist that it is the best way to boost economic development across the hemisphere.

Noah Friedman-Rudovsky/The New York Times

Photo 8.1 Hugo Chavez.

Free Trade Area of the Americas Eighth Ministerial Meeting, Ministerial Declaration (2003)

1. We, the Ministers Responsible for Trade in the Hemisphere, representing the 34 countries participating in the negotiations of the Free Trade Area of the Americas (FTAA) held our Eighth Ministerial Meeting in Miami, United States of America, on November 20–21, 2003, in order to provide guidance for the final phase of the FTAA negotiations.

2. We recognize the significant contribution that economic integration, including the FTAA, will make to the attainment of the objectives established in the Summit of the Americas process: strengthening democracy, creating prosperity and realizing human potential. We reiterate that the negotiation of the FTAA will continue to take into account the broad social and economic agenda contained in the Miami, Santiago and Quebec City Declarations and Plans of Action with a view to contributing to raising living standards, increasing employment, improving the working conditions of all people in the Americas, strengthening social dialogue and social protection, improving the levels of health and education and better protecting the environment. We reaffirm the need to respect and value cultural diversity as set forth in the 2001 Summit of the Americas Declaration and Plan of Action.

5. We, the Ministers, reaffirm our commitment to the successful conclusion of the FTAA negotiations by January 2005, with the ultimate goal of achieving an area of free trade and regional integration. The Ministers reaffirm their commitment to a comprehensive and balanced FTAA that will most effectively foster economic growth, the reduction of poverty, development, and integration through trade liberalization. Ministers also recognize the need for flexibility to take into account the needs and sensitivities of all FTAA partners.

6. We are mindful that negotiations must aim at a balanced agreement that addresses the issue of differences in the levels of development and size of economies of the hemisphere, through various provisions and mechanisms.

10. We instruct the Trade Negotiations Committee (TNC) to develop a common and balanced set of rights and obligations applicable to all countries. The negotiations on the common set of rights and obligations will include provisions in each of the following negotiating areas: market access; agriculture; services; investment; government procurement; intellectual property; competition policy; subsidies, antidumping, and countervailing duties; and dispute settlement. . . .

25. In regard to this enhanced participation of different sectors of civil society in the hemispheric initiative and increased and sustained two-way communication with civil society, we take particular note of the decision to hold meetings with civil society, in conjunction with the regular meetings of the SOC, focusing on issues that are topics of discussion in these negotiations. . . . We note that these meetings included a broad representation of FTAA government officials and civil society including business, labor, agricultural producers, NGOs, academics, rural and indigenous groups. Reports of the meetings from the

SOC, including the statements of civil society, were made available to the public on the official FTAA website. We are pleased that at least two such meetings are planned in 2004, one in the Dominican Republic on the topic of intellectual property rights and one in the United States on the topic of market access, including small business issues.

Source: Summit of the Americas Web site, http://www.summit-americas.org-Quebec-Trade/Trade/VIII%20Trade%20Ministerial%20Declaration-eng.pdf.

By the mid-1990s, investors had returned to Latin America, and the depression era of the 1980s seemed to have been overcome. In 1992, net transfers of capital showed Latin America receiving more than it paid out for the first time since 1981. But for many Latin Americans, the neoliberal model had done little to solve many of the region's most serious problems, such as debt and chronic unemployment. After implementation of the Brady Plan, total debt increased; regionwide, in 1990 Latin America was $434 billion in debt, which rose to $609 billion in 1995 and $733 billion in 2000, at which point it has mostly leveled off (e.g., it dropped slightly to $720 billion in 2005). In 2005, about 44 percent of Latin Americans lived in poverty (defined by the World Bank as less than $2 a day) a figure that represented no improvement for two decades. Although wages did rise, skilled labor benefited disproportionately, and people without such skills increasingly moved to the informal economy.

Rejection of the Washington Consensus: Cuba

In addition to the push for free trade, another high-profile issue was economic policy aimed at Cuba. For a brief time in the late 1980s, it appeared that a thaw with Cuba might be possible. Senior members of Congress (especially Democrats) went on fact-finding trips and made a variety of recommendations, such as engaging the younger functionaries of the Cuban government, writing drug trafficking treaties, and facilitating greater family contacts, all of which would put the United States in a good position when the Castro government eventually fell. These recommendations, however, were often based on the idea that without support from a Communist benefactor, Castro's days were numbered.

Indeed, Fidel Castro was in a real quandary, which only got worse in 1990 and 1991 as the Soviets ended shipments of subsidized oil, forced Cuba to sell its sugar at market prices, and removed troops from the island. For thirty years, Cuba had relied upon the Soviet Union and suddenly was adrift in a global economy with no sponsors. In the minds of many U.S. policy makers, there was no way Castro could manage to survive. Despite the calls to expand relations, the more ardent anti-Castro activists had won the ear of President George H. W. Bush, who could not ignore their political influence. Many members of Congress were also willing to listen to the argument that if the Castro regime was on its last legs, then the best plan would be to accelerate that process rather than to accommodate Fidel Castro. One step in that direction was TV Martí, which the Cuban American National Foundation (CANF), an influential and well-funded anti-Castro organization, lobbied successfully to create.

A number of U.S. policy makers viewed the situation as perfect for turning the economic screws even harder and perhaps finally forcing Fidel Castro to his knees. In particular, this meant denying Cuba access to hard currency. New Jersey Senator Robert Torricelli introduced a bill in 1992 that would become the Cuban Democracy Act (CDA). Over the years, U.S. companies had found ways around the embargo, such as creating subsidiaries in other countries that traded openly with Cuba, and the law was intended to shut off that trade by prohibiting subsidiaries from trading (by 1990, such trade reached over $500 million). In addition, it blocked any ship that had docked in Cuba from entering the United States for six months. The only "soft" part of the new law was to allow more nongovernmental contacts, such as cultural, academic, and scientific interaction. In late 1992, Torricelli said in a CNN interview that the Castro government would fall within weeks.[12]

President Bush was not enamored of the policy (and in fact had blocked efforts to introduce a similar bill in 1989) because it had the predictable effect of provoking complaints from European allies. However, when candidate Clinton began courting the Cuban American vote and announced his support for the bill, the president did an about face and said he was willing to sign it. At that time, it appeared to be political suicide to oppose such a large and vocal bloc of voters, who clearly had the sympathetic ear of Congress. Clinton even had his own reasons for opposing Castro: in 1980, while he was governor of Arkansas, Cuban refugees from the Mariel boatlift were sent to a military base in his state to be processed. The Cubans rioted, the local townspeople arrived with rifles and clubs, and Clinton blamed his loss in the 1980 gubernatorial election on that episode.

Foreign opposition to the CDA was immediately apparent. The Mexican government made a formal complaint and even issued a statement to U.S. subsidiaries that they should ignore the new law: "It is unacceptable for companies established in our country to try to place a higher value on foreign legislation in Mexican territory than national legislation."[13] In Latin America, opposition was also expressed by Argentina, Bolivia, Chile, Costa Rica, the Dominican Republic, Honduras, Uruguay, and Venezuela. The essential contention was that, aside from its effect on Cuba, the CDA was an infringement of sovereignty on countries that did not wish to become enmeshed in U.S. policy toward Cuba. Critics opposed the extension of U.S. law so far beyond its borders.

Nonetheless, when President Clinton took office, he made it clear that significant changes would not be forthcoming. For example, he dumped a nominee for the key Latin America post in the State Department (Assistant Secretary of State for Inter-American Affairs) when CANF stated its opposition, as well as its annoyance that it had not been consulted first. The administration had not interviewed potential candidates and therefore was unaware of the nominee's support for trading with Cuba.

In 1994, Republicans took both the Senate and the House of Representatives, which left the Clinton administration even less able to counter congressional initiatives. Emboldened by success, in 1995 Republican Congressman Dan Burton and Senator Jessie Helms sponsored the Cuban Liberty and Democratic Solidarity Act, which came to be popularly known as Helms-Burton. The bill had four separate sections, or "titles," all of them controversial. First, U.S. companies with property claims in Cuba could sue foreigners who "trafficked" in that property. Second, any foreign business executive who engaged in that "trafficking" would not be granted a visa to enter the United States. Third, any company buying sweeteners (such as sugar or molasses) from Cuba could not sell such products in the United States. Fourth, the United States would decrease its funding to the IMF and World Bank by the amount those institutions gave to Cuba. Fifth, the same would happen to Russia, especially given its operation of an intelligence facility in Cuba. Sixth, the U.S. president was authorized to draw up plans to send aid to Cuba once all reforms stipulated by U.S. law were implemented.

President Clinton opposed the bill, to the point that he and his advisors did rounds of talk shows and newspapers, arguing that Helms-Burton was unnecessary, given the already stringent elements of the CDA. The political pressure to sign it, however, proved too great, especially after the Cuban exile group Brothers to the Rescue had one of its planes shot down over Cuba by Mig-29 jets. Advocates of nonviolent opposition, the organization was attempting to drop leaflets, though the State Department had warned that Cuban retaliation to such activities was highly likely. In the highly charged atmosphere of the Helms-Burton debate, the deaths were framed as symbolizing the intolerance of the Cuban dictatorship. Politically unable to veto the legislation, the Clinton administration instead negotiated to include a waiver provision, whereby the president could impose a six-month waiver if the "national interest" was at stake. The retaliation against Russia could also be waived. Presidents Clinton and George W. Bush continued to utilize the waiver as a way to avoid economic and diplomatic conflict with European allies.

The European Union threatened to take the matter to the World Trade Organization, which has the authority to resolve trade disputes between member countries, but ultimately chose not to pursue the matter. The Clinton administration warned that the United States would resist any infringement on its Cuba policy, so pushing the issue could serve to destroy the WTO itself, which in 1996 was only a year old. President Clinton did promise to use the waiver provision and to "consult" Congress about removing the more controversial aspects of the law. Soon afterward, France signed a trade deal with Cuba, symbolizing Europe's disdain for U.S. policy.

The Helms-Burton law took control over the embargo out of the White House and made it law, not to be lifted until there were elections and democracy in a Cuba that did not include Fidel Castro. The president does have the waiver power, but control over Cuba policy had shifted significantly toward the legislature.

Nonetheless, pressures to ease the embargo have also been gaining steam since the 1990s. In addition to groups who believed that the embargo simply exacerbated Cuban poverty without achieving its stated objective, the voices of U.S. businesses joined in. In 1997, approximately 400 companies—including large and well-known examples like Proctor and Gamble, AT&T, Boeing, and Pepsico—came together to create USA Engage, a lobbying organization to open up trade and oppose unilateral trade sanctions, especially with Cuba. The U.S. Chamber of Commerce and a host of lobbyists for individual industries (especially in agriculture) also called for reform.

In 2002, a bipartisan group of thirty-four members of the U.S. House of Representatives formed the Cuba Working Group, with the goal of easing the embargo and allowing greater freedom of travel. Its membership would grow, averaging around fifty, and a Senate counterpart was launched in 2003 ten to fifteen senators. Members of the working group have proposed legislation, especially regarding travel, but have not yet succeeded in passing it. President Bush made clear that he would veto any such legislation, and in early 2003 his administration eliminated a category of people previously eligible to visit Cuba on educational exchanges. Restrictions extended even to sports, as in late 2005 the Treasury Department refused to allow the Cuban national team to participate in the World Baseball Classic competition in March 2006 (in 1999, the Cuban team had played—and defeated—the Baltimore Orioles, under a one-day waiver from the Clinton administration). Because one of the issues at stake was whether Cuba would receive any hard currency, Castro offered to donate any proceeds to victims of Hurricane Katrina (which hit the U.S. Gulf Coast in 2005), and the administration relented but also mentioned that it was concerned that the baseball games would "be used by the regime for espionage."[14]

States such as Illinois, Texas, Arkansas, Kentucky, and North Carolina sent trade missions to Cuba. They then pressured their representatives in Congress to enact new legislation. These members of Congress began to listen, especially because they had less to fear from the anti-Castro lobby, which was concentrated in only a few states. These efforts bore fruit, albeit meager. In 2000, for example, Congress approved limited sales of agricultural goods to Cuba, though it would not permit any financing in the United States (in other words, the transaction needed to be either in cash or financed by a third country). In this manner, Fidel Castro was able to make the first purchases of U.S. products in decades. Given the restrictions, however, more legislation would be required to facilitate large-scale transactions. One obstacle is that U.S. voters show little interest in Cuba, so easing the embargo does not translate into political support, whereas the potentially negative political effects are all too clear.

Rejection of the Washington Consensus: The Rise of Populism

There was also a reemergence of **populism** (often called "neopopulism"; the first wave of populism had taken place during the 1930s and 1940s), where newly elected presidents such as Venezuela's Hugo Chávez (a former coup plotter elected in 1998) blamed capitalism and the United States for his country's economic woes and income inequality. Chávez has even taken to referring to President Bush as "Mr. Danger." In the Brazilian presidential elections of 2002, Luiz Inacio Lula da Silva (known as "Lula") captured the imagination of the downtrodden, who felt victimized by free market reforms and excessive capitalism. In Ecuador, retired army colonel Lino Gutierrez came to power in 2000 with the aid of the military, which overthrew the sitting president, and he was vocal about protecting the country from neoliberal reforms. The foundation of his support was Ecuador's indigenous organizations, which then began to desert him, claiming he had failed to help the rural poor and was working too closely with the United States and the IMF. In 2006, Ecuador elected another populist, Rafael Correa, whose platform included unilateral restructuring of the country's debt.

Bolivian presidential candidate Evo Morales called for an end to U.S.-funded policies to eradicate coca, which he argued was harming the economic prospects

Noah Friedman-Rudovsky/The New York Times

Photo 8.2 Evo Morales.

for the country's indigenous population. His sudden surge in popularity in 2003 came at a time when Bolivian president Gonzalo Sánchez de Lozada was forced to resign on account of widespread and profound opposition to his neoliberal policies. These leaders were all tapping into a mine of deep popular discontent. Morales's election in late 2005 served to widen the economic policy gap between South American populists and the United States.

These movements reflect what Eduardo Galeano, a famous and incisive Uruguayan writer, wrote of Latin American political economy in the 1970s in his book *Open Veins of Latin America:*

> [T]he IMF, instead of attacking the causes of the production apparatus' insufficient supply, launches its cavalry against the consequences, crushing even further the feeble consumer power of the internal market: in these lands of hungry multitudes, the IMF lays the blame for inflation at the door of excessive demand. Its stabilization and development formulas have not only failed to stabilize or develop; they have tightened the external stranglehold on these countries, deepened the poverty of the dispossessed masses—bringing social tensions to the boiling point—and hastened economic and financial denationalization in the name of the sacred principles of free trade, free competition, and freedom of movement for capital.[15]

Galeano's account runs along the same lines as dependency theory. Core countries and the international institutions they control look to the developing world to ease their economic problems. Without concern for the socioeconomic consequences, they force economic reforms deemed more acceptable. Thus, underdevelopment becomes an inevitable outcome of global capitalism.

The U.S. government eyed these populist developments warily. Chávez, who was an open ally and friend of Fidel Castro, seemed especially suspect, to the point that the United States tacitly supported a coup attempt that sought to overthrow him in 2002. Because U.S. businesses and the U.S. government were some of its obvious targets, populism and popular antagonism were a source of concern. In 2002, chairman of the House International Relations Committee Henry Hyde warned that Lula was a "pro-Castro radical who for electoral purposes had posed as a moderate" and so Brazil might join Cuba and Venezuela as a "Latin axis of evil."[16] In 2006, after Morales was elected in Bolivia, Chávez would counter that Bolivia, Cuba, and Venezuela were the "axis of good."[17]

The opposition—or at least suspicion—to the United States can be viewed in realist terms. President Chávez has routinely raised the possibility of cutting oil exports to the United States and has invited investment from Iran and other adversaries of the United States as a way of creating as much political leverage as possible. Though whether such policy decisions are "evil" is open to interpretation, they are part of a political project intended to counter the hegemonic position of the United States in the context of an anarchic global political system.

Other Latin American leaders faced a difficult dilemma. They could follow the route of Chávez (and Castro before him) with fiery speeches denouncing the

United States, followed by an aggressively independent foreign policy (for example, President Chávez has worked closely with Castro to provide Cuba with oil and other necessities at subsidized prices, and referred to President Bush as the devil in a UN speech) and antineoliberal economic policies, thereby becoming an ideological enemy of the United States. Or these leaders could follow the path of Gutierrez and, to a lesser extent, Lula and attempt to work with the IMF and the United States, thereby potentially alienating their own domestic bases of support.

The Latin American reaction has not been limited to disorder or populist movements. Especially in South America, political leaders created new organizations intended to rival the economic dominance of the United States. The most prominent was the South American Common Market, or MERCOSUR, created in 1991 and composed of Argentina, Brazil, Paraguay, Uruguay, and Venezuela (which was admitted in 2006*). Bolivia and Chile became associate members in 1996, as did Peru in 2003 and Colombia and Ecuador 2004. Unlike NAFTA, MERCOSUR is also a customs union, meaning it establishes a common external tariff for all member countries. Given Chile's status as an economic exception, Chilean policy makers have resisted efforts to join any Latin American free trade group or common market and instead tried to maximize its bilateral agreements with the United States and Asia (for example, Chile joined NAFTA in 2004). The U.S. reached a bilateral free trade agreement with Peru in 2005 and Colombia in 2006 (both pending ratification) and continues similar talks with the governments of Ecuador and Uruguay.

MERCOSUR has enjoyed some success. Trade between the member countries grew fourfold between 1990 and 2000, though some of that increase may have occurred even without its existence. It has yet to become a full common market, mostly because the task of integration has been hampered by economic crises and lack of consensus. The onset of depression in Argentina in late 2001 left many wondering whether even the minimal amount of integration achieved could be sustained. Given real fears of "contagion effects," whereby crisis in one country could spread to the others, most fiscal and monetary controls have remained national.

The Argentine case illustrates some of the potential drawbacks to neoliberal reform. After suffering through the 1980s, in the 1990s under President Carlos Menem the country embarked on an ambitious plan to curb inflation and promote the stability of the Argentine peso. To achieve the latter, in 1991 the government decided to peg the peso to the U.S. dollar,[18] a decision that appeared to work very well. Argentina benefited from the dollar's stability and did not have to deal with the common problem of rapidly changing exchange rates, which can wreak havoc on trade. Cracks in the plan appeared in 1999, when Brazil devalued its currency. Suddenly, Argentina's exports to Brazil became more expensive. In addition, Argentina suffered a large budget deficit and a large amount of foreign debt, which were not alleviated by export or tax revenues.

* pending ratification

Within several years, Argentina's lack of control over its own monetary policy, such as the ability to devalue in response to shifting economic realities, brought disaster on the country, and it announced in December 2001 that it could not pay its debts. Tying itself to the U.S. dollar had ultimately achieved the opposite of what had been intended, and the growing lack of confidence led investors and citizens alike to start taking their money out of the country.

The Argentine government's response was to blame political corruption and mismanagement, but also inconsistencies in both the U.S. and IMF responses, which, some argued, did not infuse fresh capital into the country quickly enough to forestall some of the worst economic effects. The IMF, meanwhile, insisted that its recommendations had nothing to do with economic implosions in the developing world and that its main fault was to overestimate Argentina's growth potential while underestimating its ability to enact economic reforms. A senior IMF official joked, "There will always be a need for the IMF as a scapegoat of first resort![19] A 2003 study written for the Joint Economic Committee of the U.S. Congress placed the blame on Argentina and the IMF and concluded that the U.S. was concerned about protection of U.S. property rights in the country.[20] It is clear that many Latin American economies are suffering, and it is also evident that not only is finger-pointing common but also blame can be placed in numerous quarters.

Other organizations, like the Andean Pact, which includes Bolivia, Colombia, Ecuador, Peru and Venezuela, were also created with the goal of having a common market. The Andean Pact dates back to 1969, but received new attention after MERCOSUR came into being. It had largely failed in the past in that its original goal was to establish a common market by 1979. Another example is the Central American Common Market, created in 1960. The age-old dream of Central American unity has yet to become reality, and especially during the Cold War, agreements were difficult to reach. A combination of ideological hostility and economic frailty derailed the project, though renewed interests did emerge in the 1990s. All these emphases on regional organizations were intended to counter U.S. influence by denying U.S. access to them. They could provide collective leverage, a sort of economic safety in numbers.

In 2004, MERCOSUR and the Andean Pact signed a trade agreement, and subsequent meetings yielded the announcement of the South American Community of Nations, with the goal of regional integration. According to the Brazilian foreign minister, it would "strengthen the region in its trade negotiations with developed countries."[21] This is consistent with realist theory, as countries form coalitions to balance power.

One exception to U.S. exclusion is the Caribbean Basin Initiative, which included the United States, Costa Rica, Honduras, El Salvador, Guatemala, Panama, and the Caribbean (excluding Cuba) and dates to the Reagan era, when the United States hoped to unite Central America and the Caribbean against Nicaragua and Cuba. From the Latin American perspective, the economic impact has been minimal. The accord does not include sugar, and 80 percent of the countries' exports are covered in other economic agreements.

Political Economy in the Twenty-First Century

When President George W. Bush took office in 2001, free trade and market reforms had reached juggernaut status. Even the U.S. Congress, which had been deeply divided over the approval of NAFTA, had come to accept the notion that NAFTA should be expanded. To achieve that goal, President Bush requested and received fast-track authority to negotiate with Chile, which, given its recent economic history, appeared to be the best candidate for expansion of U.S. free trade agreements in Latin America. Fast-track authority refers to removing Congressional power to add amendments to agreements with other countries. President Clinton had acted with fast-track authority for NAFTA but subsequently had been unable to convince Congress to grant him that power again. One strategy the Bush administration utilized was to change the name "fast track," with its possible connotations of pulling a fast one on Congress, to "trade promotion authority." Once fast track/trade promotion authority had been established, the Bush Administration worked quickly to incorporate Chile into NAFTA.

Central American agreements were also pursued, such as the U.S.–Central America Free Trade Agreement (CAFTA). Negotiations began in January 2003, and the last country, Costa Rica, came aboard a year later. The U.S. government noted it would also seek to bring the Dominican Republic into CAFTA.[22] The U.S. Congress passed CAFTA in 2005 and the president signed it, although in early 2007 it had yet to come into effect: Central American countries had not yet come into compliance with all its requirements, and the Costa Rican government resisted final approval.

Though at times they have been less than successful, these various attempts at negotiating agreements reflect the undeniable fact that the United States and Latin America are tightly bound together economically. For example, by 2006, approximately half of U.S. trade was with the Western Hemisphere, and about 20 percent of that is with Latin America specifically. The U.S. consistently receives about half of Latin American exports. The U.S. also increasingly relies on Latin American countries for oil; nearly one third of U.S. oil is Latin American. Venezuela is the second largest exporter of oil to the United States (Canada is first; Mexico is fourth, behind Saudi Arabia). In addition, as discussed in Chapter 7, Mexico, Central America, and several Caribbean countries have come to rely heavily on remittances. The U.S. has even negotiated with Latin American countries and banks to reduce the costs associated with sending remittances.

These ties that bind are also evident in the amount of U.S. foreign direct investment (FDI) in Latin America. Although dips in FDI occur during periods of recession, in 2005 U.S. companies invested more in Latin America than any other country, reaching approximately $25 billion, which was almost 40 percent of total FDI in the region.[23] As part of economic liberalization programs, Latin American governments began selling off state-owned enterprises, and foreign investors were eager to buy them. Much of the increase of FDI in the 1990s was in public utilities, airlines, railways, steel companies, and other mining enterprises, all of which had historically been state-owned. In what sometimes seemed like a return to the past, governments would essentially bid to attract foreign investment. In the late 1990s, for example, the Intel Corporation announced it wished to open an assembly plant outside the United States. Costa Rica was successful in convincing the company to make its investment in its capital, San José. The main attraction was a Free Trade Zone, within which there were significant tax breaks, including no taxation on profits for the first eight years, then 50 percent exemption for four years after that. The government even responded to Intel's concerns about infrastructure by working on the airport and highways to make them more accessible. The efforts paid off, and in 2005 Intel announced it would open a new financial services center, which would add at least 100 additional jobs.

For Costa Rican policy makers, as well as those in many other countries, the effects of the investment made it worthwhile. It provided several thousand relatively well-paying jobs, but also raised the possibility of **backward linkages,** where Costa Rican investors could launch their own small businesses to link up with Intel. Evidence for significant backward linkages has not been easy to find, though it is indisputable that these types of foreign investments have created many new jobs. Nonetheless, working conditions in these jobs have come under scrutiny. Free trade agreements and rules of foreign investment do not necessarily provide safeguards for the workers themselves, who sometimes suffer from excessive working hours, low wages, and unsanitary conditions.

Another critical question with regard to attracting FDI goes back to some of the original concerns of dependency theorists: do these investments provide Latin American countries with a foundation for stable economic growth without the historical menace of foreign domination and control? Given the size of Intel's investment, it quickly became Costa Rica's single largest source of foreign currency. As the president of Costa Rica's Central Bank noted, "Fifty years ago we depended on coffee and bananas; today we depend on Intel."[24]

Summary and Conclusion

The 1980s was dubbed the "lost decade" in Latin America. A wave of economic implosions began in 1982, when Mexico announced it was unable to make its debt payment. All over the region, economies stagnated and millions of people suffered, as they lost their jobs and social programs were cut. The international response, spearheaded by the United States, the International Monetary Fund, and the World Bank, was to initiate market reforms that would end decades of state-led development. State spending was cut and state-run industries were privatized; tariffs were dismantled and free trade agreements constructed. The neoliberal era had been launched.

The reforms and trade agreements that accompanied this new era reflected continued U.S. hegemony but also the ways in which economic power was supplanting military power. Military force to collect debt or to force reforms was no longer the policy tool it had been in the past. However, the U.S. view that Latin American economic instability posed a security threat to the U.S. did remain. Given the tremendous economic imbalance and U.S. leverage, Latin American countries are finding fewer and fewer alternatives to the neoliberal model, given the intense pressure that is brought to bear internationally. Failure to adopt economic reforms can mean bankruptcy. The radical response has been the nascent emergence of leaders who challenge the status quo and resist international pressure to cut the role of the state in the economy. In line with realist ideas, Latin American leaders are also forming economic agreements to balance the power of the United States.

At the end of the twentieth century, Latin American economies were growing once again, but in many cases were just getting back to where they had been in the 1980s before the crash. Serious and chronic ills such as unemployment, debt, and poverty had not been stamped out by neoliberal reforms, and all too often they had actually worsened. Although the inefficiencies of import substitution industrialization had become apparent, the "Washington Consensus" seemed to offer only drastic change as a solution.

Many Latin Americans are feeling the economic pain and respond through protest and support for populist leaders who promise prosperity and freedom from international influences. This new brand of populism is gaining momentum and carries with it a strong suspicion of U.S. economic policies and international organizations. In terms of both U.S.–Latin American relations and political stability, an important question is whether neopopulism can balance the demands of its supporters while working successfully with the international actors it criticizes.

Free trade agreements also proliferated in the latter half of the twentieth century, most notably NAFTA, MERCOSUR, the Andean Pact, and the Central American Common Market. These efforts were capped by negotiations to create a hemispheric Free Trade Area of the Americas, originally set to become operational in 2005. Those negotiations, however, foundered, as many Latin American leaders questioned whether they would serve their nation's economic needs.

There is another issue integrally involved in Latin American political economy and U.S.–Latin American relations, namely, immigration. Although Mexico is the most prominent source of Latin American immigration to the United States, citizens of many countries have risked much, even their lives, to reach the United States in search of the jobs that were so scarce at home. Chapter 9 addresses the role of immigration in U.S.–Latin American relations.

Research Questions

1. United States policy makers and other proponents argue that in the long run neoliberal reforms will promote economic growth and reduce poverty. What is the rationale, and how well does it work in practice?
2. How have neoliberal policies affected democratization in Latin America?

3. What are the main pros and cons that Latin American leaders must weigh when deciding whether to join free trade agreements with the United States?
4. Have there been significant changes in the type of U.S. investment in the past fifty years? What has driven these changes?
5. Analyze the specific costs and gains associated with NAFTA. Who appears to benefit the most, and who appears not to have benefited?
6. To what degree do international organizations such as the IMF and the World Bank affect sovereignty in Latin America? Does this appear to support the arguments of dependency theorists?

Further Sources

Books

BULMER-THOMAS, VICTOR. *The Economic History of Latin America since Independence,* 2nd ed. (Cambridge: Cambridge University Press, 2003). A good historical overview of Latin American economics, beginning with the colonial legacies and concluding with the effects of market reforms in the 1990s.

CARDOSO, FERNANDO HENRIQUE, and ENZO FALETTO. *Dependency and Development in Latin America* (Berkeley: University of California Press, 1979). A translation of one of the most important works on dependency theory. One of the authors (Cardoso) later became president of Brazil and advocated the neoliberal model.

FRANKO, PATRICE. *The Puzzle of Latin American Economic Development,* 2nd ed. (Lanham, Md.: Rowman and Littlefield, 2003). An excellent and detailed introduction to Latin American political economy. It contains a clear discussion of historical background, contemporary issues, Web sites, and definitions of key terms in political economy.

GALEANO, EDUARDO. *Open Veins of Latin America: Five Centuries of the Pillage of a Continent* (New York: Monthly Review Press, 1997). As the title suggests, this is a highly critical view of foreign economic influence in Latin America, written by one of the more famous Latin American intellectuals. The book has been widely read in its original Spanish version.

PREVOST, GARY, and CARLOS OLIVA CAMPOS (Eds.). *Neoliberalism and Neopanamericanism: The View from Latin America* (New York: Palgrave Macmillan, 2002). This edited volume addresses both hemispheric and regional issues, primarily (though not exclusively) regarding political economy. It provides a good overview of Latin American perspectives.

Web Sites

Americas Program. A Web site run by the Interhemispheric Resource Center, an independent think tank critical of U.S. policy. Focusing especially on economic issues and trade, it is critical of current policies while also seeking to provide workable alternatives. The Web site has a large number of analyses, think pieces, policy briefs, and other publications, many of which center on NAFTA. http://www.americaspolicy.org.

Free Trade Area of the Americas Website. The site offers links to the structure and committees of the FTAA, discussion of key economic issues, and documents related to the negotiation of the agreement. http://www.ftaa-alca.org/alca_e.asp.

International Monetary Fund Website. The IMF Web site contains reports, analyses, press releases, and press briefings for countries all over the world, dating back to the early 1990s. An easy way to navigate the site is to choose a specific country, which is an option available on the homepage, which yields a list of reports in chronological order. http://www.imf.org.

MERCOSUR Website. The organization's own Web site—http://www.mercosur.org.uy/—has only Spanish and Portuguese as language options, but it includes all the relevant documents, meetings, accords, and agreements associated with MERCOSUR. However, another Web site linked to Mercusor is the *Mercosur Economic Research Network,* funded by a variety of national and international sources. It offers a wide range of working papers and briefs in English that address Mercosur's functions as well as its relationship to other countries and international organizations. http://www.redmercosur.org.uy/.

NAFTA Secretariat. The official Web site of the Secretariat, which is the dispute resolution center for the free trade agreement. It includes all of NAFTA's founding agreements, a discussion of disputes and their resolution, and even an option to receive email on pending cases and decisions. http://www.nafta-sec-alena.org/.

Notes

1. Franko 2003, 59.
2. Franko 2003, 101.
3. Arauz 2007.
4. Loveman 2001, 268.
5. Taibó and Marcos 2006, 63.
6. United States Department of State Web site 2006.
7. Comiti Fronterizo de Obreros Web site, http://www.cfomaquiladoras.org/dataprincipaljunio06.htm.
8. White 2001.
9. Wilkinson 2003.
10. United States Congressional Budget Office Web site 2003.
11. Ikeda 2005.
12. Azicri 2000, 189.
13. Quoted in Kaplowitz 1998, 154.
14. Curry 2006.
15. Galeano 1997, 221.
16. Forero 2003.
17. Marquez 2006.
18. Blustein 2005, 21–22.
19. Larsen 2003.
20. Schuler 2003.
21. Colitt 2004.
22. United States Trade Representative Web site.
23. Economic Commission for Latin America and the Carribean Web site 2006.
24. *The Economist* 2000.

CHAPTER 9

Latin American Immigration and U.S. Policy

	TIMELINE
1875	U.S. Congress passes first restrictive immigration laws
1891	Immigration and Naturalization Service (INS) created
1942	1964 Bracero program in place for Mexican farm workers
1986	IRCA passed
1994	California's Proposition 187 passed
1994	Operation Gatekeeper launched in California
1994	U.S. invades Haiti and repatriates refugees
1996	Illegal Immigration Reform and Immigrant Responsibility Act passed
2004	U.S. sends troops to Haiti to restore order and prevent refugee flow

Of all the issues surrounding U.S.–Latin American relations in the twenty-first century, perhaps none is as complex as immigration. Myriad laws, both state and federal, have been written since the 1980s as the influx of immigrants (both legal and illegal, sometimes called undocumented or unauthorized, referring to their lack of official documents granting them permission) has changed the face of U.S. society. By the 1980s, nearly 50 percent of all immigrants to the United States came from Latin America and the Caribbean, and by 2005 the number was 58 percent and rising.

From a theoretical standpoint, immigration is also complex. Although the United States has used power to advance its interests, the ways in which that power is wielded have varied. Control over the border—and illegal immigration—is commonly portrayed in security terms. Enforcement-oriented legislation passed in 2006 reflects that position. If we cannot establish dominion over the border, the argument goes, then all means of illegal activity—perhaps even terrorism—will ensue. Such a rationale is not limited to the United States, as illegal immigration is a high-profile topic in a number of Latin American countries, most notably Mexico. States therefore act according to their own interests as a way to block unwanted movement and activity at their borders.

At the same time, however, realism leaves a considerable theoretical gap with regard to immigration. In particular, we have to crack open the "black box" of the state to understand why certain decisions are made. It is an intermestic issue, as both Latin American and U.S. policy makers navigate the thicket of public opinion to determine the course of action. Dependency theory offers some guidance, because economic dependence plays a part. Weaker economies in Latin America cannot absorb their labor forces, and the dominant country selectively exploits a ready pool of low-paid workers. Yet dependency theory does not take the security component into account.

In the first half of the twentieth century, Latin America was a region of immigration, where people moved from one country to another and/or people came from other continents, mostly from Europe. For example, many Italians came to Argentina and Uruguay, Germans came to Argentina and Chile, and British came to Central America and parts of northern South America. There are numerous similar examples of Latin America being viewed as a place of potential opportunity. But by the 1960s, when many Latin American countries were suffering economic downturns, immigration turned to emigration, and many began making their way to the United States.

Immigration's Supply and Demand

To understand immigration's dynamics, we must view it from several different angles. First, what is the demand side? For example, for a number of different reasons, many U.S. businesses are eager to employ Latin American immigrants, sometimes to the point of actively recruiting them or arranging for their travel. Second, what is the supply side? Facing various pressures, usually economic in nature, many Latin Americans have run great risks to reach the United States. Finally, what have been the legal reactions, political ramifications, and policy prescriptions? The United States has passed numerous laws on the topic, and increasingly even Latin American governments are openly discussing it.

In addition, we need to distinguish between immigrants, refugees, and asylees. The term "immigrant" refers to people who make their way to the United States to seek employment, find a better life, or reunite with family members who made the trek in the past. A "legal" immigrant has obtained the necessary legal permits (called "visas") from the U.S. government to work, study, or join family. An "illegal" immigrant has either come across the border without any such permit or received a visa but subsequently stayed longer than it stipulated.

Refugees are fleeing political persecution, so their goal is more protection of their own lives rather than a job. If a person is outside the United States and seeking entrance to the country on the basis of persecution, he or she is a refugee, whereas a person already in the United States and seeking to stay by claiming persecution in the country of origin is called an asylee—a term used by the U.S. government to denote someone seeking asylum. In popular parlance, both are called refugees, but asylum seekers have recently become a very important part of the immigration picture in the United States. One serious policy challenge for the U.S. government has been defining "persecution" and establishing means to determine whether an individual faces sufficient threat in his or her home country to warrant allowing them to remain (or sending them back, in the case of asylees). That has proved to be a constant and sometimes acrimonious debate.

The dynamics of supply versus demand can become a deeply emotional issue. For Latin Americans, the United States can look like a beacon of opportunity, and jobs are plentiful, as U.S. companies even advertise their need for labor. Very often, men are the first to arrive, then send their earned money back home (called a **remittance**) and, in some cases, eventually try to bring their families to join them. For those unable to obtain visas, illegal immigration requires confronting the possibility of even death in the deserts and mountains of the southwestern United States to reach the "promised land." That struggle can mean months away from their spouses and children, along with constant fear of being discovered. If they are illegal, they can also easily be exploited by U.S. firms, who can avoid labor laws by telling workers they will be deported if they complain. Even if they are legal, workers do not necessarily know English well enough to understand contracts or know what their rights are under U.S. law. Furthermore, many immigrants are not well educated even in their own language, which increases the chances that they will be exploited.

The demand side is also a result of a confluence of demographic factors. Immigrants to the United States are more likely to be young adults than any other age and therefore represent an enticing pool of labor for U.S. companies.

Because the population of the United States (and other more developed countries) is increasingly older, there is a match between the demand for immigrant labor and its supply. Given the differences in fertility rates between the United States and Mexico, for example, supply and demand have been working in harmony, which means a continued influx of immigrants, both legal and illegal.

But for many U.S. citizens, the issue revolves around jobs. For them, Latin American (but especially Mexican) immigration means cheap labor—people who are willing to accept lower wages and fewer benefits. A willing U.S. worker may no longer have a chance in certain sectors—such as construction or agriculture—if companies choose to hire a foreign workforce that will accept longer hours, lower pay, and fewer benefits. These fears are greatly enhanced when U.S. unemployment rises, whether nationally or in specific U.S. states.

Unfortunately, in the United States the concerns over immigration also often take on a racist tinge. Terms such as "wetback" (referring to people who swam across the Rio Grande) came into popular usage by the post–World War II era. Although originally aimed primarily at Mexican immigrants, they became common terms for anyone of darker skin. Such terms do not differentiate between mestizos (those of mixed Spanish and indigenous lineage) and those of pure indigenous blood. To nervous U.S. citizens, they are often darker skinned and speak a different language, which makes them unknown and therefore potentially dangerous.

By the end of the twentieth century, the overtly racist and anti-Catholic rationale for restricting immigration was no longer considered acceptable, though they did not disappear. It is difficult to know how many people still hold such ideas without admitting it, but groups like the Minutemen, who coordinate their own patrols of the border, have become more mainstream and have even unsuccessfully fielded candidates for political office.

This chapter focuses mostly on Mexico, the Caribbean, and to a lesser degree, Central and South America. According to the 2000 census, 12.5 percent of the U.S. population is Hispanic, a term that the census uses interchangeably with "Latino." The former refers to someone either born in a Spanish-speaking country or with that heritage, including even U.S. citizens with origins in Spanish-speaking countries, thus leaving Brazilians, with their Portuguese heritage, in limbo. The latter tends to include Brazilians, though the label is not universally accepted. The Hispanic population has grown considerably, up from 6.4 percent in 1980 and 9 percent in 1990.

Of Hispanics in the United States, 58.5 percent are of Mexican origin. Other large groups are Puerto Ricans (9.6 percent), Cubans (3.5 percent), and Dominicans (2.2 percent). Central Americans are 4.8 percent and South Americans 3.8 percent. In the twenty-first century, even many Argentines—not traditionally a major immigrant group—have been moving to the United States in response to economic crisis; in Miami Beach, Florida, a small section has become known as "Little Buenos Aires."

Historical Background

Given the stronger economic growth and political stability in the United States than in most Latin American countries, the United States has always been a destination for Latin Americans who hope to provide better living and working conditions for themselves and their families. Until the period of the U.S. Civil War, immigration was unrestricted. Of course, until 1848 much of "the West" was still Mexican territory, but even for several decades afterward there was enough space and opportunity to allow Latin American immigrants relative freedom of movement. In fact, the U.S. government actively sought immigration to fill the needs of industry, which faced worker shortages.

Beginning in 1875, a series of measures in the U.S. Congress began a long process of immigrant restriction. That year, prostitutes and convicts were not allowed; then in 1882 the ban spread to anyone with mental illness, retardation, or "likely to become a public charge" and in 1885, those who would become contract laborers. In 1903 and 1907, the laws further encompassed epileptics, vagrants, polygamists, anyone with "radical" political beliefs or certain physical handicaps, and unaccompanied children. All of those conditions or categories were ill defined, which left much open to interpretation. Yet through the 1920s, when quotas were being placed on European immigrants, no such rules applied to Latin Americans.

The reason for this policy divergence centered on the question of whether an immigrant would seek to become a citizen. Europeans were likely to do so, but Mexicans were not, and Mexicans were much easier to deport. As a 1911 Senate report noted, "Because of their strong attachment to their native land . . . and the possibility of their residence here being discontinued, few become citizens of the United States. . . . In the case of a Mexican, he is less desirable as a citizen than as a laborer."[1]

As immigration laws became more restrictive, the power of U.S. government's immigration service increased to ensure that "less desirable" immigrants could not slip in undetected. First created in 1891, the new Immigration Service (soon to become the Immigration and Naturalization Service, or INS) took on the task of processing newly arriving immigrants.

During the Depression era of the 1930s, when unemployment in the United States hit 25 percent in 1933 and did not fall below 10 percent until 1941 (when the World War II–related industries sparked a revival), public reaction against immigrants was potent. Between 1931 and 1939, more than 400,000 Mexicans were "repatriated" to Mexico, sent home because they were deemed to be taking jobs from native-born citizens. The U.S. Border Patrol, created in 1924, became more active.

However, immigration policy closely mirrored economic prospects in the United States, because in 1942, only three years after the last repatriation, Mexican immigration was once again opened through the bracero (from the Spanish "brazo" or arm) program, which lasted until 1964. Because many U.S. workers had left to fight World War II, the government opened the borders to Mexicans seeking temporary work in agriculture. More than 4.5 million Mexican workers utilized the program, which continued after World War II because farmers claimed they could not find sufficient numbers of U.S. citizens to work in the fields. Demography also played a role in that the baby boom generation had not yet reached working age, and the rapidly growing economy required labor. Even though U.S. laws were supposed to protect the braceros from discrimination, in practice, abuses were not uncommon. The program eventually came to an end because of persistent complaints that braceros were displacing U.S. citizens.

There has always been a high correlation between U.S. public attitudes toward immigration and unemployment rates, though they can change quickly and are not always held strongly. For example, shifts in the U.S. economy and unemployment rate may change public perceptions relatively quickly.

For twenty years after the bracero program ended, the relationship between the U.S. government and illegal immigrants from Mexico was ambivalent. The INS was in charge of patrolling the border and enforcing immigration laws, but it was common knowledge that even deported illegal immigrants were likely to succeed eventually if they kept trying. This modus vivendi was accepted by the workers themselves, businesses that wished to employ them, and the U.S. public in general, which did not immediately clamor for crackdowns. Immigration reform in 1965 abolished the national quota system and replaced it with the same ceiling (20,000) for every country. Importantly, it also included provisions for family reunification, and the overall effect was to increase the number of people coming from Latin America.

Eventually, however, public opinion played a role in important legislation passed in 1986, after President Reagan had been vocal about illegal immigration for several years. In press conferences in late 1983, he made known his views, putting them in stark terms of "losing control." In October he said:

> I am going to try and get, and have been supportive of, some immigration legislation for a long time. This country has lost control of its own borders, and no country can sustain that kind of position. . . . I want to sign, as quickly as possible, immigration legislation. . . .[2]

Two months later, he made the point even more forcefully, as he faced opposition by the Democratic party in Congress:

> We have legislation . . . in the Congress right now, that we've been trying to get passed—and we've had trouble getting it passed—having to do with this entire problem and with immigrants and trying to close our borders, or control our borders. I should say, against those who are neither immigrants or refugees and who just come into the country and suddenly disappear into the whole population. But we have to a certain extent lost control of our borders. There are a great many illegal immigrants coming into our country, and we're trying with this legislation to restore it to legal immigration and at the same time keep the door open for those refugees.[3]

"This legislation" referred to Republican congressional efforts to pass a new illegal immigration bill. Only in 1986 did it finally come to fruition. The purpose of the Immigrant Reform and Control Act (IRCA) was to limit illegal immigration by penalizing employers who hired illegal immigrants, increasing funding to the border patrol, and also granting amnesty to many illegal workers already in the United States. An amnesty is a pardon, a freedom from prosecution, which in this case meant that anyone who had been in the United States illegally since January 1, 1982, could apply for legalization. Approximately 2.7 million immigrants were granted amnesty; three fourths of them were Mexican.

The amnesty portion of IRCA came as a result not of public pressure, but rather from U.S. industries that did not want to lose what had become a major part of their workforce, especially in agriculture. Indeed, there was even a provision for "special agricultural workers" who had arrived since May 1985 but worked steadily for at least three months.

The Reagan administration's intent was to curb illegal immigration, but statistics demonstrate that IRCA did not succeed in that regard. Not only did IRCA not deter illegal immigrants, but migrants who wish to reach the United States often do so. The border is too long (2,000 miles from San Ysidro, California, to Brownsville, Texas) and easy to cross, and the allure of jobs remains as strong as ever. Importantly, whether in the lettuce fields of California or the poultry-processing plants of North Carolina, countless U.S. employers are perfectly willing to hire them. No U.S. law has yet been able to stem the tide, and even periodic Border Patrol measures have been only sporadically successful. Furthermore, IRCA, by creating fairly lax enforcement rules, may have simply spawned a flourishing market in forged documents.

One prominent example of the new emphasis on enforcement was Operation Gatekeeper, begun in 1994 in the San Diego region. It involved not only more Border Patrol agents but also investment in fences, lighting (thus making night crossings more difficult), infrared technology for agents, ground sensors, helicopters, and computers. Similar efforts were launched in other western border states, with similarly dramatic names (such as Operation Safeguard in Arizona and Texas's Operation Hold the Line). Although the INS has insisted that the operation was successful, many doubt that claim. Given the consistently high levels of both supply and demand, immigrants continued to risk border crossings, sometimes further east where deterrence efforts were less evident and thus easier to avoid but also more dangerous. In addition, once in the United States they are more likely to stay than to risk a second crossing.[4]

In 1990, Congress created the U.S. Commission on Immigration Reform, which released a study in 1994, and its title ("Restoring Credibility") demonstrated the lack of consensus on immigration policy. The report noted that "reducing the employment magnet is the linchpin of a comprehensive strategy to reduce illegal immigration" but only rather helplessly remarked that current efforts were ineffective.

Photo 9.1 Crossing illegally into the United States.

U.S. Commission on Immigration Reform, "U.S. Immigration Policy: Restoring Credibility" (1994)

The U.S. Commission on Immigration Reform was created by Congress to assess U.S. immigration policy and make recommendations regarding its implementation and effects. Mandated in the Immigration Act of 1990 to submit an interim report in 1994 and a final report in 1997, the Commission has undertaken public hearings, fact-finding missions, and expert consultations to identify the major immigration-related issues facing the United States today.

This process has been a complex one. Distinguishing fact from fiction has been difficult, in some cases because of what has become a highly emotional debate on immigration. We have heard contradictory testimony, shaky statistics, and a great deal of honest confusion regarding the impacts of immigration. Nevertheless, we have tried throughout to engage in what we believe is a systematic, non-partisan effort to reach conclusions drawn from analysis of the best data available.

UNDERLYING PRINCIPLES

Certain basic principles underlie the Commission's work. The Commission decries hostility and discrimination against immigrants as antithetical to the traditions and interests of the country. At the same time, we disagree with those who would label efforts to control immigration as being inherently anti-immigrant. Rather, it is

(Continued)

both a right and a responsibility of a democratic society to manage immigration so that it serves the national interest.

CHALLENGES AHEAD

The Commission believes that legal immigration has strengthened and can continue to strengthen this country. While we will be reporting at a later date on the impacts of our legal immigration system, and while there may even be disagreements among us as to the total number of immigrants that can be absorbed into the United States or the categories that should be given priority for admission, the Commission members agree that immigration presents many opportunities for this nation. Immigrants can contribute to the building of the country. In most cases, they have been actively sought by family members or businesses in the U.S. The tradition of welcoming newcomers has become an important element of how we define ourselves as a nation.

The Commission is mindful of the problems that also emanate from immigration. In particular, we believe that unlawful immigration is unacceptable. Enforcement efforts have not been effective in deterring unlawful immigration. This failure to develop effective strategies to control unlawful immigration has blurred the public perception of the distinction between legal and illegal immigrants. . . .

In the long term, immigration policies for the 1990s and beyond should anticipate the challenges of the next century. These challenges will be substantially influenced by factors such as the restructuring of our own economy, the establishment of such new trade relationships as the North American Free Trade Agreement [NAFTA], and changing geopolitical relations. No less importantly, immigration policy must carefully take into account social concerns, demographic trends, and the impact of added population on the country's environment.

The Commission believes that significant progress has been made during the past several years in identifying and remedying some of the weaknesses in U.S. border management. Nevertheless, we believe that far more can and should be done to meet the twin goals of border management: preventing illegal entries while facilitating legal ones. . . .

Organized smuggling operations undermine the credibility of U.S. enforcement efforts and pose dangers to the smuggled aliens. . . .

The Commission believes that reducing the employment magnet is the linchpin of a comprehensive strategy to reduce illegal immigration. The ineffectiveness of employer sanctions, prevalence of fraudulent documents, and continued high numbers of unauthorized workers, combined with confusion for employers and reported discrimination against employees, have challenged the credibility of current worksite enforcement efforts. . . .

Difficulties in enforcing U.S. immigration laws have created fiscal impacts that would not have occurred had enforcement strategies been more effective. The ineffective enforcement has been due, in some measure, to a lack of political will on the part of decisionmakers, including officials and representatives of states now heavily affected by illegal immigration. Nevertheless, the federal government clearly bears a responsibility for alleviating these impacts, particularly through renewed efforts to reduce unlawful immigration. . . .

An effective procedure for prompt removal of aliens ordered deported is an essential part of a credible deterrence policy. If unlawful aliens believe that they can remain indefinitely once they are within our national borders, there will be increased incentives to try to enter or remain illegally. The Commission is reviewing the full range of issues raised by U.S. exclusion and deportation procedures and plans to issue a separate report on this subject in FY 1995. For the present, the Commission limits its specific recommendations to the removal of criminal aliens who represent the most serious threat to public safety and national security.

Since 1980, emergency circumstances in their home countries have prompted the migration of large numbers of people to the U.S. Their arrival, in turn, has created emergency circumstances within the United States. The exodus of Haitians and Cubans are only the most recent examples. An emergency can overwhelm resources and create massive problems that far outlast the emergency.

The Commission believes that a credible immigration policy requires the ability to respond effectively and humanely to immigration emergencies. Specific recommendations regarding emergencies will be the subject of a separate report in FY 1995 that will include discussion of contingency planning, interdiction, safe havens, refugee processing, asylum procedures, temporary protected status, aid to communities experiencing emergency arrivals of aliens, and other issues.

Source: http://www.utexas.edu/lbj/uscir/exesum94.html.

The next major legal attempt in the United States to address the issue of illegal immigration came in 1996 with the passage of the Illegal Immigration Reform and Immigration Responsibility Act (IIRIRA), which represented President Clinton's response to public criticism of his immigration policies. It entailed doubling the number of Border Patrol agents to 10,000 over a five-year span, building a fourteen-mile-long fence along the border, punishing immigrants who overstay their visas by not allowing them to reapply for three years, imposing harsher penalties for anyone who knowingly assists an illegal alien to falsify documents, and allowing the use of wiretaps to investigate abuses. The act also granted immigration officers greater latitude in expelling immigrants who arrive with falsified documents or no documents.

The act certainly tightened border security, but data continue to demonstrate that illegal border crossings remain at historic levels. Critics of the policy argue that immigrants' desire to cross has not waned and they have been compelled to find more remote and dangerous areas of the border, which has led to more deaths by dehydration, exposure, and hypothermia. Would-be immigrants are also paying **coyotes,** professional smugglers who employ dangerous strategies to get people across for a hefty fee. The irony is that the U.S. effort to slow down illegal immigration has led to more illegal activities in smuggling and documents.

The legislation angered a number of Latin American governments, especially in Central America, who were concerned that the bill would lead to the massive deportation of their citizens. Presidents as well as their foreign ministers repeatedly raised the issue to the Clinton administration because they were concerned about the political, economic, and social costs of an exodus back to their home countries. These entreaties were at least partially successful, and Congress provided certain exemptions for Guatemalan, Nicaraguan, Salvadoran, and Haitian immigrants already in the United States. Since the mid-1990s, Latin American embassies in the United States have been more assertively making their concerns about immigration policies known. Recent research has suggested that, over time, Latin American governments may have greater influence over U.S. policy through strategies such as encouraging U.S.-based nationals to naturalize and become more politically active, though this hypothesis remains largely untested.[5]

After September 11, 2001, the Bush administration reorganized immigration agencies by putting them under the auspices of the new Department of Homeland Security. The INS was folded into a new organization, the U.S. Citizenship and Immigration Services (USCIS). Although the functions remained the same (for example, the USCIS took over the duties of granting visas and permits), the changes reflected the new emphasis on immigration as a central element in national security.

The "Demand" Side of Immigration

Latin American immigrants come to the United States because the demand for them. Businesses in the United States have an insatiable thirst for a large pool of cheap, hardworking labor. This demand has even been labeled an addiction.[6] Although these immigrants have a profound impact on U.S. society, that is only an unintended consequence. Their main interest is economic and personal, either finding a job or joining a family member.

The U.S. government has a political incentive to assist U.S. businesses seeking better profits but also an incentive to keep that support as far away from the public eye as possible, given potential nationalist responses. Thus, "[t]hroughout the twentieth century the United States regularly encouraged or welcomed the entry of Mexican workers while publicly pretending not to do so."[7]

The demand side has made for odd bedfellows in U.S. politics. Supporters from both parties point to U.S. businesses that benefit from a constant flow of legal immigrants. Riding a wave of Republican victories in 1994, Speaker of the House Newt Gingrich argued, "I am very pro legal immigration. I think legal immigration has given America many of its most dynamic and creative citizens, and I think we would be a very, very self-destructive country if we sent negative signals on legal immigration."[8] This type of statement from a powerful Republican helped to scuttle bipartisan legislation introduced in 1993 to set an overall ceiling on the number of immigrants allowed to enter each year. One of its cosponsors, Seno Harry Reid, said that he only desired "realistic recognition that something must be done to reduce these escalating costs to ensure that our children and grandchildren do not inherit a country in which no one would want to live."[9] But Democratic President Bill Clinton agreed more with Republican Speaker Gingrich.

Meanwhile, conservative think tanks such as the Cato Institute joined forces with the liberal American Civil Liberties Union (ACLU) and the pro-Hispanic National Council of La Raza to fight congressional efforts to make cuts in legal immigration. These disparate groups came together for different reasons but with the same goal: allow legal immigrants to continue coming to the United States.

With regard to illegal immigration, strange combinations can also come together. Human rights and pro-immigrant activists address the abuses that illegal immigrants must suffer when traveling to and working in the United States, and many businesses rely on a flow of immigrants—even illegal—that they do not want to see disrupted. In some cases, businesses argue for amnesties, which can legalize their workers and eliminate the threat of raids.

Another effect of immigration has been Hispanic political clout. The 2000 presidential election was decided in Florida, where Cuban Americans are a potent political force. In California, Mexican Americans represent a group that no politician can ignore. A 2004 U.S. Census Bureau report projected that by 2030 the Hispanic population would reach 20.1 percent of the U.S. total and rise to 24.4 percent in 2050. As potential voters and also as elected officials, Hispanics have been exerting tremendous influence on U.S. politics.

The precise effects of that influence, however, are less clear. Just as "Latin America" encompasses immense complexity, so does "Hispanic," which refers to different countries of origin, different amounts of time spent in the United States, and different generations. As a result, any politician trying to court the Hispanic vote must take into account many different factors, including the fact that different groups may have different views on specific issues.

In 1976, five Hispanic members of Congress created the Congressional Hispanic Caucus (CHC), which by 2006 had twenty-one members. In 1978 they established a nonprofit organization, the Congressional Hispanic Caucus Institute, whose purpose was to create more linkages between the Hispanic population and the U.S. political system, as well as encourage greater educational opportunities for Hispanic youth.[10] The votes of the CHC demonstrate the breadth of Hispanic diversity. For example, when Congress voted in 2003 on the free trade agreement between Chile and the United States, only six of twenty CHC members were in favor. The year before, fifteen voted against granting trade preferences to the Andean countries of Bolivia, Colombia, Ecuador, and Peru. Although these legislators are deeply interested in Latin America, their voting preferences often revolve around their home district and reelection; if trade agreements are unpopular with their constituents, they vote against them.

As more Hispanic immigrants and their children gain the right to vote in the United States, it has become clear that neither the Republican nor Democratic parties have an obvious edge. For example, although the Republican party in California has been a voice for immigrant restriction, many recent Latin

American immigrants with strong Catholic backgrounds gravitate toward its conservative social message.

The political impact of Latin American immigrants is also felt in their country of origin. The 1994 presidential election in the Dominican Republic may well have been decided in New York City, where Dominicans represent the largest group of new immigrants. Although they had to return to the Dominican Republic to vote, political parties have been discussing the possibility of allowing absentee voting. In a similar vein, in 1998 the Mexican government granted voting rights in Mexico to those who had become naturalized citizens of the United States. This law serves to maintain close ties between Mexican immigrants and their homeland and gives Mexican politicians more incentive to address problems faced by immigrants and their families.

Mexican Immigration and U.S. Politics

In the past two decades, the debate in the United States has shifted from the number and status of immigrants (such as IRCA) to the political, economic, and cultural ramifications of immigration. The U.S. resentment against immigration surged at times, but the past policies of "repatriation" were gone. Sons and daughters of immigrants held important positions, even as members of Congress, and many advocate groups argued for more humane and less restrictive policies.

In the U.S. economy, immigrants—both legal and illegal—increasingly represent the backbone of the construction, agriculture, and service industries, which has led U.S. businesses to act as proponents of broader policies. Furthermore, so many immigrants have arrived over the years that they have contributed to cultural shifts. First in the border states of California, Arizona, New Mexico, and Texas, but in the 1990s also the Midwestern and Southern states, it has become common to hear Spanish being spoken, see Spanish-language advertising, hear new types of music, and taste new foods from restaurants and stores.

The U.S. fast food industry took note early on. In 1962, a man named Glen Bell in southern California opened the first Taco Bell, which paved the way for a billion-dollar market in Mexican-style fast food (altered, of course, to meet local tastes, such that the food is not the same as cuisine in Mexico). In short, Latin American immigration had become part of the mainstream, and in many parts of the United States, new hybrid cultures combined Latin American, U.S. and other cultural influences. Despite that, or in part perhaps because of it, strong opposition materialized against allowing more Hispanic immigrants. The cultural influence of Hispanics was widespread and obvious, which at times fostered greater understanding but could also spark nationalist sentiment intent on rolling it back.

California, with its large neighboring city Tijuana on the other side of the border and its economic success in the latter half of the twentieth century, was the main destination for Mexican immigration, so it is not surprising that it also became a main political battleground for immigration policy. The most prominent example was the passage of Proposition 187 in 1994, a ballot measure approved by 60 percent of the state's population. Stating that the people of California had "suffered and are suffering economic hardship caused by the presence of illegal aliens in this state," as well as "personal injury and damage caused by the criminal conduct of illegal aliens," its purpose was to deny illegal immigrants access to publicly funded programs.[11] Support for Prop 187 came from Californians who believed their tax dollars were paying for services received by people who did not pay into the system and were therefore "free riding" on health care, welfare, and education without ever contributing. They wanted to deny illegal immigrants such services, which would perhaps reduce the perception that immigrants could arrive to the United States and immediately become a drain on the state.

Immediately, opponents appealed Prop 187 to a U.S. District Court, which prevented it from being enforced, and in 1998 it was ruled unconstitutional, on the basis that immigration policy was a federal, not a state, prerogative. That ruling took the air out of similar efforts in other states (such as New Jersey). Had Prop 187 been upheld in California, it probably would have been copied elsewhere. But it had already shown the cleavages that existed not only in California but also across the country. The debate was often conflictive, defensive, and accusatory, with both sides viewing the other as having ill intentions. However, the widespread and rapid movement against the proposition also revealed that legal immigrants, especially those who were naturalized citizens, were becoming more politically active.

In 2000, Mexican President Vicente Fox came to office as a reformer, dedicated to working more closely with the United States to protect Mexican immigrants. During his campaign, he had pledged to work not only for Mexicans within his country's borders but also for Mexican immigrants living elsewhere. In his speech to Congress on his first day in office, he reiterated that commitment, saying that he "will not leave our dear migrants, our heroic migrants, on their own."

On the other side of the border, George W. Bush was sworn in January 2001. The two made public displays of mutual respect, including a statement in February 2001:

> [W]e agree that there should be an orderly framework for migration which ensures humane treatment, legal security, and dignified labor conditions. For this purpose, we are instructing our Governments to engage, at the earliest opportunity, in formal high-level negotiations aimed at achieving short and long-term agreements that will allow us to constructively address migration and labor issues between our two countries.[12]

With this exchange of friendly words (and large belt buckles), it appeared likely that immigration would become a high priority, but the events of September 11, 2001, abruptly changed everything. Hoping to head off any terrorist attempts to cross the often-porous border, the Bush administration increased security and

Vicente Fox Address to Mexican Congress (2000)

In the sphere of foreign policy, we reject any attempt at interference in our internal affairs, we condemn any intention to enforce an extra-territorial criterion in the application of laws of third parties.

We are opposed to unilateral views and to any treatment that infringes the highest rule of international law: sovereign equality under international law, sovereign equality among nations.

My administration will not leave our dear migrants, our heroic migrants, on their own, nor our companies in the face of abuses of authority or unfair international trade practices.

We will ensure that the talent we have throughout the world, in our Embassies and Consulates, becomes the best ally of their rights and a true lever of our country's economic development.

One of the things that hurts most is to see how every year hundreds of thousands of Mexicans, many of them well trained, have to emigrate to the United States and Canada—many, very many of them from Guanajuato, indeed; and from Chiapas, and Tabasco, Mexico City, Jalisco, Zacatecas, and Chihuahua and from the whole country to the United States and Canada—to find work and opportunities there which are denied to them in their own country.

To all of them I reiterate my commitment to safeguard their rights abroad and during their return to Mexico. Here we will do the essential, and we will work to ensure that they will soon find here the opportunities they went in search of, because Mexico needs them all.

Source: Mexican Government Web site http://www.presidencia.gob.mx/index.php?Art=5&Orden= Leer.

checkpoints, ensuring long waits and more difficult passage. For three years, there would be no constructive agreements.

The relationship soured considerably, made worse by Mexico's resistance to the U.S. decision to invade Iraq in 2003. In November 2003, Mexico's ambassador to the United Nations gave a speech in which he blasted the United States for wanting a "relationship of convenience and subordination"; "it sees us as a backyard."[13] Although Vicente Fox repudiated the remarks and fired the ambassador, the words seemed to epitomize the weakened relationship.

In 2004, Presidents Bush and Fox met at the former's ranch in Crawford, Texas, and announced that certain Mexican immigrants would be exempt from the new fingerprinting policy of the United States (whereby anyone from a long list of countries entering the United States must be fingerprinted and photographed to prove their identity). That built on a Bush administration proposal to provide temporary visas to illegal immigrants already in the United States, if there were no U.S. workers to fill the job, which had the same flavor as the bracero program decades earlier. The president provided no details of what was popularly known as a "guest worker" program and admitted it stood little chance in Congress. Given resistance in the House of Representatives, the only legislation to pass was authorization for 700 miles of fencing, which President Bush signed in 2006. As of early 2007, the House of Representatives had just shifted from a Republican to a Democratic majority, and the debate continued.

Both President Fox and President-elect Felipe Calderón vigorously denounced building a wall in the absence of more comprehensive immigration reform. Calderón's election marked the first application of the new Mexican law allowing citizens abroad to vote in presidential elections. It was the ninth Latin American country to have such a law.

Despite the president's relatively moderate proposal, the calls against continued immigration continued. For example, prominent political scientist Samuel Huntington argued, "The persistent inflow of Hispanic immigrants threatens to divide the United States into two peoples, two cultures, and two languages" because Hispanics were not assimilating into U.S. culture.[14] Indeed, he argued, if Mexican immigration were to stop, then U.S. wages for low-income workers would rise, debate over the use of Spanish and controversy over bilingual education would end, debate over immigrant use of government resources would conclude, and the average skills and education of the average immigrant would increase.

A 1997 report by the U.S. Commission on Immigration Reform tended not to agree with Huntington's arguments. Instead, it simply stated, "It is difficult to establish a balanced evaluation of migration's impacts because of the lack of data and the need for focused research in both countries." Differences in the type of immigrant, legal status, regional variation, gender, and other factors make generalizations difficult to sustain.

U.S. Commission on Immigration Reform, Mexico-U.S. Binational Migration Study Report (1997)

Characteristics vary by migrant type. We are able to approximate the characteristics of three "types" of migrants using combinations of several databases: *sojourner migrant* (legal or unauthorized whose principal residence is in Mexico); *settled resident* (legal or unauthorized who habitually reside in the U.S.); and *naturalized U.S. citizen* (who have met five-year legal residence and other requirements).

The characteristics of Mexican migrants reflect their "type," gender, the historical patterns of U.S. recruitment for Mexican labor, and the job market in which Mexicans continue to find work. For example, some 73 to 94 percent of sojourners are young men and more than one-half work in agriculture. About 55 percent of settlers are slightly older males, and about 13 percent work in agriculture. Women, who are a

(Continued)

smaller proportion of employed migrants, tend to work in the service economy. Naturalized citizens are long-term residents and only 54 percent are males in their early forties on average and less than 10 percent work in agriculture. A greater proportion of sojourners and settlers are employed in certain sectors of construction, manufacturing, and services than are U.S. natives or naturalized Mexican-born citizens.

Clearly, the primary motive for the migrant stream is economic; however, that does not mean Mexican migrants necessarily lack jobs in Mexico. Most migrants had some kind of work in Mexico prior to migrating. Border crossing data with large numbers of unauthorized migrants find that most had work prior to leaving. Nevertheless, the majority migrated with the intention of working in the U.S., mainly to obtain higher wages.

Mexican-born migrants tend to have low skill levels, relative both to the U.S. population at large and to other migrant groups. The sectors employing Mexican-born migrants tend to seek lower-skilled workers. They also pay low wages, accounting for the low incomes and high poverty rates of Mexican-born settlers in the United States. This situation is exacerbated by the unauthorized status of many of these migrants. Less than one-tenth of sojourners complete high school, but just over one-quarter of the settlers and well over one-third of new legal immigrants and naturalized citizens do.

Despite much continuity in origins and characteristics, migration shows increased diversity over time. Traditionally, migrants have been rural males from a subset of communities in the west central states of Jalisco, Michoacán, and Guanajuato. The new diversity shows up in changing demography, origins and destinations, and labor force characteristics. Today, Mexican migrants appear to be older, have more education, more are women, and more are coming from "new sending" states and urban areas. In the United States, Mexican migrants are highly concentrated in California, Texas, and Illinois: about 85 percent of all Mexican-born immigrants resided in these three states compared to 45 percent of all immigrants to the U.S. in 1990. At the same time, Mexican-born migrants have become attracted to new geographic destinations. Midwestern, southern and eastern states that have had few Mexican-born workers now are destinations for Mexican-born persons employed in agriculture and food processing, construction, manufacturing, and low-skill service occupations.

Migration has varied effects, producing both benefits and costs. It is difficult to establish a balanced evaluation of migration's impacts because of the lack of data and the need for focused research in both countries. We caution against overly simplistic conclusions about costs and benefits and note that the perspectives on the balance differ in each country. In Mexico, those who return most often are the sojourners, many of whom benefit from their U.S. experience. In the U.S., the settler population—often older and sometimes unauthorized, but increasingly with legal status—has relatively low skills that place it at a disadvantage relative to other U.S. residents in an "information age" economy. At the national level, economic impacts are diffuse in both Mexico and the United States. However, strong impacts are found at local and regional levels.

Violence and human rights abuses of unauthorized migrants are major sources of concern. Unauthorized migrants are sometimes victims of crimes—from attacks and abandonment by smugglers to theft, rape, and even murder—and suffer the physical consequences of difficult border crossings. Human rights abuses by federal, state, and local officials have been recorded, which is a matter of great concern for both countries. Officials in both countries have been attacked by smugglers as well. Both governments have taken action to curb these various abuses but border violence continues to be a source of tension.

There must be a careful approach to migration problems that is sensitive to differences in perspectives and build on the joint Mexican-United States commitment to foster human rights.

Source: http://www.utexas.edu/lbj/uscir/binational.html.

Immigration from Mexico is still an important and even emotional public policy issue. For Huntington and many others, the overall effect of that immigration has been pernicious, eroding the economic, social, and cultural foundations of the United States itself. There is no disputing the increases in the U.S. Hispanic population, but whether it can somehow be labeled as "good" or "bad" continues to touch deep nerves.

Increasingly, policy makers have been compelled to address the problems immigrant workers face, which at the extreme can lead to death. Immigrants—especially those in the country illegally—often take dangerous jobs that native workers do not want, and their U.S. employers take fewer steps to ensure their safety. One study found that by 2004, Mexican workers were 80 percent more likely to die in the workplace than native workers[15] and nearly twice as likely to die at work as any other immigrant group; most of those deaths occurred in the construction industry.

Illegal immigrants are highly unlikely to complain about working conditions for fear of being deported, but even legal immigrants avoid complaining because their jobs can pay many times what jobs at home (such as Mexico) pay. Also, immigrants are often not aware of their legal rights.

Nongovernmental organizations (NGOs) have emerged to provide assistance to immigrants and a forum to discuss abuses of their civil liberties, as well as promoting policies that would continue the flow of immigrants to the United States. Groups like the National Council for La Raza work to educate immigrants, residents, and naturalized citizens, as well as native-born U.S. citizens, about the state of immigration policies and protection of immigrants making their way into the United States.

The Plight of Refugees

Although immigrants, especially Mexican, often dominate the discussion, the dilemma of how to deal with refugees also flares up periodically. The most politically sensitive are Cuban, who are granted the broadest rights of any refugees.

Any Cuban able to reach land in the United States is allowed to stay, which is a right not granted to citizens of any other Latin American country.

According to the Refugee Act of 1980, a refugee is defined as "a person outside his or her country of nationality who is unable or unwilling to return because of persecution or a well-founded fear of persecution on account of race, religion, nationality, membership in a particular social group, or political opinion."[16] Because the term "well-founded" is left undefined, the law allows government officials very wide latitude in deciding who will granted refugee status. Very often, those decisions reflected political concerns: refugees from "enemy" countries, especially Cuba and Nicaragua, received open arms, but citizens of "friendly" countries, even harsh dictatorships, did not.

Ever since the revolution pushed many people out of Cuba, the U.S. government has granted Cuban immigrants a different status than anyone else. Fidel Castro has always been well aware of U.S. policies and has periodically used them for his own political advantage.

Until the 1980s, Cubans constituted by far the largest group of political refugees from Latin America. More than a million came to the United States between 1959 and the late 1980s; eventually 10 percent of the Cuban population came to reside in the United States. In the 1960s, many of the immigrants were wealthier and often tied to the Batista regime in some manner, and they were welcomed with open arms. Between 1961 and 1971, the U.S. Department of Health, Education, and Welfare paid out $730 million in subsidies to help recent immigrants; in 1960 to 1962, more than 14,000 unaccompanied children were sent to the United States in Operation "Pedro Pan" because their parents were unable to obtain visas for themselves. After negotiations with the United States in 1965, Castro opened the country's doors to allow people to leave if they wished, and the U.S. government paid for an airlift that lasted from 1965 until 1973.

The key legislation in the United States was the 1966 Cuban Adjustment Act, which made it easier for Cubans to declare themselves refugees and become permanent residents. As a consequence, Cubans enjoyed a status not conferred on citizens of any other Latin American country because the immigrant has essentially no burden of proof to demonstrate that he or she is fleeing persecution. In practice, the mere fact of coming from Cuba constitutes sufficient proof.

But by the late 1970s, the wealthier Cubans had already emigrated and the less educated (and often darker skinned) Cubans replaced them. Not coincidentally, over time the attitude of U.S. policy makers also became more ambivalent. In April 1980, thousands of Cubans stormed the Peruvian embassy in Havana in search of asylum. Responding to this pressure, Fidel Castro announced he would open the Port of Mariel to anyone who wanted to pick up Cuban relatives and take them back to the United States. President Jimmy Carter then declared that the United States would "provide an open heart and open arms for the tens of thousands of refugees seeking freedom from Communist domination."[17]

The response was a massive exodus, with 125,000 Cubans fleeing in anything that would float. Castro let them all leave, saying good riddance to such "counterrevolutionaries," and for good measure, he also released a number of convicted criminals from jail to join in. The United States was overwhelmed, and Castro had successfully maneuvered to embarrass the United States while also purging his country.

In 1965 and 1980, Fidel Castro allowed relatively open emigration to take place, which sent floods of Cubans to the United States. In both cases, the U.S. government had little choice but to accept them. In 1994, Castro once again opened Cuba's doors, but the U.S. reaction was different, as the Coast Guard picked up anyone found at sea and sent them to the naval base at Guantánamo Bay. The Clinton administration negotiated with Castro and reached an agreement whereby Cuba would deter illegal immigration and the United States would not accept any rafter found at sea but would accept a minimum of 20,000 immigrants a year, the number that had previously been announced as the maximum. In 1995, the detainees at Guantánamo were allowed to enter the United States, but only after Castro agreed that in the future he would not prosecute anyone returned to Cuba after being picked up by the U.S. Coast Guard.

The overall result has been dubbed the "wet feet, dry feet" policy, which has continued under the administration of George W. Bush. Unlike other groups (such as Haitians), Cubans who reach the mainland United States are permitted to remain, and those picked up at sea are not. One unfortunate result has been an increase in smuggling, and 5 percent of smuggled Cubans are estimated to die in the attempt.

Especially during the 1980s, questions arose about whether to accept people fleeing Central American instability, whether the government was Marxist (Nicaragua) or anti-Communist military (particularly El Salvador but also Guatemala and Honduras). Nicaragua and El Salvador were prickly cases because the United States was deeply involved in their civil wars, which were spurring on the refugee movements. But because the Salvadoran government was anti-Communist and therefore an ally, the U.S. government accepted almost no Salvadoran claims of refugee status. In Nicaragua, refugees were accepted until the end of the Sandinista regime in 1990.

Another country that deserves mention is Haiti, which had been rocked by crisis since the fall of the Jean-Claude Duvalier dictatorship in 1986. Relatively free and fair elections held in 1990 brought Jean-Bertrande Aristide to power, but he was overthrown less than a year later by the armed forces, who installed a military dictatorship. Filled with fears of repression and economic hardship, tens of thousands of Haitians boarded any vessel, no matter how unseaworthy, and tried to reach the U.S. shore, particularly Florida. Both the Bush and Clinton administrations resisted admitting Haitian refugees, even though candidate Clinton had criticized Bush for turning refugees back at sea. In 1993, the U.S. Supreme Court ruled that the Coast Guard could return to Haiti any Haitian picked up at sea, and President Clinton ordered anyone who made it to shore to be detained and sent to a camp at Guantánamo Bay, Cuba. This practice kept Haitians in refugee status, rather than the more political explosive status of asylee.

The logistics were complex and difficult, especially given the large number of people involved (the Coast Guard intercepted at least 40,000), and finally in 1994 President Clinton was on the verge of ordering an invasion of Haiti when the military government left power and Aristide was reinstalled. All refugees were then sent back. Ten years later, when rebels took up arms against Aristide, the refugee issue returned. Fearing overthrow and hoping to spur on another U.S. invasion in his favor, Aristide threatened that a wave of refugees would soon be on its way if no one acted to help him. The Bush administration chose to wait until Aristide fled the country and then began sending U.S. Marines to maintain order and prevent refugee flight. Latin American countries did not protest the decision (which included 20,000 U.S. troops and none from Latin America, though the former were soon replaced by a UN force that included Brazilian and Chilean soldiers), and the OAS did not issue any condemnatory resolutions.

The military government had not made itself popular, since it had expelled OAS and UN civilian missions, and the OAS focused mostly on protecting human rights and beseeching members states to come to the refugees' aid. Nonetheless, the Caribbean Community (CARICOM, an organization of fifteen Caribbean states) delayed granting recognition to the new government and requested the United Nations to investigate the details of Aristide's departure. In the face of U.S. and French opposition, it eventually dropped that request.

The Economic Impact of Immigration

In the United States, immigrants are a source of cheaper labor, a workforce that makes fewer demands than native-born workers, but the economic impact of immigration has been increasingly important for Latin American economies. Chapter 8 raised the issue of remittances, the money earned by immigrants in the United States and sent back home to waiting families, which have exceeded $50 billion a year. These "migra-dollars" can play an essential role in economic well-being in the home country, even to the point of reducing infant mortality by raising the standard of living.

Remittances have become so critical to Latin American economies that governments have begun discussing them openly. For example, after September 11, 2001, the president of El Salvador, Francisco Flores, launched a massive ad campaign to educate Salvadorans about potential changes in U.S. immigration policy and warn them to be vigilant about any changes that might erect an obstacle to remittances. The campaign included recorded telephone calls from President Flores to the 750,000 Salvadorans residing in the United States to remind them of the importance of the $2 billion that was wired every year to El Salvador. The 2004 presidential campaign in El Salvador also included charges by the conservative candidate that if a leftist were elected, then the United States might lose confidence in the government and begin blocking remittances.

The most common way to send remittances is through wire transfers via companies like Western Union. Thousands of transactions take place every day, often through Hispanic stores and markets that have been opened across the United States to offer immigrants the products they want from home and to provide an easy and more comfortable way to send their wages home, without concerns about feeling intimidated by stores where Spanish is not spoken.

Both costs and benefits are associated with migra-dollars. The positive side centers on the boost to the local economy. Locals have money to spend that cannot be gained by a job in the home country, and when the amounts are large, the total contribution to the national economy is significant, accounting for a strikingly large percentage (10 to 15 percent) of the gross national product. From the U.S. side, advocates of reducing remittance costs also make the point that they represent an alternative to economic aid, which does not necessarily reach the people who need it most because it has to filter through government bureaucracies, some of which are riddled with corruption.

One potential problem is economic dependence on remittances, which can fluctuate according to the U.S. economy, as well as U.S. immigration law. Although the home economy can benefit in the short term, in the longer term it is more vulnerable to sudden drops in the flow of migra-dollars. In countries like Cuba, El Salvador, and Mexico, where this type of dependence is extensive and still growing, many families (and by extension their governments) have come to count on unimpeded access to this money, which will not necessarily continue indefinitely. Dependency theorists would anticipate this outcome because Latin American economies have remained strongly attached to the United States, and thus remittances constitute yet another factor in an overall highly unbalanced relationship. And U.S. policy decisions can largely determine the continued flow of money.

Latin American presidents and policy makers have a vested interest in ensuring not only that immigrants from their country are treated humanely but also that immigrants who want to work in the United States be allowed to do so. Remittances are an obvious source of income, but the ability of unemployed workers to leave countries like Mexico takes pressure off governments that are struggling to provide jobs to their citizens. Employment in the United States thus provides a safety valve to forestall protests at home. But more and more studies are also demonstrating that the flow of immigrants can have a decidedly negative impact in Latin America, as communities are depleted and children are left without two parents (or in some cases, without both parents).[18]

Steps are being taken to cultivate more dialogue about immigration, including immigration within Latin American countries. For example, the Regional Conference on Migration (RCM) was created in 1996 to address migration-related issues in a multilateral forum. Its members are Belize, Canada, Costa Rica, Dominican Republic, El Salvador, Guatemala, Honduras, Mexico, Nicaragua, Panama, and the United States. In addition, Argentina, Colombia, Ecuador,

Jamaica, and Peru have observer status. Although the RCM does not exert any control over member countries' policies, at the very least its meetings have highlighted the need to resolve problems such as smuggling, human rights abuses (especially with women and children), and the general safety of immigrants.

Summary and Conclusion

Immigration is one of the most sensitive issues in U.S.–Latin American relations, especially for Mexico. Although U.S. citizens consider their country a "nation of immigrants," they have often favored policies to restrict immigration, and the "huddled masses" do not necessarily find open arms when they arrive. This is true even of many legal immigrants but is especially evident with illegal immigrants.

Because foreign policy is driven to a considerable extent by public opinion, U.S. immigration policy is intermestic. As realism would suggest, the United States uses power to pursue economic development and national security, but realism applies less well, given the highly complex and often changing perceptions in the United States about how to achieve those interests. It is also clear that power alone has not proved efficient in stemming illegal immigration. The U.S. government periodically admits that it has been able to do relatively little.

After an initial unrestricted period, from the 1870s until the 1940s, U.S. immigration policy became gradually more restrictive. In the latter half of the twentieth century, the U.S. government did not craft any coherent or consistent strategies to address both legal and illegal immigration from Latin America and instead responded in an ad hoc manner according to shifting pressures from the general population, businesses, and immigrant advocate groups. The bracero program, for example, was begun when World War II created a labor shortage in the United States but was abruptly ended in 1964, when unemployment ended any support for immigrant workers.

The passage of IRCA in 1986, with its inclusion of an amnesty, was intended to stem the tide of illegal immigrants, but in the past several decades the number of Latin American immigrants seeking to come into the United States illegally has continued to grow. The attacks of September 11, 2001, temporarily derailed U.S.-Mexico dialogue over border issues, as security became the main priority for U.S. policy makers, but the pressing need to establish coherent policies toward both legal and illegal immigrants eventually led President George W. Bush to advocate a new policy that included an amnesty.

The supply and demand sides of immigration demonstrate the obstacles to curtailing the number of immigrants, especially those who are illegal. The number of Latin Americans desiring to come to the United States remains high, as does the demand of U.S. employers for those workers. The many efforts to curb illegal immigration, including substantially beefing up border security, have generally not proved successful.

Immigration is also affecting the economies of many countries in the hemisphere, especially in Mexico, Central America, and the Caribbean. Millions of dollars are wired every day from the United States, and these remittances are becoming an integral part of the economies of some Latin American countries. Remittances provide both opportunities and obstacles for those economies, but either way they represent a significant effect of Latin American immigration to the United States.

Research Questions

1. Does the United States have a consistent policy toward Latin American refugees? To what degree do domestic political concerns drive that policy?
2. Analyze why the U.S. government periodically grants amnesties to illegal immigrants.
3. What are the dangers faced by immigrants trying to enter the United States illegally? What policies have been put in place to address those dangers?
4. Have there been any clear patterns to U.S. immigration policy toward Mexico after the end of the bracero program in 1964?
5. Discuss the economic impact of remittances in several different Latin American countries. To what degree have governments begun to rely on them?

Further Sources

Books

ANDREAS, PETER. *Border Games: Policing the U.S.-Mexico Divide* (Ithaca, N.Y.: Cornell University Press, 2000). A good analysis of the escalating border conflicts between the United States and Mexico, focusing on how the United States has emphasized solutions based on enforcement.

MASSEY, DOUGLAS S., Jorge DURAND, and NOLAN J. MALONE. *Beyond Smoke and Mirrors: Mexican Immigration in an Era of Economic Integration* (New York: Russell Sage Foundation, 2002). The book provides a concise discussion not only of the history of Mexican immigration to the United States but also of the precise ways in which U.S. immigration policies have failed. It concludes with a vision of what more effective policies would look like.

MITCHELL, CHRISTOPHER (Ed.). *Western Hemisphere Immigration and United States Foreign Policy* (University Park: Pennsylvania State University Press, 1992). Although dated, the book has an excellent discussion of the history of immigration policy, followed by country studies (Cuba, the Dominican Republic, Haiti, Central America, and Mexico).

SUÁREZ-OROZCO, MARCELO M. (Ed.). *Crossings: Mexican Immigration in Interdisciplinary Perspectives* (Cambridge: Harvard University Press, 1998). A good introduction to the dynamics of Mexican immigration. As the title suggests, it provides different views, grouped into history and demography, economic, social, and psychocultural, to explain different aspects of immigration from Mexico.

Web Sites

Americas Program: Border Information Clearinghouse. This Web site provides links, statistics, government documents, statements by nongovernmental organizations, and a database of immigration-oriented activists. It is run by the Interhemispheric Resource

Center, an advocacy group focused on U.S. foreign policy. http://www.americaspolicy. org/clearinghouse.html.

The Congressional Hispanic Caucus Institute. This is a non profit organization created by the Congressional Hispanic Caucus. It provides documents, press releases, publications, and policy recommendations on a wide range of issues, with immigration prominent. http://www.chci.org/.

Federation for American Immigration Reform (FAIR). The homepage of a large, strongly anti-immigration organization. It includes articles on a wide range of immigration topics, all of which are geared to demonstrating its harmful effects. http://www. fairus.org/.

National Council of La Raza. The Web site of a prominent advocacy group for Hispanic Americans. It includes discussions of farm worker rights, U.S. immigration policies (and U.S. foreign policy more generally), social security, welfare reform, and other issues. http://www.nclr.org/.

Regional Conference on Migration. The official website of the RCM, which includes official communiqués, activities, research articles on migration issues, and links to immigration-related government Web sites for each member country, as well as to other Web sites across the world dedicated to the topic. http://www.rcmvs.org/.

United States Census Bureau, Immigration. The Census Bureau homepage can be reached at www.census.gov, but going directly to the immigration page provides access to data, reports, and working papers on international immigration and the foreign-born population (both current and projected) in the United States. http://www.census.gov/ population/www/socdemo/immigration.html.

Notes

1. Quoted in Calavita 1994, 58.
2. Public Papers 1983, 1489.
3. Public Papers 1983, 1644–45.
4. Massey et al. 2002, 128–29.
5. Rosenblum 2004.
6. Suárez-Orozco 1999, 232.
7. Massey et al. 2002, 84.
8. Quoted in Reimers 1998, 133.
9. Quoted in Reimers 1998, 131–32.
10. Congressional Hispanic Caucus Institute Web site 2006.
11. Hastings Law Library Web site.
12. White House Web site 2001.
13. Weiner 2003.
14. Huntington 2004, 30.
15. Pritchard 2004.
16. United States Citizenship and Immigration Services Web site.
17. Quoted in Castro 2002, 6.
18. Aizenman 2006.

CHAPTER 10

Human Rights and Democracy

TIMELINE	
1948	United Nations Universal Declaration of Human Rights
1961	Amnesty International formed
1969	American Convention on Human Rights
1975	Helsinki Accords
1976	Amnesty International issues first report on Latin America (Uruguay)
1990	Last Latin American dictator (Chile) leaves power
1998	International Criminal Court signed; Augusto Pinochet arrested

The protection of human rights in Latin America, a region historically beset by civil strife, military actions, and foreign intervention, has been a difficult task. This chapter addresses human rights in the context of the construction of norms and agreements by U.S. and Latin American governments. As a realist perspective would suggest, the United States has been slow to include any aspect of human rights into its foreign policy, because it very often conflicts with pervading views on security and sovereignty. During the Cold War, the same was often true of Latin American governments, but in the past few decades, a renewed emphasis on human rights in Latin America has yielded new regional agreements, particularly under the auspices of the OAS. The critical question for the future is whether the United States will set aside its concerns and become a signatory to many of those agreements, even if doing so does not serve any national interest. Realist theory suggests this is unlikely, given the reluctance to delegate any authority to a nonstate actor, but there is evidence that significant changes are indeed taking place.

The issue of human rights may also be fruitfully viewed in liberal institutional terms. In the post–World War II era, international institutions—both through the UN and the OAS—have emerged and exert independent influence on sovereign countries. In that view, even if power is still a central component of international politics, governments are constrained by the evolution of new international norms about how people should be treated. This can be seen as a major accomplishment for Latin American leaders, in that it imposes a brake on U.S. actions while simultaneously empowering groups that in the past were ignored and marginalized.

Origins of Human Rights in International Law

Until World War II, the United States did not include human rights in its foreign policy toward Latin America or any other part of the world. The agony and atrocity of that war prompted the creation of the United Nations, and the United States took the lead in crafting the Universal Declaration of Human Rights in 1948. That lengthy document set forth the many aspects of human rights, but the essence is individual liberty. As Article 1 states, "All human beings are born free and equal in dignity and rights," and Article 3 asserts, "Everyone has the right to life, liberty and security of person."[1] The only way liberty can be restricted is laid out in Article 10: "a fair and public hearing by an independent and impartial tribunal, in the determination of his rights and obligations and of any criminal charge against him."

Many Latin American leaders were concerned that U.S. involvement in the UN would dampen its interest in the OAS and so pushed for a number of agreements to make it permanent. In addition to documents such as the Rio Treaty, the Organization of American States codified the same rights as the UN's in

1948 with the "American Declaration of the Rights and Duties of Man." Its preamble uses the same wording as the UN's article 1, and its own first article is taken verbatim from Article 3. In human rights, as well as many other issues, the OAS was intended to serve a similar function as the UN, but on a regional scale.

Coming on the heels of the Good Neighbor Policy, it appeared as if U.S.–Latin American relations might have turned a new corner. But as Chapter 5 illustrated, the Cold War quickly overshadowed all else, and the invasion of Guatemala, with the subsequent funding and support for military regimes, came only six years after the United States supported the idea of making human rights a global concept. When the war against Communism came to Latin America, the idea of wielding U.S. influence to protect human rights seemed absurd to policy makers, who came to view such an idea as subversive in itself. If you advocated human rights, then you were likely a shill for international Communism, and thus you were aiding and abetting the enemy, even if unwittingly. Added to the mix was the persistent belief, outlined in previous chapters, that Latin Americans themselves were culturally prone to abusing each other, so there was little point in the United States trying to stop it.

Human rights were therefore absent from U.S. policy for several decades, and the U.S. public showed no inclination to pressure their elected representatives in that direction. Gripped by fear of Communist aggression, popular opinion mostly supported U.S. intervention in Latin America for many years and was not concerned about the existence of dictatorships if they kept the United States "safer." Invasions received relatively little scrutiny.

Nor was human rights much of an issue for Latin American presidents and military leaders, who, to varying degrees, also believed that the potential threat of instability and/or internal "subversion" precluded such niceties. Even in Chile, with one of the strongest histories of democracy in the region in the postwar period, the 1948 Law for the Permanent Defense of Democracy outlawed the Communist party and, especially when combined with already existing emergency power legislation, legalized the systematic harassment of domestic opposition. Constitutions in Chile and elsewhere routinely allowed for the suspension of civil liberties in times of "emergency."[2] Weaving human rights into the fabric of politics would have to wait—and in some cases, the waiting continues.

Nonetheless, human rights gradually became more prominent in international agreements. Ratified in 1969, the American Convention on Human Rights is a comprehensive document on civil and political rights; economic, social, and cultural rights were not addressed until almost two decades later in the Protocol of San Salvador. The American Convention on Human Rights covers a wide range of rights: of personal liberties, due process of law, freedom of religious expression, of thought and expression, assembly and association, as well as rejection of the death penalty (with a caveat for countries that currently had the death penalty). The United States would not ratify the treaty until 1977 under President Jimmy Carter.

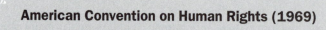

American Convention on Human Rights (1969)

Article 1. Obligation to Respect Rights

1. The States Parties to this Convention undertake to respect the rights and freedoms recognized herein and to ensure to all persons subject to their jurisdiction the free and full exercise of those rights and freedoms, without any discrimination for reasons of race, color, sex, language, religion, political or other opinion, national or social origin, economic status, birth, or any other social condition. . . .

Article 4. Right to Life

1. Every person has the right to have his life respected. This right shall be protected by law and, in general, from the moment of conception. No one shall be arbitrarily deprived of his life.

2. In countries that have not abolished the death penalty, it may be imposed only for the most serious crimes and pursuant to a final judgment rendered by a competent court and in accordance with a law establishing such punishment, enacted prior to the commission of the crime. The application of such punishment shall not be extended to crimes to which it does not presently apply.

3. The death penalty shall not be reestablished in states that have abolished it.

4. In no case shall capital punishment be inflicted for political offenses or related common crimes. . . .

Article 7. Right to Personal Liberty

1. Every person has the right to personal liberty and security.

2. No one shall be deprived of his physical liberty except for the reasons and under the conditions established beforehand by the constitution of the State Party concerned or by a law established pursuant thereto.

3. No one shall be subject to arbitrary arrest or imprisonment.

4. Anyone who is detained shall be informed of the reasons for his detention and shall be promptly notified of the charge or charges against him.

5. Any person detained shall be brought promptly before a judge or other officer authorized by law to exercise judicial power and shall be entitled to trial within a reasonable time or to be released without prejudice to the continuation of the proceedings. His release may be subject to guarantees to assure his appearance for trial.

6. Anyone who is deprived of his liberty shall be entitled to recourse to a competent court, in order that the court may decide without delay on the lawfulness of his arrest or detention and order his release if the arrest or detention is unlawful. . . .

7. No one shall be detained for debt. This principle shall not limit the orders of a competent judicial authority issued for nonfulfillment of duties of support. . . .

Article 12. Freedom of Conscience and Religion

1. Everyone has the right to freedom of conscience and of religion. This right includes freedom to maintain or to change one's religion or beliefs, and freedom to profess or disseminate one's religion or beliefs, either individually or together with others, in public or in private.

2. No one shall be subject to restrictions that might impair his freedom to maintain or to change his religion or beliefs.

Article 13. Freedom of Thought and Expression

1. Everyone has the right to freedom of thought and expression. This right includes freedom to seek, receive, and impart information and ideas of all kinds, regardless of frontiers, either orally, in writing, in print, in the form of art, or through any other medium of one's choice.

2. The exercise of the right provided for in the foregoing paragraph shall not be subject to prior censorship but shall be subject to subsequent imposition of liability, which shall be expressly established by law to the extent necessary to ensure:

   a. respect for the rights or reputations of others; or

   b. the protection of national security, public order, or public health or morals.

3. The right of expression may not be restricted by indirect methods or means, such as the abuse of government or private controls over newsprint, radio broadcasting frequencies, or equipment used in the dissemination of information, or by any other means tending to impede the communication and circulation of ideas and opinions.

Article 15. Right of Assembly

The right of peaceful assembly, without arms, is recognized. No restrictions may be placed on the exercise of this right other than those imposed in conformity with the law and necessary in a democratic society in the interest of national security, public safety or public order, or to protect public health or morals or the rights or freedom of others.

Article 16. Freedom of Association

1. Everyone has the right to associate freely for ideological, religious, political, economic, labor, social, cultural, sports, or other purposes.

2. The exercise of this right shall be subject only to such restrictions established by law as may be necessary in a democratic society, in the interest of national security, public safety or public order, or to protect public health or morals or the rights and freedoms of others.

3. The provisions of this article do not bar the imposition of legal restrictions, including even deprivation of the exercise of the right of association, on members of the armed forces and the police. . . .

Source: http://www.oas.org/OASpage/humanrights.htm.

Between 1973 and 1975, thirty-five countries (including the United States and the Soviet Union) gathered in Helsinki, Finland, for the first meeting of the Conference on Security and Cooperation in Europe, which culminated in the 1975 Helsinki Accords. The purpose of the meetings was to defuse tensions between the two major powers, with agreements reached on peaceful settlement of disputes and refraining from the use of force. In addition, however, the Helsinki Accords outlined key civil rights, such as freedoms of expression, belief, and thought, as well as avoiding discrimination on the basis of gender, race, religion, or minority status.

The result was that although U.S. presidents tended to dismiss the issue, they were unable to avoid it entirely. In fact, the Helsinki Accords were intended to highlight pervasive human rights violations in the Soviet Union, which therefore kept human rights on the U.S. policy radar. There was still strong resistance, however, to making human rights a part of U.S. policy toward any non-Communist area of the world. Cuba was thus frequently a target of U.S. rhetoric, but U.S.-supported military governments were not. Still, in 1974 and 1975, Congress did begin calling on the State Department to issue reports on the human rights record of countries receiving security assistance.

A Human Rights Interregnum: President Jimmy Carter

In 1977, President Jimmy Carter took office in the aftermath of the Vietnam War and the Watergate scandal that forced President Richard Nixon to resign. Public confidence in the government was low, and cynicism about foreign policy was high. Especially among Democrats, the 1975 Church Committee also had an important impact, as it highlighted the direct ways in which administrations had worked to undermine democracy (even by assassination) and promote military governments.

During the Nixon and Ford administrations, some Democrats in Congress had made various efforts to block aid to dictatorships but faced an uphill battle not only among their colleagues, but more firmly in the White House. Even during the Carter administration, Congress wavered. In 1977, for example, the House of Representatives voted to deny funds to the Argentine dictatorship yet the very next day approved restoring aid to the Somoza dictatorship in Nicaragua. Carter would also cut aid to Brazil, Chile, El Salvador, Guatemala, and Uruguay, which in turn would lead to complaints in Latin America about U.S. "interventionism." The president also worked personally to gain the release of political prisoners.

This was, many argued, the only way the United States could get the attention of repressive governments, which would listen not to airy speeches but only to the cold reality of being denied money. Opponents argued that not only was it a blatant case of interventionism but also that Latin American militaries would simply find other countries that did not make human rights a sticking point, where they could purchase weapons and spare parts and develop training programs.

In 1977, President Carter created the Bureau of Human Rights and Humanitarian Affairs, which would later become the Bureau of Democracy, Human Rights, and Labor, thus placing human rights in a more prominent position within the U.S. government. A commission headed by Senator Edward Kennedy (D-MA) had recommended its creation in 1968, but both Congress and the Nixon and Ford administrations gave it little support. The position of "coordinator" for human rights existed briefly at the end of the Ford administration (though the coordinator did virtually nothing), but Carter brought it to the cabinet level, and its staff and prominence grew. It now includes a Human Rights and Democracy Fund, allocating $31 million for projects around the world, such as election monitoring, human rights documentation, strengthening women's advocacy groups, and creating the office of a special prosecutor.

The response in Latin America to President Carter's initiatives was decidedly mixed, given the varieties of democracies and dictatorships in the region in the late 1970s. In Chile, Augusto Pinochet called for a national **plebiscite** in 1978 in the face of several U.S. policy shifts. In December 1975, the Kennedy Amendment (named for Senator Edward Kennedy, who had taken a special interest in Chile) became law, which prohibited Chile from receiving military aid or training and from purchasing weapons (though Secretary of State Kissinger added a number of weapons to already existing contracts, saying the new law did not cover them). Then in 1977, the United States cosponsored a United Nations resolution condemning human rights abuses in Chile (the Nixon and Ford administrations tended to abstain from such votes). Presidents Carter and Pinochet had met at the Panama Canal signing ceremony in 1977, and Carter had made plain the need for UN human rights observers in Chile. Pinochet's own rage at this affront is clear as he called for the plebiscite, which was worded:

> In the face of the international aggression unleashed against the government of the fatherland, I support [General] Pinochet in his defense of the dignity of Chile, and I reaffirm the legitimate right of the republic to conduct the process of institutionalization in a manner befitting its sovereignty.[3]

President Carter had spurred real interest in democratization that did not disappear after he left office. Even during the Reagan administration, the U.S. Congress became more active in denying funds to Latin American governments that systematically violated human rights. As one former foreign service officer and human rights activist notes, "While there was no spurt of congressionally initiated legislation as in the mid-1970s, the strengthening of the Kennedy Amendment showed how much ground those concerned with human rights had gained in Congress."[4]

There were already antidictatorial voices coming from Latin America, and they gained steam in the 1980s. Perhaps the most vocal was Costa Rican President Oscar Arias Sánchez, who played an important role in mediating the deadly conflicts in El Salvador, Honduras, and Nicaragua. The Nicaraguan civil war was especially problematic, because the Reagan administration long refused to negotiate with what it considered an outlaw Communist regime. With Arias's leadership, in 1987 progress was made and a peace plan put into place. For his efforts, Arias received the Nobel Peace Prize that same year. In an impassioned speech accepting the award, Arias spoke directly to the powerful countries waging ideological war: "let Central Americans decide the future of Central America. Leave the interpretation of and the compliance with the Peace Plan to us."

Oscar Arias Sánchez, Nobel Peace Prize Acceptance Speech (1987)

When you chose to honor me with this prize, you chose to honor a land of peace: you chose to honor Costa Rica. When, in this year of 1987 you fulfilled the wish of Alfred E. Nobel to encourage efforts for peace in the world, you chose to encourage the efforts to secure peace in Central America. I am most grateful for this recognition of our search for peace. All of us in Central America are grateful. . . .

Peace is not only a matter of noble words and Nobel lectures. We already have an abundance of words, glorious words, inscribed in the declarations of the United Nations, the World Court, the Organization of American States and a network of international treaties and laws. We need deeds which respect these words, which honor the commitments avowed in these laws. We need to strengthen our institutions of peace, such as the United Nations, to ensure that they are used on behalf of the weak as well as the strong. . . .

In Central America we do not seek solely peace, nor solely a peace to be followed one day by political progress. Instead we seek peace and democracy together, indivisible: an end to the shedding of human blood which is inseparable from an end to the violation of human rights. We do not judge, much less condemn, the political or ideological system of any nation which is freely chosen and not exported. We cannot impose on sovereign states models of government which they themselves have not chosen. But we can and do insist that every government respect the universal rights of man, whose value transcends all national borders and ideological labels. We believe that justice and peace can prosper only together, never apart. A nation which mistreats its own citizens is more likely to mistreat its neighbors. . . .

I know that you join us in our call to the members of the international community, and in particular to those nations of East and West which have much more power and resources than my small nation can ever hope to wield. To them I say with the greatest urgency: let Central Americans decide the future of Central America. Leave the interpretation of and the compliance with the Peace Plan to us. Support the efforts for peace in our region, not the forces of war; send us not swords but ploughshares, not spears but pruning hooks. If, for your own purposes, you cannot stop hoarding the weapons of war, then in the name of God, at least leave us in peace.

I am from that Latin America whose face is marked by deep traces of suffering, which record the exile, torture, prison and death of many of her men and women. I am from that Latin America still exhibiting totalitarian regimes which are the shame of the human race.

America is marked by profound scars. In the very years that she is seeking a return to freedom, the advent of democracy is revealing for the first time the horrible trail of torture, exile and death left by the dictators. America has enormous problems to overcome. The inheritance of an unjust past has been aggravated by the tragic actions of tyrants, to producing external debt, social insensitivity, economic destruction, corruption, and many other evils in our societies. These evils are in plain view for anyone to see them. . . .

Central America is halted at a terrible crossroads. Faced with the agonizing problems of poverty, there are those who from the mountain or from the government call for dictators of new ideological creeds, ignoring the cry for freedom of so many generations. Next to the grave evils of generalized misery, evils defined in the North-South context, the East–West conflict is brewing. Where the problems of poverty meet ideological struggle, the fear of freedom raises a cross of ill omen for Central America.

Perhaps it was in hours as difficult for Central America as those in which we live today, perhaps it was in premonition of the present crossroads, that Rubén Dario—the greatest poet of our America—wrote these lines in the conviction that history would change its course:

Pray, generous, pious, and proud;
pray, chaste, pure, heavenly, brave;
intercede for us, supplicate for us,
for already we are almost without sap and bud,
without soul, without life, without light, without Quixote,
without feet, without wings, without Sancho
and without God.

I assure the immortal poet that we shall not renounce our dreams, fear wisdom, or flee freedom. I assure him that in Central America we shall not forget Quixote, we shall not renounce life, we shall not turn our backs on the human spirit, and we shall never lose faith in God.

I am one of five men who signed an accord, a commitment which consists, in great part, in the act of desiring peace with all one's soul.

Source: Nobel Prize Web site http://nobelprize.org/nobel_prizes/peace/laureates/1987/ariaslecture.html.

The Role of Nongovernmental Organizations

Especially when dictatorships reigned widely in Latin America, the most important actors addressing human rights were not necessarily associated with governments, but rather were nongovernmental organizations (NGOs). Dedicated to the rights of the oppressed and frustrated by government inaction or dissembling, they moved to fill what they viewed as the vacuum of leadership.

Until the 1970s, NGOs remained largely peripheral to policy making in Washington, D.C. They lacked the resources and experience necessary to lobby effectively. But as international protests against dictatorship and repression spread, so did the NGOs. The most prominent, Amnesty International, was founded in 1961 by a British lawyer trying to free two Portuguese citizens imprisoned for political reasons by their military government. Its work, based on the tenets of the UN's Universal Declaration of Human Rights, became so widely recognized that it was granted the Nobel Peace Prize in 1977. It was only in 1976, however, that it opened an office in Washington, D.C., and worked to make abuses in Latin America a priority. Its first report on Latin America centered on torture in Uruguay, and with the help of Congressman Ed Koch (D-NY), that information was put directly into the *Congressional Record*.

There are other important human rights NGOs as well. Human Rights Watch was created in 1978 to monitor whether Soviet bloc countries were abiding by the Helsinki Accords, but subsequently it took on a life of its own. The Washington Office on Latin America (WOLA) was founded in 1974 as a reaction against U.S. support for dictatorships in the hemisphere. More so than other NGOs, its explicit purpose is to influence legislation.

Prominent domestic NGOs in Latin America have included the Madres de la Plaza de Mayo (Argentina); the Vicaria de Solidaridad, a Catholic church–based human rights group in Chile; the Academy of Human Rights in Mexico; the Fundación Arias in Costa Rica; and the Comisión Andina de Juristas in Peru. In the past several decades, the list of such organizations has become very long.

These and many other NGOs also formed part of an international human rights network, and the 1973 coup in Chile was the "watershed moment" for the creation of that network.[5] NGOs had already begun the work of placing human rights abuses in the context of international law, and Latin American organizations began to form and work closely together. Aside from working with sympathetic legislators (in all countries) to bring Latin American human rights issues into focus, publicity is perhaps the greatest lever these NGOs have. The human rights networks collected information and stories from many of the people who had suffered, which was then disseminated to the entire world, thus putting pressure on governments to take action. This is referred to as "leveraging."[6] Through leveraging, "ordinary persons without political power convince a spokesperson more powerful than themselves to deal with authorities."[7]

These networks included of parts of intergovernmental organizations, international NGOs, domestic NGOs, private foundations, and parts of some governments. Members of these groups played a greater role in drafting international law than has often been acknowledged, working both at the United Nations and the Organization of American States from their beginnings. In this way, "international human rights pressures can lead to changes in human rights practices, helping to transform understandings about the nature of a state's sovereign authority over its citizens."[8]

During the 1980s, the number and diversity of such networks expanded, which made them more effective in producing changes of policy by both governments and international organizations (such as the OAS). Successful publicizing meant they were also able to raise more funds, both private and public.

By the 1990s, it was far more difficult for the United States or the OAS to paper over human rights violations or unconstitutional changes of government in the region. Although such changes did occur (e.g., in Peru in 1990 and Ecuador in 2000), the outcry was far greater than in the past, and as a result some similar efforts failed (e.g., Guatemala in 1993 and Paraguay in 1996).

The NGOs have worked closely with OAS institutions such as the Inter-American Court of Human Rights. Although many Latin American NGOs and human rights groups have the information necessary to lodge complaints, they lack the legal experience and money to construct a legal case while also paying for witnesses and lawyers to attend hearings. Currently, the IACHR does not pay for any of those activities, so they often fall on the shoulders of wealthier NGOs based in the United States.

The NGOs have also contributed to a better understanding of the dilemmas faced by groups in Latin America who traditionally had received little attention, such as women and indigenous groups. Marginalized in their own societies and bereft of international attention, in NGOs these groups found recognition that their rights were equally important as everyone else's.

In South America, military dictatorships usually brought with them very conservative notions about the "proper" role of women in society and politics. For example, in 1975 the president of Uruguay announced his country would not participate in UN activities celebrating the International Women's Year because they would serve to "aggressively launch women into the arena of political battles that are occurring in the world today. . . . It is clear that at the root of all these attempts there is a materialist philosophy and underlying them is the Marxist conception of state and society . . . to which we can in no way adhere."[9]

Until the early 1980s, violence against women was not on the agenda for the women's movement or for international human rights groups, in Latin America or elsewhere. The United Nations first addressed the issue in 1985, but in Latin America the OAS Inter-American Convention on the Prevention, Punishment, and Eradication of Violence against Women was not signed until 1994. It called on states not only to protect women from physical, sexual, and psychological abuse but also to call attention to the problem, change their laws, and even modify the very cultural contexts that tolerated such abuse. The inclusion of women's issues under the rubric of human rights has thus been slow but nonetheless steady.

Indigenous groups had traditionally been mistreated irrespective of the type of government in power, and they have received more than token attention only in the past several decades. Largely as a result, their only avenue for political change has been rebellion, which in turn has brought on a negative reaction from Latin American governments and the United States. In recent years, indigenous demands were at the heart of a coup in Ecuador (2000) and the forced departure of Bolivian presidents (2003 and 2005), and as discussed in Chapter 8, the Mexican Zapatistas continue to make their demands for land reform and autonomy in Chiapas. In these and other countries, indigenous

Inter-American Convention on the Prevention, Punishment, and Eradication of Violence against Women (1994)

Article 1

For the purposes of this Convention, violence against women shall be understood as any act or conduct, based on gender, which causes death or physical, sexual or psychological harm or suffering to women, whether in the public or the private sphere.

Article 2

Violence against women shall be understood to include physical, sexual and psychological violence:

a. that occurs within the family or domestic unit or within any other interpersonal relationship, whether or not the perpetrator shares or has shared the same residence with the woman, including, among others, rape, battery and sexual abuse;

b. that occurs in the community and is perpetrated by any person, including, among others, rape, sexual abuse, torture, trafficking in persons, forced prostitution, kidnapping and sexual harassment in the workplace, as well as in educational institutions, health facilities or any other place; and

c. that is perpetrated or condoned by the state or its agents regardless of where it occurs.

Article 7

The States Parties condemn all forms of violence against women and agree to pursue, by all appropriate means and without delay, policies to prevent, punish and eradicate such violence and undertake to:

a. refrain from engaging in any act or practice of violence against women and to ensure that their authorities, officials, personnel, agents, and institutions act in conformity with this obligation;

b. apply due diligence to prevent, investigate and impose penalties for violence against women;

c. include in their domestic legislation penal, civil, administrative and any other type of provisions that may be needed to prevent, punish and eradicate violence against women and to adopt appropriate administrative measures where necessary;

d. adopt legal measures to require the perpetrator to refrain from harassing, intimidating or threatening the woman or using any method that harms or endangers her life or integrity, or damages her property;

e. take all appropriate measures, including legislative measures, to amend or repeal existing laws and regulations or to modify legal or customary practices which sustain the persistence and tolerance of violence against women;

f. establish fair and effective legal procedures for women who have been subjected to violence which include, among others, protective measures, a timely hearing and effective access to such procedures;

g. establish the necessary legal and administrative mechanisms to ensure that women subjected to violence have effective access to restitution, reparations or other just and effective remedies. . . .

Article 8

The States Parties agree to undertake progressively specific measures, including programs:

a. to promote awareness and observance of the right of women to be free from violence, and the right of women to have their human rights respected and protected;

b. to modify social and cultural patterns of conduct of men and women, including the development of formal and informal educational programs appropriate to every level of the educational process, to counteract prejudices, customs and all other practices which are based on the idea of the inferiority or superiority of either of the sexes or on the stereotyped roles for men and women which legitimize or exacerbate violence against women;

c. to promote the education and training of all those involved in the administration of justice, police and other law enforcement officers as well as other personnel responsible for implementing policies for the prevention, punishment and eradication of violence against women;

d. to provide appropriate specialized services for women who have been subjected to violence, through public and private sector agencies, including shelters, counseling services for all family members where appropriate, and care and custody of the affected children;

e. to promote and support governmental and private sector education designed to raise the awareness of the public with respect to the problems of and remedies for violence against women;

f. to provide women who are subjected to violence access to effective readjustment and training programs to enable them to fully participate in public, private and social life;

g. to encourage the communications media to develop appropriate media guidelines in order to contribute to the eradication of violence against women in all its forms, and to enhance respect for the dignity of women;

Article 9

With respect to the adoption of the measures in this Chapter, the States Parties shall take special account of the vulnerability of women to violence by reason of, among others, their race or ethnic background or their status as migrants, refugees or displaced persons. Similar consideration shall be given to women subjected to violence while pregnant or who are disabled, of minor age, elderly, socioeconomically disadvantaged, affected by armed conflict or deprived of their freedom.

Source: OAS Web site, www.oas.org/juridico/english/treaties/a-16.html

groups are exerting greater political power, which can be directed against the U.S. free trade and drug policies.

The challenge of asserting indigenous rights is exemplified by the inability of the OAS to forge an agreement. The Proposed American Declaration on the Rights of Indigenous Peoples was drafted in 1997, eight years after the Inter-American Commission on Human Rights began discussing it; the original intent was to assert indigenous rights in recognition of the 500th anniversary of Europe's arrival in the region in 1492. The proposal has yet to be completed. Although all countries in the hemisphere have offered objections and suggestions, as have indigenous organizations, one problem for the United States is the notion, as stated by the U.S. delegate in 2002, that the document "should not set forth an obligation since this is a declaration, an expression of aspirations, and not a convention" and that "We also have difficulty with a requirement that states shall adopt special measures against discrimination; we prefer a formulation which encourages states to take measures. . . ."[10] The point is that an "obligation" would potentially encroach on existing U.S. laws. Other countries, such as Colombia, continue to express concern that negotiations have been drawn out over a decade without a concrete result. As discussed later, the United States has often been reluctant (or simply unwilling) to ratify OAS agreements on human rights.

The Role of the OAS

Especially once the region's dictatorships (with the exception of Cuba) gave way to elected governments by 1990, the Organization of American States has crafted a number of resolutions intended to strengthen the hemisphere's commitment to the protection of human rights. As Table 10.1 demonstrates, the United States has declined to ratify any of them after the Carter administration, while the thirty-four other countries in the hemisphere have been far more willing.

The argument against ratification centers on sovereignty and the possible authority such agreements could exert over U.S. citizens. Both executives and legislators in the United States have argued against allowing any court outside their borders to exert any authority, arguing that such an arrangement could even prove unconstitutional. For example, former Secretary of State Henry Kissinger wrote that the United Nation's International Criminal Court (which could call citizens of any country to stand trial for "gross violations" of international law), created in 1998, "represents such a fundamental change in U.S. constitutional practice that a full national debate and the full participation of Congress are imperative."[11] Kissinger's own personal interest in the matter is considerable, as his support for the Chilean coup and dictatorship has often been cited as a potential case for the ICC.

For the same reasons, until 2006 the United States not only refused to ratify the ICC but sought to punish countries that do not agree to provide waivers for the U.S. military, so it becomes a security issue as well. Colombia, for example, is a signatory to the ICC and was threatened with a cut in aid in 2003. Eventually

Table 10.1 Major OAS Documents on Human Rights (as of 2007)

Name	Latin American Signatories	Ratified by United States?
American Declaration of the Rights and Duties of Man (1948)	26	Yes
American Convention on Human Rights (1969)	26	Yes (in 1977)
Protocol to the ACHR to Abolish the Death Penalty (1990)	9	No
Inter-American Convention to Prevent and Punish Torture (1985)	20	No
Inter-American Convention on Forced Disappearance of Persons (1994)	16	No
Inter-American Convention on the Prevention, Punishment, and Eradication of Violence against Women (1994)	31	No
Inter-American Convention on the Elimination of All Forms of Discrimination against Persons with Disabilities (1999)	20	No

Source: OAS Web site.

the Colombian government convinced the United States that all security and aid personnel were already protected by a 1962 agreement between the two countries. The incident underlined the continued concern the United States had with the dictates of international human rights law. Other countries—such as Bolivia, the Dominican Republic, El Salvador, Honduras, Nicaragua, and Panama—agreed to exempt U.S. nationals. Yet Brazil, Costa Rica, Ecuador, Paraguay, Peru, Uruguay, and Venezuela all refused to acquiesce, thus accepting the potential loss of aid in the name of preserving sovereignty. Interestingly, in 2005 the head of U.S. Southern Command, Army Gen. Bantz Craddock, argued against any military-related ICC penalties to a congressional panel, saying they would have "unintended consequences" because Latin American militaries would go elsewhere for training.[12] Largely because of such resistance from the U.S. military, in 2006 restrictions on military aid were lifted for countries that still had not signed waivers.

Despite U.S. efforts to control it, international law has spread in unanticipated ways, such as when judges of one country issue arrest warrants for crimes not committed on their own soil. That is precisely what happened in October 1998 to Augusto Pinochet, the former president of the military government in Chile (1973–1990). Spanish judge Baltasar Garzón sent an international warrant for Pinochet's arrest while the former dictator rested in London after back surgery. The charges were murder, conspiracy to murder, hostage taking, torture, and kidnapping. Pinochet would remain under house arrest for fifteen months while the British government deliberated about whether to extradite him to Spain.

In 2000, the British government found a loophole that would extricate it from the controversy by ruling that Pinochet—by virtue of age and health problems—suffered from "dementia" and therefore should be released. A Chilean Air Force plane was waiting, and the retired general was whisked away before any new arrest warrants (which were coming from other European countries) could be delivered.

Even though Pinochet was freed, the case reverberated globally, in a manner consistent with liberal institutional theory. In the past, the accused that were held under international law had been defeated in some manner (e.g., Nazis and the Nuremberg Trials or Rwandan Hutus facing the ICC), but Pinochet had never been defeated in battle and had enjoyed extensive support even within his own country. Human rights law was now moving—albeit with halting steps—toward eliminating impunity even for victors. The U.S. government remained opposed to giving up any sovereignty in such matters and followed Kissinger's argument that international trials would become politicized and used as platforms by biased judges for political purposes (though the Clinton administration did declassify a large number of documents that would be used in the Pinochet case). This aspect of human rights law is so new that it remains to be seen how it will develop, but already it has been argued that the Pinochet saga compelled the Chilean government to pressure its own courts to bring more cases to trial. However, he died in December 2006 before any court could prosecute him.

Relations with Latin American Militaries

Especially after the Cold War began, one of the most troublesome human rights issues was the relationship between the U.S. government and the armed forces in Latin America. An explicit trade-off was made, whereby the United States accepted sometimes gross violations of human rights if they were done in the name of combating the global threat of Communism. Chapter 7 addressed the ways in which U.S. policy makers were well aware of the torture, deaths, and disappearances, but rationalized that a Communist dictatorship would be worse. Human rights activists faced an uphill struggle to cut aid or otherwise call attention to the governments committing those abuses, especially in Central America.

With the exception of Costa Rica, which abolished its military in 1948, Central America suffered devastatingly violent civil wars and/or repressive governments during much of the Cold War. Particularly during the Reagan administration, military spending aimed at El Salvador and Honduras increased sharply. In El Salvador, the United States paid out $300 to $500 million a year throughout much of the 1980s, and Honduras received $100 to $300 million in the same period, and these numbers do not include money spent on the Contras fighting the Nicaraguan government. In South America, the support was more symbolic than financial, as the United States helped to legitimize military rule but did not funnel anywhere close to the same amount of money as it did in Central America. For Latin America as a whole, U.S. military spending actually decreased from the highs reached in the 1960s. Grant military aid (excluding El Salvador and Honduras) declined from an average of about $110 million a year in 1969 to $35 million in the mid-1980s. The number of Latin American soldiers coming to the United States for courses and training dropped from a high of 9,000 in 1962 to approximately 2,000 in the 1980s.

The precise influence of the U.S. government on Latin American militaries has been a matter of some dispute. Some agree with the School of the Americas Watch, which argues that training at the SOA "has left a trail of blood and suffering in every country where its graduates have returned."[13] The training and the weapons have often been used for repression. Others counter that it is often difficult to trace a clear line between U.S. spending/training and the military's activities and that overall U.S. influence underwent a decline from its high in the early Cold War. The abuses of School of the Americas graduates thus amounts only to "a few foul balls," in the words of a former SOA instructor.[14] This was due in part because Congress began imposing limits on aid to countries with poor human rights records. When President Carter took office, he quickly moved to cut military aid to Argentina, Bolivia, and Chile, and over time he criticized and/or reduced funding to dictatorships across the region.

Yet it is indisputable that aside from aid and training, the United States offered its rhetorical support for many dictatorships and militaries that were clearly violating the human rights of their citizens. To U.S. presidents, dictatorships were nascent democracies facing sabotage from unpopular guerrillas, and groups like the Contras were simply "freedom fighters" trying to restore political and economic liberties to embattled Nicaraguans. Very often, U.S. officials gave clear "green light" signals to governments, a tacit understanding that the United States would not criticize the regime as it handled problems of mutual interest. The green light, sometimes even given privately, contradicted official statements about democracy and human rights.

The human toll in Latin American countries whose militaries received either concrete or tacit support from the U.S. government is stunning in its magnitude, especially as truth commissions complete the laborious task of counting the dead. More than 3,000 Chileans were killed for political reasons during the Pinochet years (1973–1990). In neighboring Argentina, 20,000 died during the 1976–1983 military government. When the FMLN geared up its activities in El Salvador in the early 1980s, the death toll reached upwards of 60,000. Between 1980 and 2000, 69,000 Peruvians were killed in the war against insurgencies. Between 1962 and 1996, 200,000 Guatemalans died, 90 percent at the hands of government forces.

These numbers do not register the vast numbers of people who were imprisoned, tortured, and otherwise abused, or the suffering of their families and friends, who waited anxiously to find out if they would survive. The psychological scars continue to run deep as well. In Ariel Dorfman's play *Death and the Maiden* (1991) the protagonist encounters a man she believes was her torturer by recognizing his voice; she had always been blindfolded (she also identified him through the music he always played, Schubert's "Death and the

Maiden"). She faces a whirlwind of emotions, most notably terror and retribution, and tries to decide whether to kill him. For many Latin Americans, the dictatorships came to an end, but the fear and psychological suffering did not.

In the 1990s, with the disappearance of the specter of Communism, U.S. policy toward Latin American militaries underwent changes. At the Western Hemisphere Institute for Security Cooperation, formerly the School of the Americas, human rights instruction has been integrated into every course. Where once soldiers were taught the "fallacies of Communist theory" in any class they took, now they are taught how to incorporate human rights awareness into military operations, which, according to instructors at the school, "is actually the cutting edge of regional military teaching for the armed forces and the police in the applied Human Rights process."[15] From that perspective, the U.S. military is well equipped to teach Latin American soldiers how to combat threats while avoiding the excesses of the Cold War. Human rights activists remain highly skeptical.

The 1995 *United States Regional Security Report of the Americas* came out of the first meeting of defense ministers in the hemisphere, and it emphasized the goal not only of democratic elections but also of democratic control of the armed forces. Subsequent meetings reiterated those points. As part of this overall effort at promoting democracy, the Center for Hemispheric Defense Studies opened in 1997 in Washington, D.C. Its purpose is to educate both officers and civilians in democratic defense policy, including the nuts and bolts of forging military budgets.

Critics claim that institutions such as these serve no positive purpose, that regardless of their stated goals, they retain the essential element of teaching Latin American militaries how to control their own populations. Supporters, however, believe that inclusion of human rights and democracy can instill a greater sense of duty, honor, and respect for life to soldiers who otherwise might not learn such values. As one proponent put it, "The school's [SOA] annual budget is less than that of a small junior college. In return, it averts wars that cost half a billion dollars a day."[16]

The U.S. Congress also made its mark on military policy in recent years. For example, in 2000 it passed (and President Bill Clinton signed) a massive $1.3 billion package of military and economic aid to Colombia (dubbed "Plan Colombia," it is examined in greater detail in Chapter 11). Congress had insisted that a human rights certification be granted for military assistance to Colombia, and this certification would be made (or denied) after meetings conducted by the U.S. government and NGOs (including Amnesty International, Human Rights Watch, and the Washington Office on Latin America). Nonetheless, this example also demonstrates the limits of both congressional and NGO influence; the latter achieved consensus that the human rights conditions had not been met, but President Clinton decided later in the year to waive those conditions in the name of national security. As had happened many times in the past, the president's perception of a security threat took precedence over everything else. That would be even more pronounced with President George W. Bush after 9/11.

Nonetheless, the ways in which human rights became a normal part of the policy process both within the United States and across the hemisphere may allow a certain degree of optimism. Human rights issues can be contested, but they can no longer be ignored. As Kathryn Sikkink argues:

> Outcomes still depend on political struggles, "fought out issue by issue, day by day," where human rights advocates require skill, energy, and fortuitous circumstances to prevail. A major accomplishment of the human rights movement has been to discipline and change U.S. foreign policy and subject its impact on human rights to scrutiny.[17]

This is in line with liberal institutional theory. The work by human rights activists increased the profile of the issue, and international agreements took it on. It is consequently more problematic for the United States to ignore it.

The Case of Cuba

Although U.S. policy toward Cuba finds few allies around the world, even many of Castro's firmest supporters backed away from him in 2003, when he began imprisoning more than seventy political dissidents and summarily executed three men who had attempted to hijack a ferry to sail to Florida. In Europe, where leaders have usually viewed U.S. policy toward Cuba with a resigned weariness, Castro was harshly criticized. He responded that Cuba did not need Europe, "a group of old colonial powers historically responsible for slave trafficking, looting and even the extermination of entire peoples."[18]

The United Nations Human Rights Commission (HRC) passed a resolution in 2003 (approved even by Mexico) calling for Cuba to accept a UN envoy to investigate human rights, which Castro refused. Cuba was, in fact, reelected to a position on that commission, which highlighted the depth of skepticism in the international community toward U.S. policy, as the United States had already been voted off the commission in 2001. In addition, the European Union announced it would not curtail economic aid to the island.

Yet despite Cuba's presence on the commission, in April 2004 it narrowly passed another resolution, introduced by Honduras, rebuking Cuba for human rights violations and urging "that full civil and political rights be granted to the Cuban people with full participation and freedom of opinion without fear or reprisals."[19] It also repeated the previous call to allow a UN envoy to visit and investigate the accusations of human rights abuses. The Cuban government's response was to accuse Honduras of being a tool of the United States.

The renewal of repression in Cuba was linked to the development of the Varela Project. The Cuban constitution provides for a national referendum to be called if sufficient signatures are obtained. The Varela Project was a petition calling for democratization in Cuba, including freedom of speech and association, an amnesty for political prisoners, the ability to run private businesses, and free and fair elections. It therefore represented a total rejection of the Castro regime.

Its sponsors delivered 11,000 signatures (and ultimately claimed to have 20,000) in May 2002, timing it precisely the day before former president Jimmy Carter was scheduled to arrive in Havana to meet with Fidel Castro.

The Cuban government rejected the petition, arguing that it misinterpreted the constitution, which it said did not allow citizens to amend the constitution themselves (the U.S. Constitution does not allow for such an action either). He also accused the United States of meddling in Cuban affairs, because the head of the U.S. Interest Section (in the absence of diplomatic relations, there is no embassy) James Cason had met with Cuban dissidents to discuss political transition. With provocative statements and connections to Castro opponents, Cason was transformed into a high-profile transmitter of the Bush administration's Cuba policy. Soon Castro also began cracking down on democratic activists, declaring them tools of Cason's machinations, which led to the 2003 roundup of dissidents.

President Bush maintained his public stance of calling for the end of the Castro regime. In May 2002 he announced his Initiative for a New Cuba, which reiterated many of the criteria of the Helms-Burton Law (and even echoed the Varela Project), such as calling for free elections, freedom of speech and assembly, release of political prisoners, and opening up the Cuban economy. The overall message of U.S. policy was that relations simply could not be normalized as long as Fidel Castro remained in power.

In 2004, President Bush went a step further with the Commission for Assistance to a Free Cuba, which was intended to identify ways to "help the Cuban people bring an expeditious end to the Castro dictatorship."[20] Its recommendations amounted to eliminating the lifelines that Fidel Castro had constructed, such as tourism, access to hard currency, and foreign investment. The key proposal was to limit dollar remittances and family visits, as well as the amount of money that could be spent on such visits. This measure went too far even for many Castro opponents, who lamented their inability to wire more money to their relatives. In that sense, President Bush took a position that reflected a harder line than in the past.

Castro reacted immediately and negatively. He led a large rally in Havana and announced the closing of stores that accepted dollars, which had become common, exempting only gasoline, some food items, and personal hygiene products. Castro blamed the United States for the measure, which forced Cubans to rely on rations and stores (with more depleted stocks) that accepted only pesos. Later in 2004, he would outlaw dollar transactions. Years after the Cold War's end, the economic and rhetorical war between the two countries remained as intense as ever.

For many years, U.S. presidents have lobbied skeptical Latin American governments to support the embargo and to condemn Fidel Castro in international settings such as the OAS and the UN. In the OAS, such efforts were easier during the Cold War, especially when military governments ruled a number of countries. The Cuban government was expelled from the OAS in 1962 (though Cuba as a country officially remains an OAS member), and Castro routinely vilifies it as a tool of U.S. imperialism.

Nonetheless, the OAS has also issued reports criticizing the human rights situation in Cuba. The 2002 report of the Inter-American Commission on Human Rights found that the Cuban government was violating the human rights of its own citizens by refusing to call free elections and was violating its own constitution by refusing to accept the petition of the Varela Project.[21] It also cited reports by Amnesty International, the Inter-American Press Association, and dissident organizations within Cuba that detailed the illegal detention, assaults, and harassment of journalists and activists. The report concludes, "By law and in practice, the Cuban State has imposed limitations and restrictions on freedom of expression, assembly and association for so long and to such an extent that those limitations and restrictions have by now become government routine."[22] Thus, although most Latin American governments do not support U.S. punitive actions against Cuba, they decry the dearth of freedom there. When it received the report, the Cuban government replied that it did not recognize the authority of the commission.

The State of Democracy in Latin America

Certainly, liberal democracy is the political system most propitious for respect of human rights, in which not only do citizens enjoy the full panoply of rights but also all security forces are controlled by elected civilian authorities and are fully accountable for all their actions. With the exception of Cuba, Latin American governments are currently in power by virtue of free elections, but the foundations of democracy are generally still weak. Control over the military and police remains an aspiration rather than an accomplishment, and large portions of the population remain marginalized, sometimes with no effective political voice at all.

Particularly troubling is the low level of support for democracy among Latin Americans. In 2004, the United Nations Development Program issued a report based on interviews with 19,000 citizens spanning the region, completed in conjunction with the non profit NGO Latinobarómetro, which has conducted numerous similar surveys since 1995. The results were sobering and underlined how Latin Americans are not convinced that democracy is the most preferable form of government.[23]

Across Latin America only 2.3 percent believed that "government fulfills its promises," and 64.6 percent agreed with the statement that government officials "do not fulfill their promises because they lie to win elections." Even more problematic is that 54.7 percent agreed that they would support an authoritarian government if it solved economic problems; 43.9 percent did not think that democracy is capable of solving the country's problems. The study also concluded that although "democrats" and "nondemocrats" are spread throughout the entire population, Latin Americans who do not identify themselves as "democrats" tend to be younger and believe that they will be worse off than their parents. But there are also many parents themselves who believe their children will be worse off. Those who support democracy tend to be better educated, which also poses a challenge in a region with weak educational institutions.

The dilemma is that the rule of law undergirding human rights requires a democratic system, but support for democratic rule remains weak across the region. If, as the data suggest, people believe that democracy cannot resolve their economic problems, then they are more likely to support some type of political system (even if not necessarily a traditional military dictatorship) prone to ignore both regional and international human rights laws and conventions.

As with virtually all other aspects of human rights, there is no consensus regarding the "proper" role of the United States in fostering greater regional support for democracy. The U.S. government has focused largely on free market policies, centered on the idea that capitalism will provide economic opportunities for individuals, which in turn will make them believe that democracy benefits them. Critics disagree, at times strenuously, citing the increases in income inequality and poverty and the widespread sense of disenfranchisement.

In the post–Cold War era, the U.S. government has acted in defense of Latin American democracy. In 1993, Guatemalan President Jorge Serrano attempted a self-coup (known in Spanish as an "autogolpe"), which meant suspending the constitution and dissolving the legislature. In response, the Clinton administration froze economic aid and insisted that he restore democracy. Ultimately the Guatemalan military ultimately compelled his resignation. In 1996, Paraguayan army commander Lino Oviedo refused a presidential order to resign, and coup rumors quickly emerged. The U.S. ambassador immediately announced support for the president, even providing him safe haven, and Oviedo was eventually imprisoned.

In Peru, the United States had accepted the 1992 autogolpe of President Alberto Fujimori, but after a fraudulent (and unconstitutional) election in 2000, U.S. policy shifted. His widespread unpopularity, abuses of human rights, authoritarian tendencies, and then a scandal linking the Peruvian military to the Colombian FARC led to increased U.S. pressure, which then played a role in his decision to resign and seek asylum in Japan in 2000. As Chapter 11 will demonstrate, however, U.S. support for democracy has been more problematic after 9/11.

Summary and Conclusion

Before World War II, the issue of human rights was not a factor in U.S.–Latin American relations (or, in fact, international relations in general). The savagery of the war and especially the Holocaust vaulted human rights to the fore and made them a central part of the creation of the United Nations and the Organization of American States. However, the Cold War, with its emphasis on security over all else, quickly shifted human rights to the policy backburner, where it would remain until the 1970s.

As realism would predict, protection of human rights is a casualty of security, and as a consequence it took years for the issue to become relevant. Even after the Cold War, the United States was loath to sign either global or hemispheric agreements, arguing that they would infringe too much on sovereignty. In the era of the "war on terror," this policy stance is unlikely to be altered significantly. Change has been more noticeable in Latin America, where policy calculations differ from those in the United States.

The resurgence of human rights as a policy priority for Latin America came as a result of the new military dictatorships that were taking over in the region beginning in the 1960s, particularly because they were forcing out elected governments in countries like Chile and Uruguay that had enjoyed relatively long histories of stability and democratic elections. The Chilean dictatorship of General Augusto Pinochet became the epitome of what was wrong with human rights in the region, and his regime was a target for human rights activists.

In addition, at that time the development of human rights NGOs provided a forum that had not existed before. Even if the U.S. and many Latin American governments were reticent to speak out against Cold War allies, NGOs could, thereby putting pressure on the U.S. Congress and the international community to take action. This poses a challenge to the realist perspective, in that nonstate actors may gradually be forcing a powerful country to rethink policies and perhaps orient them in ways that are not consistent with its perceptions of security interests.

The end of the Cold War obviously changed the security perceptions of U.S. policy makers and created an opportunity to put the weight of the executive and legislative branches behind human rights policies. The U.S. attitude toward its relationship with Latin American militaries changed to the extent that human rights became an explicit part of military training.

After September 11, 2001, the issues of human rights and security were once again complicated. Chapter 11 will focus on the changes that took place when the global "war on terrorism" went into full swing. Given the military nature of the perceived threat, Latin American armed forces once again became the preferred conduit for U.S. defense policy, and the militaries themselves made it clear that, given the security issues at stake, they should be on the front lines of the new war. The consequence of this shift remains a vital issue in U.S.–Latin American relations.

Research Questions

1. What are the most prominent differences in U.S. policy regarding human rights during the Cold War versus the post–Cold War period?
2. What are the relative merits of realist and liberal institutional theories for analyzing human rights?
3. In what ways have international NGOs aided domestic NGOs in Latin America to protect human rights? Use the cases of one or two specific countries.

4. How effective does the United States appear to have been over time in reducing the human rights abuses committed by Latin American militaries?
5. How much influence has the U.S. Congress had over the human rights policies of the United States?
6. How prominent have the rights of women and indigenous groups in Latin America become in recent years? Use specific countries to illustrate.

Further Sources

Books

CLEARY, EDWARD L. *The Struggle for Human Rights in Latin America* (Westport, Conn.: Praeger, 1997). A clear summary and theoretical synthesis of the development of human rights as an important issue in Latin America, with attention to the growth of both grassroots organizations and transnational networks that put pressure on military governments.

DAVIS, MADELEINE (Ed.). *The Pinochet Case: Origins, Progress, and Implications* (London: Institute for Latin American Studies, 2003). Taken together, the essays in the book analyze the Pinochet case itself and also the importance of international law, the role of the military in Latin America, and the relationships between national and international courts.

KECK, MARGARET E., and KATHRYN SIKKINK. *Activists beyond Borders: Advocacy Networks in International Politics* (Ithaca, N.Y.: Cornell University Press, 1998). A groundbreaking book that addresses the ways in which international human rights activists had a dramatic impact on international and national policies and laws. Although it is not focused exclusively on Latin America, it dedicates a chapter to the region.

SCHOULTZ, LAR. *Human Rights and United States Policy toward Latin America* (Princeton, N.J.: Princeton University Press, 1981). Although dated, the book provides an in-depth analysis of the development of human rights issues in U.S. policy and the complicated process by which human rights activists (both within the U.S. Congress and from NGOs) were successful (or not) at influencing that policy.

SIKKINK, KATHRYN. *Mixed Signals: U.S. Human Rights Policy and Latin America* (Ithaca, N.Y.: Cornell University Press, 2004). An excellent book by an expert on the issue, emphasizing not only the "mixed signals" that the United States has sent in past decades but also the promise of important shifts that have taken place in U.S. policy. In particular, she argues that human rights advocates have been central to pushing the U.S. government to incorporate human rights in its policy toward Latin America.

Web Sites

United Nations, Human Rights Section. Part of the UN Web site is dedicated to human rights. It includes the entire text of the Universal Declaration, in addition to a wealth of other documents, treaties, and commission reports on a variety of topics, such as protection of women's rights, children, racial discrimination, and political persecution. http://www.un.org/rights/index.html

Amnesty International, Americas. This section of the Amnesty International Web site focuses on the Western Hemisphere. It has links both to regions and to specific countries. Each country link contains reports, dating back over a decade, on issues that AI has raised and its perceptions of actions being taken by the government of that country. http://web.amnesty.org/library/engworld/2am.

Human Rights Watch, Americas. Like Amnesty International, HRW has a specific section on the Americas. It frequently updates its press releases on current events related to human rights abuses and links to each country that has reports dating back to 1989. http://www.hrw.org/americas.

Inter-American Commission on Human Rights. The Web site of this OAS commission provides text of all human rights agreements and documents, along with press releases, speeches, annual reports (from 1970 to the present), and special reports. It also includes many country studies dating back to the 1960s. http://www.cidh.oas.org.

Latin American Network Information Center (LANIC), Human Rights. The University of Texas provides a very useful Web site that has links to a large number of topics and organizations. For human rights, it includes direct links to regional organizations, NGOs in Latin American countries and in the United States, research resources, and publications on human rights. http://lanic.utexas.edu/la/region/hrights/.

Notes

1. UN Web site.
2. Loveman 1993.
3. Quoted in Loveman 2001, 275.
4. Barnes 2004, 310.
5. Sikkink 1996, 63.
6. Sikkink 1996, 65.
7. Cleary 1997, 119.
8. Keck and Sikkink 1998, 116.
9. Quoted in Schoultz 1981, 15.
10. U.S. Department of State Web site 2003 (b).
11. Kissinger 2001, 93.
12. Bachelet 2005.
13. School of the Americas Watch Web site.
14. Ramsey 1997, 225.
15. Ramsey and Raimondo 2001, 112.
16. Ramsey 1997, 245.
17. Sikkink 2004, 208.
18. BBC News Web site 2003.
19. U.S. Department of State Web site 2004.
20. U.S. Department of State Web site 2004.
21. Organization of American States Web site 2002.
22. Organization of American States Web site 2002.
23. United Nations Development Program Web site.

CHAPTER 11

Drug Trafficking and Terrorism

<table>
<tr><td colspan="2">**TIMELINE**</td></tr>
<tr><td>1980</td><td>Shining Path formed</td></tr>
<tr><td>1986</td><td>President Ronald Reagan announces "War on Drugs"; U.S. certification policy begins</td></tr>
<tr><td>1992</td><td>Bombing of Israeli embassy in Buenos Aires</td></tr>
<tr><td>1992</td><td>Shining Path leader Abimael Guzmán captured</td></tr>
<tr><td>1994</td><td>Bombing of Jewish community center in Buenos Aires</td></tr>
<tr><td>2000</td><td>"Plan Colombia" goes into effect</td></tr>
<tr><td>2001</td><td>U.S. attacked by Al Qaeda terrorists</td></tr>
<tr><td>2003</td><td>U.S. allows Colombia to use funds for both drug traffickers and guerrillas</td></tr>
</table>

Concern over terrorism and political violence in the Americas is nothing new. For the United States, the existence of some type of armed threat was routinely the rationale employed for using force, including invasion, to protect its national security. The assumptions of realism clearly held during the Cold War, and the new specter of a global threat that emerged after September 11, 2001, brought the issue of the use of power to protect and advance national interests back to the fore. A militarized response, in which police and armed forces are prominent, once again took center stage.

In Latin America, the perception of political violence and terrorism is not monolithic. Some governments advocate the same policies as the United States; others seek alternate solutions. Even in countries where the government has launched military initiatives, prominent groups sometimes oppose such measures and argue that the interests of the United States do not mesh with national concerns.

Thus, in an international system characterized by anarchy, states are likely to clash over the response to perceived terrorist threats. Realist theory would posit that states faced with such potentially serious threats will behave according to their own interests and probably form coalitions that reflect shared interests. In the context of U.S.–Latin American relations, this can foster discord, as the hegemonic power's assertions of terrorist threats are not widely shared. For example, should an Andean coca grower be viewed as a cog in the drug-trafficking machine or as a peasant growing a crop his family has been cultivating for millennia?

The word "terrorism" itself is a loaded term, nebulous and open to interpretation. As mentioned in Chapter 6, Latin American guerrillas viewed themselves as freedom fighters, while the U.S. government and Latin American militaries preferred more negative labels. In the 1980s, a new type of threat emerged, associated with drugs, that would soon take a lion's share of U.S. policy attention, especially in the Andean region. These narco-terrorists were driven by profit and not ideology. Later, the U.S. "war on terror" would intensify U.S. attention on other potential terrorist threats, connected to the Middle East. In fact, senior analysts in the U.S. Defense Department wrote a memo after September 11 that proposed launching attacks in South America as "a surprise to the terrorists."[1] The notion that Latin American governments would also be unpleasantly surprised was not examined.

The Nature of Terrorism

Merely defining the concept is a slippery undertaking, with hundreds of definitions sprouting up from all directions, often based on ideological bias. A unique aspect of terrorism, however, is that it is deliberately perpetrated on "innocents," that is, people who are not directly participating in a given political conflict. In a prominent text on terrorism, Cindy Combs offers the following definition:

> A synthesis of war and theater, a dramatization of the most proscribed kind of violence—that which is perpetrated on innocent victims—played before an audience in the hope of creating a mood of fear, for political purposes.[2]

The U.S. government's legal definition is even broader. Title 18 (Chapter 113B, section 2331) of the U.S. Code defines "terrorism" as something that "appears" to be intended "to intimidate or coerce a civilian population; to influence the policy of a government by intimidation or coercion; or to affect the conduct of a government by mass destruction, assassination, or kidnapping."[3] Because the definition hinges on the word "innocent" or "civilian," terrorism is in the eye of the beholder. And governments have often affixed the terrorist label to political opponents, thereby legitimizing their persecution.

There is also a difference between terrorism perpetrated by individuals or groups and **state-sponsored terrorism,** which refers to terrorist acts organized and directed by governments. Currently, most terrorist acts in Latin America are committed by individuals or groups; during the Cold War, state-sponsored terrorism was much more prevalent, as dictatorships forged state policies of killing political enemies.

What varies even more is the appropriate response to the organization or group deemed to be terrorist. The most common answer has been military—fighting fire with fire—but this solution has been controversial, both within the United States and in individual Latin American countries.

So where has terrorism arisen in Latin America? Four organizations are listed by the State Department as "designated foreign terrorist organizations" (of which there are thirty-seven worldwide): the Colombian Revolutionary Armed Forces (FARC), the Army of National Liberation (ELN), the United Self-Defense Forces of Colombia (AUC), and Peru's Shining Path. In addition, the United States has identified terrorist activities in drug production and trafficking, guerrillas (mostly in Colombia), paramilitary violence, and support for extrahemispheric groups linked to political violence in other areas of the world (most notably the Middle East). A quantitative study of terrorist activity concluded that "**nongovernmental terrorism** in Latin America is more likely to occur in poorly institutionalized democracies characterized by electoral liberties, but at the same time by widespread human rights violations."[4] This description certainly fits both Colombia and Peru.

Latin Americans themselves are less certain that terrorism is a hemispheric problem or that the "global war" on terrorism is directly relevant to them. A useful illustration of the divergence is a comparison between the opinion of the main U.S. military representative in the Americas, the commander in chief of the United States Army Southern Command (SOUTHCOM), and Latin American public opinion.

General James Hill testified to a U.S. congressional panel in April 2004 about the threat of terrorism in Latin America. He said the United States "must take comprehensive measures in our region to combat international terrorism," including strengthening Latin American militaries and expanding their roles, which would be the main way to combat terrorists who "bomb, murder, kidnap, traffic drugs, transfer arms, launder money and smuggle humans."[5] Those statements stand in contrast to public opinion, because in only two countries (Colombia and Peru) do a majority of citizens believe terrorism is a "serious problem" in their country.[6] Taken together, 57 percent of Latin Americans also opposed U.S. military force in Afghanistan as a way of fighting terrorism (with a high of 80 percent in Argentina).

Because there is no consensus on whether a threat of terrorism even exists, it is not startling that U.S. solutions to its perceived threats are coming under scrutiny in Latin America. For example, the U.S. invasion of Iraq was widely denounced. Chile and Mexico were nonpermanent members of the UN Security Council when the United States attempted to garner support for invasion. Both countries publicly opposed a UN stamp of approval on the invasion, which scuttled U.S. hopes of obtaining a resolution for the use of force. Other governments signaled their disagreement, with Brazilian President Lula saying, "No one gave the United States the right to judge what is good and what is bad for the world."[7]

The countries that did support the Iraq invasion were small nations in Central America and the Caribbean (such as the Dominican Republic, El Salvador, Honduras, and Nicaragua). After the 2004 withdrawal of Spanish troops from Iraq, however, the Dominican Republic, Honduras, and Nicaragua followed suit. The overall point is that support for the U.S. global war on terrorism is shallow in Latin America.

Terrorism and Drugs

In the 1970s, the appetite for drugs, especially cocaine, in the United States rose dramatically. The Nixon administration was the first to address the problem officially by launching a domestic "war on drugs" in 1971, and President Nixon even appointed Elvis Presley as an honorary drug agent after a White House meeting. President Reagan made the topic even more prominent in 1986; his own drug war emphasized utilizing the U.S. military for purposes of interdiction. He did not, however, choose a drug addict as his celebrity ally. Significantly, this new war officially elevated drugs to the level of a national security threat, thereby greatly widening the potential responses.

Also in 1986, the United States began the policy of "certifying" countries before they could be eligible each year to receive antidrug funding. It represented Congress's attempt to force the president to prove that countries were "cooperating fully," with decertification signifying that money would not be granted. Other penalties, such as negative U.S. votes on loans from the International Monetary Fund and the Inter-American Development Bank, were also possible but not mandated by law. Although some Latin American countries (for example, Bolivia in 1995 and Colombia in 1996 and 1997) have been decertified at one point or another, the vast majority of countries are certified even if their record of fighting drugs is not stellar. The reason is that cutting off aid drastically limits U.S. influence, so that in the case of Peru, for example, the U.S. government acknowledged the growth of the coca industry but argued certification was necessary to ensure U.S. involvement in the economy and the protection of human rights. Similar arguments have been made for other countries. The president has the option of providing continued assistance to noncooperating countries if it is deemed in the national interest, and presidents have used this waiver extensively. Regardless, the **certification** process is viewed as insulting in Latin America.

As the demand for drugs in the United States soared, the profit to be made from cultivation, processing, and trafficking soon became immense. The country initially affected the most was Colombia, and it would continue to bear the brunt of the drug wars. The tremendous profit margins sparked violence, and rival groups in Colombia fought to seize as big a slice of the pie as possible. Throughout Latin American history, groups that employed violence most often offered an ideological rationale, even if only for public consumption. Drug-related terrorism lacks ideology and is instead focused on power and profit. It takes the form of intimidating elected officials and judges through bombings, assassinations, kidnappings, and extortion. It creates a climate of fear within which it is difficult to build effective political institutions.

Since 1999, the United Nations has published the annual *World Drug Report,* and the 2004 edition demonstrates the scope of the problem. Colombia accounts for the majority of the world's cocaine, and both Mexico and Colombia showed significant production of the opium poppy (which becomes heroin). The UN report did, however, estimate that the cultivation of coca bushes in Bolivia, Colombia, and Peru had dropped, though in Colombia the decrease only brought it back to the levels seen in the mid-1990s. One disturbing trend was that drug consumption in Latin America, which historically had been low, has been on the rise since 1995, especially in Brazil and Colombia but also in Central America and the Caribbean. Estimating the total profits associated with illicit drugs in Latin America is a tricky business, because drug traffickers don't tend to inform the authorities how much money they are illegally making. As a result, the estimates vary widely, but tend to hover between $2 billion and $6 billion a year.

The Latin American view of drugs and U.S. policy is complex. Despite scant support for the violence associated with drugs, there are indigenous movements that believe U.S. policy unfairly fails to distinguish between terrorists and indigenous populations that have been growing and chewing coca for millennia. There is concern about governments' ability to combat drug-related terrorism,

Figure 11.1 Cocaine Consumption Trends in Latin America

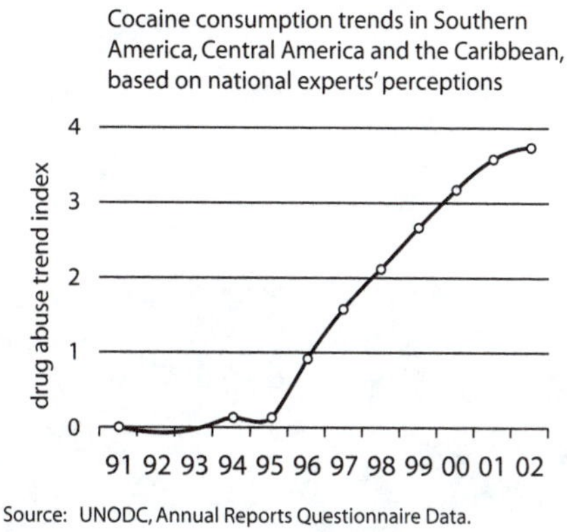

Cocaine consumption trends in Southern America, Central America and the Caribbean, based on national experts' perceptions

Source: UNODC, Annual Reports Questionnaire Data.

Source: United Nations *World Drug Report* (2004).

but there is also resentment that the United States uses blunt instruments such as the certification process to compel Latin America to fight the drug war its way.

Terrorism and Drugs: The Case of Colombia

The Colombian case illustrates many of these complexities. Colombia is blessed by tremendous natural resources (including oil), but part of the blessing became a curse in that large expanses in remote areas have the perfect climate and soil for coca. Although Colombian presidents sought positive relations with the United States for many years (including sending troops to Korea in 1951), they crafted foreign policies that were consciously independent of the United States, including opposition to U.S. intervention in Central America (with leadership in the Contadora Group), participation in the Non-Aligned Movement, and seeking Latin American solutions to the debt crisis. The upsurge in drug-related violence, however, served to emphasize the power imbalance, as Colombia would shift its foreign policies in response to pressure from the U.S. government, which held the purse strings to enormous amounts of aid. In the past, Colombian presidents had been reluctant to use military force. The U.S.–Colombian relationship broke down in the early 1990s, as the United States accused President Ernesto Samper of being ineffective and tied to the drug cartels, even labeling Colombia a "narco-state."[8]

Particularly since the 1980s, virtually all Colombian violence is fueled by drug money. In addition to the drug traffickers themselves, the already existing Marxist guerrilla groups—the FARC and ELN—began taking "taxes" estimated at 10–15 percent for each transaction between coca growers and drug traffickers, which nets approximately $500 million a year. Although the FARC and the ELN continue to espouse their Marxist revolutionary messages (the

Scott Dalton/The New York Times

Photo 11.1 Colombia coca production.

FARC's Web site emphasizes the mission of revolution to advance the cause of the oppressed), they have become closely associated with the drug trade.

Added to this volatile mix are paramilitary groups, the private armies originally funded by landowners who wanted armed protection from the guerrillas. The largest of these, the AUC, has committed more acts of terrorism in recent years than any other group in Colombia (on occasion in conjunction with the military) and also has tapped into the drug trade. As one experienced observer notes, "All of Colombia's armies seemed to assume, barring clear proof to the contrary, that everyone in their path was suspect, a potential 'military target.'"[9]

The Colombian government considered itself under siege, and in late 1998 President Andrés Pastrana proposed a program to combine Colombian and international funds to fight the war on drugs, largely military but including a comprehensive program of economic development. What became known as "Plan Colombia" involved requesting aid from both Europe and the United States, a total of $7.5 billion, $4 billion of which would come from the Colombian government. European leaders who, Pastrana hoped, would contribute humanitarian assistance, did not, but in January 2000, the Clinton administration agreed to pay $1.6 billion. Given concerns within Congress that Colombia could become "another Vietnam," the administration framed it almost entirely in antidrug terms. Plan Colombia has been renewed every year, and by late 2006 the Colombian government estimated that $10.65 billion had been spent.[10] Consistently, more than 80 percent of the funds go to the military and police.

Plan Colombia (1999)

INTRODUCTION

Colombia finds itself on the threshold of the twenty-first century proud but threatened, facing an historic challenge to establish and consolidate a society within which the State may exercise its true authority and fulfill its fundamental obligations, in accordance with the Constitution:

". . . To serve the community, promote the general welfare and guarantee the effectiveness of the principles, rights, and duties enshrined in the Constitution; to facilitate the participation of all into the decisions that affect them and in the general economic, political, administrative, and cultural life of the nation; to defend national independence, to maintain territorial integrity and to assure peaceful coexistence and the perpetuation of a just order."

Today, all of these objectives are at stake. Our greatest responsibility as a government is to construct a better and more secure country for the generations of today and tomorrow and to assure that the State becomes a more effective force for tranquility, prosperity, and national progress. We ought to construct a social justice State that protects all citizens and maintains their rights to life, dignity, and the rights of belief, opinion, and press. . . .

There can be no doubt that Colombia suffers the problems of a State that as yet has not been able to consolidate its power, with a lack of confidence in the capacity of the armed forces, police, and judicial systems, of the ability to guarantee the permanence of order and security; a crisis of credibility in different levels and services of government; and corruption in the conduct of the public and private sectors. All of this has been fomented and aggravated by the destabilizing effects of narcotrafficking, which with its vast economic resources has generated indiscriminate violence, and the same time has undermined our values to a point that can only be compared to the era of prohibition in the United States.

. . . In sum, the aspirations of the Colombian people and the labors of the government have been frustrated by narcotrafficking, and this has complicated the efforts of the government to fulfill its constitutional duties. A vicious and perverse cycle of violence and corruption has exhausted the resources necessary for the construction and success of a modern State.

We understand that the achievement of our objectives will depend on a social and governmental process that will probably last many years, years in which it will be of vital importance to obtain a lasting consensus within society, where people understand and demand their rights, but also stand ready to fulfill their duties. . . .

The negotiations with the insurgent groups, already initiated by my government, constitute the nucleus of our strategy, since it is critical to resolve a conflict that for forty years has served as a source of obstacles to the creation of a modern and progressive State that Colombia must urgently create. The search for peace and the defense of democratic institutions demands constant effort, faith,

(Continued)

and persistence to successfully combat the inherent pressures and doubts in a process so full of difficulties

The fight against narcotrafficking is another of the important themes of Plan Colombia. Our strategy seeks to improve the alliance between countries that are producers and consumers of narcotics, based on principles of reciprocity and equality. The traffic in illicit drugs constitutes a complex transnational threat, a destructive force in all societies, that carries with it unimaginable consequences for the consumers of this poison, and overwhelming effects, starting with the violence and corruption generated by its immense profits. No solution will be achieved with mutual recriminations between producer and consumer countries. Our efforts will never be sufficient unless they form part of an alliance of true international reach to combat narcotrafficking. . . .

However, we have to recognize that now, twenty years after the arrival of marijuana cultivation in Colombia, together with the increased production of coca and poppy, narcotrafficking is growing in importance as a destabilizing force; it is a cause of distortions in our economy, a reversal of the advances made in the redistribution of land, a source of corruption in society, and multiplier of violence, and a negative factor in the investment climate and worst of all, it serves as a source of growing resources for armed groups. . . .

On the road to success, we also need reforms in the heart of our institutions, especially in the armed forces, with the goal of strengthening the law and recovering the confidence and security of all Colombians in every corner of the country. To consolidate and maintain the rule of law, it is critical to have strong armed forces and police, responsible and agile in their responses, with an obvious commitment to peace and respect for human rights. We will work without cease toward this goal, convinced that our primordial obligation as a government is to guarantee that our citizens may exercise their fundamental rights and liberties without fear.

But at the same time, the strategy for peace and progress depends upon the reform and modernization of other institutions, so that the political process can function as an effective instrument of economic progress and social justice. In this sense, we must reduce the causes and factors that generate violence, through the opening of new roads for social participation and the creation of a collective conscience that holds the government accountable for the results. Our strategy in this area includes a specific initiative to guarantee that within five years there will be universal access to education and an adequate health system, with special attention to the most vulnerable and abandoned sectors.

Additionally, we will try to reinforce local administration with the aim of making it more sensitive and to provide a more rapid response to the necessities of citizens. Similarly, we will foster the active participation of the general population in the fight against corruption, kidnapping, violence, and the displacement of people and communities in conflict zones.

Lastly, Colombia needs help to strengthen its economy and to generate employment. The country needs better and fairer access to international markets for our competitive products. The collaboration of the United States, the European community, and the rest of the international community is essential for the country's economic development. This same development will serve as a force to combat narcotrafficking, since it promises alternatives of legal employment for those who otherwise would resort to organized crime or to insurgent groups that feed off narcotrafficking. . . .

There are reasons to be optimistic about Colombia's future, especially if we receive a positive response from the international community regarding our efforts to bring general prosperity accompanied by social justice. This will allow Colombians to advance toward a lasting peace.

Translated by the author (original in Spanish).

Source: http://embajadausa.org.ve/wwwh176.html#001.

Largely because of the intermestic concern that the public would view a war against guerrillas a potential "quagmire" like Vietnam, for years the U.S. government had distinguished between drug traffickers and guerrillas in Colombia, which meant funding efforts to fight the former but not the latter. Narco-terrorists were thus viewed as an international problem, whereas guerrillas represented a domestic Colombian issue, to be left to the Colombian government. In 2002, the Bush administration announced that the distinction would no longer be made. In practice, however, the two had been blurred for some time, despite the U.S. government's public insistence that U.S. military aid would be directed only to counternarcotics missions. Under pressure from the U.S. Congress, which was concerned about human rights violations, in 1997 the Clinton administration worked out an agreement whereby military aid would be restricted to specific parts of Colombia to ensure it was being used only to fight drug traffickers. In 2000, however, these "designated areas" were defined as the "entire national territory of the Republic of Colombia."[11] The Colombian government insisted that it was impossible to separate the two, and President Bush eventually agreed.

President Alvaro Uribe was elected in 2002 on a platform of restoring security to the country. He announced, for example, that the military would be employed to retake the Switzerland-sized territory in southern Colombia that had been ceded to the FARC in 1999 by President Pastrana as part of a failed peace agreement. His use of emergency powers (which include suspension of normal constitutional rights) was popular, and within months his approval rating was 74 percent.

Uribe has also been very canny in placing Colombia's violence in the broader context of the U.S. war on terrorism. Even as he supported the Bush administration's preparations to invade Iraq, Uribe argued that drugs posed "a more serious menace than Iraq," so "why don't they consider an equal, similar deployment to put an end to this problem."[12] Although the United States did not commit to such a deployment, in 2004 it did double the number of U.S. military personnel (from 400 to 800), primarily to protect oil pipelines—an increasingly common target—from sabotage.

The War on Drugs in Bolivia and Peru

Although Colombia is the epicenter of the drug trade, Bolivia and Peru are also important source countries. From the so-called **balloon effect**, whereby squeezing in one country leads to greater production in another, production shifted to Colombia when counterdrug policies were expanded in Bolivia and Peru. Coca cultivation never came close to disappearing, however, and the two countries have tended to evince more opposition to U.S. drug policies than Colombia and are less eager to use military force in rural areas.

Led by president and former military dictator Hugo Banzer, in 1998 the Bolivian government launched Plan Dignidad, an aggressive military effort that led to major decreases in coca cultivation and much improved relations with the United States. Popular support for such measures have been mixed. In rural areas, it is quite low, but dissatisfaction has also been on the rise in urban areas, where the issue is viewed as involving sovereignty and nationalism. Tensions between the United States and Bolivia continually surface because of the stiff resistance of coca growers, or **cocaleros,** to what they view as policies being imposed by the United States, leaving the Bolivian government in the unenviable position of standing between U.S. pressure and domestic opposition. Even Bolivian military officers involved in eradication can feel guilty: "We know that what we are doing here causes these people to go hungry. Alternative development projects don't provide income. This makes us the bad guys."[13] The U.S. State Department's International Narcotics Control Strategy Report (INCSR) for 2005 noted with clear impatience that the Bolivian government "seemed more concerned with containing possible confrontations with cocaleros through negotiation and concessions than with the consistent application of the rule of law."[14] Indeed, Evo Morales's election in late 2005 marks a new twist in the U.S.–Bolivian relationship, because he stands firmly behind the right of peasants to grow coca for their own consumption.

In Peru, the drug trade as a whole equals $1.2 to $2 to 4 billion, or approximately 2 to 4 percent of Peru's GDP. The debt crisis in the 1980s spurred migration toward the coca-growing regions, and the trade quickly expanded. During the tenure of Alberto Fujimori (1990–2000), there were numerous reports of drug-related corruption in the government, especially his shadowy advisor, Vladimiro Montesinos. As in Bolivia, the Peruvian government has always faced rural opposition to eradication. In 2003, cocaleros successfully blocked a major highway and forced government concessions on where eradication would take place. In February 2004, there was even a congress of coca growers in Lima, which advocated the marketing of coca-based products, such as energy beverages, flour, chocolate, cakes, shampoo, toothpaste, and cosmetic creams. Furthermore, efforts by the government to negotiate gradual eradication have been opposed by the United States. The U.S. ambassador argued that the Peruvian government should not negotiate with coca farmers (whom he labeled "narco-farmers"): "This [negotiation] focus does not take into account a fundamental element: that illegal crops are the principal ingredient drug traffickers use to make coca paste and cocaine. Coca growers, as such, become the suppliers of drug trafficking."[15] The 2005 INCSR also lamented "the increased support by members of Congress for cocalero demands for more permissive coca laws."

Transshipment Countries: The War on Drugs in Mexico

Drug trafficking and violence affects other Latin American countries primarily in the context of transshipment, as drugs pass through from source countries on their way to waiting customers in the United States. Although Mexico has long been one source of marijuana and poppy, its long border with the United States transformed it into the primary launching pad for bringing cocaine into the United States.

In 1995, high-level meetings between U.S. and Mexican officials set in motion greater military contacts, and by 1996 almost 1,000 Mexican soldiers began receiving training in the United States. After 2000, newly elected president Vicente Fox (who broke the nearly 70-year grip on power by the Partido Revolucionario Institucional, or PRI) proposed making the drug issue one of public order rather than national security and removing the Mexican army from the drug war, but these proposals were shelved under U.S. criticism.

The connection between drug trafficking and corruption is a source of friction, as the U.S. government has accused high-ranking Mexican officials (including cabinet members, state governors, and presidential advisors) as having ties to drug traffickers. A Swiss study determined that Raúl Salinas, the brother of former president Carlos Salinas (1988–1994) controlled the flow of drugs in and out of the country during his brother's term.[16] The Fox administration initiated anticorruption programs (one of which included consultation by former New York City Mayor Rudy Guiliani) that have decreased—though not eliminated—the considerable distrust between U.S. drug officials and the Mexican government.

"Winning" the War on Narcoterrorism

Unlike a conventional war in which one side is clearly defeated, the war on drugs, like the war on terrorism more generally, is multifaceted and rarely yields obvious victory. From a strictly military point of view, "winning" would mean defeat of the major terrorist groups in countries like Colombia, but such a victory is far from certain. Given access to immense funds, the FARC remains strong and, despite changes in leadership and efforts to provide amnesties in exchange for giving up armed struggle, so has the AUC, while the violence originating with the drug traffickers themselves has also continued largely unabated. Organized crime related to drugs remains a critical dilemma across the region, especially in the Andean countries, Central America, and Mexico (in the parlance of U.S. policy, guerrillas and drug traffickers tend to be viewed jointly as "terrorists," even though the latter is oriented more toward profit than toward politics).

From a Latin American point of view, "winning" would involve eliminating the incentives—especially monetary—that prompt citizens to grow coca and distribute it. Programs aimed at crop substitution—meaning subsidies to grow legal crops such as corn, coffee, rice, cotton, heart of palm, black pepper, pineapple, bananas, passion fruit, and macadamia nuts—by and large have not been successful. Convincing the rural population to grow these new crops has been difficult, as an immediate problem is that they do not yield the same profit and, in many cases, are harder to grow than coca (which is a hardy plant that grows quickly). A 2004 report by the General Accounting Office admitted that start-up costs for alternative crops were too high. In one instance, a project to grow coffee foundered because it would require up to five years to meet the standards of the specialty coffee market, and U.S. buyers were unwilling to travel to evaluate it in the first place.[17] In addition, the U.S. domestic policy of agricultural subsidies that protects U.S. farmers makes it harder for Latin American farmers to sell alternative products in the U.S. market. The Andean Trade Promotion and Drug Eradication Act, passed in 1991 and extended in 2006 (though only for six months), grants Bolivia, Colombia, Ecuador, and Peru preferences for certain exports. Approximately 5,600 products are listed (such as apparel, jewelry, footwear, leather, watches, cacao, and lumber), though politically sensitive items (such as cotton) are not because the foreign policy is largely intermestic. Allowing such goods through trade preferences can spark a domestic political backlash in the United States.

In part, success can also be measured in the reduction of land acreage used for coca cultivation. In 2004, the U.S. State Department announced that Colombian coca cultivation was down 33 percent in the 2002–2004 period and down 22 percent overall in Bolivia, Colombia, and Peru.[18] However, a combined view of the three countries paints a different and more volatile picture, in which total area dropped in 2003 but only after large increases in 2001–2002, and in which overall cultivation has remained fairly constant for over a decade.

Unfortunately, even success can have serious consequences. For example, the most common strategy to eradicate coca plants is aerial spraying of herbicides. Private contractors (usually U.S. citizens) fly small planes to spray from the air. Although the U.S. government considers aerial spraying a highly effective way to eradicate coca, from the ground the perspective is strikingly different. Because legitimate farmers can live close to coca plantations and aerial spraying is imprecise (pilots fly as high as possible to avoid being shot at), their legal crops are often destroyed as well. There is also fear that people are being sprayed (which causes blisters and poisoning) and that water sources may become contaminated.

Victory would also entail a reduction in the amount of narco-terrorist violence. In a 2003 speech to the United Nations, Colombian President Alvaro Uribe noted that in the first nine months of the year, the number of homicides decreased by 22 percent, kidnappings by 34.7 percent (though that brought the number of kidnappings down only to 1,485), victims of illegal road blocks declined 49 percent, and the number of "massacres" by 35 percent.[19] Those gains seem impressive but must be viewed in the context of the spread of violence across Colombia's borders. In 2002, more than a hundred people were

Table 11.1 Hectares of Coca Cultivation in Bolivia, Colombia and Peru, 1991–2005

	1991	1992	1993	1994	1995	1996	1997	1998	1999	2000	2001	2002	2003	2004	2005
Bolivia	47,900	45,500	47,200	48,100	48,600	48,100	45,800	38,000	21,800	14,600	19,900	24,400	28,450	24,600	25,600
Colombia	37,500	37,100	39,700	44,700	50,900	67,200	79,500	101,800	122,500	136,200	169,800	144,450	113,850	114,100	144,000
Peru	120,800	129,100	108,800	108,600	115,300	94,400	68,800	51,000	38,700	34,200	34,000	36,000	31,500	27,500	38,000
Totals	206,200	211,700	195,700	201,400	214,800	209,700	194,100	190,800	183,000	185,000	223,700	204,850	173,450	166,200	207,600

Source: INCSR Reports, 1999–2007.

killed in Ecuador as the FARC moved through porous rural borders to find supplies and even built its own radio station. The FARC has similarly moved into neighboring Panama and Venezuela.

For many Latin Americans, there is also the question of why the war is being fought in the first place. Peasants struggling to subsist are certainly not much concerned whether more middle-class teenagers in the United States become addicted to crack, and they wonder why they are caught in the middle of a battle they view as utterly removed from them. Political leaders like Evo Morales in Bolivia criticize U.S. policy, which they say is just another example of imperialism: "The fight against drug traffickers is a pretext for the US to dominate Latin America—for the US to dominate our people—to violate our sovereignty."[20] Suspicion about U.S. objectives remains high. Dependency theorists would follow a similar line of thought, as the drug trade could be viewed as yet another example of how Latin American economies are driven by the demands of the developed world. In addition, the fact that peasants engage in the drug trade is indicative of a failure of the Colombian economy to produce jobs. Persistent underdevelopment thus further fuels the drug trade.

Moreover, the drug war can be measured in terms of demand in the United States. As the Peruvian novelist and former presidential candidate Mario Vargas Llosa argues, "Production exists because a market exists, near irresistible goad to produce. Farmers can increase their earnings fivefold, tenfold, sometimes one hundredfold by planting coca instead of traditional crops."[21] Given the booming market, it is extraordinarily difficult to stop production. The White House Office of National Drug Control Policy estimates that in 2000 there were 2.7 million chronic users of cocaine and 3 million occasional users in the United States, and combined they spent $35 billion. The use of cocaine has dropped from the highs of the mid-1980s (when more public attention was finally paid to the epidemic), but has remained generally level since 1990. The money to be made remains massive.

Ideological Violence

Although the drug trade is the engine of much violence in Latin America, there are still pockets of ideologically motivated organizations that seek the overthrow of governments. Aside from the FARC, one of the most deadly is in Peru. The Sendero Luminoso ("Shining Path") was the brainchild of a philosophy professor, Abimael Guzmán. Organized in the 1970s, it was based on Marxist ideology, and through the 1980s it led a violent and relentless campaign; according to Peru's Truth and Reconciliation Commission, it was directly responsible for 54 percent of the 69,000 deaths caused by guerrilla war.[22] Shining Path's goal was even more extreme than most Marxist organizations in Latin America because it wanted to destroy all existing institutions and create a peasant society loosely based on the ideas of Mao Zedong, the former Chinese Communist dictator. The commission estimated that at its height, Shining Path had approximately

5,000 members, which "speaks of an exceptional ferocity," given the number of deaths it caused.

Unlike drug policy, the U.S. and Peruvian governments were of one mind when it came to deciding what methods were necessary to face the problem. Under the leadership of President Fujimori, Peru made significant advances against Shining Path and even caught Guzmán in 1992. (He was then dressed in a striped prison outfit and placed in a public cage, where he ranted against the government and announced that the revolution would cost a million deaths.)

With the encouragement of the U.S. government (despite a brief snag in relations when Fujimori dissolved Congress in a "self-coup" in 1992), Fujimori had utilized all measures at his disposal to fight terrorism. The downside, however, was the erosion of Peruvian democracy, which was already teetering on the brink. Antiterrorist legislation laid waste to due process. Furthermore, Fujimori had empowered the national intelligence agency and, with the assistance of his advisor Vladimiro Montesinos, utilized it in the name of security to spy on the entire country, especially his political enemies. The mounting corruption charges would eventually prompt Fujimori and Montesinos to flee the country in 2000. The former would successfully seek asylum in Japan (in 2005, he flew to Chile, where he was immediately arrested; as of early 2007, he awaited extradition hearings), whereas the latter would be arrested and eventually imprisoned. Peru's political institutions have yet to recover.

Religious Extremism

The U.S. government has charged that support for religious extremists, especially those originating in the Middle East, is a growing problem in Latin America. Two major attacks did occur in Argentina, the 1992 bombing of the Israeli Embassy and the 1994 bombing of a Jewish cultural center, which combined accounted for more than a hundred deaths. These attacks were linked to the Iranian government (including the ambassador) and received considerable international attention, but fortunately similar terrorist activities did not appear either in Argentina or in other countries. However, the issue of Middle Eastern–based activity became far more prominent for the United States after September 11, 2001. Of central concern were not attacks per se, but rather money laundering and weapons trafficking.

In particular, the so-called Triborder Area that intersects Argentina, Brazil, and Paraguay has long been a haven for illicit activity, most notably money laundering, and the United States considers it a center of support for Middle Eastern terrorism. According to the United States, this support includes smuggling and drug trafficking for the purpose of raising funds for Hezbollah, Hamas, Islamic Jihad, and even Al Qaeda. Although Latin American governments in the subregion deny links to terrorism, the United States has pushed for increased military presence in what it terms "ungoverned areas."

Even before September 11, 2001, the U.S. government had begun working to redefine its defense policies to account for the end of the Cold War. This effort was partly multilateral, as beginning in 1995 the defense ministers of the region met to discuss the defense issues facing the hemisphere (by 2006, five subsequent meetings had been held). This led to a 1995 National Security Strategy for the Americas that was updated again in 2000. Arguing that the primary threats would be transnational in nature, the document stated, "The United States is unequivocal in its opposition to terrorism and committed to take whatever steps are necessary to protect American lives, property, and interests."[23] The word "whatever" soon manifested itself in military terms.

As a whole, the strategy bore a great resemblance to Cold War policy, though unlike the past, it specifically emphasized the development of democratic civil-military relations, human rights, and accountability. It also contained an echo of the past in terms of acknowledging the relationship between economic deprivation and political unrest, which in turn could contain the seeds of drug trafficking and violence. But where the Alliance for Progress had called for development projects, in the twenty-first century the United States instead emphasized capitalism, free markets, free trade, and economic integration.

United States Security Strategy for the Americas (2000)

The past decade has brought about a period of unprecedented transition in the hemisphere. The end of armed conflict in Central America and other improvements in regional security have coincided with renewed emphasis on democratic principles and free market economics throughout the Americas. . . . Many Latin American nations have made enormous advances in democratic governance. The hemisphere's leaders are committed to strengthening democracy, justice, and human rights. They have pledged to intensify efforts to promote democratic reform, subordinate their militaries to democratic civilian authorities, protect the rights of migrant workers, improve the civil and criminal justice systems, and encourage a strong and active civil society. . . .

While traditional security concerns continue to exist, the principal security concerns in the hemisphere now are transnational in nature. They include drug trafficking, arms trafficking, money laundering and other organized crime, illegal immigration, and terrorism. These threats could undermine the sovereignty, democracy, and national security of nations in the hemisphere. Working bilaterally and multilaterally through the OAS and other organizations, the countries of the region have reaffirmed their commitment to combat together the serious challenges posed by these transnational threats. . . .

TERRORISM

Latin America is not immune to the actions of international terrorist groups and the resultant threat of terrorism. Extrahemispheric actors were linked to Hizballah car bomb attacks against Israeli targets in Buenos Aires in 1992 and 1994. Some regional terrorism is rooted in long-standing internal strife. In Colombia, for example, there are two main groups—the Revolutionary Armed Forces of Colombia (FARC) and the National Liberation Army (ELN)—and a league of criminal paramilitary groups which engage in extensive terrorist activity. These groups threaten the lives of Colombians and other citizens and the security and development of the region. In Peru, the Sendero Luminoso (Shining Path) and Tupac Amaru Revolutionary Movement (MRTA) remain potential threats even after both suffered severe reversals in the mid-1990s at the hands of government security forces.

The United States is unequivocal in its opposition to terrorism and committed to take whatever steps are necessary to protect American lives, property, and interests. Our goal is to investigate terrorist attacks fully and capture perpetrators as quickly as possible, not only to put them out of action but also to deter would-be imitators. The United States will bring to justice those who commit acts of terrorism against American interests. Countries in the hemisphere must work together to eliminate terrorist sanctuaries, counter state-supported terrorism and employ all available legal means to punish terrorists.

DRUG TRAFFICKING

The Andean Ridge states of Colombia, Bolivia, and Peru produce the vast majority of the world's cocaine as well as a significant amount of heroin. Lesser quantities of heroin are cultivated in Mexico. Efforts to eradicate crops or interdict them en route show progress in terms of hectares destroyed and kilograms seized, but the volume of drugs available on the streets of countries across the hemisphere, including the United States, remains unacceptably high. . . .

The illicit drug trade has a direct impact on domestic security and social stability of every country in the hemisphere. The United States will continue to support eradication, interdiction of regional air-bridges, anti-trafficking efforts on maritime and riverine routes, alternative crop development, and reform of judicial systems and law enforcement agencies, while simultaneously promoting intensive demand reduction at home. The United States will pursue opportunities to foster greater intraregional counterdrug cooperation, taking into account the role of the armed forces, police forces, and law enforcement personnel associated with the counterdrug effort varies from country to country. The United States seeks to achieve a counterdrug alliance in this hemisphere, one that might serve as a model for enhanced cooperation elsewhere in the world. . . .

The United States has long defined its security interests in the Western Hemisphere in terms of peace, stability, and prosperity. . . . With the end of the Cold War, the United States adjusted its diplomatic and military posture to the new realities of the hemisphere. The focus of U.S. policy shifted to achieving increased interoperability for purposes of international peacekeeping and to better respond to humanitarian crises in the hemisphere, encouraging the institutionalization of democratic norms within defense establishments and engaging in cooperative security initiatives to include combating transnational crime.

(Continued)

On the economic front, the United States seeks to advance the goal of an integrated hemisphere of free market democracies by building on the economic integration process begun by NAFTA. Formal negotiations to initiate the Free Trade Area of the Americas (FTAA) by 2005 are underway. The United States will also continue to work with the IMF, the World Bank, the Inter-American Development Bank, the governments of the Western Hemisphere and the private sector to help the transition to integrated, mature, free market economies.

STRATEGY FOR THE AMERICAS

In pursuit of these objectives, the Department of Defense has a five-pronged strategy. First, the Department of Defense will *remain engaged in the hemisphere*. . . . Second, the Department of Defense will *support efforts to ensure democratic control of defense and law enforcement institutions*. . . . Third, the Department of Defense will *support efforts to strengthen effectiveness, legitimacy, and transparency of regional and subregional security structures and regimes*. . . . Fourth, the Department of Defense will *support cooperative approaches to the peaceful resolution of border disputes and response to transnational threats and humanitarian crises*. . . . Finally, the Department of Defense will seek *to build mutual confidence on security issues and develop long-term bilateral and multilateral cooperation among defense ministries and security forces*.

Source: United States Security Strategy for the Americas. United States Department of Defense, Office of International Security Affairs (2000).

The Role of the OAS

After the rancor of the Cold War, the 1990s saw a period of greater consensus in the Organization of American States on the subject of terrorism. Resolutions passed in 1996 and 1998 paved the way for the creation in 1999 of the Inter-American Committee against Terrorism (CICTE), which began meeting in 2001 to discuss how member states could cooperate through the auspices of the OAS to combat the problem.

In the wake of September 11, 2001, the OAS moved quickly to show solidarity with the United States and to debate antiterrorist measures. Ten days later, a meeting of the foreign ministers passed a resolution condemning the attacks and calling on all countries to "take effective measures" against terrorists, though also emphasizing the need to protect human rights, civil liberties, and democracy.

Interestingly, the OAS has faced the same dilemma as the United Nations in failing to define "terrorism." Because of the difficulties inherent in differentiating a "freedom fighter" from a "terrorist," the strategy of individual governments has often been to criminalize certain activities and label the perpetrators (and their supporters) as terrorists. In that vein, the Inter-American Convention against Terrorism, passed in 2002, looks to international agreements (especially through the

United Nations) to specify terrorist activities, such as seizure of aircraft, taking of hostages, and bombings. The convention thus calls for member states to share intelligence, freeze assets, deny asylum, transfer suspects, tighten borders, and prosecute money laundering. By 2004, thirty-three of thirty-four member countries had signed it—the only country not to sign is Dominica, a small Caribbean island—and ten had ratified. The United States ratified in late 2005.

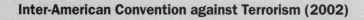

Inter-American Convention against Terrorism (2002)

Article 1. Object and Purpose

The purposes of this Convention are to prevent, punish, and eliminate terrorism. To that end, the states parties agree to adopt the necessary measures and to strengthen cooperation among them, in accordance with the terms of this Convention. . . .

Article 3. Domestic Measures

Each state party, in accordance with the provisions of its constitution, shall endeavor to become a party to the international instruments listed in Article 2 to which it is not yet a party and to adopt the necessary measures to effectively implement such instruments, including establishing, in its domestic legislation, penalties for the offenses described therein. . . .

Article 5. Seizure and Confiscation of Funds or Other Assets

Each state party shall, in accordance with the procedures established in its domestic law, take such measures as may be necessary to provide for the identification, freezing or seizure for the purposes of possible forfeiture, and confiscation or forfeiture, of any funds or other assets constituting the proceeds of, used to facilitate, or used or intended to finance, the commission of any of the offenses established in the international instruments listed in Article 2 of this Convention. . . .

Article 7. Cooperation on Border Controls

The states parties, consistent with their respective domestic legal and administrative regimes, shall promote cooperation and the exchange of information in order to improve border and customs control measures to detect and prevent the international movement of terrorists and trafficking in arms or other materials intended to support terrorist activities. . . .

Article 8. Cooperation among Law Enforcement Authorities

The states parties shall work closely with one another, consistent with their respective domestic legal and administrative systems, to enhance the effectiveness of law enforcement action to combat the offenses established in the international

(Continued)

instruments listed in Article 2. In this context, they shall establish and enhance, where necessary, channels of communication between their competent authorities in order to facilitate the secure and rapid exchange of information concerning all aspects of the offenses established in the international instruments listed in Article 2 of this Convention.

Article 15. Human rights

1. The measures carried out by the states parties under this Convention shall take place with full respect for the rule of law, human rights, and fundamental freedoms.

2. Nothing in this Convention shall be interpreted as affecting other rights and obligations of states and individuals under international law, in particular the Charter of the United Nations, the Charter of the Organization of American States, international humanitarian law, international human rights law, and international refugee law.

3. Any person who is taken into custody or regarding whom any other measures are taken or proceedings are carried out pursuant to this Convention shall be guaranteed fair treatment, including the enjoyment of all rights and guarantees in conformity with the law of the state in the territory of which that person is present and applicable provisions of international law. . . .

Source: http://www.oas.org/main/main.asp?sLang=E&sLink=http://www.cicte.oas.org.

Even countries with governments suspicious of the United States concurred with the need to fight terrorism. At CICTE's 2004 meeting, the Venezuelan delegate asserted that his country "condemns terrorism in all its forms" while focusing also on the desirability of cooperation.[24] Brazil offered its support and emphasized the need to reduce poverty as a means to limit the temptation and rationale to join terrorist organizations. The reactions of other countries were similar, in terms of acknowledging the general threat of terrorism while highlighting the need for continued multilateral discussions.

The exception to OAS activities, of course, remains Cuba. The United States maintains that Cuba should be labeled a "state sponsor" of terrorism, with the argument that Fidel Castro allowed members of the Spanish terrorist group ETA as well as the Colombian FARC to come to Cuba. Outside the United States, there is little acceptance of the notion that Cuba represents any sort of terrorist threat and, as mentioned in Chapter 8, diplomatic and trade relations between Cuba and other Latin American countries are expanding.

Immediately after September 11, 2001, Fidel Castro gave a speech condemning terrorism and sent a letter to UN Secretary General Kofi Annan expressing Cuba's support for antiterrorist resolutions. Anti-Castro activists believed none of it and argued that someone who had espoused terrorism was in no position to condemn it. The U.S. government took the same position, continuing to list Cuba as one of only seven countries worldwide to be labeled as "state sponsors of terrorism" (the others were Iran, Iraq, Libya, North Korea, Syria, and Sudan) because it allowed members of terrorist organizations (such as ETA from Spain and the Colombian FARC) safe haven in Cuba.

Labeling Cuba a security problem rang more hollow after a 1998 U.S. Defense Intelligence Agency study concluded that Cuba did not represent a conventional threat to the United States. The report caused an uproar in Congress and prompted a letter by Secretary of Defense William Cohen to Senator Strom Thurmond to assure him and other members of Congress that despite Cuba's lack of threat, he "remain[ed] concerned" about Cuba gathering intelligence about the United States, as well as its "potential to develop and produce biological agents."[25]

In May 2002, Undersecretary of State for Arms Control and International Security John Bolton (who later would be a highly controversial UN ambassador) gave the Bush administration's view of Cuba in a speech titled "Beyond the Axis of Evil."[26] Arguing that the Cuban threat was "underplayed," he said that, given its ability to develop weapons of mass destruction, Cuba was a "rogue state" similar to the "axis of evil" (Iran, Iraq, and North Korea). The 1998 report was dismissed as "unbalanced."

Castro scoffs at the idea that he can be lumped into the same category as Al Qaeda, and in speeches he routinely refers to the Bush administration as "neofascist" and dictatorial. After the preemptive attack by the United States against Iraq in March 2003, Castro also began speaking regularly of the possibility that Cuba could be next: "In Miami and Washington they are now discussing where, how and when Cuba will be attacked or the problem of the Revolution will be solved."[27]

A critical question facing any effort to combat terrorism is whether it damages the slow process of democratization in Latin America. In official documents and speeches, the U.S. government has reiterated its commitment to democracy and human rights, but the effects of antiterrorist policies have raised concerns. In particular, critics have questioned whether a renewed emphasis on intelligence gathering, the use of the military to fight domestic enemies, and martial law may erode the gains made since the end of the Cold War: "The danger is that once again the very highest levels of government are sending signals that the goal of fighting terrorism justifies the violation of human rights."[28]

The U.S. policy response to the threat (or perceived threat) of terrorism in Latin America has been military in nature, whereby Latin American militaries are encouraged, funded, equipped, and trained, and this type of reaction became more pronounced after 2001. For fiscal year 2006, the Bush administration requested $908 million in military and police aid to Latin America and $1.03 billion for social and economic programs.[29] Even during the Cold War, military aid was usually only half of the total assistance package, and now they are almost even.[30]

Summary and Conclusion

Terrorism in Latin America comes in different forms, some more virulent than others. The threat varies widely across the region, different political actors define "terrorism" in different ways, and the legacies of dictatorship and repression in many countries leave serious concerns about using a military solution. During the Cold War, the solution often became worse than the problem, given the thousands killed in the name of national security.

For the U.S. government, realist assumptions are prevalent. Terrorism and the drug trade are national security threats and must therefore be met with force. Echoing the Cold War, the argument goes that not only does the use of counterterrorist force improve U.S. security but also it contributes to the process of democratization in Latin America.

With regard to drug-related terrorism, the country most beset by violence is Colombia, where the government faces a three-headed hydra of drug traffickers, guerrillas, and paramilitaries, all of them well armed from the profits of the drug trade. In the past several years, Colombian presidents have advocated a stronger military response, and U.S. funding for the military elements of Plan Colombia have reached into the billions; the number of U.S. soldiers in Colombia is also rising.

The idea that drugs should prompt a military response is not universally accepted in Latin America, particularly in Andean countries with long histories of indigenous use of coca. Backlashes to U.S. drug policies have already appeared, along with skepticism that U.S. definitions of terrorism should apply to the region. But increasingly, the U.S. government has emphasized Latin American links to Middle Eastern terrorist organizations. As a result, U.S. policy has shifted noticeably toward encouraging the use of Latin American militaries to address all potential threats.

Research Questions

1. Analyze the potential problems and benefits of using crop substitution as an incentive to stop the production of coca.
2. What have been the most effective means of defeating terrorist threats in Latin America? To what degree have these means affected democracy?
3. What are the parallels between the current "war on terrorism" in Latin America and the "war on Communism" during the Cold war? Are there key differences?
4. Analyze the development of the "certification" policy. How effective has it been in combating drug traffickers?
5. Have Latin American countries interpreted the threat of terrorism differently than the United States has? In what ways, and why?

Further Sources

Books

CRANDALL, RUSSELL. *Driven by Drugs: U.S. Policy toward Colombia* (Boulder, Colo.: Lynne Rienner, 2002). A concise and well-written analysis of the formulation of U.S.

policy, the decision-making process within the U.S. government, and the manner in which drugs have become the overriding factor in the U.S. relationship with Colombia.

THOUMI, FRANCISCO E. *Illegal Drugs, Economy, and Society in the Andes* (Baltimore: Johns Hopkins University Press, 2003). An interesting analysis of the drug trade focusing on its effects in Bolivia, Colombia, and Peru. This includes socioeconomic factors, racial differences, and how rural populations have been affected by antidrug policies.

VELLINGA, MENNO (Ed.). *The Political Economy of the Drug Industry: Latin America and the International System* (Gainesville: University Press of Florida, 2004). A useful edited volume, with authors from Latin America, Europe, and the United States. It includes specific country studies, as well as sections on money laundering, the drug industry, and transnational crime.

YOUNGER, COLETTA A., and EILEEN ROSIN (Eds.). *Drugs and Democracy in Latin America: The Impact of U.S. Policy* (Boulder, Colo.: Lynne Rienner, 2005). This edited volume provides not only both case studies of numerous countries and overall assessment of the effects of U.S. drug policy but also a substantial Latin American voice. It is the result of a three-year study by the Washington Office on Latin America.

Web Sites

OAS, Inter-American Committee against Terrorism. This is the official site of the counterterrorist organization within the OAS. It contains all the relevant hemispheric documents on the topic, in addition to news and press releases, resolutions, and events. It also includes a useful list of links to other international Web sites dedicated to the issue of terrorism. http://cicte.oas.org.

Truth and Reconciliation Commission (Peru). Available in both English and Spanish, this is the official Web site of the commission, and it includes the entire text of the final report (nine separate volumes detailed the violence). It also provides complete descriptions of the commission's work, funding, press releases, and transcripts of meetings with individuals and political parties. http://www.cverdad.org.pe/.

FARC. The FARC's official site (which is only in Spanish) is often the source of its communication with the government, and it provides its own (highly skewed) view of society and politics. It is a sophisticated site, with a large number of press releases, interviews, articles, and discussions of specific issues. http://www.farcep.org/.

Plan Colombia. The Colombian government dedicated a Web site to the various aspects of Plan Colombia, though of course it is only in Spanish. However, it contains a considerable amount of information about not only fighting narco-trafficking but also programs for economic and social development. It also includes an option to receive email updates about the plan. http://www.plancolombia.gov.co/.

United Nations Office on Drugs and Crime. The Web site provides reports and data not only on drugs (such as the World Drug Report) but also on terrorism more generally. Although the focus is global, the search engine can be used to find information on specific countries or regions. http://www.unodc.org.

Notes

1. Hosenball and Isikoff 2004.
2. Combs 2003, 10.

3. U.S. Code Online.
4. Feldman and Perälä 2001, 1.
5. Epstein 2004.
6. Lagos 2003, 97.
7. Quoted in Martynov 2003, 94.
8. See Crandall 2002.
9. Kirk 2003, 182.
10. *El Tiempo* 2006.
11. National Security Archive Web site www.gwu.edu/~nsarchir/.
12. Kirk 2004.
13. Ledebur 2005, 157.
14. INCSR 2005 www.state.gor/p/inl/rls/nrcrpt/.
15. Quoted in Rojas 2005, 217.
16. Morris 1999.
17. General Accounting Office 2004.
18. Green 2004.
19. United Nations Web site 2003.
20. BBC News Web site 2000.
21. Quoted in Clayton 1999, 279.
22. Truth and Reconciliation Web site.
23. National Security Strategy 2000.
24. Organization of American States Web site.
25. U.S. Department of State Web site 1998.
26. U.S. Department of State Web site 2002.
27. Quote from *Granma*: http://www.granma.cu/documento/ingles03/015.html.
28. Sikkink 2004, 218.
29. Latin America Working Group 2005.
30. Latin America Working Group 2003.

Glossary

Autogolpe: Spanish for "self coup." A political process whereby a president suspends the constitution and dissolves government institutions that block his or her power.

Backward linkages: When local businesses are launched as a means to link up with a multinational corporation that has established an industry in the country.

Balloon effect: Like a balloon, when coca production is "squeezed" in one area, it expands in a neighboring area. It refers primarily to the Andean region.

Banana republic: Derogatory reference to a small country (usually Central American or Caribbean) that is deemed backward and weak.

Capital flight: When investors believe that a country is experiencing a level of instability that may endanger their capital, they move it to banks in a different country. This, in turn, tends to exacerbate instability.

Certification: The process by which the United States determines whether a given country is participating sufficiently in the fight against drug trafficking; denial of certification entails the loss of certain types of aid.

Chicago Boys: In the 1970s, a group of Chilean government officials, many of whom had been educated at the University of Chicago's Department of Economics, applied their education by drastically reducing the role of the state in the economy.

Cocaleros: The Spanish name for people—particularly in Bolivia and Peru—of indigenous descent who commonly farm coca.

Coyotes: Professional smugglers who bring Latin American immigrants illegally into the United States.

Debt swapping: The process by which debtor countries exchange current loan conditions (e.g., interest and payment schedules) for different ones, thus avoiding short-term economic crisis.

Disappeared: An individual who was arrested for political reasons but was never seen again.

Domino effect: During the Cold War, a line of dominoes became a metaphor for Latin American countries. If one domino is pushed—that is, if one country fell to Communism—then the others next to it would also begin falling.

Embargo: The prohibition of trade with a specific country, for political reasons.

Fascism: An ideology that focuses on the unity and harmony of a country, embodied in a single leader; it is highly nationalist and antidemocratic.

Guerrilla: A Spanish term that refers to a type of irregular soldier who uses small units, knowledge of terrain, support of the local population, and hit-and-run tactics to defeat an enemy that is more powerful (such as a standing army).

Import-substitution industrialization (ISI): A strategy of economic development that entails protecting certain native industries with tariffs, thus substituting native goods for foreign imports. The goal is to remove those tariffs once native industries have become competitive.

International Criminal Court: A United Nations court that entered into force in 2002. It can prosecute individual citizens from participating states for the crimes of genocide, crimes against humanity, and war crimes. It has the authority to act if the member state is unwilling or unable to do so.

Iran-Contra: The term refers to the scandal in the 1980s, in which officials of the Reagan administration secretly sold weapons to Iran and used the proceeds to continue illegal funding to the Contra rebels in Nicaragua.

Liberation theology: A current of thought in the Catholic Church in Latin America, mostly prominently in the 1970s and 1980s. It argued that the church had an obligation to take active steps to liberate the poor and dispossessed; it was highly controversial because priests became deeply involved in politics. It was condemned by the Vatican.

Lost Decade: The devastating economic decline in Latin America in the 1980s led many observers to label it as lost, as poverty and unemployment rose.

Maquiladoras: A factory, usually on the Mexican side of the U.S.-Mexico border (though they can exist in any country), that receives materials or parts tariff-free from the United States, then assembles them and exports the finished product back to the United States.

Nationalization: The process by which a state takes ownership of a specific asset, usually from a private individual or corporation.

Neoliberalism: An economic strategy based on capitalist market principles, with a minimal role for the state and a strong emphasis on private enterpreneurship.

Nongovernmental organizations: Organizations without formal ties to governments that focus on issues they believe governments have not adequately addressed, such as human rights.

Nongovernmental terrorism: Terrorist activity that is perpetrated by individuals or groups not formally associated with a government.

Pan-Americanism: The idea that there exists a commonality among nations of the Americas that binds them together and should make cooperation easier.

Petrodollars: A reference to money made by oil-producing states from the sale of oil, which is then reinvested into Western banks. In the 1970s, U.S. banks began to lend that money in large quantities to Latin American countries.

Plebiscite: A vote in which the entire electorate chooses whether to accept or reject a specific proposal; also known as a referendum.

Populism: A style of political leadership in which a highly charismatic individual organizes a large following based on criticism of the status quo and established political institutions; it is often comprised of people who previously had been marginalized.

Remittance: Earnings made by migrant workers that are sent back to the workers' home country.

Shock therapy: Popular term for the rapid market-oriented reforms put in place by many Latin American governments.

State-sponsored terrorism: Terrorist activity that is perpetrated by agents of a government.

Structural adjustment: The process by which debtor countries are compelled to transform their economies in order to qualify for new loans and receive debt relief. It entails a neoliberal focus on privatization and free trade.

Tariff: A tax imposed on foreign imports. It is used to raise revenue and also to protect domestic industries.

Washington Consensus: A term used to describe the belief in the United States and in international financial institutions that neoliberal policies constitute the most effective way of promoting economic development.

White man's burden: The perception in the United States (and Europe) of an obligation to "civilize" countries with darker skinned natives, thus teaching them how to run a country "correctly."

Bibliography

ABBOTT, PHILIP K. "Terrorist Threat in the Tri-Border Area: Myth or Reality?" *Military Review* (September–October 2004): 51–55.

ABC News Website. "Americans Split on Relations with Cuba." May 13, 2002. http://www.abcnews.go.com/sections/world/DailyNews/cuba_poll020513.html (accessed April 13, 2004).

ACEREDA, ALBERTO, AND WILL DERUSHA. *Selected Poems of Rubén Darío: A Bilingual Anthology* (Lewisburg, Pa.: Bucknell University Press, 2001).

ACHING, GERARD. *The Politics of Spanish American Modernismo* (Cambridge: Cambridge University Press, 1997).

ADELMAN, JEREMY. *Republic of Capital: Buenos Aires and the Legal Transformation of the Atlantic World* (Stanford, Calif.: Stanford University Press, 1999).

AIZENMAN, N. C. "Vibrant Village Quieted as Salvadorans Go North." *Washington Post,* May 8, 2006.

ALLISON, GRAHAM, AND PHILIP ZELIKOW. *Essence of Decision: Explaining the Cuban Missile Crisis, 2nd ed.* (New York: Longman, 1999).

ANDREAS, PETER. *Border Games: Policing the U.S.-Mexico Divide* (Ithaca, N.Y.: Cornell University Press, 2000).

ARAUZ, SERGIO. "Director de Centros Penales renuncia por 'frustración' de no conseguir votos del FMLN." February 28, 2007. http://www.elfaro.net/secciones/Noticias/20070226/noticias13_20070226.asp.

ARÉVALO, JUAN JOSÉ. *Fabula del tiburón y las sardinas.* (Caracas: Monte Avila Editores, 1980).

ARKIN, WILLIAM M. "Venezuela: Fumbling a Pop Up." *Washington Post,* November 1, 2005.

ARNSON, CYNTHIA. *Crossroads: Congress, the President and Central America, 1976–1993, 2nd ed.* (University Park: Pennsylvania University Press, 1993).

ASTORGA, LUIS. "Mexico: Drugs and Politics." In Menno Vellinga (ed.), *The Political Economy of the Drug Industry: Latin America and the International System* (Gainesville: University Press of Florida, 2004): 85–102.

ATKINS, G. POPE. *Latin America in the International Political System, 3rd ed.* (Boulder, Colo.: Westview Press, 1995).

ATKINS, G. POPE, AND LARMAN C. WILSON. *The Dominican Republic and the United States: From Imperialism to Transnationalism* (Athens: University of Georgia Press, 1997).

Avalon Project at Yale Law School. Documents in Law, History and Diplomacy. http://www.yale.edu/lawweb/avalon/intdip/interam/intam13.htm.

AZICRI, MAX. *Cuba Today and Tomorrow: Reinventing Socialism* (Gainesville: University Press of Florida, 2000).

BACHELET, PABLO. "U.S. Aid Threatened by Global Court Pact." *Miami Herald,* October 23, 2005.

BAKER, PETER, AND BILL BRUBAKER, "Bush Hails International Ethanol Production." *Washington Post,* March 9, 2007.

BALDWIN, DAVID A. *Neorealism and Neoliberalism: The Contemporary Debate* (New York: Columbia University Press, 1993).

BARBER, WILLARD F., AND C. NEALE RONNING. *Internal Security and Military Power: Counterinsurgency and Civic Action in Latin America* (Columbus: Ohio State University Press, 1966).

BARNES, Jr., HARRY G. "U.S. Human Rights Policies and Chile." In Debra Liang-Fenton (ed.), *Implementing U.S. Human Rights Policy* (Washington, D.C.: United States Institute of Peace Press, 2004): 299–329.

BARTLEY, RUSSELL H. *Imperial Russia and the Struggle for Latin American Independence, 1808–1828* (Austin: Institute of Latin American Studies, University of Texas, 1978).

BATISTA, FULGENCIO. *The Growth and Decline of the Cuban Republic* (New York: Devin-Adair, 1964).

BBC News Website. "Bolivia Wages War on the Coca Leaf." June 6, 2000. http://news.bbc.co.uk/1/hi/world/americas/778100.stm.

BBC News Website. "EU Unfazed by Castro Rebuff." July 28, 2003. http://news.bbc.co.uk/2/hi/americas/3101651.stm.

BEATTIE, PETER M. *The Tribute of Blood: Army, Honor, Race, and Nation in Brazil, 1864–1945* (Durham, N.C.: Duke University Press, 2001).

BEMIS, SAMUEL FLAGG. *The Latin American Policy of the United States: An Historical Interpretation* (New York: Harcourt, Brace and Company, 1943).

BERMANN, KARL. *Under the Big Stick: Nicaragua and the United States since 1848* (Boston: South End Press, 1986).

BESCHLOSS, MICHAEL R. *Taking Charge: The Johnson White House Tapes, 1963–1964* (New York: Simon & Schuster, 1997).

BESCHLOSS, MICHAEL R. *Reaching for Glory: Lyndon Johnson's Secret White House Tapes, 1964–1965* (New York: Simon & Schuster, 2001).

BIERCK, Jr., HAROLD A. (Ed.). *Selected Writings of Bolivar* (New York: Colonial Press, 1951).

BLASIER, COLE. *The Hovering Giant: U.S. Responses to Revolutionary Change in Latin America* (Pittsburgh: University of Pittsburgh Press, 1976).

BLUSTEIN, PAUL. *And the Money Kept Rolling In (and Out): Wall Street, the IMF, and the Bankrupting of Argentina* (New York: Public Affairs, 2005).

BOLIVAR, ALBERTO. "Peru." In Yonah Alexander (ed.), *Combating Terrorism: Strategies of Ten Countries* (Ann Arbor: University of Michigan Press, 2002): 84–115.

BREA, JORGE A. "Population Dynamics in Latin America." *Population Bulletin* 58, 1 (March 2003): 1–36.

BULMER-THOMAS, VICTOR. *The Economic History of Latin America since Independence, 2nd ed.* (Cambridge: Cambridge University Press, 2003).

CABESTRERO, TEÓFILO. *Blood of the Innocent: Victims of the Contras' War in Nicaragua* (Maryknoll, N.Y.: Orbis Books, 1985).

CALAVITA, KITTY. *U.S. Immigration Law and the Control of Labor, 1820–1924* (London: Academic Press, 1994).

CALLCOTT, WILFRID HARDY. *The Western Hemisphere: Its Influence on United States Policies to the End of World War II* (Austin, University of Texas Press, 1968).

CAMPOS, CARLOS OLIVA. "The United States, Latin America, and the Caribbean: From Panamericanism to Neopanamericanism." In Gary Prevost and Carlos Oliva Campos (eds.), *Neoliberalism and Neopanamericanism: The View from Latin America* (New York: Palgrave Macmillan, 2002): 3–27.

CARDOSO, FERNANDO HENRIQUE, AND ENZO FALETTO. *Dependency and Development in Latin America* (Berkeley: University of California Press, 1979).

CAVALLO, ASCANIO. "El menu con que la Casa Blanca espera a la Presidenta." *La Tercera* (Chile), May 28, 2006.

CENTENO, MIGUEL ANGEL. *Blood and Debt: War and the Nation-State in Latin America* (University Park: Pennsylvania State University Press, 2002).

CHESTER, ERIC THOMAS. *Rag-Tags, Scum, Riff-Raff, and Commies: The U.S. Intervention in the Dominican Republic, 1965–1966* (New York: Monthly Review Press, 2001).

CLAYTON, LAWRENCE A. *Peru and the United States: The Condor and the Eagle.* (Athens: The University of Georgia Press, 1999).

CLEARY, EDWARD L. *The Struggle for Human Rights in Latin America* (Westport, Conn.: Praeger, 1997).

CLINTON, WILLIAM J. *A National Security Strategy for a Global Age.* http://www.globalsecurity.org/military/library/policy/national/nss-0012.pdf.

COLITT, RAYMOND. "South American Nations Agree to Regional Pact." *Financial Times,* November 4, 2004.

COMBS, CINDY C. *Terrorism in the Twenty-First Century, 3rd ed.* (Upper Saddle River, N.J.: Prentice Hall, 2003).

CONNIFF, MICHAEL L. *Panama and the United States: The Forced Alliance* (Athens: University of Georgia Press, 2001).

CORRADI, JUAN E. "Prelude to Disaster: Weak Reform, Competitive Politics in Argentina."

In Carol Wise and Riordan Roett (eds.), *Post-Stabilization Politics in Latin America: Competition, Transition, Collapse* (Washington, D.C.: Brookings Institution Press, 2003).

COTTAM, MARTHA. *Images and Intervention: U.S. Policies in Latin America* (Pittsburgh: University of Pittsburgh Press, 1994).

COVARRUBIAS, ANA. "Mexico: The Challenges of a Latin American Power in the U.S. Backyard." In Frank O. Mora and Jeanne A. K. Hey (eds.), *Latin American and Caribbean Foreign Policy* (Lanham, Md.: Rowman and Littlefield, 2003): 13–30.

CRANDALL, RUSSELL. *Driven by Drugs: U.S. Policy toward Colombia* (Boulder, Colo.: Lynne Rienner, 2002).

CRANDALL, RUSSELL. *Gunboat Democracy: U.S. Interventions in the Dominican Republic, Grenada, and Panama.* (Lanham, Md.: Rowman and Littlefield, 2006).

CRUZ, JEFFREY N. *U.S. Remittance Policy and the Western Hemisphere.* Congressional Hispanic Caucus Institute Policy Brief, 2003.

CULLATHER, NICK. *Secret History: The CIA's Classified Account of Its Operations in Guatemala, 1952–1954* (Stanford, Calif.: Stanford University Press, 1999).

CURRY, JACK. "Cuba Makes Cut for the Classic." *New York Times,* January 21, 2006.

DAVIS, HAROLD EUGENE, JOHN J. FINAN, AND F. TAYLOR PECK. *Latin American Diplomatic History: An Introduction* (Baton Rouge: Lousiana State University Press, 1977).

DAVIS, MADELEINE (Ed.). *The Pinochet Case: Origins, Progress, and Implications* (London: Institute for Latin American Studies, 2003).

DESCH, MICHAEL C. *When the Third World Matters: Latin America and United States Grand Strategy* (Baltimore: Johns Hopkins University Press, 1993).

DOMÍNGUEZ, JORGE I. *To Make a World Safe for Revolution: Cuba's Foreign Policy* (Cambridge: Harvard University Press, 1989).

DONATO, KATHARINE M., JORGE DURAND, AND DOUGLAS S. MASSEY. "Stemming the Tide? Assessing the Deterrent Effects of the Immigration Reform and Control Act." *Demography* 29, 2 (May 1992): 139–57.

Economic Commission for Latin America and the Caribbean. *Foreign Investment in Latin America and the Caribbean.* April 2006. http://www.eclac.org/cgi-bin/getProd.asp?xml=/publicaciones/xml/2/24302/P24302.xml&xsl=/ddpe/tpl-i/p9f.xsl&base=/tpl-i/top-bottom.xslt.

The Economist. "The Americas: Chip Shop Afire in Costa Rica," January 8.

EISENHOWER, MILTON S. *The Wine Is Bitter: The United States and Latin America* (New York: Doubleday, 1963).

El Tiempo (Colombia). "En el Plan Colombia se han gastado 10.650 millones de dólares, reveló el Departamento de Planeación." September 15, 2006.

EPSTEIN, JACK. "GENERAL SEEKS BOOST FOR LATIN AMERICAN ARMIES." *San Francisco Chronicle,* April 30, 2004.

EVANS, PETER. *Dependent Development: The Alliance of Multinational, State, and Local Capital in Brazil* (Princeton, N.J.: Princeton University Press, 1979).

FARNAM, ARIE. "Colombia's Civil War Drifts South into Ecuador." *Christian Science Monitor,* July 2, 2002.

FELDMAN, ANDREAS, AND MAIJU PERÄLÄ. *Nongovernmental Terrorism in Latin America: Re-Examining Old Assumptions.* Kellogg Institute Working Paper 286 (July 2001).

FIFER, J. VALERIE. *United States Perceptions of Latin America, 1850–1930: A "New West" South of Capricorn?* (Manchester and New York: Manchester University Press, 1991).

FITCH, J. SAMUEL. "Democracy, Human Rights, and the Armed Forces in Latin America." In Jonathan Hartlyn, Lars Schoultz, and Augusto Varas (eds.), *The United States and Latin America in the 1990s: Beyond the Cold War* (Chapel Hill: University of North Carolina Press, 1992): 181–213.

FORERO, JUAN. "Latin America's Political Compass Veers toward the Left." *New York Times,* January 19, 2003: 4.

FOWERAKER, JOE, TODD LANDMAN, AND NEIL HARVEY. *Governing Latin America* (Cambridge, UK: Polity Press, 2003).

FRAGOMEN, Jr., AUSTIN T. "The Illegal Immigration Reform and Immigrant Responsibility Act of 1996: An Overview." *International Migration Review* 31, 2 (Summer 1997): 438–60.

FRANKO, PATRICE. *The Puzzle of Latin American Economic Development, 2nd ed.* (Lanham, Md.: Rowman and Littlefield, 2003).

GALEANO, EDUARDO. *Open Veins of Latin America: Five Centuries of the Pillage of a*

Continent (New York: Monthly Review Press, 1997).

GAMARRA, EDUARDO A. "Has Bolivia Won the Drug War? Lessons From Plan Dignidad." In Menno Vellina (ed.), *The Political Economy of the Drug Industry: Latin America and the International System* (Gainesville: University Press of Florida, 2003): 25–52.

General Accounting Office. "Efforts to Develop Alternatives to Cultivating Illegal Crops in Colombia Have Made Little Progress and Face Serious Obstacles." GAO-02-291, February 2002.

General Accounting Office. "U.S. Nonmilitary Assistance to Colombia Is Beginning to Show Intended Results, but Programs Are Not Readily Sustainable." GAO-04-726, July 2004.

GIL, FEDERICO. *Latin American–United States Relations* (San Diego: Harcourt Brace Jovanovich, 1971).

GIL, HENRY. "The Point of View of Latin-America on the Inter-American Policy of the United States." *Proceedings of the American Political Science Association* 8 (1911): 164–72.

GILDERHUS, MARK T. *The Second Century: U.S.–Latin American Relations Since 1889.* (Wilmington, Del.: Scholarly Resources, 2000).

GLEIJESES, PIERO. *Shattered Hope: The Guatemalan Revolution and the United States, 1944–1954* (Princeton, N.J.: Princeton University Press, 1991).

GLEIJESES, PIERO. "The Limits of Sympathy: The United States and the Independence of Spanish America." *Journal of Latin American Studies* 24, 3 (October 1992): 481–505.

GOODWIN, Jr., PAUL B. "Initiating United States Relations with Argentina." In T. Ray Shurbutt (ed.), *United States–Latin America Relations, 1800–1850: The Formative Generations* (Tuscaloosa: University of Alabama Press, 1991): 102–21.

GREEN, ERIC. "U.S. Officials Confirm Colombia Curtailing Narco-Terrorism." United States Department of State, International Information Programs. October 28, 2004. http://usinfo.state.gov.

GUEVARA, CHE. *Guerrilla Warfare, with Introduction and Case Studies by Brian Loveman and Thomas M. Davies, Jr* (Lincoln: University of Nebraska Press, 1985).

GUNDER FRANK, ANDRE. *Capitalism and Underdevelopment in Latin America* (New York: Monthly Review Press, 1967).

HANSON, GORDON H. "What Has Happened to Wages in Mexico Since NAFTA? Implications for Hemispheric Free Trade." *National Bureau of Economic Research Working Paper 9563* March 2003.

HARRISON, LAWRENCE E. *The Pan-American Dream: Do Latin America's Cultural Values Discourage True Partnership with the United States and Canada?* (New York: Basic Books, 1997).

HASLAM, JONATHAN. *The Nixon Administration and the Death of Allende's Chile: A Case of Assisted Suicide* (New York: Verso, 2005).

Hastings Law Library Web Site. "Text of Proposition 187." http://traynor.uchastings.edu/cgi-bin/starfinder/16432/calprop.txt.

HEALY, DAVID. *James G. Blaine and Latin America* (Columbia: University of Missouri Press, 2001).

HENRY, O. *Cabbages and Kings* (Garden City, NY: Doubleday, 1904).

HOLDEN, ROBERT H., AND ERIC ZOLOV. *Latin America and the United States: A Documentary History* (New York: Oxford University Press, 2000).

HOSENBALL, MARK, AND MICHAEL ISIKOFF. "Fighting Terror by Attacking . . . South America?" *Newsweek* 144, 6 (September 8, 2004).

HUNTINGTON, SAMUEL P. *Who Are We: The Challenges to America's National Identity* (New York: Simon & Schuster, 2004).

HURRELL, ANDREW. "The United States and Latin America: Neorealism Re-Examined." In Ngaire Woods (ed.), *Explaining International Relations Since 1945* (Oxford: Oxford University Press, 1996): 155–78.

IKEDA, NESTOR. "Fox: Dissenters Unneeded for Trade Zone." Associated Press Financial Wire, November 4, 2005.

JOHNSON, JOHN J. *Latin America in Caricature* (Austin: University of Texas Press, 1980).

JOYCE, ELIZABETH. "Packaging Drugs: Certification and the Acquisition of Leverage." In Victor Bulmer-Thomas and James Dunkerley (eds.), *The United States and Latin America: The New Agenda* (Cambridge: Harvard University Press, 1999): 207–25.

KAPLOWITZ, DONNA RICH. *Anatomy of a Failed Embargo: U.S. Sanctions against*

Cuba (Boulder, Colo.: Lynne Rienner, 1998).

KATZ, JONATHAN M. "U.N. Seat Contest Heating Up." *Miami Herald*, September 5, 2006.

KECK, MARGARET E., AND KATHRYN SIKKINK. *Activists beyond Borders: Advocacy Networks in International Politics* (Ithaca, N.Y.: Cornell University Press, 1998).

KEOHANE, ROBERT O., AND LISA L. MARTIN. "Institutional Theory as a Research Paradigm." In Colin Elman and Miriam Fendius Elman (eds.). *Progress in International Relations Theory: Appraising the Field.* (Cambridge, MA; MIT Press, 2003): 71–107

KINSELLA, DAVID. "No Rest for the Democratic Peace." *American Political Science Review* 99, 3 (August 2005): 453–57.

KIRK, ROBIN. *More Terrible Than Death: Massacres, Drugs, and America's War in Colombia* (New York: Public Affairs, 2003).

KIRK, ROBIN. "Colombia and the 'War' on Terror: Rhetoric and Reality." *The World Today*, March 2004: 14–16.

KIRKPATRICK, JEANE. "Dictatorships and Double Standards." *Commentary* (November 1979): 34–45.

KISSINGER, HENRY. "The Pitfalls of Universal Jurisdiction." *Foreign Affairs* 80, 4 (2001): 86–96.

KLARÉN, PETER F. "Lost Promise: Explaining Latin American Underdevelopment." In Peter F. Klarén and Thomas J. Bossert (eds.), *Promise of Development: Theories of Change in Latin America* (Boulder, Colo.: Westview Press, 1986): 3–35.

KORNBLUH, PETER. *The Pinochet File: A Declassified Dossier on Atrocity and Accountability* (New York: New Press, 2003).

KORNBLUH, PETER (Ed.). *Bay of Pigs Declassified: The Secret CIA Report on the Invasion of Cuba* (New York: New Press, 1998).

LABAQUI, IGNACIO, AND GABRIELA RODRÍGUEZ LÓPEZ. "Argentina and the IMF: It Takes Two to Tango." FLACSO-Argentina Working Paper, May 2002.

LAFEBER, WALTER. *The New Empire: An Interpretation of American Expansion, 1860–1898.* (Ithaca, N.Y.: Cornell University Press, 1963).

LAFEBER, WALTER. *Inevitable Revolutions: The United States in Central America* (New York: W. W. Norton, 1984).

LAFEBER, WALTER. "Thomas C. Mann and Latin American Policy." In Thomas J. McCormick and Walter LaFeber (eds.), *Behind the Throne: Servants of Power to Imperial Presidents, 1898–1968* (Madison: University of Wisconsin Press, 1993): 166–203.

LAGOS, MARTA. "Terrorism and the Image of the United States in Latin America." *International Journal of Public Opinion Research* 15, 1 (March 2003): 95–101.

LANGLEY, LESTER D., AND THOMAS SCHOONOVER. *The Banana Men: American Mercenaries and Entrepreneurs in Central America, 1880–1930* (Lexington: University Press of Kentucky, 1995).

LAROSA, MICHAEL, AND FRANK O. MORA. *Neighborly Adversaries: Readings in U.S.–Latin American Relations* (Lanham, MD: Rowman and Littlefield Publishers Inc, 1999).

LARSEN, FLEMMING. "Argentina and the IMF: The Need for Perspective." *Crises and Exiting Crises Roundtable*, November 18–22, 2003. http://www.imf.org/external/np/speeches/2003/111803.htm.

LATANÉ, JOHN HALLADAY. *The United States and Latin America.* (New York: Doubleday, Page, 1920).

Latin American Weekly Report. "Peru: Seeking New Markets for Coca." March 5, 2004.

Latin America Working Group. "Paint by Numbers: Trends in U.S. Military Programs with Latin America and Challenges to Oversight." August 2003. Available at http://www.cipon-line.org/facts/PaintByNumbersFinal.pdf.

Latin America Working Group. "Erasing the Lines: Trends in U.S. Military Programs with Latin America." December 2005. Available at http://www.wola.org/media/erasing_the_lines_05.pdf.

LEDEBUR, KATHRYN. "Bolivia: Clear Consequences." In Coletta A. Youngers and Eileen Rosin (eds.), *Drugs and Democracy in Latin America: The Impact of U.S. Policy* (Boulder, Colo.: Lynne Rienner, 2005): 143–84.

LEOGRANDE, WILLIAM M. *Our Own Backyard: The United States in Central America, 1977–1992* (Chapel Hill: University of North Carolina Press, 1998).

LEONARD, THOMAS M. *Encyclopedia of Cuban–United States Relations* (London: McFarland, 2003).

LEONARD, THOMAS M. *United States–Latin American Relations, 1850–1903: Establishing a Relationship* (Tuscaloosa: University of Alabama Press, 1999).

LEONARD, THOMAS M. *Central America and the United States: The Search for Stability* (Athens: University of Georgia Press, 1991).

LEVINSON, JEROME, AND JUAN DE ONÍS. *The Alliance That Lost its Way: A Critical Report on the Alliance for Progress* (Chicago: Quadrangle Press, 1970).

LEWIS, JAMES E. *The American Union and the Problem of Neighborhood: The United States and the Collapse of the Spanish Empire, 1783–1829.* (Chapel Hill: University of North Carolina Press, 1998).

LINDSEY, BRINK. "The Miami Fizzle—What Else but Cancun Redux?" *Wall Street Journal* November 28, 2003: A-9.

LOVEMAN, BRIAN. *The Constitution of Tyranny: Regimes of Exception in Spanish America* (Pittsburgh: University of Pittsburgh Press, 1993).

LOVEMAN, BRIAN. *For la Patria: Politics and the Armed Forces in Latin America* (Wilmington, Del.: Scholarly Resources, 1999).

LOVEMAN, BRIAN. *Chile: The Legacy of Hispanic Capitalism* (New York: Oxford University Press, 2001).

LOVEMAN, BRIAN, AND THOMAS M. DAVIES. *Che Guevara: Guerillas Warfare* (Lincoln: University of Nebraska Press, 1985).

MARICHAL, CARLOS. *A Century of Debt Crises in Latin America* (Princeton, N.J.: Princeton University Press, 1989).

MARQUEZ, HUMBERTO. "Morales, Chávez, and Castro Begin a New "Left Axis."" IPS-Inter Press Service, January 4, 2006.

MARTYNOV, BORIS. "Latin America and Terrorism." *International Affairs* 49, 4 (2003): 87–96.

MASSEY, DOUGLAS S., JORGE DURAND, AND NOLAN J. MALONE. *Beyond Smoke and Mirrors: Mexican Immigration in an Era of Economic Integration* (New York: Russell Sage Foundation, 2002).

MCPHERSON, ALAN. "Misled by Himself: What the Johnson Tapes Reveal about the Dominican Intervention of 1965." *Latin American Research Review* 38, 2 (2003): 127–46.

MCSHERRY, J. PATRICE. *Predatory States: Operation Condor and Covert War in Latin America* (Lanham, Md.: Rowman and Littlefield, 2005).

MITCHELL, CHRISTOPHER. "Introduction: Immigration and U.S. Foreign Policy toward the Caribbean, Central America, and Mexico." In Christopher Mitchell (ed.), *Western Hemisphere Immigration and United States Foreign Policy* (University Park: Pennsylvania State University Press, 1992): 1–30.

MITCHELL, CHRISTOPHER. "The Future of Migration as an Issue in Inter-American Relations." In Jorge I. Domínguez (ed.), *The Future of Inter-American Relations* (New York: Routledge, 2000): 217–36.

MORLEY, MORRIS, AND CHRIS MCGILLION. *Unfinished Business: America and Cuba after the Cold War, 1989–2001* (New York, Cambridge University Press, 2002).

MORRIS, STEPHEN. "Corruption and the Mexican Political System: Continuity and Change." *Third World Quarterly* 20, 3 (1999): 623–43.

NACLA Report on the Americas. "Colombian President Alvaro Uribe who has radically escalated Colombia's internal war in his first 100 days in office, has seen his popularity rating rise to levels far higher than those enjoyed by his two immediate predecessors." *NACLA Report on the Americas* 36, 3 (November–December 2002): 5–6.

NEWTON, WESLEY P. "Origins of United States–Latin American Relations." In T. Ray Shurbutt (ed.), *United States– Latin America Relations, 1800–150: The Formative Generations.* (Tuscaloosa: The University of Alabama Press, 1991): 1–24.

NIXON, RICHARD M. *Six Crises.* (New York: Simon and Schuster Inc., 1962).

NORDEN, DEBORAH L., AND ROBERTO RUSSELL. *The United States and Argentina: Changing Relations in a Changing World* (New York: Routledge, 2002).

NUNN, FREDERICK M. *The Time of the Generals: Latin American Professional Militarism in World Pespective.* (Lincoln: University of Nebraska Press, 1992).

OFFNER, JOHN L. *An Unwanted War: The Diplomacy of the United States and Spain over Cuba, 1895–1898* (Chapel Hill: University of North Carolina Press, 1992).

Organization of American States Web site 2002, Inter-American Commission on Human Rights, "Annual Report: Cuba." http://www.cidh.org/annualrep/2002eng/chap.4a.htm (accessed April 15, 2004).

OPPENHEIMER, ANDRES. "Latin America's Unlikely Foes: Hispanic U.S. Congressmen." *Miami Herald*, March 14, 2004.

ORRENIUS, PIA M., AND MADLINE ZAVODNY. "Do Amnesty Programs Reduce Undocumented Immigration? Evidence From IRCA." *Demography* 40, 3 (August 2003): 437–50.

PASTOR, ROBERT. *Condemned to Repetition: The United States and Nicaragua* (Princeton, N.J.: Princeton University Press, 1987).

PASTOR, ROBERT. *Not Condemned to Repetition: The United States and Nicaragua* (Boulder, Colo.: Westview Press, 2002).

PAZ, OCTAVIO. *One Earth, Four or Five Worlds: Reflections on Contemporary History* (San Diego: Harcourt Brace Jovanovich, Publishers, 1985).

PÉREZ, LOUIS A. *Cuba between Empires: 1878–1902* (Pittsburgh: University of Pittsburgh Press, 1983).

PÉREZ, LOUIS A. *Cuba and the United States: Ties of Singular Intimacy* (Athens: University of Georgia Press, 1990).

PÉREZ, LOUIS A. "Cuba: Sugar and Independence." In Thomas M. Leonard (ed.), *United States–Latin American Relations, 1850–1903: Establishing a Relationship.* (Tuscaloosa: The University of Alabama Press, 1999): 35–57.

PETERSON, HAROLD F. *Argentina and the United States, 1810–1960* (New York: State University of New York, 1964).

PIKE, FREDRICK B. *Chile and the United States, 1880–1962: The Emergence of Chile's Social Crisis and the Challenge to United States Diplomacy* (Notre Dame, Ind.: University of Notre Dame Press, 1963).

PION-BERLIN, DAVID. "The Pinochet Case and Human Rights Progress in Chile: Was Europe a Catalyst, Cause, or Inconsequential?" *Journal of Latin American Studies* 36, 3 (August 2004): 479–505.

PREVOST, GARY, AND CARLOS OLIVA CAMPOS (Eds.). *Neoliberalism and Neopanamericanism: The View from Latin America* (New York: Palgrave Macmillan, 2002).

PRIEST, DANA. *The Mission: Waging War and Keeping Peace with America's Military* (New York: W. W. Norton, 2003).

PRITCHARD, JUSTIN. "AP Investigation: Mexican Worker Deaths Rise Sharply Even as Overall U.S. Job Safety Improves." Associated Press (March 2004).

RAAT, W. DIRK. *Mexico and the United States: Ambivalent Vistas* (Athens: University of Georgia Press, 1996).

RABE, STEPHEN G. *Eisenhower and Latin America: The Foreign Policy of Anticommunism* (Chapel Hill: University of North Carolina Press, 1988).

RABE, STEPHEN G. *The Most Dangerous Area in the World: John F. Kennedy Confronts Communist Revolution in Latin America* (Chapel Hill: University of North Carolina Press, 1999).

RAMSEY, RUSSELL W. *Guardians of the Other Americas: Essays on the Military Forces of Latin America* (New York: University Press of America, 1997).

RAMSEY, RUSSELL W., AND ANTONIO RAIMONDO. "Human Rights Instruction at the U.S. Army School of the Americas." *Human Rights Review* 2, 3 (April–June 2001): 92–116.

REAGAN, RONALD. *Speaking My Mind: Selected Speeches.* (New York: Simon & Schuster, 1989).

REIMERS, DAVID M. *Unwelcome Strangers: American Identity and the Turn Against Immigration* (New York: Columbia University Press, 1998).

RIDELY, JASPER. *Maximilian and Juárez.* (New York: Ticknor and Fields, 1992).

ROBERTSON, WILLIAM SPENCE. *France and Latin-American Independence.* (New York: Octagon Books, 1967).

ROBINSON, LINDA. "Terror Close to Home." *U.S. News and World Report* 135, 11 (October 6, 2003).

RODRÍGUEZ DÍAZ, MARÍA DEL ROSARIO. "Mexico's Vision of Manifest Destiny during the 1847 War." *Journal of Popular Culture* 35, 2: 41–50.

ROJAS, ISAÍS. "Peru: Drug Control Policy, Human Rights, and Democracy." In Coletta A. Youngers and Eileen Rosin (eds.), *Drugs and Democracy in Latin America: The Impact of U.S. Policy* (Boulder, Colo., Lynne Rienner Publishers, 2005): 185–230.

ROSECRANCE, RICHARD. *The Rise of the Trading State: Commerce and Conquest in the Modern World* (New York: Basic Books, 1986).

ROSENBLUM, MARC R. "Moving beyond the Policy of No Policy: Emigration From Mexico and Central America." *Latin*

American Politics and Society (Winter 2004): 91–125.

SAN MARTIN, NANCY. "'Dollarization' Keeping Cuba Afloat." *Miami Herald,* September 1, 2003.

SARMIENTO, DOMINGO F. *Life in the Argentine Republicin the Days of the Tyrants, or Civilization and Barbarism* (New York: Collier Books, 1961).

SATER, WILLIAM F. *Chile and the United States: Empires in Conflict* (Athens: University of Georgia Press, 1990).

SCHLESINGER, STEPHEN, AND STEPHEN KINZER, *Bitter Fruit: The Story of the American Coup in Guatemala* (Cambridge: Harvard University Press, 1999).

School of the Americas Watch. www. soaw.org

SCHOONOVER, THOMAS D. *The United States in Central America, 1860–1911: Episodes of Social Imperialism and Imperial Rivalry in the World System* (Durham, N.C.: Duke University Press, 1991).

SCHOULTZ, LARS. *Human Rights and United States Policy toward Latin America* (Princeton, N.J.: Princeton University Press, 1981).

SCHOULTZ, LARS. *National Security and United States Policy toward Latin America* (Princeton, N.J.: Princeton University Press, 1987).

SCHOULTZ, LARS. *Beneath the United States: A History of U.S. Policy toward Latin America.* (Cambridge: Harvard University Press, 1998).

SCHULER, KURT. "Argentina's Economic Crisis: Causes and Cures." Summary of Report for the Joint Economic Committee, United States Congress, June 2003. Accessed through http:// www.house.gov/jec/imf/ 06-13-03.pdf.

SHEPARD, ALICIA C. "A Crackdown Leading Nowhere." *Washington Post,* July 13, 2003.

SHIFTER, MICHAEL. "Breakdown in the Andes." *Foreign Affairs* 83, 5 (September–October 2004): 126–38.

SIKKINK, KATHRYN. "The Emergence, Evolution, and Effectiveness of the Latin American Human Rights Network." In Elizabeth Jelin and Eric Hershberg (eds.), *Constructing Democracy: Human Rights, Citizenship, and Society in Latin America* (Boulder, Colo.: Westview Press, 1996): 59–84.

SIKKINK, KATHRYN. *Mixed Signals: U.S. Human Rights Policy and Latin America* (Ithaca, N.Y.: Cornell University Press, 2004).

SMITH, JOSEPH. "The First Conference of American States (1889–1890) and the Early Pan American Policy of the United States." In David Sheinin (ed.), *Beyond the Ideal: Pan Americanism in Inter-American Affairs* (Westport, Conn.: Praeger, 2000): 19–32.

SMITH, PETER H. *Talons of the Eagle: Dynamics of U.S.–Latin American Relations* (New York: Oxford University Press, 1996).

SMITH, WAYNE. "Crackdown in Cuba." *Nation,* May 12, 2003.

SNYDER, JACK. "One World, Rival Theories." *Foreign Policy* (November–December 2004): 53–62.

STANSIFER, CHARLES L. "United States–Central American Relations, 1824–1850." In T. Ray Shurbutt (ed.), *United States–Latin America Relations, 1800–1850: The Formative Generations.* (Tuscaloosa: University of Alabama Press, 1991): 25–45.

STRUCKMAN, ROBERT. "New Airing for Old Grievances about Southwest Land." *Christian Science Monitor* 93, 69 (March 6, 2001): 2.

SUÁREZ-OROZCO, MARCELO M. "Crossing: Mexican Immigration in Interdisciplinary Perspectives." In Marcelo M. Suárez-Orozco (ed.), *Crossings: Mexican Immigration in Interdisciplinary Perspectives* (Cambridge: Harvard University Press, 1998): 5–50.

SUAREZ-OROZOC, MARCELO M. "Latin American Immigration to the United States." In Victor Bulmer-Thomas and James Dunkerley (eds.). *The United States and Latin America: The New Agenda* (Cambridge, MA: Harvard University Press, 1999): 227–44.

TAIBO II, PACO IGNACIO, AND SUBCOMANDANTE MARCOS. *The Uncomfortable Dead* (New York: Akashic Books, 2006).

THOMAS, HUGH. *Cuba, or the Pursuit of Freedom* (New York: Da Capo Press, 1998).

THORP, ROSEMARY. *Progress, Poverty and Exclusion: An Economic History of Latin America in the 20th Century* (Washington, D.C.: Inter-American Development Bank, 1998).

THOUMI, FRANCISCO E. *Illegal Drugs, Economy, and Society in the Andes* (Baltimore: Johns Hopkins University Press, 2003).

TICKNER, ARLENE B. "U.S. Subordinate, Autonomous Actor, or Something in Between?" In Frank O. Mora and Jeanne A. K. Hey (eds.), *Latin American and Caribbean Foreign Policy* (Lanham, Md.: Rowman and Littlefield, 2003): 165–84.

TORRES, MARÍA DE LOS ANGELES. *In the Land of Mirrors: Cuban Exile Politics in the United States* (Ann Arbor: University of Michigan Press, 1999).

Truth and Reconciliation Web site (Peru). http://www.cverdad.org.pe/ingles/pagina01.php.

TUCHMAN, BABARA W. *The Zimmerman Telegram* (New York: Ballantine Books, 1958).

United Nations Web site. "Universal Declaration of Human Rights." http://www.un.org/Overview/rights.html.

United Nations Web site. "Statement by H.E. Mr. Alvaro Uribe Velez, President of Colombia." September 30, 2003. http://www.un.org/webcast/ga/58/statements/coloeng030930.htm.

United Nations Development Program Web site. "La democracia en América Latina" (2004). http://democracia.undp.org/Default.asp.

United States Citizenship and Immigration Services Web site. "Refugee Definition." http://uscis.gov/graphics/services/refugees/Definition.htm.

United States Department of State Web site. "Briefing on the Selection of the Latin American Seat for the United Nations Security Council, Iran, and Other Matters" (October 19, 2006). http://www.state.gov/p/io/rls/rm/74826.htm.

United States Department of State. "Background Note: Mexico" (October 2006). http://www.state.gov/r/pa/ei/bgn/35749.htm (accessed December 2006).

United States Department of State. "Patterns of Global Terrorism 2002: Western Hemisphere Overview" (April 30, 2003). http://www.state.gov/s/ct/rls/crt/2002/html/. (accessed April 20, 2004).

United States Department of State. "U. S. Intervention on Articles II–VI, Human Rights of the OAS "Draft American Declaration on the Rights of Indigenous Peoples."

February 26, 2003 (b). http://www.state.gov/p/wha/rt/oas/20812.htm (accessed April 25, 2004).

United States Department of State Factsheet. "Fewer Than 500 Latin American Refugees Admitted to U.S. in 2003." January 16, 2003.

United States Department of State Web site. "U.N. Criticizes Cuba's Treatment of Dissidents, Journalists." April 15, 2004. http://usinfo.state.gov/xarchives/display.html?p=washfile-english&y=2004&m=April&x=20040415170629cwniktebul0.6980097.

United States Department of State Web site. "Report to the President: Commission for Assistance to a Free Cuba." 2004. http://www.state.gov/p/wha/rt/cuba/commission/2004/c12237.htm.

United States Department of State Web site. "Beyond the Axis of Evil: Additional Threats from Weapons of Mass Destruction." May 6, 2002. http://www.state.gov/t/us/rm/9962.htm (accessed April 13, 2004).

United States Department of State Web site. "Defense Secretary's Letter to Thurmond on Cuban Threat." May 6, 1998. http://usinfo.state.gov/regional/ar/us-cuba/def6.htm (accessed April 13, 2004).

United States Trade Representative Web site. http://www.ustr.gov (Accessed September 23, 2004).

U.S. Code Online. Title 18, Chapter 113B, Section 2331, "Definitions." http://frwebgate.access.gpo.gov/cgi-bin/getdoc.cgi?dbname=browse_usc&docid=Cite:+18USC2331.

VALDERRAMA, MARIANO, AND HUGO CABIESES. "Questionable Alliances in the War on Drugs: Peru and the United States." In Menno Vellinga (ed.) *The Political Economy of the Drug Industry: Latin America and the International System* (Gainesville: University Press of Florida, 2003): 53–69.

VEESER, CYRUS. *A World Safe for Capitalism: Dollar Diplomacy and America's Rise to Global Power* (New York: Columbia University Press, 2002).

VELLINGA, MENNO (Ed.). *The Political Economy of the Drug Industry: Latin America and the International System* (Gainesville: University Press of Florida, 2004).

WADHAMS, NICK. "U.S. Stance Against Venezuela Has Dangers," *Miami Herald* July 19, 2006.

WALTZ, KENNETH. *Theory of International Politics* (New York: McGraw-Hill, 1979).

WEBB-VIDAL, ANDY. "Gutierrez Loses Backing of Indigenous Groups." *Financial Times* February 17, 2004: 2.

WEEKS, GREGORY. "Almost Jeffersonian: U.S. Recognition Policy toward Latin America." *Presidential Studies Quarterly* 31, 3 (2001): 490–504.

WEEKS, GREGORY. "Fighting the Enemy Within: Terrorism, the School of the Americas, and the Military in Latin America," *Human Rights Review* 5, 1 (October–December 2003): 12–27.

WEINER, TIM. "Mexico's Envoy to U.N. Is Fired after Criticizing U.S. Policy." *New York Times* November 18, 2003.

WHITE, MARCELINE. "Women and FTAA." *Foreign Policy in Focus* (March 2001): 1–2.

White House Web site. "Joint Statement by President George Bush and President Vicente Fox towards a Partnership for Prosperity."

February 16, 2001. http://www.whitehouse.gov/news/releases/2001/02/20010220-2.html.

WILKINSON, DANIEL. "Labor and the FTAA: A Cautionary Tale." *Human Rights Watch Commentary* (November 21, 2003). http://www.hrw.org/editorials/2003/ftaa112103.htm (accessed April 29, 2004).

WOOD, BRYCE. *The Making of the Good Neighbor Policy* (New York: Columbia University Press, 1961).

WOOD, BRYCE. *The Dismantling of the Good Neighbor Policy* (Austin: University of Texas Press, 1985).

WOODWARD, JR. RALPH LEE. *Central America: A Nation Divided* (New York: Oxford University Press, 1999).

YOUNGER, COLETTA A., AND EILEEN ROSIN (Eds.). *Drugs and Democracy in Latin America: The Impact of U.S. Policy* (Boulder, Colo.: Lynne Rienner, 2005).

ZUBOK, VLADISLAV, AND CONSTANTINE PLESHAKOV. *Inside the Kremlin's Cold War: From Stalin to Khrushchev* (Cambridge: Harvard University Press, 1996).

Index